Saved by Cocktails:

a Manual and Diary of Discovery for the Home Bartender

By David Swords

Saved by Cocktails:
a Manual and Diary of Discovery for the Home Bartender

2nd edition
Edited by Steven R. Poore
Design by Kristian Gustafson
Photos of cocktails by Marianne Wafer

Library of Congress Cataloging-in-Publication has been applied for.
ISBN 979-8-9925381-0-6

Acknowledgments

A diary is by nature chronological. Seems only right that those who brought it to life should be thanked in that order.

First, Jenny, who suggested a diary of what we were drinking two weeks into the Covid Pandemic, had the intuition that we would need a drink in the evenings, that the isolation could last, and that we should make essential use of our home bar. She's a beauty who knows things, feels things, and graces life.

Second, our friends from the Luggnuts—Rick Lugg, Ruth Fischer, Dan Morrissey, Mitch Simon, Rick Pollak, and Ann and George Saunderson—at outdoor gatherings on cold New Hampshire Pandemic nights bravely drank our early experimental traveling cocktails.

Third, our son Al, sent home from college in his second semester, made the best of underage drinking with his friends Skylar Hathorn, Max Phillips (who came with his own double-rocks glass), Carter MacLean, and unnamed others in the Ol' Bean Bar, where we lived, learning enough that two weeks past his 21st birthday Al started work as a professional bartender. He is fulfilling the moon-eyed prediction of the teacher who licensed him that, "Someday you're going to make someone a wonderful bartender." Better sooner than later.

Fourth, Tim and Beth Goodrich, Jenny's parents, whose plight changed our lives, and for the better. Beth needed cocktails as much as I did, and Tim loved, still loves, them even more.

Fifth, Rick Lugg, his wife, Ruth, along with Mark and Elise Kendall have been the friends who first supported and then committed to our Chimes @ Midnight project. They have willingly taken the oath to, "Forswear thin potations" and do their best to keep the faith nightly.

My friend of fifty years, Steve Poore, with moral support from his bartending wife Rochelle, talked sports, politics, and cocktails with me unerringly for two years and then edited the book. Long ago he taught me the difference between "bring" and "take," which saddles him with responsibility for any errors you find. If you bring the perspicacity to discover what Steve did not, then we'll both take your recommendations. Good luck with the hunt.

Finally, we made new friends, mariners all, through shared cocktails in Florida, especially Quinn and Roy, Rich and Patricia, and Duncan and Pat. In New Hampshire, other friends—Kyle and Susi, Laura and Brick—contributed curiosity and enthusiasm.

We may have been saved by cocktails. We surely were saved by these people.

Table of Contents

Saved by Cocktails:
a Manual and Diary of Discovery for the Home Bartender

Foreword, 2022

The diary that I kept from March 23, 2020, until May 8, 2021, captures what we drank, who we were, what we thought, how we acted, and parts of what the world did during the Covid Pandemic. The strength and the weakness of a diary are that it presents events as they happen, and us as we were, with the glow, fire, and obliviousness of the moment. People, it turns out, are like Heraclitus's river: no one is the same for long. Over time memory seems to become diminishingly reliable unless saved in print.

And thank goodness for the cocktails. Spirits, in particular "hard alcohol," the main ingredient in nearly every cocktail, have the deserved reputation of ruining lives, fortunes, families, health, friendships, marriages, values, even virtue itself. Yet, alcohol has had vital roles in nearly every human culture from prehistoric times (see, for example, Slingerland, *Drunk*; Forsyth, *A Short History of Drunkenness*). If alcohol is the very foundation of evil, or one of its pillars, how can this be so?

More than one answer exists, but for our little purposes during the Great Covid-19 Pandemic of 2020 and 2021, cocktails at the end of the day brightened us by lifting the perils, defeats, uncertainty, and loneliness of the hours. Beginning with their myriad flavors on the tongue, ascending to their first welcome touch of the brain, often at least seeming to improve conversation or contemplation, they buoyed our spirits in hard times. Their ritual preparation was a welcome task; their unending variation a precious difference; their way of taking us to a limit that we could choose to cross or not a welcome decision, whatever the consequence.

The introduction that follows, written in May 2020 as the pandemic settled in, held true. For me, thinking about cocktails and writing about them daily in this diary became rewards in themselves, in the drinking, discovery, writing, and now in looking back. Without the infinite time granted by the pandemic, events of the day would inevitably have ruled life, and I could never have had the steady patience, resolve, or diligence to write so much over so long.

The modest ambition with which the project began, as an offhand suggestion by my wife Jenny to record what we were drinking each day, allowed time for entries to become a habit that was never far from mind. As the pandemic settled in, the May 2020 introduction suggested we think of the isolation and the cocktails as a voyage in the exploratory sense of not knowing where we would go or when or how it would end. We could not know, for example, that the metaphorical voyage would become an actual voyage, both on the high seas and in our living circumstances. The journal ends thirteen and one-half months after it began, when Jennifer, Alex our son, and I are vaccinated and return to New Hampshire after living the winter in Florida aboard a sailboat.

The Diary

Early in the diary cocktails rule the stage, from March, through April, and into May 2020. Trips to the grocery felt dangerous because we had little understanding of how the virus spread, but we had to eat, and we had to drink. By May our cocktails were ranging broadly enough that some weeks we spent more on spirits than on food. As our tastes widened, general matters of preparation, such as how to build a cocktail and the amount of bitters in a dash, begin to appear as subjects to be investigated. Gradually, as the effects of the pandemic—such as businesses closing their doors for good, the dawning social effects of isolation on behavior, and the howls of a consequential presidential election—take the stage, the diary begins to look beyond cocktails.

In July Jenny's parents moved into their RV replica of a boxcar, sited on our property in New Hampshire, partly thinking they would be protected from the virus that scourged Florida. Sadly, two elderly couples and one widow from three neighborhood houses reacted by calling in town officials hoping to have the boxcar removed. Their antipathy set in motion a cascade of events.

In September we committed to selling our house and leaving the town where we had lived happily for 15 years, raising our son. After investigating a move to places more hospitable to "auxiliary dwellings" along the Maine or New Hampshire coast, in October we bought a sailboat in Florida. In November we sailed from Tampa, around Key West, and on to Stuart on the east coast. Daunting mishaps occurred along the way, largely my fault. No one died. Donald Trump lost the election, and the aftermath, and my take on it, especially January 6, are necessarily recounted. We sold our New Hampshire house and spent most of the winter in Stuart helping to care for Jenny's aging dad. Through all of this we settled a lot of questions about preparing and enjoying cocktails that are an original, we hope entertaining, exploration of how to be a good home bartender.

The Cocktails

But how is this book different from other cocktail manuals? First, the entries are rarely prescriptive, which is to say, the recipes seldom require certain brands of this rum, that bourbon, or a particular gin. Nor are the recipes simply descriptive, naming contents and amounts, letting you choose the brands. If you move chronologically through the diary, you'll find that it is experimental, comparing one cocktail with another of its genre and working to test whether ingredients different from the ones usually indicated can be improvements. An easy example is lemon versus lime; sometimes you will prefer the one experts have not considered. The main point we wish to make is that our tastes and tongues, moods and preferences change, are different from one person to the next, and cannot be contained by "definitive" recipes.

Initially, I hoped to learn to make from memory the cocktails guests in our house were likely to order, the "classics." Instead, I learned to decide on the drink of the night based on many factors: the season, the temperature, curiosity about something new or yearning for what is proven, Jenny's preference, tastes of any guests, and the ingredients we have on hand. One advantage is that memory plays almost no part. But a bigger advantage, useful to any home bartender, is that rather than Jack and Coke or vodka and soda-water, guests discover, and invariably love, cocktails they would never know without you.

All of this has led to a reliable and delightful process. As evening comes, I decide on a cocktail, gather the ingredients, and if they include citrus, squeeze what we need into a bottle. In mixing cocktails, I follow a pattern. Anything that will play against the main spirit, including vermouth, amari, and liqueurs goes in first. Next, I add the sweetener, such as simple syrup, grenadine, honey syrup, Benedictine, or orgeat. The main spirit or spirits are next, followed by citrus, and finally bitters and garnish. The order, in my mind, washes the jigger of the tastiest ingredients, which may or may not really matter. I do not add ice until all ingredients are in the stirring glass or shaker. More important, if I am distracted the order helps guard against inadvertently omitting anything. Adding ice last decreases dilution. And a dash is 1/8 teaspoon.

Onward

I began regularly enjoying cocktails more than 50 years ago as a teenager in New Orleans. Beginning in the early part of this century, Jenny and I had an elaborate home bar in the 1792 Ol' Bean Tavern, in New Hampshire. But it was not until the infinite time afforded by the pandemic that cocktails became an almost daily indispensable part of our lives. With luck, this book will be a shortcut for you to find your way to the satisfactions that continue to intrigue us and our friends. Always we live by the admonition of our spiritual guide Sir John Falstaff to, "Forswear thin potations!"

Introduction—May 2020

On First Looking into Chapman's Homer—John Keats

Much have I travell'd in the realms of gold,
And many goodly states and kingdoms seen;
Round many western islands have I been
Which bards in fealty to Apollo hold.
Oft of one wide expanse had I been told
That deep-brow'd Homer ruled as his demesne;
Yet did I never breathe its pure serene
Till I heard Chapman speak out loud and bold:
Then I felt like some watcher of the skies
When a new planet swims into his ken;
Or like stout Cortez when with eagle eyes
He star'd at the Pacific and all his men
Look'd at each other with a wild surmise—
Silent, upon a peak in Darien.

The best poetry, in the way it elevates an event, a sight, a feeling is a lot like the moment when alcohol begins to touch our brains with its magic. That first cocktail on an evening peels away the cares of the day on one hand and transports us to a better world on the other. Relief juxtaposed with surprise is a powerful drug that helps explain why profoundly important rituals in virtually every civilization and even prehistoric gatherings have been built on the effects of alcohol.

As I write in May 2020, the Covid-19 pandemic rages. We're shut-ins at home, where endless time with nowhere to go is a monstrous curse for some. The teenager who lives in our house, banished from his first taste of campus life, in worse straits than one of Ulysses' sailors in Polyphemus's cave, finds himself imprisoned by two monsters who give him no chance to escape; bark absurd lectures; and require, more or less, soiled dishes to be returned—eventually—to the kitchen. For others, almost as if unwillingly strapped to their masts by petty local tyrants, the Siren call of maskless freedom stirs their Constitutional souls to fits of anguish, rage, and arms bearing.

Many of us, by contrast, in the spirit of thousands of years of human tradition, elect to drink. Time, we come to realize once past our teenage years and stuffed into the maw of real life, vanishes, as songwriter Chris Smither puts it, "In those days we were young, and we lived 'em one by one/Now we hardly see 'em, they don't walk, they run." But then, out of the blue, along comes a pandemic and some of us, at least, get not only a taste of, but are lucky enough to live in (and perhaps live through), infinite time. In this unfair world, those who take joy and inspiration from infinite time woke in March to a garden of earthly delights, where liquor stores are designated essential by the State. It was almost as if when cocktail time rolled around, in our house at about 6:00 each evening, the spirits of our ancestors gently moved us to crack open the bottle, break out the ice, measure the vermouth.

Jenny and I had been enjoying this ritual for the first two weeks of the lockdown when she suggested a "cocktail diary." Whatever she meant, the idea quickly, naturally, to me meant a voyage, embarking to unknown destinations where in martini-glass islands we discover Keats's realms of gold. Provisioning held dangers in sorties to the liquor store, but the adventure, like all great adventures, seemed worth the risk. And with that, we set sail on a voyage where, as I write, no end is in sight.

Some Personal Background to Get Us to the Present

For many years, going back to business trips to Brussels in the mid 1980s, I had been mostly a beer drinker, although one who liked cocktails, especially during corporate-sponsored evenings at high-end restaurants. My dad drank an Old Fashioned or two in our New Orleans home every night when my brothers and I were children; our mother, a poor cook, made a perfectly good one. I have always loved an Old Fashioned as well as a Manhattan, Sidecar, Sazerac, Dark and Stormy, Gin & Tonic, Margarita, Martini,

and probably a few other classics. But those were rare, especially after the beer renaissance came to New England during the past decade. Central New Hampshire is a perfect place from which to launch day trips to the Alchemist, Hill Farmstead, Lawson's, Schilling, Treehouse, Trillium, and many other great breweries.

Meanwhile the cocktail renaissance had taken on its own life. We had adumbrations of it in New Hampshire, such as a speakeasy-style bar in Concord, but I lacked any clear understanding or knowledge in visiting, say, New York City, that bars besides Bemelmans at the Carlyle Hotel, or in London, The American Bar at the Savoy, were rising. We saw small distilleries and bought their products but beyond the few old standards knew little about how to deploy them… Hmmm… here in Infinite Time I can't resist digressing further, to memories unvisited in decades, to consider whether they could help clarify the present.

The Chemistry of Drinking

At age 14, recently moved back to our hometown of New Orleans, I needed a chemistry lab. Not a chemistry set, which in those days came in small, medium, or large metal boxes, with little bottles of harmless chemicals, and a booklet of boring experiments in which, unmiraculously, liquids performed such feats as changing color. No explosions. I needed the real thing with beakers, flasks, and scales, racks of test tubes, and chemicals bought individually, rather than en masse, from a real chemical supply house (oh! Curtin Chemical, how I loved you) and that included hydrochloric, nitric, and sulfuric acids; silver and potassium nitrate; sulfur; mercury; iodine crystals and ammonium hydroxide, the stuff of explosives.

Somehow my parents indulged this fascination, blind to the explosive dreams, and my dad found a wooden shed someone wanted hauled away. So we hauled, and I rebuilt it with windows, shelves, a pitched roof that barely leaked, and counters for measuring, weighing, and mixing. After school, I'd head for the lab and mix mostly explosives, even trying to make gunpowder and nitroglycerine, until some combination of iodine crystals and ammonium hydroxide, a heatless explosion, blew up in my face, the only permanent injury being an end to any career as a chemist.

That is, the chemist career ended until the Ol' Bean's Bar—the Ol' Bean Tavern is the house where we live in New Hampshire—spoke to my neighbor, and we became home brewers. The beer we made was pretty good, and it was chemistry. Meanwhile, sometime during the decade, breweries opened all over New England, and I bought enough of their beer that guests, especially the band I was in, the Luggnuts, that practiced at our house, became less and less interested in our beer. Meanwhile, double IPAs grew to be ubiquitous, and distinguishing one from another became like distinguishing among good wines.

I had always made a few classic cocktails for myself or guests, especially on special occasions such as, for example, Ramos Gin Fizzes (a New Orleans thing) for a baby shower Jennifer hosted one Sunday morning. Four or five years ago, inspired by a poet's drinking recommendations, I took up Martinis, and someone gave me a copy of Ted Haigh's (the self-styled Dr. Cocktail) *Vintage Spirits and Forgotten Cocktails*. Two summers before the pandemic struck, I found the Corpse Reviver No. 2 in that book, and it was like magic, proof that cocktails are not only chemistry, they are alchemistry, turning confections of base raw materials into gold. Cocktails also are explosive. Once you've mixed, stirred or shaken, strained, poured, and garnished, you've got lightning in a glass that tastes like nectar of the gods, whatever that taste may be. The inspiration revived my corpse such that I gave cocktails near daily, serious attention.

Such attention included reading, in no programmatic way, past and present books about cocktails and collecting a small library of them. Old ones, such as the seminal *Savoy Cocktail Book*, are easily found in excellent used editions on the Internet. Abe Books, for example, is a good source. Even better, small bookshops in England, Canada, and the United States now seek out used books about cocktails and more than a few stock any they can find. As cocktail bars have opened, the most successful practitioners have published their own excellent books giving us modern sources for modern tastes. And finally, among other online resources, an especially satisfying website, *euvs-vintage-cocktail-books.cld.bz*, is a near comprehensive library of known books dating from the 1820s to the 1940s about the drinks bartenders make. The library houses digital copies to page through, making one feel as if he has traveled back in time. Using it costs nothing but your well spent time. Finally, we have included a bibliography in case, along the way, you want to enjoy these and other resources. That said, the alchemist's laboratory is a bar, and let's get to yours.

The Pleasures of Your Bar

If you're reading this, you must love a good bar. The thing is, unless you live in a city, at best ride the bus or walk to work and stop in for a few drinks on your way home, you'll visit a good bar only occasionally. If a pandemic comes along, all the bars, but not the liquor stores, shut down, unless you live in a daring state, say, Texas or Michigan, and believe you can shoot your way out of a pandemic. In short, if you like a bar, you need one in your house or apartment that is open whenever you say. Nor is need too strong a word. The home bar should not be optional if your plans include reliably and frequently enjoying life, escaping cares, feeling magically better at the end of a terrible day with the help of spirits.

When I was a kid back in the 50s expecting Russia to blow us up, a few people built bomb shelters deep underground, stocked them with canned food, and, I suppose, hoped for the day that their investment would pay off. It never did, happily for the rest of us, although I think the children of those bomb-shelter builders are hoarding assault rifles with hopes, spurred by the pandemic, of putting them to use on their liberal neighbors. You know, what fun is a bomb shelter if no one is blowing you up or an assault rifle if no one is taking away your rights? ("If nobody hates you, nobody knows you're alive."—Chris Smither, again.) Now we look less likely to be exploded than, as we've done for more than two months now, to stay sheltered as the nature we've betrayed fights back, sending storms, economic and social chaos, and pestilence our way. Given this, odds are you're going to need a bar of your own, at best on high ground and with pocket shutters (formerly crudely known as Indian shutters) that repel assault rifle rounds in the event that your President succeeds in starting a cultural civil war, as our present one seems pretty eager to do.

We've all got a liquor cabinet, closet, cupboard, shelf, pocket, or drawer where we store the booze. But really, too often the space is an afterthought, a modest, probably less convenient storage niche than the kitchen cabinet where you keep canned goods. If you're going to make cocktails a ritual for yourself and loved ones with the care, goodwill, and art that mark a high point of middle-class hospitality today and that have signaled success and a welcoming spirit to guests in virtually every civilization for 5,000 years, you need a proper bar.

I've been determined to use an extended metaphor to give this diary a framework, a device to enrich the experience of exploring cocktails together. Extended metaphors in service of (mostly) non-fiction are risky, typically become trite and self-indulgent. I'm a sailor, so self-indulgence is surely at play if the metaphor is that during this pandemic we are all on a risky voyage. In this, we resemble early explorers who did not know what the nautical miles held, such as whether they would pitch over the edge of the earth. Until now, today's voyages have had destinations and schedules. Our pandemic voyage, if we tentatively allow the metaphor, does not. And now that we've both been warned, let's give the metaphor a shakedown cruise.

Setting Sail in a Pandemic

During a pandemic that requires we sequester, our home and the bar in it are much like a ship at sea. A ship is a world unto herself, and you'll want to be certain—once you've fitted her with bar tools and spirits—that yours is well supplied with staples: ice, toothpicks, straws, citrus, sugars and syrups, egg white, cherries, and perhaps olives or cocktail onions. And booze. These cocktail ingredients are as needed as food and perhaps more important. If food is the fuel, the bar and its spirits are the bridge from which we chart the course and steer the ship along its journey, giving us courage and a reason to live. Some weeks here at the Ol' Bean we spend more on alcohol and its accoutrements than on food. Food is for the body, spirits for the soul, for morale, for remembering and for forgetting, for giving us a reason to keep wind in our sails. If you are the officer in charge of the bar, you will need to keep your deck supplied and trim; glasses spotless; shelves organized; tools to hand; workspaces clean, efficient, and uncluttered.

A vital part of your work will be to keep your ship, your world, off the rocks (although we'll often take our cocktails on the rocks). You'll want to watch for the lee shore of anxiety, looking ahead and calculating

the prospects of storms and other perils you will face. Caring for the crew begins with caring for yourself, which in the context of a bar means knowing and, usually, observing limits.

Wait, don't put this book back on the shelf; it emphatically is NOT a book about moderation. To begin with, we're addressing together drinking cocktails you build at home in the bar you fashion. Right now, even neighbors who could walk or crawl home, aren't allowed. Driving should be no issue whatsoever. An immediate advantage is that you'll prepare any cocktail exactly as you like, with real grenadine, fresh citrus, the version of any spirit you prefer most. You'll find immense variety to address hot days or cold nights.

In his masterly, sadly neglected work *The American Language,* Supplement One, H.L. Mencken writes,

> The principal manuals for bartenders list hundreds [of cocktails]: in the Savoy
> Cocktail Book *there are actually formulae for nearly 700. I have myself invented
> eleven, and had nine named after me. William Warren Woolcott and I once employed
> a mathematician to figure out how many could be fashioned of the materia
> bibulica ordinarily available in a first rate bar. He reported that the number was
> 17,864,392,788. We tried 273 at random, and found them all good, though some, of
> course, were better than others (page 260. Thanks to Bob Nardini for steering me to
> Mencken on this subject).*

Over time, you'll build a store of ingredients that are fairly imperishable and a few inexpensive ones that are perishable. You may find one drink or just a few that so deeply satisfy your tastes, talents, and turpitude that you won't need any others. Or you may explore from now till the last ding dong of doom and love pretty much every coupe, Nick and Nora, or rocks-glass island you visit. We'll have to see.

Caution: This Voyage Can Be Dangerous

The pandemic has created vast, deep unease. Millions of jobs lost, nearly every job threatened. New, solitary ways of working. And no place to go at the end of the day. Anxiety settles into the pit of your stomach and invades your uneasy sleep. I'm guessing millions of marriages will fail from the shock of togetherness.

The beginnings of Prohibition, among the worst stains on American good sense, on par I'd say with the election of Donald Trump by a minority of citizens (or on second thought, not quite that bad), came in the early and middle Nineteenth Century. Farmers, in effect sequestered on isolated plots of land, as humans had for thousands of years, made do with whatever fermentable fruits or grains were to hand and drank, drank a lot. As a result, farms became neglected, wives abused, families bereft, and ultimately the demand for abstinence arose amid those who suffered. We do not want a repeat of this in your home.

The ancient Greeks, patriarchs of western thought—Homer, Thales, Socrates, Plato, Aristotle, Euripides, to name only a few—all were enthusiastic tipplers from whose cultural experience at least two Commandments made for the drinking person have stood across time, distance, and cultures: *meden agan* (nothing too much) and *gnothi sauton* (know thyself). The Greeks loved evenings of uncontrolled wine drinking, so all of them understood, as Odysseus says,

> *It is the wine that leads me on, the wild wine,*
> *that sets the wisest man to sing at the top of his lungs,*
> *laugh like a fool—it drives the man to dancing. . . it even*
> *tempts him to blurt out stories better never told. (Wilson 216)*

Knowing that many such evenings lay ahead, the Greeks kept before them the ideas that we must limit ourselves and know our personal limits. Again, "nothing too much" did not require being moderate; rather, it meant stopping short of doing more harm than good.

"Know thyself" means that each of us handles spirits differently and that for some this means four, five, six cocktails, while for most of us one, two, or three is the limit. The Greek comic playwright Euboulus had this to say about numbers of drinks: "For sensible men I prepare three kraters: one for health, one for love and pleasure, and the third for sleep. After the third one is drained, wise men go home" (Forsyth 60). Turns out, the number for me is three, though none of us is forever wise.

According to Euboulus here's what happens if I continue past three, "The fourth krater is not mine because it belongs to bad behavior. The fifth is for shouting. The sixth for rudeness and insults, the seventh for fights. The eighth is for breaking the furniture, the ninth for depression, and the tenth for madness and unconsciousness." How did he know?

In general, gin seems gentler than bourbon, rye, or cognac of the same proof, or so I believe. Rum, if not 151 proof, stands somewhere in between, and tequila can be dangerous. I seldom venture beyond three cocktails in an evening and four, especially four made with tequila, send me aground on the shoals of regret. Most cocktails contain between 2 and 3 ounces of alcohol, so 6 to 9 ounces is pretty safe, by which I mean, sleep is peaceful, I don't wake up in the night, the next day have no headache or other noticeable after effects. Another 2 to 3 ounces is an altogether different story.

At home, you are both bartender and customer. One job of a good bartender, as important as his or her mixological gifts, is to listen to the customers, ourselves included. As we carefully prepare what they/we think they/we want, it's important to measure what they/we might prefer. Our job can help them/us to feel at least temporarily safer, cared about, and more sanguine through the use of the medicine, the alchemistry, of alcohol. What I am fumbling to say is that as a bartender, even if preparing cocktails only for yourself, modeling good humor, hopefulness, understanding, discernment, judgment, and courage are part of the territory. Sound inflated? Anyone who grows up with a drunk in the house, as opposed to a parent who likes to drink, knows it is not.

As we all do, the bartender faces the discomforts and hazards of the unknown. Storms, monsters, villains, heartless gods and goddesses, our own appetite and curiosity, all pose dangers. The taste and effects of an especially fetching cocktail after a haunting day may lead a person to drink himself into a stumbling, mumbling, zombie-like corpse while the evening is young. As a veteran of roughly 55 years of serious drinking, I know the condition well. Beware! Because you too have surely had nights when too much was not enough, let us strive together to plumb the depths of intoxication without drowning in them, becoming neither sober nor too drunk. We'll travel better if by understanding our weaknesses we can find ways to give them scope, without ruin. It is possible to abhor moderation, which I do, yet believe in limits.

The Ritual and the Marriage

A ship's discipline and deeper enjoyment of the cocktails you will create come from making the cocktail hour a ritual. To practice the ritual, having a regular time to begin settles and centers the mind as we prepare to savor the evening's first drink. Considerable pleasure may come from pondering in advance the evening's offering. I often don a nice shirt, freshen up before going to the bar. Preparing the bar by gathering ice and setting out the chosen ingredients and glasses makes for a sanctified atmosphere before the first sip. Ritual quiets the noise of the day and prepares us, not simply to swallow a cocktail but to savor it, think about its flavors, awaken the parts of the tongue, contemplatively.

Deep into the first cocktail, I nearly always begin to feel it reanimating my soul, thanks to the 2 to 3 ounces of alcohol in that first glass. My preference during the pandemic is to start this drink at about 6:00 (4 bells) before doing anything toward dinner or other evening chores.

After the first cocktail has been drunk, stage two begins for me as dinner time approaches. The moment demands discipline. If barbecuing, I start the fire, put the potatoes or corn on, and only then make a second cocktail. If cooking indoors, I do the most burdensome chores of food preparation before mixing a second cocktail. Of course, it is possible that your better half will move off to the kitchen, while you happily retreat to where you do your best work, behind the bar, making drinks for both of you.

Once dinner is cooking, or if quickly made and on the table, we require a second cocktail. Here, an overlooked, little regarded marriage of food and spirits demands attention. All of us have drunk innumerable bottles of red or white wine with dinners that command one or the other. We have also used cocktails as aperitifs, a Negroni or Manhattan, at fine restaurants, or when dining at home with friends, before moving on to wine. With casual food we often prefer beer. And of course, spirits alone (a glass of cognac, port, or Green Chartreuse) or certain cocktails (how about a Sazerac, please?) are excellent after dinner. But the cocktail with dinner is absurdly, ludicrously, sadly, needlessly disregarded, and I don't know why!

Let's change that, make the world and the culinary moment an altogether better place. For example, a Martini, especially one with vermouth and orange bitters, rather than a glass of cold gin, pairs beautifully with fish. The fish is hot, the Martini cold and doesn't overpower the fish; the fish makes the Martini more drinkable. Together, each highlights the flavors of the other. Even better, you'll find cocktails to go with practically any food you love.

Setting up Your Bar

Getting the voyage started is fun on its own, and then supplying and using the bar are even more fun. The project need not be expensive, but happily it can be. (And think of the money saved by not drinking in commercial bars.) Your bar might have modest dimensions, the liquor kept out of sight, or it can be the main attraction of your home. Your bar can be part of the kitchen in a small apartment, it can be in the corner of a comfortable room where you entertain, it can be a man cave, or it can be a whole wing of your house. Wherever it is, however, your bar should not be an afterthought.

At best a bar has a freezer, sink, and a refrigerator, all of which can be found in kitchens, where you're likely to have counters, shelves, cabinets, glassware, knives, spoons, and some of the ingredients that take turns in cocktails. When we set-up the kitchen in a dwelling to which we've just moved, why not make suitable provisions for the bar a priority rather than an afterthought? If you've been in a place for 30 years, why not rethink how to configure a space so that the place of cocktails in your life is designed, organized, and efficient rather than closeted? Old place or new, confining and constraining make it much harder to enjoy the mighty pleasures of cocktails.

Planning the bar is an engineering, economic, and spiritual problem you'll—with the help of experiences in these pages—have to solve for yourself. But a bar hidden in low-lying cabinets is like a sailboat on a trailer. Getting set-up to use takes time, takes effort better employed in making and drinking, and as a result, use will diminish. A boat kept in the water with sails hanked on year in, year out will be used exponentially more than a sailboat on a trailer. A bar with glassware, tools, ice, and ingredients convenient to preparation will be more efficient, creative, diverse, and fun than one in a closet.

Prohibition has had many evil, lasting effects. Among them, its insidious influence can still be felt in the notion that spirits must be kept out of sight, that making apparent our drinking habits signals we're unwholesome and probably poor models for our children. As a result, in many, perhaps most middle-class homes, the bar is an afterthought or sequestered inconspicuously, much as we are at the moment.

Prohibition began as a woman's issue because husbands too often drank so much that families suffered. Soon it became a Christian cause as well, which is patent nonsense. Jesus himself was not only a drinker, but especially at the Last Supper clearly associated his blood with wine, leading to the sacrament of communion. Jesus's first miracle, in fact, was at a wedding in Cana where, as the festivities ran short, Mary said to him, "They have no more wine" (Forsyth 77). He stepped in, helped out by turning something like 120 gallons of water into wine, which the New Testament makes clear is a fine thing and to be celebrated. If alcohol was good enough for Jesus, why not start by tossing useless inhibitions and treating cocktail time as the valuable ritual it is, deserving of its own temple?

Stepping up to a bar is a lot like approaching an altar, and you're the priest. People love to watch a capable bartender, to ask questions, to admire the cocktail priest as he transubstantiates liquor into soul. Don't be nervous if you have not yet worn the priestly robes or learned the secret codes and incantations. You are now on the Path, and, between us, it's a gentle, uplifting stroll.

In arranging the bar to spread the word to your parishioners, think about how to prepare and serve drinks with as few steps as possible so that you can concentrate on delivering the sermon. If you can keep your feet planted and reach the spirits easily, conversation and concentration are both easier. An ice bucket in a sink next to the bar helps on the front and back end of a cocktail. (Or, better, keep your ice in a freezer that serves only the bar.) Keeping your choices of spirits and mixers visible so that you can lay hands on what's called for without thinking about where it might be, and then returning the bottles to their spots, makes you much more efficient and approachable.

But let's get out of the sacramental weeds. The idea is simple: design your bar, don't hide it. Down the road, if the bar becomes integral to your life, and resources allow, you can redesign and move it with the benefit of experience.

With that, shall we cast off? The best news is that you can design how you take this voyage, making cocktails day by day or looking around for ones that suit a particular mood. Either way, you might consider taking notes. They will in time become your ship's log, and the best guide you can have to the cocktails you love most.

Part I: Infinite Time

Entry 1: 23 March 2020 Monday—The Martini

The long, researched first entry is like nothing else you'll find here. It serves as a beginning, however, by demonstrating that cocktails have historical roots, may change with the times, often deserve tasting in their older forms…are not one thing. Diary entries can't change over time, but since writing this I've researched Martinis much more extensively. A whole book on the subject, The Silver Bullet *by Lowell Edmunds, is terrific.*

We've got to start somewhere, so why not begin with an investigation from the weekend just past of a highly evolved, ever evolving classic? Martinis are a drinker's drink, boozy and powerful, so they get right to the point. We'll try to do the same.

My longtime friend Phil loves to order his Martini as follows: "Do you have Beefeater? Yes? Yes. So, I'd like a Beefeater Martini, very dry. I mean very, very dry—perhaps wave vermouth in the direction of the glass—shaken, served up, with an olive." The last time I saw Phil place this order, weeks before the pandemic, the bartender, a real, knowledgeable bartender, replied, "I think you want a glass of gin, no vermouth, no bitters, shaken, and served up?" Yes, what Phil and much of the world these days mean when they order a Martini is a glass of cold gin.

For a year or two, I "refined" my Martini taste. This required trying the major London dry gins, and some other more floral, inappropriate gins, deciding Beefeater was my choice too. I also followed the advice of a hard-drinking poet that the Martini must be as cold as possible and so I kept, still keep, a bottle of Beefeater in the freezer. This poet was of the school (come to think of it, Phil had a brief career as a poet) that a whiff of dry vermouth was plenty, but I liked adding a capful of Noilly Pratt, which I kept on the shelf, not in a refrigerator, where vermouth, red or white, should be kept after opening.

I drank many, many of these Martinis, mostly stirred, some shaken, and to tell the truth, loved the effect without really liking the drink. Rather than savoring each sip, I'm pretty certain I grimaced, though without ever going so wrong as to use vodka.

Let's look at the history. As guide for this journey into the Martini, last night I used Robert Vermeire's recipes from *Cocktails: How to Mix Them (1924)*. Simply identified as "Robert" on the title page of his book, Vermeire was Belgian but plied his trade in London and Paris as well as Brussels, and thanks to his book was an authoritative bartender of the age. He begins with what he describes as the "original Martini," advising, that it "should always be made with Martini-Rossi Vermouth" exactly to his specifications.

Vermeire's Gin Cocktail from 1924

Fill the bar glass half full with broken ice and add:
1 dash orange bitters
1/6 gill of Martini-Rossi Vermouth
2/6 gill of Gordon's Dry Gin
Prep: Stir and strain into a cold cocktail-glass. Squeeze lemon-peel on top.

For orange bitters I used Regans'; for vermouth, 1 oz Martini-Rossi; for gin, 2 ozs Beefeater, thus preserving Robert's ratios. Sweet but very good. No one would use red vermouth in a martini today.

Vermeire's original, however, is quite different from the real original. The two earliest authoritative manuals for bartenders are by Jerry Thomas (1862) and by his rival Harry Johnson (1888).

First, Thomas's 1862 recipe for a gin cocktail could be construed as the original, original Martini... sort of:

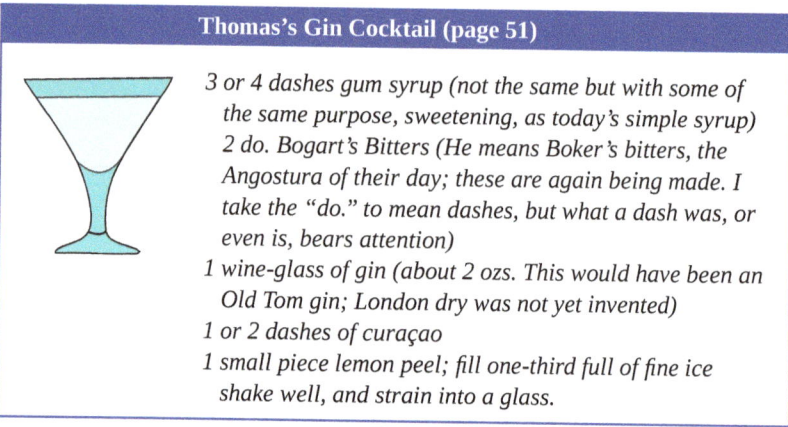

Thomas's Gin Cocktail (page 51)

3 or 4 dashes gum syrup (not the same but with some of the same purpose, sweetening, as today's simple syrup)
2 do. Bogart's Bitters (He means Boker's bitters, the Angostura of their day; these are again being made. I take the "do." to mean dashes, but what a dash was, or even is, bears attention)
1 wine-glass of gin (about 2 ozs. This would have been an Old Tom gin; London dry was not yet invented)
1 or 2 dashes of curaçao
1 small piece lemon peel; fill one-third full of fine ice shake well, and strain into a glass.

The recipe starts, anyway, with gin and aims mostly to tart it up. The gum syrup and curaçao stood in place of Vermeire's later red vermouth.

Harry Johnson's more complicated recipe in *New and Improved Bartender's Manual or How to Mix Drinks of the Present Style*, pages 38-39, is called a Martini and is as follows:

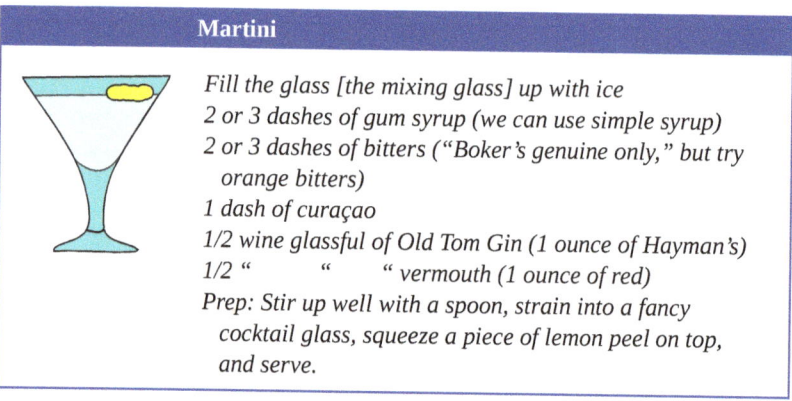

Martini

Fill the glass [the mixing glass] up with ice
2 or 3 dashes of gum syrup (we can use simple syrup)
2 or 3 dashes of bitters ("Boker's genuine only," but try orange bitters)
1 dash of curaçao
1/2 wine glassful of Old Tom Gin (1 ounce of Hayman's)
1/2 "   "   " vermouth (1 ounce of red)
Prep: Stir up well with a spoon, strain into a fancy cocktail glass, squeeze a piece of lemon peel on top, and serve.

And here vermouth makes its appearance, moving the Martini toward Robert's. Obviously, by 1924 the Martini had changed a great deal in the direction—dry gin, vermouth—that we recognize today.

Vermiere also offers a "medium" version Martini, which halves red and dry vermouth and has equal amounts of vermouth and gin, a kind of "perfect" Martini.

Medium Martini
2 ozs gin (Beefeater) 1 oz sweet vermouth (Dolin Rouge) 1 oz dry vermouth (Dolin Dry) 2 dashes orange bitters

As it turns out, this proto-Martini is terrific. In particular, the dry vermouth left a dry mouthfeel, which I'd never experienced before in a cocktail and loved. Does it seem odd that today we use dry vermouth in a Martini, but when we want a dry Martini reduce or eliminate the vermouth? In the Medium Martini, suppose we halved the red vermouth and used 1.5 ozs of white, maybe call it a Three-Quarter Martini? I think it's worth a try, but for now will leave the discovery to anyone who ever reads this… with luck, Jennifer, who will make one for me.

Only three years after Vermeire, in 1927, Harry McElhone's *Barflies and Cocktails* became the first book I can find to include only French (dry, white) vermouth in a Martini:

The ratios would be acceptable to many of us today. The gin may have been meant as London dry.

Martini Cocktail
2/3 gin 1/3 French vermouth Orange or angostura added if required Prep: Shake well and strain into cocktail glass.

Shaking versus Stirring

Note the advice to "shake" rather than "stir," a Martini practice some have ascribed to James Bond, for which he can be only anachronistically blamed. In these early manuals, shaking and stirring are applied in ways I cannot fathom. Today we typically stir drinks that exclude citrus, shake those that contain citrus, egg white, or milk. Exceptions exist, as in the Bond Martini, but they are rare. Our forebears seem to have had other, lost-to-me criteria to guide their stirring and shaking.

Okay, a lot of head-scratching detail here but not pointless. The Martini is a cocktail with which to begin this diary because it is protean, can be bent to whatever flavors suit you. In other words, even iconic cocktails have no Platonic form. Rather, an individual cocktail changes with the particular brand of spirit you prefer (Tanqueray or Beefeater), the kind or number of dashes of bitters you like, the specific ingredients (red vermouth, white vermouth, no vermouth), up or on the rocks, shaken or stirred, garnished or not, the glassware you use (we draw the line at plastic) and remains a Martini, Manhattan, Old Fashioned, Sazerac, or what have you.

Tonight's Martini

Here's where all of this has taken me tonight, and I'm going to need a lot of these if diary entries take this long (all day) to write.
1.5 ozs gin. Cold Beefeater
1/2 oz dry vermouth. Dolin Dry
1-2 dashes orange bitters

The dose of vermouth and bitters takes the ragged edge off the gin. This version is not quite where I find each sip a moment to be savored and where I look longingly as the glass moves to empty. But it is a step in that direction.

In conclusion, Phil's glass of gin, like revenge best served cold, is a Martini. If we had to draw a line as to what is not a Martini, I would say vodka is going too far. But that is bias, not science. As my daddy would urge, *de gustibus non est disputandum*.

24 March Tuesday

Editing comment: The next two entries show that I was groping for an approach to the Diary and had not quite gotten there. That is, presenting a cocktail without its recipe seems in retrospect to have been dumb. Luckily, in this at least, I learned quickly.

Jenny and I each drank double Chartreuse Swizzles, from *101 Cocktails* (Monti 58). A delicious drinkable cocktail for a summer day but the complexity of Chartreuse, along with interactions with the other ingredients (pineapple juice, lime juice, and Falernum) make this a cocktail to savor.

Chartreuse Swizzle

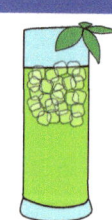

1.5 ozs Green Chartreuse
1 oz pineapple juice (Dole's was okay)
¾ oz lime juice
½ oz falernum (Taylor's Velvet Falernum)
Prep: Mix in a Collins glass and serve with crushed ice. Mint sprig for garnish.

Two ingredients in the Swizzle deserve special attention:

Green Chartreuse: A 110 percent liqueur, made in a French monastery for 500 years, and like its little sister Yellow Chartreuse, comprising some 130 botanicals, for which the recipes are known only to a couple of monks in a generation. My father always kept a bottle and on special occasions after dinner would offer it in a tiny glass to guests along with cognac. It has long been used in three cocktails (Last Word, Bijou, Widow's Kiss) but is now used in others such as tonight's Swizzle and the Naked and Famous. As a result of the increasing popularity and very limited production it has become quite expensive.

Falernum: Some bars now make their own, but Taylor's Velvet Falernum is excellent and widely available. A sugar, lime, rum liqueur, different versions are flavored with spices such as cloves and nutmeg. Relatively few people I know have heard of falernum, but it is essential, especially for many great summer cocktails.

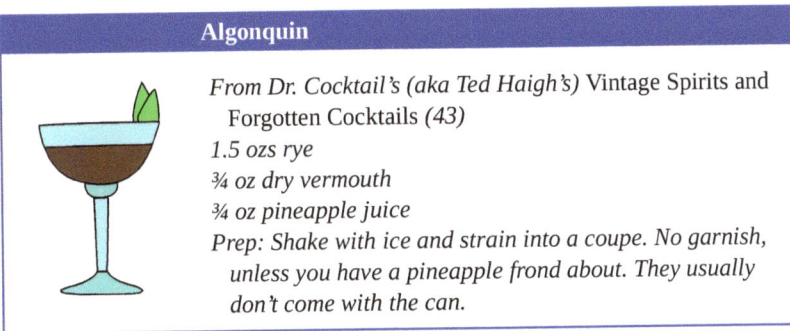

Corpse Reviver No. 1

from Fine and Classic Cocktails *(Corpse Reviver No. 1)*
1.5 ozs cognac
¾ oz calvados
¾ oz Italian vermouth
"To be taken before 11 am or whenever steam and energy
are needed."—Harry Craddock (51)

---

25 March Wednesday

Algonquin

From Dr. Cocktail's (aka Ted Haigh's) Vintage Spirits and
Forgotten Cocktails (43)
1.5 ozs rye
¾ oz dry vermouth
¾ oz pineapple juice
Prep: Shake with ice and strain into a coupe. No garnish,
unless you have a pineapple frond about. They usually
don't come with the can.

Could be canned pineapple juice is not great, though we used it last night in the Chartreuse Swizzles, and it was fine. Neither sweet nor sour, perhaps the combination of rye and pineapple is too unusual. Drunk in honor of New York as the city struggles with the Covid 19 pandemic.

Derby

Based on the recipe in Vintage Spirits and Forgotten
Cocktails (110)
2 ozs bourbon
1 oz Italian (sweet) vermouth
1 oz orange curaçao
1.5 ozs lime juice

Excellent. A genre of cocktail that uses sweet (Antica Formula and curaçao), sour (lime), and the base spirit (Buffalo Trace bourbon) to yield an alchemical mixture. Dropping a mint leaf on top gives the drink an aroma that complements the taste of the cocktail. Take it over a mint julep any day.

26 March Thursday

This was to be a day of abstinence. But, in the afternoon New Hampshire's Republican governor issued a stay-put order, and at the same time we learned the young daughter of people we know here in our small, sheltered town has Covid-19, diagnosed, but not tested, owing to the scarcity of tests, which screams that the incidence of plague is far greater than statistics report. In short, a day of abstinence was impossible.

The bad news and cocktail hour arrived together, necessitating a quick search for an appropriate drink, and what could lift the spirits more than forever being able to say to a good bartender, "Make me a Millionaire"?

Mostly, cocktails are intense, small drinks that will buzz but not KO a person. In extremis, one should maintain the proportions but raise the amounts, as I have done tonight. Many Millionaires have been invented, and we'll examine those as the plague allows. Tonight's base recipe is Dr. Cocktail's variation on Harry Craddock's Millionaire No. 1 from *The Savoy Cocktail Book*.

Here is one way she or he would go about it:

Millionaire

In the Dr. Cocktail's recipe (207), Myers's Rum is the base spirit:

2 parts Myers's Original Dark Rum

1 part sloe gin (see note below)

1 part apricot brandy (bottom shelf is fine, which will be "apricot flavored brandy")

1 lime. These organic fruits appear in supermarkets in different sizes, different states of readiness. Slice along the fruit's equator, squeeze both hemispheres into your shaker, and let the gods determine how much comes out.) Most limes in the US are Persian limes, which are small but can be counted on to produce enough juice for a normal cocktail. Originally, the smaller but more intense key limes were what people had and used. Today, these are for pies, not drinks. That said, the recipe calls for 2 parts lime as opposed to the one lime I used.

Prep: Shake and strain into a cold cocktail glass; garnish with a lime wedge or wheel.

Sloe Gin

As teenagers in the 1960s, many males of my generation believed sloe gin to be a sweet spirit invented to seduce girls. Imagine my surprise, more than 50 years later, on discovering that sloe gin has other uses, other tastes. Sloes are the fruit of the blackthorn, a bush that grows, so far as I know, only in England. Some of the English are deeply enough committed to this oddity that they collect sloes and infuse them into their favored gin. Otherwise, the only reliable (and, really, excellent) alternative is Plymouth Sloe Gin.

The stature of the lime affects the balance of sweet and sour in the drink. Until the tail end of my life, Myers's was the sole dark rum I knew about. Study, and experience, reveal alternatives. Cuban rum (Havana

Club), Jamaican rum (Myers's is Jamaican, but others, such as Appleton, are excellent), Dominican rum, Barbados rum, Bermuda rum, Nicaraguan rum, Guyana rum, Haitian rhum, all the outcomes of history and circumstance, may present a drink that suits you better. My favorite, from this dispiriting night is Pusser's Rum (from the British Virgin Islands), the daily ration of sailors in the Royal Navy from 1655 until 1970.

Whatever your rum preference, this is a first-rate cocktail. It balances sweet and sour and the mix of rum and sloe gin creates a richness to be savored. "Bartender, make me a Millionaire!" (Haigh 207). Or even better, I'll make myself a Millionaire!

And what about the other Millionaires? The Modern Cocktail on page 46 of *Barflies and Cocktails* resembles the Millionaire No. 1 in that it includes as the base spirit, scotch rather than rum, and sloe gin. But it also has orange bitters, absinthe, and gomme syrup.

Most Millionaires omit sloe gin. Starting with *The Savoy's:*

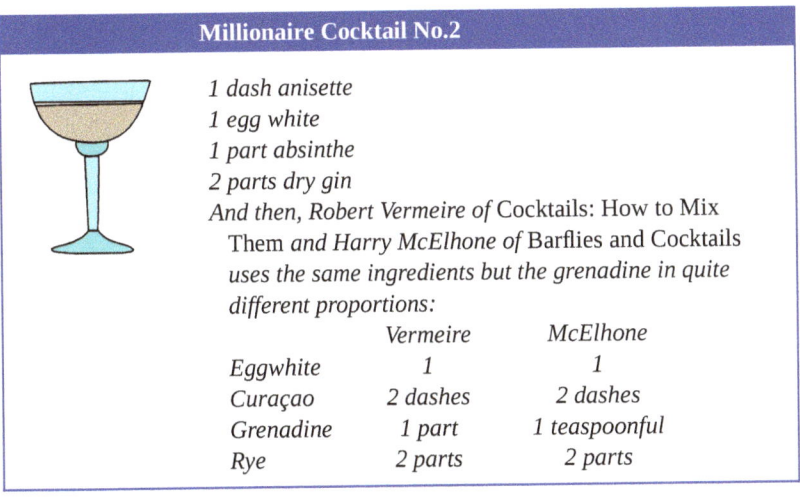

Millionaire Cocktail No.2

1 dash anisette
1 egg white
1 part absinthe
2 parts dry gin
And then, Robert *Vermeire of* Cocktails: How to Mix Them *and Harry McElhone of* Barflies and Cocktails *uses the same ingredients but the grenadine in quite different proportions:*

	Vermeire	McElhone
Eggwhite	1	1
Curaçao	2 dashes	2 dashes
Grenadine	1 part	1 teaspoonful
Rye	2 parts	2 parts

The definitive Millionaire? As Shakespeare put it, "What you will."

27 March Friday

At sea. I'm thinking, given our nautical metaphor, that "at sea" will signal we didn't drink, for some obscure reason.

28 March Saturday

Friday was a dry day, which makes drinks on Saturday, especially as part of the first Luggnuts virtual gathering, all the better. The Luggnuts?

We're a local band of senior citizens who have been playing together for about eight years. We practice here at the Ol' Bean in part because the pub has space to keep our electronic gear such as speakers, soundboard, and Mitch Simon's drums set up. Until Covid struck, we typically practiced once a week and made use of the pub afterward, often talking till late in the evening. Now, like every musician, we're on our own.

The heart of the band is Ruth Fischer, wife of Rick Lugg, for whom we are named. She plays violin, mandolin, and sings; has had musical training; has a good ear; and is the soul of honesty about almost everything in life. She is a Quaker. Ruth went to school at Earlham College, known as the "fighting

Quakers." This fighting drink is mostly, though not entirely on the Internet, forgotten:

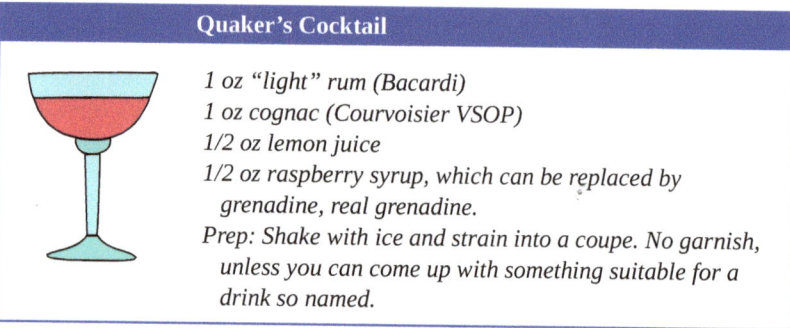

Quaker's Cocktail

1 oz "light" rum (Bacardi)
1 oz cognac (Courvoisier VSOP)
1/2 oz lemon juice
1/2 oz raspberry syrup, which can be replaced by
grenadine, real grenadine.
Prep: Shake with ice and strain into a coupe. No garnish,
unless you can come up with something suitable for a
drink so named.

The first occurrence that I've found of this drink is in *Barflies and Cocktails*, 1927. The recipe includes a cartoon drawing of a pensive Quaker looking, perhaps, for divine direction. Hard to say. The same recipe is in *The Savoy Cocktail Book,* though without comment or illustration. But try also the version in *Schofield's Fine and Classic Cocktails.*

Jenny and I drank Quaker's Cocktails while we saw everyone through Zoom, which seems to be the favored meeting software of the moment. Worked fine, seeing everyone in their separate homes, if awfully sad.

29 March Sunday

I first came cross this New Orleans drink in Great Barrington, Massachusetts, just before the pandemic, the night that our bartender, David Guenette, at No. 10 Castle Street, pointed out that Phil's version of a Martini was a glass of cold gin. As we entered the restaurant and sat at the bar, Phil announced us to be a couple of Louisiana boys, and David offered a Cocktail de la Louisiane. Suited me.

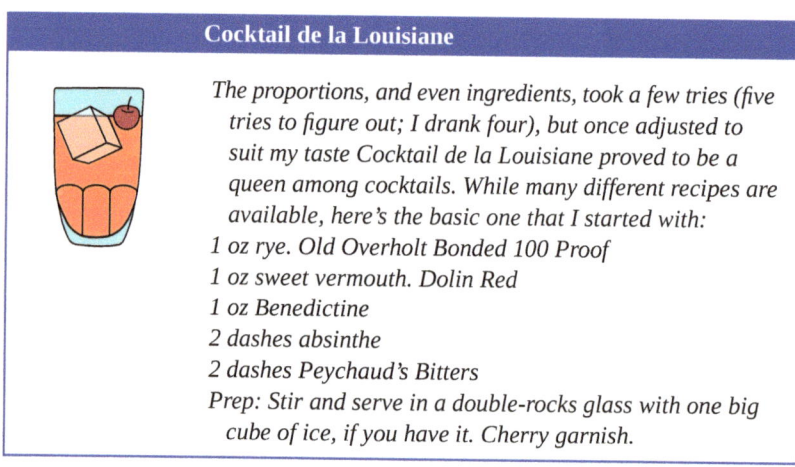

Cocktail de la Louisiane

The proportions, and even ingredients, took a few tries (five
tries to figure out; I drank four), but once adjusted to
suit my taste Cocktail de la Louisiane proved to be a
queen among cocktails. While many different recipes are
available, here's the basic one that I started with:
1 oz rye. Old Overholt Bonded 100 Proof
1 oz sweet vermouth. Dolin Red
1 oz Benedictine
2 dashes absinthe
2 dashes Peychaud's Bitters
Prep: Stir and serve in a double-rocks glass with one big
cube of ice, if you have it. Cherry garnish.

And this proved too sweet for me, though Jenny liked it. I quickly made another version with 1.5 ozs Old Overholt and 0.5 oz Benedictine, and that version was excellent.

We'll come back to this queen, but trying to work out how David, an excellent bartender, might have made up this cocktail was fun. Someday I hope to be able to ask him in person.

30 March Monday

The Knickerbocker, an ancient drink is a Tiki cocktail served nearly 100 years before Trader Vic invented them, pre-dating the old Knickerbocker Hotel on Times Square by nearly 40 years, where it later became the house drink and then disappeared, leaving us to wonder what a bartender at the rebuilt, Emirati-owned Knickerbocker Hotel would offer up today, were they opened, which of course they are not. We hope a confection worthy of this classic.

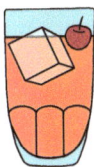

Cocktail de la Louisiane

The proportions, and even ingredients, took a few tries (five tries to figure out; I drank four), but once adjusted to suit my taste Cocktail de la Louisiane proved to be a queen among cocktails. While many different recipes are available, here's the basic one that I started with:

1 oz rye. Old Overholt Bonded 100 Proof
1 oz sweet vermouth. Dolin Red
1 oz Benedictine
2 dashes absinthe
2 dashes Peychaud's Bitters
Prep: Stir and serve in a double-rocks glass with one big cube of ice, if you have it. Cherry garnish.

Drinking this at home with family, and so not needing a lovely presentation, I dropped a spent, squashed half lemon or lime into the glass and poured the drink over it. Don't do this. For rum, I tried Myers's (Jamaican), Pusser's (Virgin Islands), Goslings Black Seal (Bermuda), and St. James (Martinique). Aren't we the island savants? And weren't we drunk? All are dark and all good. My favorite was the relatively unusual St. James, which is a *rhum agricole*. The other rums in this list are from islands in the British sphere; Martinique is, of course, French.

Basics of Rum

So, what's the difference? The British rum is distilled from molasses, a by-product of the production of sugar from cane. As for the French, during the Napoleonic wars the British blockaded the French islands in the Caribbean, preventing them from shipping sugar to their mother country. Napoleon encouraged scientists (scientists, like Dr. Fauci, not charlatans that our Dear Leader seems to prefer; Napoleon was no fool) to find other sources of sugar, and shortly they were able to counter the blockade by producing it from beets in France. As a result, the French islands had a large surplus of sugar cane and so began to produce rum directly from sugar cane juice rather than molasses.

The result, rhum agricole, is a distinctive flavor which seems to me to work especially well in the Knickerbocker. Thus, we have a Dutch name for a cocktail from New York, applied to an anachronistic tiki drink, improved by French island rhum. Finally, and I do not know the historic reasons, but the national spirit of Brazil, called cachaça, like French rhum agricole, is distilled from sugar cane juice. (Do with that what you will.)

Making Your Own Grenadine

If you were to use grenadine in place of the raspberry syrup, cocktail cognoscenti demand real grenadine, which is made from pomegranates. This is harder to find than the red sweetener posing as grenadine but is available, and self-identified, in good liquor stores. On the other hand, you can easily and cheaply make your own grenadine from POM Wonderful pomegranate juice. Use a cup, or half cup, of both the pomegranate juice and sugar (more if you'll use a lot of grenadine, less if you'll use it sparingly) being sure the sugar dissolves entirely. Dissolving is easier and faster with superfine sugar, a good ingredient to keep on hand in a home bar. You can mix the sugar and POM in a Ball jar and shake like hell. Come back later and shake hard again until the sugar dissolves. Keep the grenadine in a refrigerator; it will mold if you don't. Or, add a tablespoon of cheap vodka and it will keep indefinitely in the refrigerator.

Afterword: Having studied the Knickerbocker and rum, you might be as surprised as I was to discover the variation that follows as one of the two Knickerbockers presented in *The Savoy Cocktail Book:*

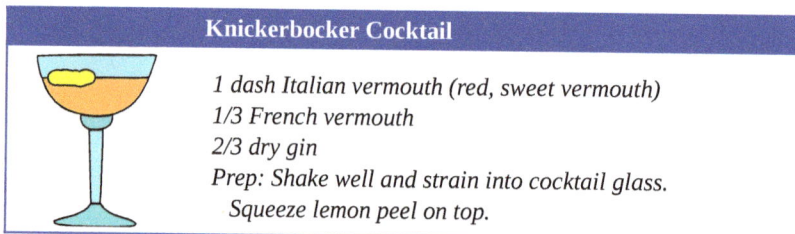

Knickerbocker Cocktail

1 dash Italian vermouth (red, sweet vermouth)
1/3 French vermouth
2/3 dry gin
Prep: Shake well and strain into cocktail glass.
  Squeeze lemon peel on top.

WHAT?! Yet another Martini trying to find its proper name and alcoholic incarnation. Where did he get this? Not only that, but along the way to the Martini in *The Savoy Cocktail Book*, we find the Marguerite Cocktail.

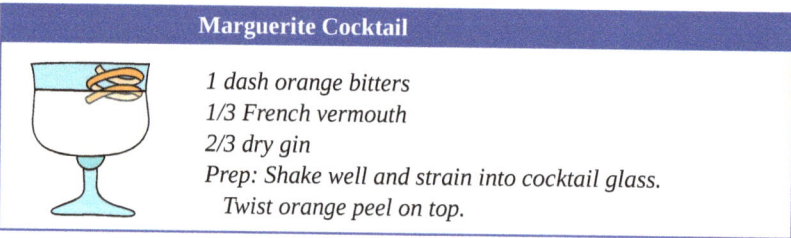

Marguerite Cocktail

1 dash orange bitters
1/3 French vermouth
2/3 dry gin
Prep: Shake well and strain into cocktail glass.
  Twist orange peel on top.

Which is close to many a modern-day Martini. Go figure.

31 March Tuesday

At sea, luckily. Since the first day of this cocktail diary, I've been Tristram Shandy, from Lawrence Sterne's unique 18th Century novel of that name, attempting to write my autobiography and, even in quarantine, tracking only a small part of 24 hours, falling ever farther behind. The real reason for a day away from cocktails is not to give the liver a break. Rather, it is to give the diarist time to catch up.

1 April Wednesday

Thanks to yesterday's pause I've had time to go to the grocery and observe quarantine protocol upon returning (step in a bucket of bleach and water on the porch, wipe down the grocery bags, strip in the laundry room, and shower is my approach); research and prepare a pretty complicated, potentially tasty, meal; write most of a song; exercise; and do the needed research to make this evening's choice of cocktail a good one. Result: the Jack Rose. It is a good one and rightly regarded as a classic.

This ancient, for a time lost, simple, inexpensive, effective, regionally appropriate cocktail deserves historical understanding and, so long as the research does not require days of abstinence, it'll be done. Just don't hold your breath, or hold back, before it is. Drink up!

To begin, the ingredients: applejack, lemon or lime juice, grenadine or (in the drink's original form, raspberry syrup). Three ingredients, but within that small world, room to explore and almost no way to run on any serious, so to speak, rocks.

Jack Rose

2 ozs applejack. While other applejack is now being made, Laird's is the original.

3/4 oz grenadine or raspberry syrup. Some recipes call for less and this is a de gustibus *matter; formulate your own preference. I like either sweetener, and either is enough to give the Rose a distinctive pink hue.*

1 oz lemon, lime or 1/2 oz of each. Just use what you have or what is ready to be cut.

Prep: Strain into a chilled coupe or Martini glass, something that allows the color to come through. For garnish, a Luxardo cherry adds to the pink, but a twist of lemon or lime would be fine.

Applejack and Apple Brandy

Laird's New Jersey distillery was the oldest in North America, dating from 1780, and Robert Laird served in the American Revolution. George Washington asked Laird for his applejack recipe and is said to have made and sold applejack based on it from the distillery he started at Mt. Vernon. Today, Laird's makes many versions of its apple-based spirits. The most ubiquitous, Laird's Applejack, is 80 proof, in which apple is blended with neutral spirits. It is inexpensive, usually under $20 for a 750 ml bottle. While I love the flavor of a Jack Rose, the taste of the applejack is pretty much lost in it among the lemon/lime, grenadine/raspberry syrup. Worth trying will be Laird's Apple Brandy and its 100-proof applejack [Note: Since the entry this has proven to be true. Always buy the Apple Brandy *if you can find it!] Some recipes use half applejack and half calvados. Seems a needless complication to me, but no reason exists, if you have calvados around, for not giving straight calvados a go. Hmmm, sounds like an idea for tonight. For a good discussion of applejack see Haigh 107-109.*

At least one very old Jack Rose recipe, 1927, Harry McElhone's of the New York Bar in Paris, requires 1/3 applejack, 1/3 calvados, 1/6 gin, 1/12 French vermouth,1/12 Italian vermouth, 1/6 orange juice, and 1/6 lemon or lime juice, along with enough grenadine to give the Rose its color. Talk about making the simple extravagantly complicated. I wonder why McElhone did not specify 1/12 lemon and 1/12 lime juice? And by my count, the ratios add up to 8/6. Huh?

Afterword. It occurred to me that a dash of bitters might be interesting and, sure enough, Jim Schwarz, *The Classic Craft Cocktail Recipe Book*, recommends a dash of Peychaud's. *The Home Bartenders' Guide and Songbook*, by Charlie Rowe and Jim Schwenck, omits the citrus and uses equal parts applejack and gin, sounding dangerous. Take your pick.

> *So long as it looks like a Rose, call it Jack,*
> *For by any other name it won't be as sweet.*
> *The simple version is delicious and cheap.*

2 April Thursday

Today we left the field of classic cocktails in favor of two newly invented ones that, as it turns out, are classic knock-offs. First, Mercy, Mercy from a fellow named Jim Schwarz who is apparently a well-known bartender in San Diego; this one appears in *The Classic Craft Cocktail Recipe Book*, page 133. Second, from *Death & Company of NYC*, the May Fair (Kaplan, Fauchald, and Day 166). Both are stirred, not shaken. The recipe for a Mercy, Mercy is easily available on the Internet. The May Fair recipe is not.

Mercy, Mercy

2 ozs gin (I used Beefeater)
1/2 oz Aperol
1/2 oz Cocchi Americano (if you lack Cocchi Americano use Lillet Blanc instead)
Prep: Stir, strain into a chilled cocktail glass. Garnish with an orange twist.

Obviously this is a variation of the Negroni (gin, Campari, sweet vermouth, orange peel or wheel garnish), could even be a Negroni (Aperol, like Campari, is an amaro, a type of Italian liqueur, though a bit less forceful; Cocchi Americano is vermouth and sweet, but it is white, not red). As such, the Mercy, Mercy is a good before dinner drink. We'll call the Negroni a type and look for other variations [see 25 December for a Negroni recipe. Variations in this book include the Mercy, Mercy, Scorched Earth, Novara, and Boulevardier.]

The recipe in *Death & Company: Modern Classic Cocktails* is very specific, and shown below along with what came to hand, since I lack their resources, which, by the way, is a significant flaw of their very good book. That is, *Death & Company* has every cocktail-related ingredient known, including many they prepare or invent themselves. While the bar at the Ol' Bean is well stocked, we have the precise ingredients for few of their cocktails and can make-do with others. Still, we're able to prepare somewhere between one in five or one in ten of the cocktails in the book. Looks like a good excuse to visit NYC…someday (he writes wistfully).

May Fair

1 oz Tanqueray London Dry Gin (I used Beefeater)
1/2 oz Krogstad Aquavit (Nope)
1/2 oz Linie Aquavit (I had only Linie Aquavit and so used 1 oz of it)
1 oz house sweet vermouth. (They mix their own from one part Dolin Rouge and one part Punt e Mes. The Bean has both and could give this a try. But last night I used Antica Formula, my favored red vermouth for most drinks.)
1/4 oz Benedictine
2 dashes Angostura Bitters
2 dashes House Peychaud's Bitters. (They mix two parts Peychaud's with one part Bitter Truth Creole Bitters. I used regular Peychaud's.)

And with all of that, what we have is a variation of [fanfare] one of my favorites: the Vieux Carré, in which the chief spirit is rye, and, I'd say, cognac stands in place of Aquavit. Is the May Fair, or the version of it I was able to make, good? Oh yes. Would it replace a Vieux Carré? No. Does the May Fair stand well enough on its own to keep as part of the repertoire? Hmmm, this could call for testing the two cocktails together, and I will leave the reader to it. Aquavit does not see a lot of use, so why not also investigate it as a cognac substitute in a Vieux Carré? Oh, the world of cocktails is a fine place to live, especially during a pandemic!

3 April Friday

Today the greatest of books about cocktails, *Imbibe* by David Wondrich, arrived. If Michael Jackson was the sage of the world of beer, Wondrich is his equal, or better, in the world of cocktails, a scholar and hunter, though one of the greatest joys of cocktails is that you need not hunt for them. You make your own! Wondrich's quest is to explore the history of the cocktail and the individuals who comprise it. In setting the stage, he describes the low regard Europeans had for American intellectualism in the early 19th Century. We had no literature, painting, science, or philosophy worth their time. But we invented the cocktail, the importance of which Wondrich captures in a memorable paragraph:

Now, admittedly, mixed drinks are not paintings, sculptures, novels, or poems. They are disposable and, frankly, not a little bit disreputable, standing roughly in relation to the culinary arts that American motorsports do to automotive engineering or hot jazz to musical composition: they smack of improvisation and cheap effects and even the most august of them lack the cachet accorded to fine wines, old whiskies, and cognac brandies. They are easily abused: they can degrade lives and even destroy them. Even if appreciated in moderation, they are appreciated in surroundings that rarely lead to detached meditation of truth and beauty (if those are not the same thing) or constructive engagement with the great moral and social questions of the age. And yet neither are they contemptible. A proper drink at the right time—one mixed with care and skill and served in a true spirit of hospitality—is better than any other made thing at giving us the illusion, at least, that we're getting what we want from life. A cat can gaze upon a king, as the proverb goes, and after a Dry Martini or a Sazerac Cocktail or two, we're all cats. (Imbibe, 10)

In his foreword, Wondrich advises that *Imbibe* is a long book and that we should settle in with an Old Fashioned or a Presidente. For the evening, we chose the latter, but after such a paragraph we would not have balked at even a frozen purple daiquiri. The Presidente is very feminine to my eyes and a beauty.

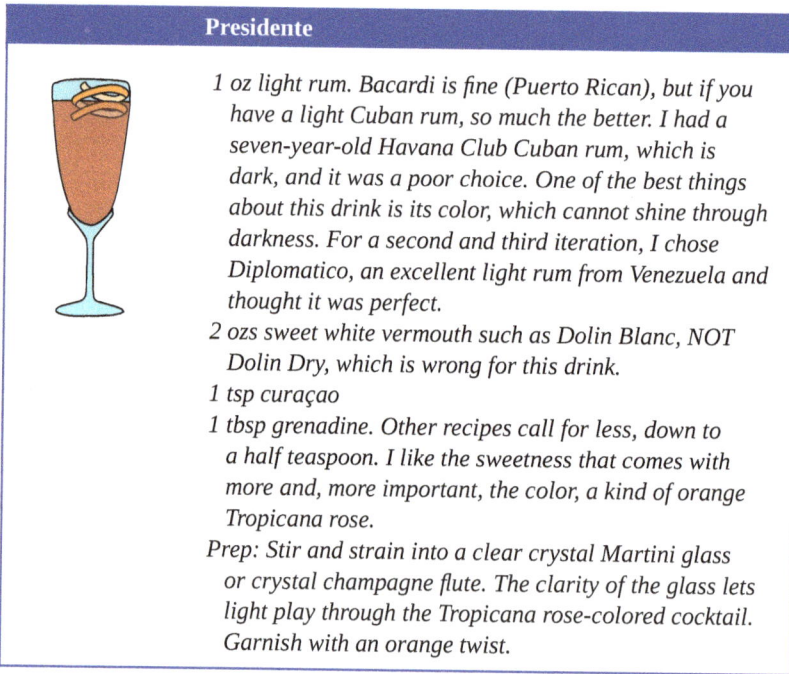

Presidente

1 oz light rum. Bacardi is fine (Puerto Rican), but if you have a light Cuban rum, so much the better. I had a seven-year-old Havana Club Cuban rum, which is dark, and it was a poor choice. One of the best things about this drink is its color, which cannot shine through darkness. For a second and third iteration, I chose Diplomatico, an excellent light rum from Venezuela and thought it was perfect.

2 ozs sweet white vermouth such as Dolin Blanc, NOT Dolin Dry, which is wrong for this drink.

1 tsp curaçao

1 tbsp grenadine. Other recipes call for less, down to a half teaspoon. I like the sweetness that comes with more and, more important, the color, a kind of orange Tropicana rose.

Prep: Stir and strain into a clear crystal Martini glass or crystal champagne flute. The clarity of the glass lets light play through the Tropicana rose-colored cocktail. Garnish with an orange twist.

The Presidente, given the role of light and color in the pleasures of this cocktail, might be the most beautiful drink of all, a beauty to be admired, nor would I call it a "cheap effect."

4 April Saturday

Sours

Three ingredients, a base spirit (rum, gin, tequila, whisky, brandy, applejack, or even vodka), lime or lemon, and sweetener comprise a class of drink called sours. Add a bit of soda water to a sour, and you have another class of drink, the daisy. The Daiquiri is a classic sour: rum, lime, and sugar. Nothing simpler, nothing better.

Because these cocktails have much in common (both are sours) and can be served on similar occasions, say, in summer, why not explore the Daiquiri and Margarita together? The Daiquiri and yesterday's Presidente begin with white rum and are seminal Cuban cocktails, the one shaken because citrus based, the other stirred and relying on liqueurs. The nearly as simple Margarita is Mexican, of course, and at their original best these cocktails are cultural statements, though often degraded into highballs as frozen, colored, or artificially flavored, compromised catastrophes. Until Saturday I'd never made, perhaps never drunk, a real Daiquiri. Now, happily, there is no going back.

Befitting their warm, Latin origins these cocktails are ideal summer drinks for hot days. Generally, in the U.S., the Daiquiri seems far less popular than the Margarita. In my hometown, New Orleans, however, where it is nearly always hot, drive-through frozen-daiquiri chains sell outrageously colored giants dispensed in plastic that would seem to belie this observation. In fact, however, such monstrosities have helped relegate an excellent cocktail to the realm of kid's stuff. The recipe…

Daiquiri

2 ozs rum. Most recipes call for white rum, especially Bacardi (Ruth and Jenny's first version last night). I like the "funky" Haitian Barbancourt white (Rick and I had this). Venezuela's Diplomatico white is excellent. If you want gold rum, Pirat (the second version Rick and I had) was good. You might also try a high-end Jamaican rum, say, Appleton. In any event, use what you've got but probably nothing too dark such as Myers's or Gosling.

1 oz lime juice. Note that the ratios are the same as in a Margarita. With any cocktail, use only freshly squeezed citrus.

3 barspoons of superfine sugar. If simple syrup, 3/4 oz. As always, adjust the ratio to suit your palate.

Prep: Shake and strain into a chilled cocktail glass. Garnish with a lime twist.

Every recipe calls for the Daiquiri to be served up, without ice. I've found that where chilling the glasses is difficult, using the ice from the shaker gives you a Daiquiri on the rocks, lets you sip at leisure, and does not dilute the drink appreciably.

Here is proof that perfection and simplicity need not be strangers. The drink is easily prepared one at a time or by the pitcher. To find the version that exactly accords with your taste, comparing different rums should be fun. The simplicity of a Daiquiri enables the flavor of the rum to come through more intensely, I believe, than does tequila in a Margarita. From Harry Craddock, *The Savoy Cocktail Book*, by way of Joseph Hergesheimer's San Cristobal de la Habana:

> The moment had arrived for a Daiquiri. It was a delicate compound; it elevated
> my contentment to an even higher pitch. Unquestionably, the cocktail on my table
> was a dangerous agent, for it held in its shallow glass bowl slightly encrusted with
> undissolved sugar the power of a contemptuous indifference to fate; it set the mind
> free of responsibility; obliterating both memory and tomorrow, it gave the heart an
> adventitious feeling of superiority and momentarily all the celebrated, the eternal
> fears. Yes, that was the danger of skillfully prepared intoxicating drinks… The word

"intoxicating" adequately expressed their power, their menace to orderly, monotonous resignation. A word, I thought further, debased by moralists from its primary ecstatic content… but then, with a fresh Daiquiri and a sprig of orange blossom in my button-hole, it meant less than nothing (54-55).

The Margarita was invented sometime between 1929 and 1961 in Mexico, Texas, or California, a latecomer compared with relatives, Daiquiri, Presidente, and Knickerbocker. Yet, none of the origin myths I've seen claims those cocktails influenced the birth of the Margarita.

Margarita

2 ozs tequila. Either silver or reposado. No need to use expensive tequila.

1 oz fresh lime juice

1 oz orange liqueur. Usually recipes specify Cointreau. I prefer curaçao, which is FAR cheaper. Triple secs other than Cointreau, such as Grand Marnier, are fine too. Suit yourself.

1/2 oz sweetener. The perfect sweetener for this drink, and one otherwise underrated for use in cocktails, is agave, easily found in a grocery. If you use curaçao you may want more sweetener than if you use Cointreau.

Prep: Shake, of course. If you like your Margarita on the rocks, just pour everything into a single-rocks glass. If you prefer your Margarita up, use a coupe. If you want it frozen, I can't help you. Garnish with a lime wheel.

Salting a Rim

If you like a salted rim, rub spent lime on the outside of the glass and twirl it through Diamond Crystal kosher salt. The lime on the outside keeps the salt there rather than inside. Where it could spoil your drink. Why so specific about the salt? The usual choice in most groceries is between this one and Morton's. The difference comes from the way the two are dried, and the process Diamond Crystal uses lets their salt cling to and stay better on the rim.

5 April Sunday

At sea.

6 April Monday

Manhattan from Wondrich

2 dashes of bitters (Angostura is what he recommends, and everyone uses anyway)
1 dash of absinthe (he indicates this is optional)
2 ozs whisky (rye generally, here Old Overholt)
1 oz Vino Vermouth (that is red vermouth, here Antica Formula)
A little (1/4 tsp) maraschino (I prefer a little syrup from the Luxardo Cherries)
Prep: Stir well. Strain and serve in a cold coupe.

7 April Tuesday

[Note: In the recipe below I used ratios rather than ounces, thinking, I believe, it was a more universal approach. Two days later went back to ozs. You'll note in the brief discussion of limes and lemons, ozs work, parts do not.]

Perhaps the most forgotten great cocktail, from a forgotten time (Prohibition), invented by a forgotten star (Tommy Millard), during a lost (not just forgotten) moment of inspiration for all the right reasons (defying a stupid government) is the Twelve-Mile Limit. Before telling this story let's go right to the ingredients that comprise the drink in hopes of inspiring you to enjoy one while reading on.

Twelve-Mile Limit

4 parts rum.
2 parts VSOP cognac. Here, take your pick.
2 parts rye. I typically use the standard Old Overholt, an excellent price and versatile mixer.
2 parts lemon. I've given up measuring lemon and lime by the ounce. Their ratios seem not to be critical, so do what is convenient. A lime usually yields a bit more than an oz a lemon twice as much.
2 parts real pomegranate grenadine.
Prep: Shake hard and strain into a chilled Martini glass; coupe; or at best, a champagne flute. Garnish with lemon twist.

This cocktail is heavy on spirits, but rum is its foundation. I don't know this for a fact but believe that the right rum either makes or breaks the drink. The recipes call for white rum, and the most common is Bacardi. It is, however, the wrong choice: too light. For a while I've used white Diplomatico from Venezuela, highly rated, but our liquor store had none so I bought a white *rhum agricole* from Haiti, Barbancourt, and used it. This Haitian *rhum* seems made for the Twelve-Mile Limit. It blends beautifully with the other spirits and stands out at the same time. The taste is heavenly.

33

Such a delicious and dangerous cocktail, the kind you could impulsively drink down by the bucket only to find yourself waking on the front lawn in your underwear. Be careful! If you're curious about Tommy Millard, you can find him in Wikipedia. He is worth a look with a Twelve-Mile Limit in hand.

8 April Wednesday

Another Prohibition sour. I tried this one with 100 proof Old Overholt Rye and with 101 proof Wild Turkey Bourbon to go with Dolin Dry White Vermouth. On the last round, running short of real pomegranate grenadine, switched to Rose's. Photos of this cocktail showed brilliant red but steadfastly insisted on using real grenadine, which for me created a pale orange drink. The Rose's was indeed tarted up, brilliant red, and not so good. That is, the Scofflaw proved that if you venture outside the law of using real grenadine do not expect a great drink.

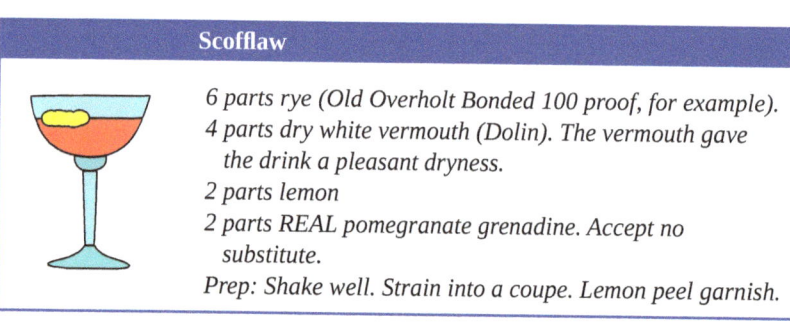

Scofflaw

6 parts rye (Old Overholt Bonded 100 proof, for example).
4 parts dry white vermouth (Dolin). The vermouth gave the drink a pleasant dryness.
2 parts lemon
2 parts REAL pomegranate grenadine. Accept no substitute.
Prep: Shake well. Strain into a coupe. Lemon peel garnish.

To my palate, while this cocktail is fine, it lacks the richness of the rum, rye, cognac combination of the Twelve-Mile Limit; seems wrong that the Scofflaw is far easier to find, is much better known. Could be all in the name.

Canadian Whisky
Some early recipes specify Canadian whisky for a Scofflaw because it was said to be mostly rye and a good substitute for rye. Not so. Even today, Canadian whisky can have any percentage of rye the distiller likes, including none at all. Worse, with apologies to my Canadian friends, it is light on flavor.

Note the difference in spelling. In the US and Ireland, whiskey includes an 'e'; in the UK, Canada, and Japan, it has no 'e'. Whiskey in the US and Ireland; whisky in the UK, Canada, and Japan.

9 April Thursday

At sea.

10 April Friday—Good Friday

What is a symbolically appropriate cocktail for this Good Friday of the Coronavirus Pandemic? Blood and Sand? Corpse Reviver? Fancy Free? Last Word? Daisy de Santiago (surely not)? Zombie? Howl on the Hill? The last, from *Death & Company* page 178, has the gravity appropriate to the occasion.

> *The Spoon and the Shaker*
> *As good a rule as "Love thy neighbor."*
> (Do not recall where I got this…)

A complex drinker's drink, which is to say, alcohol dominates. If you don't relish the combinatory possibilities of alcohol, move on. Importantly, the drinks I've made are NOT, cannot be, Howls on the Hill. As usual with *Death & Company's* (*D&C's*) highly sophisticated New York City cocktails, people out here in the hinterland, where provincial liquor stores are the best we can do, must come as close to *D&C* ingredients as our cash, interest, and retailers enable. But limited as we are, I'd say that on Pandemic Good Friday 2020, the Ol' Bean Tavern feels on the cusp of resurrection.

To begin, the *D&C's* invention has two rums: 1.5 ozs El Dorado 15-year rum (I doubt a rum this expensive has ever crossed the New Hampshire border); 0.5 ozs Santa Teresa 1796 rum (not a chance).

In place of these unobtainable rums, I used 1.5 ozs of St James and 0.5 oz of 7-year-old Cuban on the first drink. On drink two, St James alone. On drink 3, Barbancourt. On drink 4 (yes, I had a hangover) Pusser's. The blend was lost on me. I'd add of the *D&C* recipe that if a 15-year-old rum cannot stand on its own, what's the point of giving it 15 years to mature? And, indeed, the St James on its own and the Barbancourt, a white rum, each were excellent. The first was richer, deeper. But the white rum introduced a cleanness amidst the other complex spirits that stood out as very fine. And finally, the Pusser's, a rum I like a great deal in other drinks, was bad in this one.

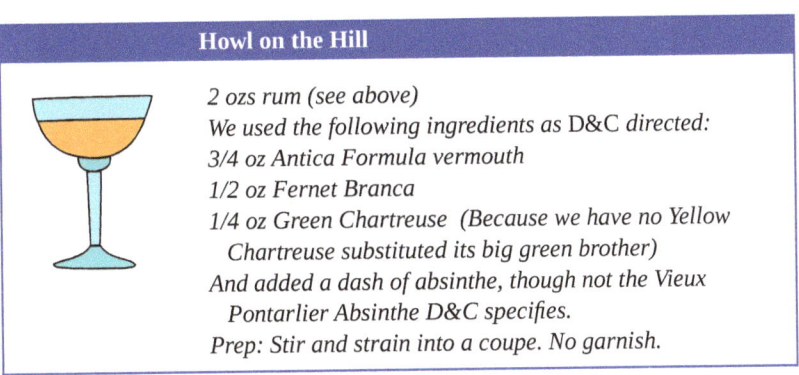

Howl on the Hill

2 ozs rum (see above)
We used the following ingredients as D&C *directed:*
3/4 oz Antica Formula vermouth
1/2 oz Fernet Branca
1/4 oz Green Chartreuse (Because we have no Yellow
*   Chartreuse substituted its big green brother)*
And added a dash of absinthe, though not the Vieux
*   Pontarlier Absinthe D&C specifies.*
Prep: Stir and strain into a coupe. No garnish.

The St James and Barbancourt versions were excellent, possibly cocktails I'll return to often. But the question is, what is this drink? It cannot be a Howl on the Hill, or can it? Is the, ahem, spirit of a cocktail some Platonic form such that the particular brands or manifestations within a brand (yellow versus green) don't matter? Or is that the same as saying I am my brother (oh my, not that!)? Among the glories of drinking, and I say this sober, if hungover, are its many ponderables.

11 April Saturday

Considered a day of abstinence owing to last night's over enthusiasm, but at the last minute, post dinner, decided that was a poor idea. Looked for something simple, and the Gimlet appeared in *Schofield's Fine and Classic Cocktails*. Based on their recipe, it was clear that a Gimlet is a gin-based Daiquiri and last Saturday we learned to love Daiquiris. So I made a couple as follows:

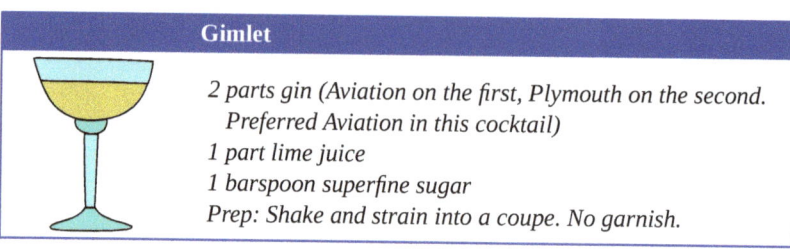

Gimlet

2 parts gin (Aviation on the first, Plymouth on the second. Preferred Aviation in this cocktail)
1 part lime juice
1 barspoon superfine sugar
Prep: Shake and strain into a coupe. No garnish.

A very English drink, and we have been watching an English detective series, so I sipped slowly, joyfully, while watching. Lime and sugar love spirits, all of them. And what could be simpler? Except, looking back to yesterday's question, the drink was not, or may not have been, a Gimlet. What?

Rose's Lime Juice

Rose's Lime Juice Cordial is what. That is, the Schofield's notion that a Gimlet does not require Rose's, which is sweetened lime juice that does not spoil on the shelf, originally invented to prevent scurvy, is by many lights just plain wrong. Oh my. What's in a name?… or an ingredient?

12 April Sunday—Easter

What else, on Easter, but the Corpse Reviver No. 2. This classic from *The Savoy Cocktail Book* was itself revived by Dr. Cocktail. The wonder is how it could have died away in the first place. Awhile back our 18-year-old son introduced the Corpse Reviver No. 2 to his friend Carter, who found a way to buy the ingredients and now makes them nightly for his family. Apparently, the Corpse Reviver is Carter's favorite liquid. Frequently we find ourselves short of lemons at the Ol' Bean owing to late night reviving by our son.

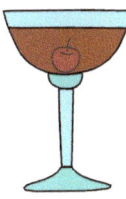

1 part gin. I began the night with Ford's, and it was my favorite. Next in preference was Aviation. Plymouth seemed a bit too sweet, and Beefeater lacked character. Emphatically, any of these, and surely many others, is fine.

1 part Lillet Blanc or Cocchi Americano. Either of these is a modern substitute for the original Kina Lillet, now long gone. Some recommend one, some the other. I have read that Cocchi Americano is nearer to the original, but who knows? Last night used Cocchi Americano and it was excellent. But so is Lillet Blanc, which is available at our local liquor store and is inexpensive.

1 part lemon juice

1 part Cointreau. I also used orange and later blue curaçao. Neither is a substitute for Cointreau in this drink and the blue is to be avoided for its color alone. Even the orange tinges this lovely drink enough that I'll not use it again. I will try Grand Marnier.

3 drops (not dashes) of absinthe [What is a dash? You'll see that the question puzzled me considerably. The diary describes how to produce consistent dashes later, but for now it is enough to say that a dash is 1/8 teaspoon and that a dash is not the same thing as a "shake" or a "drop."]

Prep: Shake and strain into a chilled coupe. Garnish by letting a Luxardo cherry sink to the bottom.

This is a drink nearly anyone will love, its equal portions are easy to remember, and so it seems a candidate for a house drink that will surprise and delight most guests, that will make the bartender look good. The cocktail is still uncommon enough that most people will not have heard of it, giving them the pleasure of a delicious discovery. Even the name is a pleasant talking point (not just on Easter), deriving from a class of mid-19th Century drinks meant to cure hangovers. In short, why not add the Corpse Reviver No. 2 to your repertoire?

13 April Monday

A day of abstinence. Lent, for me, lasts only a day and can show up any time, making me holier than thou.

14 April Tuesday

The Alamagoozulum and the Jack Rose Redux

The what? When people, or computers, read this a thousand years from now, they may not know that Corona Virus 19 can deprive us of our senses of smell and taste. The Alamagoozulum surely kills any virus long before its evil effects are rendered owing to the cocktail's gigantic booziness. But first, let's look again at the Jack Rose (see April Fool's Day).

Jack Rose Redux

A typical, simple sour, relying on applejack, which at our last review, really did not hold up, was lost in the citrus and grenadine. Much as we love Laird's, the historical idea of Laird's as our oldest and surviving New World distillery, and much as we love the $15.99 cost of a bottle of Laird's Applejack, it will not do for a Jack Rose.

With that in mind I sprung for a far pricier apple brandy, something like $37, I think. From the Copper and Kings' Distillery this 100-proof apple brandy, Floodwall, stood up and stood out. For a few dollars more, the New Hampshire Flag Hill Distillery has a much-awarded apple brandy, Josiah Bartlett, but that will be for another time. Why doesn't applejack work? By definition, it includes neutral grain spirits, as much as 80 percent, besides alcohol distilled from apple and, as a result, has a less intense apple flavor. We can't seem to get Laird's apple brandy in New Hampshire, a bad break.

For some time I have followed the edict of all serious cocktail writers and used pomegranate grenadine, except for a one-time trial of Rose's, which proved their point. As it happens, I had run low on the Powell and Mahoney that I have been using, but had Infused Grenadine Syrup from Master of Mixes, which is made with 15% cherry and pomegranate juice (that's the total juice). Much better than Rose's, this will do in a pinch, and it makes the Jack Rose quite red, which the tastier Powell & Mahoney does not. In short, now that we have acceptable apple brandy, work still needs to be done finding the right grenadine. It is unfortunate and thoroughly unpoetic that Rose's will not work.

On to the **Alamagoozulum**

The word does not appear in the *Oxford English Dictionary*, never has, probably never will. But the recipe for this cocktail, owing to the alphabetical make-up of the word, appears first in Dr. Cocktail's *Vintage Spirits and Forgotten Cocktails* (38-39), which tells us that the Dr. was willing to stake his book's reputation on this oddly named oddity. It is an oddity.

First, the Alamagoozulum is, as I think its name suggests, enormous: eight ingredients and a lot of booze. Among Dr. Cocktail's lost confections, it is anomalous by its size. Typically, cocktails are potent, but small, in general including 2 to 3 ounces of alcohol. This one has 5.5 ounces, including 1.5 ounces of the 120 proof Green Chartreuse. Second, it has 1/2 oz of Angostura bitters; bitters are usually measured in dashes, or even drops, almost never in ounces! Third, Dr. Cocktail's recipe calls for Genever, or Dutch gin, a basic 19th Century ingredient but rarely called for in 21st Century America (I had part of a bottle left over from a trip to Amsterdam years ago). And while this next ingredient, egg white, is not unusual, it's hardly a commonplace. Let's look then at how to make this monster:

Alamagoozulum

1/2 egg white? Okay, how do you measure half an egg white? But here you go:
1/2 egg white (I now use egg whites in a carton. Try 1/2 oz)
2 ozs Genever (substituted Beefeater)
2 ozs water (Water? Just water?)
1.5 ozs Jamaican rum (such as Myers's or Appleton)
1.5 ozs gomme syrup (simple syrup will do)
1.5 ozs Yellow or Green Chartreuse
0.5 oz orange curaçao
0.5 oz Angostura bitters
Prep: Shake long and hard and strain into a very large, chilled coupe or coupes.

Was not crazy about this complicated confection but down the line, perhaps another try?

15 April Wednesday

Manhattan

This great, classic, simple drink deserves careful preparation and top-shelf ingredients. Or maybe it is so grand it doesn't require top-shelf ingredients. In *Death & Company's* second book, it is the mother of a whole class of cocktails. But first…

Old Overholt Rye

For tonight's Manhattans, I used Old Overholt Bonded 100 Proof Rye. A few words about Old Overholt. The regular 80 proof is bottom shelf, at about $20 a 750 ml bottle. Modern bar guides, including Dr. Cocktail's Vintage Spirits and Forgotten Cocktails, *often recommend it, and down the years in good bars I've visited this is often the house rye. It mixes well with other ingredients where you have no need for a pricey (and they can be very pricey) rye. As I write, the overlord company Jim Beam is making some changes to Old Overholt that sound promising, which will include raising the proof from 80 to 86, but the price should increase only $1.*

Further, Old Overholt is truly storied. From Pennsylvania, it has sold commercially since 1810. In 1919 the brand passed from the Overholt family into the hands of one of their partners, Andrew Mellon. Prohibition took effect in 1920, and in 1921 Mellon became Secretary of the Treasury, responsible for issuing "medicinal whiskey licenses." Of course, he issued a license to himself.

Over the years Carnegie sold the brand, and after Prohibition, rye fell out of favor. Despite hard times, Old Overholt, much changed in character, continued through various owners and today is distilled in Kentucky by Jim Beam. The bottom-shelf version today is a Kentucky style whose grain bill includes corn and is aged 3 years, not the 4 required to be bottled in bond.

Bottled in Bond

Bottled in bond is the result of an 1897 federal law that came about because whiskey was being badly adulterated. Bonded means the whiskey (any spirit can be bonded but practically only whiskies are) is the product of one distillery and one distiller in one season, barreled for at least four years, and bottled at exactly 100 proof.

Rules for Rye and Bourbon

By the way, in the United States a rye whiskey must be 51 percent rye, just as bourbon must be 51 percent corn. The other 49 percent of grain can be anything, and, for rye whiskey bottled in Kentucky, that often will include significant corn, and in the case of Old Overholt, malted barley as well. Really, there is nothing "straight" about straight rye or bourbon.

Anyway, a couple weeks back I bought Bonded Old Overholt, still reasonably priced at $25. This is a fairly new product, and turns out, a good one. Richer than their regular rye, the Bonded version will be the Ol' Bean house rye, at least until the 86-proof version appears, and then we will see. The Manhattan recipe:

Manhattan

2 ozs Old Overholt Bonded 100 Proof Rye
1 oz Antica Formula Italian vermouth. First time we've had Manhattans with this vermouth, and, oh my goodness, the drink is Platonic. Still, we'll try Cocchi di Torino and perhaps even Punt e Mes. I mean, once you've found your way to Platonic why not go for Perfect? At any event, for Manhattans and other cocktails requiring sweet vermouth, Antica Formula yields a far richer cocktail than more common Rossi.
2-4 dashes Angostura or Peychaud's bitters or any combination. Try orange bitters and even absinthe. I like bitters, but my tastebuds are more sensitive some days than others. If yours are similar, it'll be good to find a day when your taste buds are especially acute, discover what you like, and stay with it through dull days.
Prep: Serve up in a cold coupe. Garnish with Luxardo cherry.

16 April Thursday

At sea, preparing for a drinking weekend

17 April Friday

Oh my, such a night. Here's the cocktail menu: Diamondback, Blue Moon, Hanky Panky, Jungle Bird. I made all of these, but the Blue Moon and Hanky Panky were for Jenny.

Diamondback
2 ozs Old Overholt Bonded Rye, or similar. 1/2 oz Yellow Chartreuse (or Green will do) 1/2 oz apple brandy (or calvados) Prep: Stir with ice and strain into a cold coupe.

The drink originated in the early 1950s in the Diamondback Lounge of the Lord Baltimore Hotel. It is an end-of-the-night-if-you're-not-driving boozy confection. Most recipes call for Yellow Chartreuse, but Green is acceptable.

And this is about all I recall. Wonder why. We'll have to come back to the other cocktails. I'm saving the next Diamondback for a very blue moon.

18 April Saturday

The voyager must be prepared for the unexpected, a cocktail that looks promising and falls flat or a recipe that wrongs a storied drink. The Park Avenue looks right, but in my versions, both of them, it was not. The Mai Tai presented by the Schofield brothers was uninteresting but rescued on an adjusted second attempt. Dr. Cocktail spends little time on this drink; I'll mostly follow suit.

Park Avenue
2 ozs gin. I made two back to back, the first with Beefeater, the second with Plymouth. 3/4 oz pineapple juice. I use the canned kind from Dole, and in other cocktails it has been fine. But the others also include citrus, either lemon or lime, which is fresh. Here, with canned pineapple by itself, the juice fragrance and liveliness fail. Perhaps fresh pineapple? 3/4 oz sweet vermouth. Into the Beefeater version went Antica Formula and into the Plymouth, Cocchi di Torrino. The latter was notably flatter, but neither was the former very interesting. Could be that a more moderate vermouth, say Dolin red, would suit this cocktail better. 2 tsps orange curaçao. Not really forward here. Prep: Shake and serve up by straining into a cold coupe.

We could experiment with any of the ingredients. Or, we could simply leave this to the swells of Park Avenue and move on.

Invented in 1944 by the famed Trader Vic (Victor Jules Bergeron), or perhaps by his competitor Don the Beachcomber (Don Beach), the Mai Tai is the seminal Tiki Drink.

Mai Tai (from the Schofield Brothers)

1 oz Jamaican rum (e.g. Myers's or Appleton)
1 oz aged rhum agricole (e.g. Barbancourt 15 year old)
1 1/4 oz lime juice
1/3 oz orange curaçao
1/3 oz orgeat
1 dash Angostura bitters
Prep: Shake and pour into an ice-filled rocks glass. Mint sprig and lime wheel garnish.

Orgeat

About orgeat (or/zhat). This almond sweetener is worth having in your bar and easily found. It can overpower a cocktail with its scent, but the flowery fragrance is lovely when used appropriately. I keep a large bottle of Difford's on hand, and it does not go bad.

19 April Sunday

A perfect early spring day (yesterday it snowed), keeping everyone outdoors, and by day's end, we're exhausted. Meanwhile in faraway New Orleans my friend Michael rode his bike to the French Quarter, which without people or traffic, showed well and put me in mind of perhaps my favorite cocktail, the Vieux Carré (which is, of course, French for old quarter and often used as a synonym for French Quarter, though likely to be mispronounced as VOO Karry).

Mostly in this age, and perhaps in others, people have a cocktail, or spirits in some other form, that they will drink nightly at home or order in a restaurant or bar. These drinkers, and I may prove to be one, try new drinks in, say, a proper cocktail bar, but at home are unlikely to have the ingredients for these rare flowers or, really, to know what those ingredients are. As a result, they stay with the familiar.

My dad drank an Old Fashioned, or two, every night. One of my brothers, while less religious about nightly, loves an Old Fashioned often, as do I. Martini, Gin or Vodka and Tonic, Whiskey Sour, Manhattan, Margarita, even an Aperol Spritz or Negroni, Jack on the rocks, single malt neat, red or white wine, beer, we tend to find what we like, often influenced by parents, sometimes by trends or travels, and mostly stay with it. In part this diary is an attempt to find and rest on a handful of favored cocktails.

The Vieux Carré—invented by Walter Bergeron at the Monteleone Hotel in the French Quarter in 1938, almost disappeared, and is included among Dr. Cocktail's *Forgotten Cocktails* (280)—may be nobody's regular. But it could be. It could become my regular.

The drink commands a group of bourbon or rye-based, bitters-dependent perennials—the Manhattan, Old Fashioned—and the closely related, Louisiana-originated Sazerac and Cocktail de la Louisiane. The Vieux Carré is distinguished, however, because it elegantly includes versions of the ingredients that enliven each of the other cocktails in this group. Let's begin with the recipe:

Vieux Carré

1 oz rye but you could use bourbon
1 oz cognac, and I'd recommend VSOP
1 oz sweet vermouth. Take your pick, but I like, as usual,
   Antica Formula or Dolin Rouge
1/2 tsp Benedictine
2 dashes Angostura Bitters
2 dashes Peychaud's Bitters
Prep: Stir, serve up or on the rocks. Garnish with a cherry
   or lemon twist or both.

Exactly twice the number of ingredients in a Manhattan (rye, vermouth, Angostura Bitters) or an Old Fashioned (bourbon, sweetener [whether sugar or some other, such as my favorite, maple syrup], Angostura bitters); and two ingredients up on a Sazerac (rye, sugar, Peychaud's Bitters, absinthe), the Vieux Carré, shall we say, comprehends it cousins, including the less known Cocktail de la Louisiane (rye, Benedictine, sweet vermouth, absinthe, Peychaud's Bitters), which is still one ingredient short.

All of these New Orleans cocktails predate the Vieux Carré by more than 50 years, and it is a safe bet that before inventing his own, Bergeron had made hundreds or thousands of each. The ingredient that the Vieux Carré shares with none of the other cocktails in this line-up is cognac. And therein lies irony and its nearly inseparable companion, history.

But rather than look back, let's look forward. Maybe you like the list of ingredients but lack some of them. If so, how about fashioning a Vieux Carré-like cocktail. Perhaps bourbon or rye, apple brandy or calvados, sweet vermouth, Cherry Heering, and a couple of bitters? Intriguing? Down the road, let's tell each other how this turns out.

Meanwhile, I first came across the Vieux Carré only a few years ago with my brother at the bar of the Black Birch Restaurant in Kittery, Maine. We were each drinking a well-prepared Old Fashioned served properly on one big rock, and lamenting that Peychaud's Bitters, another New Orleans product, were used only in the Sazerac. Our bartender, Alex, piped up to ask, "Would you like a Vieux Carré?" Turns out that Peychaud's Bitters are used in many cocktails, but in none to better effect than this one.

The principal reason for making Sunday April 19, 2020, a Vieux Carré night was a pandemic-style cocktail call with our friends Mitch and Susan. Mitch loves a Manhattan, but knowing that I love an Old Fashioned, he promised to drink one during the call. I thought a Vieux Carré, which to me is a Manhattan on steroids, would be the right way to acknowledge Mitch's preference. As with a Manhattan, the Vieux Carré can easily be fine-tuned to your particular tastes, and, indeed, its extra ingredients allow for even more artful combinations.

20 April Monday

At sea, except… keeping to our New Orleans theme, a Sazerac.

Sazerac

 *Wash a single-rocks glass with absinthe, which is to say add a tsp and swirl it until the glass is coated. Most manuals say to discard the absinthe that remains, but why would you do that, at least if the cocktail is for you or your wife? Waste not; drink it. The absinthe probably will not cause you to go mad. Put the glass in your fridge or freezer if handy while you blend the other ingredients by stirring with a barspoon.*
2 ozs rye
3 dashes Peychaud's Bitters
1/2 - 1 oz simple syrup
Pour the blended Sazerac into the coated glass. Garnish with a cherry, lemon twist, or both.

21 April Tuesday

Jambalaya, food of the gods, at least the ones who dwell in Louisiana, is a favorite dish among a few of us in New Hampshire, including our friend Rick Lugg. Ingredients, proper ones, would seem to be impossible to find so far from their native land, but it turns out, one smokehouse in Claremont, New Hampshire, for some deeply mysterious reason, makes good smoked chicken; fine andouille sausage; and the key, truly unlikely ingredient, tasso, which is a smoked, very spicy ham. You cannot find these many places, and the tasso can only be ordered, so Rick, on his own, put in a large order, asked how much my brother wanted and how much we wanted, and then—gratis—delivered these to our house, risking his life braving the pandemic.

Our son Al loves jambalaya, and we used this as the way for him to learn, under my experienced eye, how to go about preparing it. I showed him how to sharpen a chef's knife with a steel; how to make the spice mix; how to chop onions, bell pepper, celery, and garlic; and how to dice the meats. Then we combined everything in the Dutch oven in the right order, cooked them in the evening, and had a Zoom call with Rick and Ruth, who were eating the jambalaya Rick made. Meanwhile, the cocktail of the day, a carryover from Sunday's Vieux Carré exploration, was Cocktail de la Louisiane (see 29 March 2020).

First thing to say is that just as the Vieux Carré was a delicious companion with ribs and potatoes (did I mention that?), the sweet, cooling Cocktail de la Louisiane was wonderful with the savory, spicy jambalaya. But here's the thing: I expected a poor version of the Vieux Carré, a drink not quite as profound that could not take the measure of its sister. I was wrong.

Then, things got interesting, leading to a digression about another seminal New Orleans drink, the Sazerac.

Sazerac

In the 1700s and 1800s New Orleans is a cognac town, not surprising given its strongly French culture. In 1795, Antoine Peychaud moves from Haiti (before it was called Haiti) to New Orleans. He is an apothecary who carries with him the family recipe for a bitters that contains anise and comes to sell it from his shop on Royal Street in the French Quarter as Peychaud's Bitters. By 1838 Peychaud includes his bitters as part of a no-doubt-restorative pharmaceutical cocktail served in an egg cup, called a coquetier. (From this plausible history, by the way, various New Orleanians have inferred that the word "cocktail" derives from coquetier and that this makes the Sazerac the oldest cocktail. This is nonsense.)

But here's a real problem. In about 1850, Sewell T. Taylor sold his bar, the Merchants Exchange Coffee House, and became an importer of spirits, in particular of Sazerac de Forge et Fils, while the new owner of the bar changed its name to Sazerac Coffee House. The story goes that the coffee house's Sazerac Cocktail was made with cognac from Sazerac de Forge et Fils and spiced with Peychaud's Bitters.

David Wondrich, however, says that "The first time we hear of a specific Sazerac Cocktail is in 1899" (Imbibe, 238), but he notes that to find a Sazerac, "you had to go to the venerable (if oft rebuilt) Sazerac House Bar at 116 Royal Street," and goes on to describe the bar as a necessary stop for tippling tourists by 1900. The bar, and the formula for Peychaud's Bitters were owned by the W.C. Handy Company, which was also selling a line of pre-mixed cocktails that included the Sazerac.

All three of these stories could be true. That is, Antoine Peychaud may have invented what came to be called the Sazerac in the early to mid-Nineteenth Century. Sewell and Bird may have taken Peychaud's recipe and used their favorite cognac both to name the cocktail and to prepare it. And so, by the time Wondrich finds the drink in print, New Orleanians may have been drinking Sazeracs for decades. And indeed, by 1899, Sazeracs were being made not with Sazerac de Forge et Fils cognac. They were made with rye, so if the cocktail was invented lately, why name it for a cognac?

The reason for the change to rye was phylloxera. In the early 1860s an aphid from American grape vines, helped by quick passage on newly sailing steam-powered vessels, invaded and began destroying French vineyards. As a result, New Orleans' preferred spirit for mixing cocktails became much harder to obtain, more expensive, and soon lost its pre-eminent position. Among the losses was the Sazerac to rye and even to bourbon.

But what about the Cocktail de la Louisiane? After downing that first excellent, less sweet version, it occurred to me to experiment with how the past might have tasted, to learn whether New Orleans' phylloxera-forced migration to spirits besides cognac could have left something worth knowing behind. And indeed, could the Cocktail de la Louisiane originally have been, as was the Sazerac and, for example, the Brandy Crusta, cognac based?

22 April Wednesday

To be certain that last night's revelatory Cocktail de la Louisianes were no chimerical result of enthusiasm, itself conjured by the VSOP cognac, I brewed up what I thought to be the definitive version.

2 ozs VSOP cognac
1/4 oz DOM Benedictine
1 oz Antica Formula sweet vermouth
2 dashes absinthe
2 dashes Peychaud's Bitters.
Prep: Stir, strain into a cold Martini glass, garnish with
a cherry.

And there you have a cocktail that will soothe a parched soul any, or every, evening. We'll return to the Cocktail de la Louisiane for historical reasons, but for now, since we're in New Orleans, let's linger for a bit and enlarge our exploration with color from the present and the past.

This morning, my daughter Mel texted that her husband, Commander CJ Joyce, is about to become XO of the air squadron at the Navy's Alvin Callender Field in Belle Chasse, Louisiana, across the Mississippi from New Orleans. They live in Corpus Christi, but will move their three boys, now 8, 6, and 4 (or thereabouts) to New Orleans and are looking for a house on the West Bank, near the Navy base. Try to bear with this familial digression, which will add color, like Cherry Heering, and depth, like Green Chartreuse, as we segue into insights about cocktails. I'll even postulate that one could argue some bored god has assembled this confluence of naval command and Louisiana cocktails as evidence of universal order.

Mel and CJ met in the Navy when they were stationed in Oklahoma City, but both grew up in, and near, New Orleans, and have family still there (not me). Mel's mother, Cindy Noble, grew up in Belle Chasse, in a home in Noble Manor, a subdivision her father invented, in a house that seemed determined to fall over, helped by falling oaks, nearly as soon as Charlie Noble built it. Charlie had been a Navy pilot and mustered out at Alvin Callender. My beloved, widowed grandmother was secretary to the XO at Alvin Callender for years. She would rise early, drive to Morning Call Coffee Stand in the French Quarter for coffee and beignets, then take the Algiers ferry across to work. When my dad, as commanded by mother, left the Air Force, he found work in Houston, where we lived until mother commanded a return to New Orleans. And so our family, with three boys, moved there from Texas, just as Mel's family, with three boys, will presently.

Nor do the strange parallels end there, but you've got the picture. With luck, the French Quarter will help to give those grandboys a sense of wonder and curiosity about how cultures come to be and thrive through language, architecture, music, beignets, and in some useful ways, blends of spirits. To make the point, let's consider what may be New Orleans' oldest surviving cocktail, the Brandy Crusta.

Seldom made until the 21st Century cocktail revival brought it back to life, and even now a rarity, the cocktail is one whose origin is not in doubt. The first bar guide published, Jerry Thomas's 1862 *Bar Tender's Guide*, includes it, noting that the drink was invented in New Orleans by Joseph Santini.

Brandy Crusta
2 ozs brandy (VSOP cognac) 1/2 oz curaçao 2 tsp maraschino liqueur 1 oz lemon juice Prep: Sugar the rim of the cocktail glass (sound familiar? Think Sidecar). Combine ingredients over ice and shake. Strain into a brandy snifter and garnish with a lemon peel.

A relatively new French Quarter bar, the Jewel of the South, has made the Brandy Crusta its signature drink. Have not been there. Can't wait.

23 April Thursday

At sea.

24 April Friday

Might be vanity, or a shred of nearly lost hope, but how could an old feller pass up a drink named Between the Sheets.

Between the Sheets
1 oz VSOP cognac 1 oz light rum 1 oz orange liqueur (perhaps Pierre Ferrand Dry Orange Curaçao) 1 oz lemon juice Prep: Shake and strain into a cold coupe. Orange peel garnish.

The Bartender's Measure
It is important to say (and could be I've said it before) but the actual recipe for this classic calls for 3/4 oz of each ingredient. That, however, is a bartender's measure meant to fill a glass but save—and make—money to pay salaries. At home, we have no such demands, and good sense requires that we fill the jigger, and our happily swooning brains, with full ozs. Think of it. At 3/4 jigger times per cocktail, you'll swallow 3 ozs, rather than the 4 ozs, you'll drink at the 1 oz measure.

In three cocktails at 3/4 oz per ingredient you imbibe 9 ozs rather than 12 ozs. That, my dear, is one precious drink of difference where time saved, effects felt, infinitely outweigh dollars.

Oh, and the cocktail is a good one.

25 April Saturday

Because the old ways are the best, we rarely look at newly invented cocktails. But once in a while, whether to prove the maxim or to prove it wrong, we'll try something new, as tonight. Invented by Jamie Boudreau, a famous person as bartenders go, in at least one sense this drink harks back to Jerry Thomas's famously dangerous Blue Blazer, one old drink that I hope never to make. The drinks have fire in common.

The key to making a Rubicon is order.

Rubicon

2 ozs gin. Tried this with Beefeater, Aviation, and most happily with Hayman's Old Tom, which was tastier than the others
1/2 oz Luxardo Maraschino liqueur
1/2 oz lemon juice
1 sprig fresh rosemary
1/2 oz Green Chartreuse
Prep: Begin by curling the sprig of rosemary into the bottom of a double-rocks Old Fashioned glass. Pour the Green Chartreuse over it. In your shaker, combine the gin, Luxardo, and lemon juice, but do not yet add ice. Next, in a Lewis bag, crush enough ice to (later) fill the rocks glass. Now, add ice to the shaker and quickly light the Chartreuse and rosemary that are in the rocks glass. As it burns in the glass, shake the gin, Luxardo, and lemon juice hard, 10 or 15 times. Once shaken, strain the contents over the rosemary to douse the fire, and, finally, fill the glass with your crushed ice.

What did we think? This drink is subtle. It is a lot of trouble to make and for your trouble you get its subtle smoky flavor. Could be I didn't get the thing just right, but probably won't come this way again soon. Would be fun to find it on a menu at, say, Jamie Boudreau's bar. Otherwise, the old ways are the best (excepting the Blue Blazer).

26 April Sunday

Tallying all the cocktails for which you could find a recipe is about as hopeless as finding the date the first cocktail was served or the world made by some god or gods. Yet, once in a while, the cocktail hour rolls around (I've recently moved it from 6:00 to 5:00 pm for reasons to be discussed), and no particular one has presented itself. Today, in search of something unusual—after the Rubicon, the theme of the weekend—I went to *Death & Company*, the section they call "Classic and Vintage Cocktails" and found the Port au Prince, an otherwise nearly unknown, or at least unreported, classic.

As almost always happens with *Death & Company*, well provisioned as the Ol' Bean Tavern bar has become, we lack some of the specific ingredients or brands they call for. Most significantly, the recipe below, then, uses different rum from their recipe, but it turns out, rums perhaps better suited to the spirit of the drink.

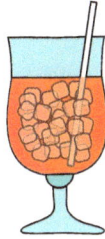

1 oz Barbanourt white rhum agricole *which I have previously reported using as a substitute for an unobtainable rum in* Death & Company's *Howl on the Hill. Of course, this rum is Haitian, made the French way from cane juice rather than molasses. An excellent choice for a cocktail named for Haiti's capital.*

1 oz Havana Club 7 year old. This too departs the D&C *recipe but seemed excellent. I used it only in this first iteration of the cocktail, but that was really because once the Havana Club is gone, I'll need to take another international trip through duty free to buy a bottle, a Covid impossibility.*

1/2 oz Barbancourt 15 year old. D&C loves to mix rums (which I complained about in the Howl on the Hill). Their recipe calls for 1/4 oz of a 151 proof rum, so I could have added more of this standard proof bottle to come up to the alcohol content of their version. In subsequent drinks I omitted the Havana Club and used 1.5 ozs each of the two Barbancourts. Next time will give St James, from Martinique, a try. At any rate, the two Haitian rums are delicious and suit the spirit of this cocktail.

3/4 oz Velvet Falernum. An ingredient most home bars lack, but if you like Tiki cocktails, of which this is an example, you'll need Falernum, available in high-end liquor stores.

3/4 oz lime juice (or thereabouts). I stuck with one-half a lime, whatever that came to.

1/2 oz pineapple juice. Canned Dole tasted good to me.

1/4 oz grenadine. I am now a believer in real pomegranate, which, we have noted (see 30 March 2020), is easily made from POM Pomegranate Juice. But, no one ever uses the juice in a jar of Luxardo cherries, which is thick, sweet, and delicious on its own. I've used up the cherries in a jar and have ample syrup. Why not give this a try as a sweetener? Will report.

1 tsp ginger syrup. A typical D&C *variation on the traditional version of this cocktail, but, to me, a very good one. You can find ginger syrup in a supermarket.*

6 dashes of orange bitters. I decided to use orange bitters. D&C calls for Elemakule Tiki Bitters, which I've never seen. Orange seemed more in the spirit of the drink than Angostura or Peychaud's, and the heavy dose makes the bitters important. Was very happy with the choice.

As I noted, the Port au Prince is a Tiki cocktail, invented by Don the Beachcomber, one of the two founders of that tropical branch of cocktail making. Typically, such cocktails are served in their own tall, ice-filled glasses.

We have a couple of lovely hand-blown pilsener glasses made in Vermont. Using a Lewis bag (you should have one by now) and mallet bought for the purpose (any rubber-headed or wooden hammer would suffice), I proceeded as follows:

1. Mixed the ingredients in the shaker without ice.
2. Filled the Lewis bag with what I estimated would fill one of the pilsener glasses.
3. Pounded the ice inside the bag until crushed. Takes a couple of blows, no more. You don't want powder.
4. Filled the glass with the crushed ice.
5. Added ice to the shaker and short-shook (that is, shake briefly so as not to dilute it) the cocktail.
6. Strained contents into the ice-filled pilsener glass.
7. Garnished with three Luxardo cherries. Add a piece of pineapple if you have it.
8. A straw is a nice touch. Eating the ice as you drink is fantastic too.
9. Departed for cocktail heaven.

This will be an impressive summer cocktail that could, and given its complexity, probably should be mixed in quantity in advance of a small gathering.

27 April Monday

At sea sailing back from Port au Prince.

28 April Tuesday

Mango Salsa's Toronto (variation) Cocktail
1.5 oz rye (Old Overholt Bonded)
0.5 ozs bourbon (Eagle Rare)
0.5 ozs Cynar
0.25 ozs Luxardo Maraschino
0.25 ozs Fernet Branca
Prep: Stir with ice serve up, strained into a cold coupe.

The Toronto Cocktail is longstanding and justly famous, a riff on the Manhattan and especially the Vieux Carré. Often made with Canadian whisky or a good rye, here, combining bourbon and rye, makes for a richer drink. The more peculiar variation in this cocktail, however, is Cynar, an amaro (as in the amari Campari and Aperol) made partly from artichokes. Its flavor is strong, distinctive, and workable in the Toronto. Is it an improvement on the traditional, which includes no Cynar and more Fernet Branca. Or could it entirely replace the Fernet Branca? You'll have to decide.

29 April Wednesday

One useful understanding of this mostly *in situ* voyage has been testing different versions of grenadine and learning, as the doctors of cocktail assert, that real pomegranate grenadine is the only grenadine that will do. Problematically, during this long pandemic, the New Hampshire Liquor Store stocks only faux grenadine, so we've been in danger of running short. No need, as I recorded earlier, but will repeat.

Again, Make Your Grenadine with POM Wonderful. The popular juice POM (well, they make blueberry POM too, so be sure to check the label) is pure pomegranate, available at most any supermarket, including ours. Buy a bottle, get a Ball jar, mix one cup of POM with one cup of superfine sugar, put the lid on tightly, and shake like hell. It'll take a few times shaking, but soon enough, the sugar dissolves, and you've got grenadine that cannot be bettered. Keep it in the refrigerator; down the road I'll let you know how long mine keeps… if it lasts.

The presence of freshly made grenadine requires testing, and the perfect cocktail is, well, a Secret. Okay, the Pink Lady is no secret, but Dr. Cocktail believes it needs to be or some swells might spurn it in favor of what they deem more manly confections, hence the Secret Cocktail. Fine with me.

Secret Cocktail (or Pink Lady)

1.5 ozs gin. I tried both Beefeater and Plymouth; each is fine, though I prefer Plymouth. Experiment with what you have, like, or want to use up, as always. I also tried splitting the amount of gin and apple brandy (1 oz each) but felt the 1.5:0.5 ratio worked a bit better.

0.5 oz apple brandy. Again, don't use the cheap Laird's Applejack unless it's all you have. I've been using Floodwall from New Hampshire Flag Hill Distillery and like it plenty.

0.75 oz lemon juice or thereabouts.

0.25 oz grenadine (or perhaps a bit more, but less than 0.5 oz)

0.5 oz egg white or one egg white. I made a dessert, pot de creme au chocolat, the other day that called for yolks only and so saved the whites all together, which makes a measurement, since separating whites is not really feasible, difficult. Waste not and use what you have when it's a Pink Lady who is waiting.

Prep: First, dry shake (that is, shake without ice) to help emulsify the egg white. Then, shake like hell with ice and strain into a chilled coupe glass, or any clear glass that shows off the lovely pink and the soft froth, and garnish with a cherry.

Strong enough to feel but delicate and pretty. Why wouldn't a fellow want to drink with such a lady?

How to Treat Lemons and Limes

By the way, I've learned a trick. Take the fruit out of the refrigerator and let it warm before making cocktails. Or, leave lemons and limes out of the refrigerator altogether; they last just as well out as they do in. Before squeezing the juice from a lemon or lime, roll the fruit on your bar top. This helps free the pulp from the rind, and you'll end up with a bit more of the juice.

30 April Thursday

At sea.

1 May Friday

We decided to revisit the Presidente, not realizing that it was one-sequestered-month ago, Friday, April 3, that I had gotten David Wondrich's *Imbibe* from our local bookstore, and in scanning its early pages with great anticipation, found that Wondrich recommended the Presidente as a help for the thirsty reading of his tome. In the course of following his sound advice we learned the drink was delicious and lovely to look at, or really, look through.

First impressions hold, Presidente is as beautiful, even more beautiful, than we remembered. But since April 3, we've tried other rum, or *rhum*, and learned to build on experience. So tonight, we discovered not just a beautiful, elegant Presidente, but the Platonic Presidente. Let me introduce you:

Presidente Redux

1.5 ozs white rum, for us Barbancourt. Remember, dark rum, or rhum would surely taste fine, but half (I mean it) the pleasure of this drink is its color, which dark rum would spoil. Besides, the Haitian Barbancourt has character in all the right ways. Not saying we will try no others, say rum from Guyana, or that the Venezuelan Diplomatico that we used last time lacks in any way, but the Barbancourt was great. Additionally, we tinkered with the proportion of rhum to Dolin Blanc. At first we tried 2:1 rhum to vermouth and the 1:2 reverse. Ultimately we decided the 3 ounces are best evenly divided.

1.5 oz Dolin Blanc white vermouth. Not the Dolin Dry, which is too sour. The Blanc is soft, which is a great part of this cocktail's appeal.

1/4 oz orange curaçao

1 tsp real (as in made from POM) grenadine

1-3 dashes Angostura bitters

Prep: Stir, strain, garnish with a Luxardo cherry.

Stare and drink!

2 May Saturday

Given the choice between the Honeymoon Cocktail, which she has never had, and a San Martin, which she has never had, Jennifer chose the latter, suggesting, perhaps, that at this time of life one need have no alcohol-fueled illusions about romance.

Nor had I tried one of these, but Wondrich loves them while cautioning that they come in many guises. The recipe he chooses (see below), the original, or as near to it as one can come after 120 years, is excellent and likely to be the best place to begin. That said, before beginning I peeked into *Difford's Guide* and other online sources, discovering that if anything, Wondrich underestimated the variety of this cocktail. Going back to Juliet's question, "What's in a name?" one could argue that it is only the name that is real. A San Martin constructed with nearly endless variation, is music that can be played in any key, fast or slow, sung reverently or ironically, and we still know it for what it is, a San Martin. How wonderful for the plucky bartender whose instincts, talent for blending, and curiosity lead to mystical places only he or she might ever go.

Here is Wondrich's starting point:

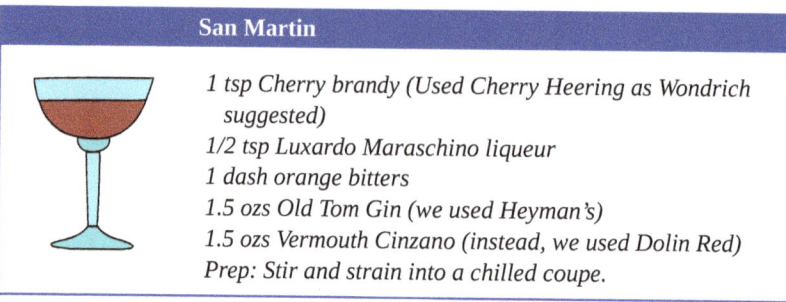

San Martin
1 tsp Cherry brandy (Used Cherry Heering as Wondrich suggested)
1/2 tsp Luxardo Maraschino liqueur
1 dash orange bitters
1.5 ozs Old Tom Gin (we used Heyman's)
1.5 ozs Vermouth Cinzano (instead, we used Dolin Red)
Prep: Stir and strain into a chilled coupe.

The original recipe works admirably, yet, as soon as one begins to type "San Martin Cocktail" into Google, here's what happens:

Mr. Boston = gin (not specific) + sweet vermouth (any) + Green or Yellow Chartreuse Huh?

Esquire is more specific though not much like the original:

London dry gin + Italian (i.e., sweet) vermouth + Yellow Chartreuse

Difford's, which has most any cocktail, shows an Avenue San Martin as:

BarSol Mosto Verde Italia Pisco (search me) + Amaro CioCiaro + raw runny honey + lime juice + ginger sugar syrup

And by way of illustration, here is one more:

Cardamaro + Calvados (Le Compte) + dry vermouth (Dolin)

As the principal spirit we've gone from Old Tom gin, any gin, to London dry, to pisco (a type of brandy, originally from Peru) to Calvados. Vermouth, sweet or dry, makes it into most, though not all, versions. I like this because within the loose structure we have plenty of room to play. For example, only the day before I'd bought my first bottle of Yellow Chartreuse. Green is a fantastic mixer with gin, adding profundity to a drink as a concoction of cloistered monks should. Over the course of the evening, I eased out the maraschino in favor of half an ounce of the Yellow Chartreuse. Delicious and perhaps only the beginning of a course of elaborate scientific trials of this fine cocktail.

3 May Sunday

The first signs of summer, especially a temperature where T-shirts replace flannel, appeared unexpectedly today, prompting investigation of a genuine summer cocktail, the Mojito. It is not just the weather, however, that makes this cooling drink a good choice; it is the modern supermarket. Specifically, many of the ingredients you need for a proper cocktail are available nearby, things such as Fever-Tree or Q tonic and soda water, or Goslings ginger beer, Peychaud's Bitters, and efficient citrus squeezers. The main ingredient critical for the Mojito, mint, comes in small plastic packaging among the fresh spices. If you unpack the mint and put it into a coffee cup with water, even dried out it regains freshness and keeps happily.

The recipe that struck me as most sensible is based on *Death & Company's*, with my own flourishes:

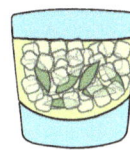

Mojito

6 mint leaves lightly muddled with
1 oz lime juice in the shaker and with
3/4 oz simple syrup. A sweetener that gets little attention
*   except in tequila cocktails, agave (like mint, available in*
*   a plain old supermarket these days), goes well with rum,*
*   especially dark rum. And sure enough, one try persuaded*
*   Jenny and me that it seemed to suit Mojitos better than*
*   simple syrup.*
1-2 dashes Angostura Bitters
2 ozs rum. As to the rum, take your pick. I like the Haitian
*   Barbancourt white but found the Venezuelan white*
*   Diplomatico even more interesting, and a dry Haitian*
*   St. James equally good. I think whatever rum you prefer*
*   should be happy in this drink.*
Prep: Once you have lightly muddled the mint, lime, and
*   agave, add the bitters and rum and shake with ice.*
*   Pour the whole into a double rocks glass and fill it with*
*   crushed ice. Don sunglasses, sip, and be cool.*

4 May Monday

At sea

5 May Tuesday—Cinco de Mayo

Yes, we could have, probably should have, had a Margarita. But why be like every other American? So we tried the Honeymoon, truth told a bit of a disappointment.

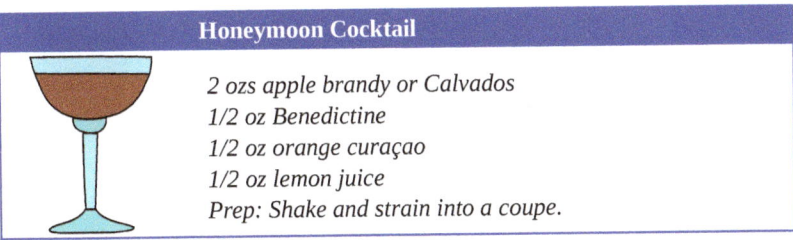

Honeymoon Cocktail

2 ozs apple brandy or Calvados
1/2 oz Benedictine
1/2 oz orange curaçao
1/2 oz lemon juice
Prep: Shake and strain into a coupe.

From *Forgotten Cocktails*, and perhaps best left that way. Still, on the right evening, trying for a second honeymoon might be just the thing.

6 May Wednesday

We learned today that our friend, Captain Charly Belden, committed suicide last week. Charly was a died-in-the-wool mariner, mostly a sailor, but earned his livelihood with TowBoatUS rescuing boaters in trouble. We hired Charly to captain *Sea Sisters* on the voyage up from Charleston. His sister, a veterinarian, lives in Haverhill, Massachusetts. He liked to visit her and made it a practice to let us know so that we could sail, dine, drink, or all three. He loved his children; I know only Marlon, his son, who is a talented young fellow in many ways. Charly was enthusiastic, always lively, and is about the last person I'd have expected to turn to suicide.

Old Fashioned

Anyway, and because it is very strong, an Old Fashioned seemed the right drink for the night. The cocktail gets its name because it is made in the "old-fashioned way." That is, originally cocktails had three ingredients, the base spirit, bitters (because they were medicinal), and sugar. I have a personal relationship to the Old Fashioned, beginning with my parents; it was the drink my dad favored after work, prepared by mother, who either made or bought pre-made, fairly sweet, Old Fashioned mix. In that period, 50s, 60s, 70s, 80s (not that I lived at home all those years), the drink was out of fashion because considered old fashioned most places, though never in New Orleans, and we thought of it as a southern drink. I recall ordering one in San Antonio in about 2010, a big hotel, and the bartender was utterly baffled, looked it up in a book, and made a dreadful, undrinkable mess. (Texas fancies itself more western than southern, I suppose, except in politics, with apologies to Houston and Austin.) Through most of the two-thousand-teens here in New England, an Old Fashioned typically came with soda water, another abomination, especially since adding water turned it from a cocktail into a highball and, sacrilege, weakened it. But somewhere along in the teens, the series *Madmen* re-popularized the Old Fashioned, and today it is stylish. At any good bar you can expect it to be prepared well, and at the Bean, prepared perfectly.

Old Fashioned	
	*Not less than 2 ozs bourbon. Some prefer rye, but for a southerner, this drink demands bourbon. I like Eagle Rare. You make the drink in a double rocks glass, and David Embrey advises that after it is mixed, you fill the glass with ice, preferably large cubes or one big rock, so that the ice melts slowly, and then pour bourbon until it is 3/8 inch from the rim of your glass. Let us not count how many ounces that could be.* *1/4 - 1/2 oz maple syrup. It's best to heat the syrup first in the microwave just enough to take the chill off, so that it mixes more easily with the bourbon. The maple syrup is regional, made here in New Hampshire, and works beautifully with bourbon. Mostly people use simple syrup, Demerara sugar, or sugar cubes. Go ahead. But maple syrup is better.* *1 to 2 dashes Angostura Bitters* *Prep: Put the maple syrup, bitters, and a bit of bourbon into your rocks glass and stir until you're confident they're mixed. Then, fill the glass with ice and after that, bourbon to the carefully measured 3/8-inch mark. Add a twist of lemon, orange, or a cherry. I used to prefer the cherry but have come to love the lemon.*

Be advised: Don't allow yourself more than two of these in an evening.

…Here's to Captain Charly.

7 May Thursday

At sea.

8 May Friday

Back when I worked for a living, among the happiest days and nights were those with Ebook Library, a group of people sympathetic to one another from around the globe who loved to spend time together. During those times, and I think beginning at an American Library Association meeting in Dallas at the Adolphus Hotel, the Sidecar became our company drink. I'm not sure how it happened, but then, those hazy origins are just as well left in the far reaches of time. The bartender at the hotel, however, was especially good at sugaring the rim of the glasses, creating a firm, thick layer, a necessary part of this classic cocktail that, curiously, sometimes uneducated or lazy bartenders skip.

Sugaring a Rim

Sugaring deserves a paragraph of its own. Historically, the first cocktail for which the practice came about was the Brandy Crusta, invented by Joe Santini at his New Orleans bar in, roughly, the 1860s. At the time, cognac was popular, especially in New Orleans owing to its French ties, and the Brandy Crusta was the first cocktail to introduce lemon as a mixing ingredient. A decade later, as the phylloxera pox descended on French vineyards, brandy lost prominence to other spirits, though in Paris, anyway, it had returned by World War I, which, according to David Embury, is where a friend of his, an English captain who got around on a motorcycle with a sidecar, became the inventor of tonight's cocktail. But back to sugaring and on to its own paragraph…

A bar requires many forms of sweetener. Some are sprits in their own right such as Benedictine or, in the Sidecar, a triple sec such as Cointreau. But you also need grenadine, and perhaps raspberry and orgeat syrups on hand. I've been keen about agave for rum as well as tequila-based drinks and about maple syrup for the Old Fashioned. Of course, regular simple syrup is vital, and for many purposes, superfine sugar is the best resource. But besides all of those, and others unmentioned, for sugaring a rim, you'll want the plain granular sugar used in the kitchen. Just as rimming a Margarita glass goes best with Diamond Crystal Kosher Salt, rimming a Sidecar glass goes best with regular sugar. Superfine, that is, melts too easily. You'll want to work your mouth around the rim as you drink a Sidecar, at least I do, and superfine sugar will dissolve from sources of moisture besides your lips and tongue. Additionally, you want a cold glass and, if it's handy, keeping glasses in the freezer is excellent. If not, fill your glass with ice, but not water and let it cool while you add ingredients for the Sidecar to a shaker. Then, pour the ice used to cool the glass into the shaker. Quickly wipe the glass dry, moisten the outer rim with your spent lemon half, and roll the rim through the table sugar. I try to coat the entire rim thickly and evenly.

It will be worth trying other orange liqueurs, such as Grand Marnier and curaçao. The latter always interests me for its rich taste and low cost. Works for a Margarita, which is quite similar in concept (spirit, citrus, curaçao, agave, rimmed glass), so why not for a Sidecar?

That said, here's to my friends at Ebook Library: May we all drink many a Sidecar on our own, together, and at the Ol' Bean.

9 May Saturday

As I've said, I am on the side of "old ways, old things, are the best." As such, one point of this diary has been to discover just the right mix of an old cocktail, say a Vieux Carré, that would make it the only drink I ever need. But then, along the way, other cocktails have shown their glory, and so I became converted reluctantly and lately to the notion that any of many, but historical, cocktails mixed perhaps more than one way, could be even better.

Yet, from time to time no cocktail for the evening readily presents itself, and thanks to the omnipresence of the Internet where a multitude of sites proffer cocktails, I'll find myself led to the present, in forms such as the New Toronto Cocktail, a variation on a Manhattan and not a bad one. But not compelling either. Or I'll sometimes turn to *Death & Co.* for ideas, usually variations of classics, though typically the Bean's comparatively modest holdings require stretching the bounds of their prescriptions to generic medicines rather than the brand names they specify. The results are tasty, but again, not life changing.

Tuxedono2.com

And then this past week I stumbled on tuxedono2.com, a mysterious website that has the right recipes for classic cocktails, is smartly written, easy to use, thoroughly versed in cocktail literature and history, and modest. Click "About" and you learn only that the brains behind this site are, apparently, topped by red hair. So yesterday, perhaps as counterpoint to the Sidecar, lacking a direction, I turned to tuxedono2.com and, I'm not quite sure how, landed on the Black Betty.

The author, we'll call him or her Tux2, says the Black Betty was created in Seattle by Chris Good of Canon. Canon is also where Jamie Boudreau, perhaps the best-known contemporary bartender, hangs his hat. On the other hand, Saveur has a vastly different recipe for a Black Betty, though at least in the same family, saying it came from Sydney, by Max Greco of Vasco. Cocktail confusion being what it is, others claiming to be Black Betty dress in tequila, rye, bourbon, Southern Comfort, even—goodness, so non-discriminating— peach schnapps, and adorn themselves with citrus, club soda, and egg. Let us not be misled. Whatever claims the others make to being the original or the real Black Betty, for the evening we can be happily monogamous with Black Betty as Tux2 brings her out.

Black Betty

1 oz dark rum. Take your pick; you can hardly go wrong. We tried dark rum from Guyana (Pyrat), Haiti (St. James), and Jamaica (Myers's). If you like "funk," go Haitian; this confection brings it powerfully to the front. If you prefer something less unilateral, either of the others is excellent. I'm looking forward to trying every dark rum we have in this Betty.

1 oz Fernet Branca. This dark amaro, which is to say an Italian bitter, from Milan, is ancient (1845), herbal, and powerful. It can easily overwhelm a cocktail, but not Betty. (Fer NET Bran ka)

1 oz Amaro Montenegro. Another amaro but from Bologna, brand new to the Bean (though I've long eyed it on the shelf at the New Hampshire Liquor Outlet) adds another 40 or so ingredients to the 27 (I think) of Fernet Branca. Think now of Betty as a very, very complicated mix of wonderful possibilities.

1/2 oz sherry. Chris Good's recipe specifies Lustau Pedro Jimenez made from the solera method. Tux2 suggests trying sherry, port, or madeira. A California tawny port was handy, so I used it.

Prep: Stir, serve in a double rocks glass. After stirring, I poured everything, including the ice, carefully into the rocks glass and added more ice until the drink just barely covered it. We buy our ice from the grocery, cocktail cubes, and a five-pound bag costs $0.30 more than a bag of regular ice. So I do not easily throw cubes away, and just to say, the cubes used to stir the drink must have the ingredients on them, so why not keep them, so to speak, in the mix? I'll have more to say about ice another time. Garnish with orange twist.

Black Betty in the glass is dark with a red glow, a beckoning beauty. And her kiss is sublime, a commingling of scents and tastes takes you into her chamber. If you can, sit quietly before a fire silently bathing your senses in liquid pleasure.

10 May Sunday

From Black Betty to Scorched Earth

Here's a first. In the course of this diary I've never returned to a drink from one day to the next but was so smitten by Black Betty, that by the time cocktail hour rolled around on Mother's Day, she was the only one for me. As it happened, Saturday I'd laid hands only on port, replacing the sherry normally used, but Sunday both sherry (Jerez Solera Lustau, exactly the one called for by Canon) and madeira appeared. Have not tried madeira, and the sherry of course was good, but port gives Betty this beguiling ruby that is, to me, irresistible. On the other hand, thinking aloud, could we substitute a red vermouth for the sherry, port, madeira addition? Hmmm?

Amari, Vermouth and Fortified Wines

Amaro is the Italian word for bitter, and amari are bitter, though often with an opposing sweetness. The best known amari are probably Campari and Aperol, but dozens exist in many different styles from all over Italy.

How do amari differ from Italian vermouth (which is to say red, sweet vermouth that you would use in a Manhattan)? Fundamentally, amari are liqueurs that begin with grain alcohol, whereas vermouths are fortified wines that begin with grapes. From their different beginnings, however, the two become more alike in that they are next infused with some combination of herbs, fruits, citrus, roots, and so on. Some vermouths are infused such that they become a "vermouth amaro." One other thing about vermouths: once opened, keep them refrigerated. They spoil if you do not. Amari need not be refrigerated.

Sherry, port, and madeira, like vermouth, are fortified wines, which is to say, alcohol beyond that produced by fermentation is added to them. But unlike vermouth, nothing is infused into sherry, port, or madeira.

Suppose in Black Betty we replaced sherry with vermouth? The notion may not be farfetched. A Negroni includes equal parts Campari and red vermouth with gin. Tux2 links the Scorched Earth, which is a very high-test Negroni, to the Black Betty, as embracing similar extremes with different spirits.

<table>
<tr><td colspan="2" style="background:#3a4a8a;color:#fff">Scorched Earth</td></tr>
<tr><td></td><td>

1 oz mezcal. I'd never tried mezcal but had a bottle just in case. The good bartender tries to foresee a future unbounded by the present.

1 oz Cynar. This artichoke-based amaro has a character all its own; sweeter than other amari, it strikes me as playing much the role of a vermouth, at least in this cocktail and, of course, because it supports my theory that Black Betty might like a vermouth in place of sherry. Lately, Cynar seems to appear regularly in recipes.

1 oz Campari

2 dashes orange bitters

Prep: Stir, serve in a double rocks glass topped up with ice, and garnish with an orange twist.

</td></tr>
</table>

If you like a Negroni, and have a bottle of mezcal, you must try the more intense Scorched Earth. Meanwhile, we'll soon return to the Black Betty made with vermouth, but which one?

11 May Monday

Planned to be at sea, but our Simon Pierce coupe glasses arrived and, wisely, Jennifer said we should try them out. She got no argument from me.

Jenny loves a Manhattan, especially for the cherry, so that's where we went. Thanks to our discovery of great vermouth, I no longer go to things such as a Perfect Manhattan. Rather:

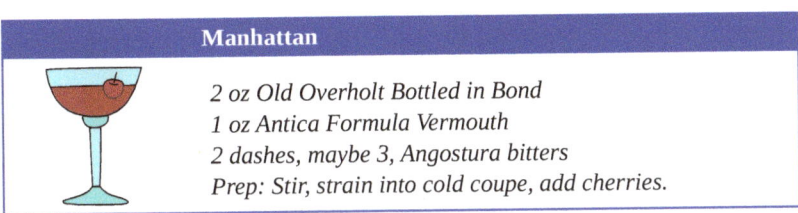

Manhattan

2 oz Old Overholt Bottled in Bond
1 oz Antica Formula Vermouth
2 dashes, maybe 3, Angostura bitters
Prep: Stir, strain into cold coupe, add cherries.

Nothing better. You can call this recipe the standard. Good as it is, however, lots of variations are worth trying.

12 May Tuesday

At sea.

13 May Wednesday

With Black Betty and the discovery of tuxedono2.com, our cocktail adventure seems to have taken an unexpected turn toward the new. But do not worry, in this world, the new understands its debt to the past.

A YouTube channel called "How to Drink," is a lot of fun and Greg, the guy who makes the drinks, is a wit who appears to be making a living and building a reputation with his channel. Lots of these booze channels exist; mostly I ignore the others but often watch Greg.

The Hanky Panky is an old-line cocktail invented at the Savoy by Eva Coleman, predecessor to Harry Craddock, author of the seminal *The Savoy Cocktail Book*. When we sat at the Savoy's American Bar in February, Jennifer ordered a Hanky Panky and on the spot declared it her favorite cocktail. Craddock's recipe is 2 dashes Fernet Branca, 1 oz Italian vermouth, 1 oz London dry gin with an orange twist.

I had other possibilities in mind for Jenny tonight, but stumbled on Greg's Swanky Panky, leading to another change of plans. Here you go…

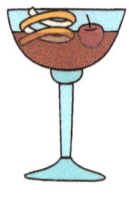

Swanky Panky

2 oz Antica Formula vermouth. This, of course, is my favored sweet vermouth, and finding it the basis of the drink proved intriguing.

1 oz Aviation Gin, which is a good American-made dry gin but not especially juniper forward. We go through a lot of this gin.

1 oz rye, for which we use Old Overholt Bottled in Bond. Gin and rye are usually strangers, but turns out, they shouldn't be.

2 dashes Fernet Branca, just as Harry Craddock says.

Prep: Stir, strain into chilled coupe, Jennifer likes a cherry. Or stick with the orange twist. Or use both.

From the first taste we knew this was delicious and an improvement on its mother cocktail, now Jennifer's former favorite.

My real goal for the evening had been (1) to continue exploring cocktails from Tux2 and (2) to have no more than one of any. No longer am sure how the Abbey appeared, perhaps because I have an old orange whose peel has been sacrificed to many twists and whose pulp probably deserves a better fate than simply being thrown onto the compost. Anyway, the Abbey came up:

Abbey

1.5 ozs gin (Plymouth)

3/4 oz Cocci Americano (or Lillet Blanc)

3/4 oz orange juice. This old orange is a blood orange. I'm thinking it should have gone to the compost unsqueezed.

1 or 2 dashes orange bitters.

Prep: Double strain, using both the strainer for the shaker and a mesh strainer to avoid pulp from the orange going into the new coupe. Garnish with cherry.

First taste was unpromising, which seems to happen often to me. Jenny tried it and agreed. The cocktail was mild tasting, and perhaps compared with the more forceful Swanky Panky it paled. As I drank more, however, the Abbey grew on me, and could be I'll come back for another try. Maybe, maybe not. The orange juice alone may have accounted for the failure.

Drank Abbey quickly and got up to move along, with the choice I'd laid out between a Corn 'n Oil and a Sawyer. Corn' n Oil is a classic that's been on my list for months, and I was headed that way but re-read the recipe for the Sawyer. Blame it on the bitters.

Bitters and Cocktails: A Brief History

Bitters predate cocktails, were sold as medicine for centuries, and if they were in reality snake oil, the alcohol in them must have made a patient temporarily feel better long enough to at least seem cured. I'm guessing most medicine chests at home had a favorite bitter, and families of believers passed their remedy along from one generation to the next. But as did common remedies when I was a child—cod liver oil, paregoric, my mother's cooking—bitters tasted, well, like medicine. More of the active ingredient, alcohol, would obviously improve the effect and many a patient would have believed it improved the taste. Soon, some American housewife probably added a bit of sugar to encourage a screw-faced child to take his medicine, first showing the way by sampling a bit herself. And thus, from bitters, alcohol, sugar, and mother, the cocktail was born, America's first great, revolutionary, ubiquitous, and most enduring, invention.

Once the cocktail took on a life of its own, became "medicine" in its own right, it began to evolve until, by the mid and late 19th Century, bitters had become a minor ingredient, consigned to dashes rather than doses, or sometimes, and increasingly more often in the 20th and 21st Centuries, left out altogether as, first citrus, and soon fortified wines and liqueurs such as vermouth, amari, Chartreuse, and others took on the role bitters formerly played.

Today, however, a visit to your liquor store shows a renewed life for bitters and a flowering of artisanal versions. We should not be surprised—although you could have knocked me over with a gentian root—that cocktails in which bitters contribute by the ounce rather than the dash are on the cusp of leading a modern return to old-fashioned ways.

The first of these that I have tried is the Sawyer, and if any bitters-based cocktail is better, well, my grandmother had a friend who was addicted to paregoric.

Sawyer

2 ozs gin. Started with Plymouth, moved to Beefeater. No opinion yet about a path and expect to try others soon. Advice is to use a juniper-forward London Dry such as Tanqueray, but we'll see.

1/2 oz lime juice

1/2 oz simple syrup

1/2 oz Angostura Bitters. For the two I've made at this writing, I mistakenly used only 1/4 oz Angostura. And the drink was spectacular. Tonight it is the full Monty.

1/4 oz Peychaud's Bitters. And you see here that it will be easy enough and a refreshing experiment to calibrate the ratios of the bitters to your taste. I love Peychaud's for their New Orleans origin and have been pleased to see them show up in ever more cocktails. More Peychaud's in this cocktail might be just what the doctor ordered.

1/4 oz orange bitters. Tux2 points out the original version of the cocktail indicated Regans' and Fee Brothers orange bitters, so why not try both?

Prep: Combine, shake with ice, strain into a chilled coupe.

This is above all a sipping cocktail. Linger over it while Brahms First Symphony plays late in the evening, replenish part way through, and whatever ails you will be cured.

14 May Thursday

At sea.

15 May Friday

Something in the air, here a mass of thunderstorms, together with the time of week—and a pandemic—led to more introspection about drinking, thanks, perhaps, to more drinking, than is even usual. Jenny was on the phone from 8:00 am on; I had a really stiff neck; 5:00 pm rolled past, and the Trinidad Sour had reached its time.

One ounce, and in many versions 1.5 ounces of Angostura are the beginning, middle, and end of the powerful Trinidad Sour. Can you drink Angostura bitters straight, perhaps with a bit of orgeat? Clearly an end-of-the-night cocktail, because otherwise it would so dominate your taste buds that whatever else you drink could be anything. If you're from Louisiana, hardly any one ingredient can overpower your sense of taste. That is, we're accustomed to the intense effects on the tongue of cayenne pepper, tasso, the holy trinity (in Louisiana cooking, chopped onion, bell pepper, and celery), bourbon on the rocks. Other ingredients must find ways to support, perhaps enhance, but inevitably give way to these dominators. And so it is with Angostura bitters in the Trinidad Sour.

Cocktails, and especially highballs that use ice to cool and ameliorate—as does water in light beer or grain alcohol in blended spirits—suit some tastes, nor do we wish to be insensitive. But ameliorating notions live in a world outside the orbit of this journal.

Here's the thing about a Trinidad Sour: mix it, shake it, strain it, drink it. Glass empty, pour the ice from the bottom side of your shaker and the leftover Trinidad from the top side into your glass, and as if by magic, you have a second cocktail—strong, curative, intense.

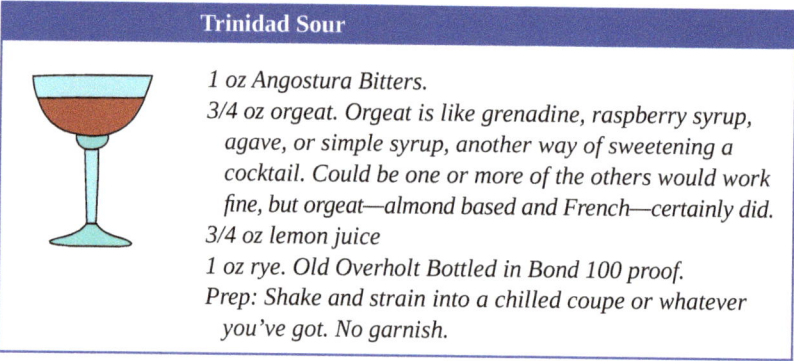

Trinidad Sour
1 oz Angostura Bitters.   3/4 oz orgeat. Orgeat is like grenadine, raspberry syrup, agave, or simple syrup, another way of sweetening a cocktail. Could be one or more of the others would work fine, but orgeat—almond based and French—certainly did.   3/4 oz lemon juice   1 oz rye. Old Overholt Bottled in Bond 100 proof.   Prep: Shake and strain into a chilled coupe or whatever you've got. No garnish.

Consider your socks knocked off. And don't forget to use the ice from the shaker once your glass is empty. Let nothing go to waste.

Angostura Bitters

Originally made in Venezuela, the factory, if that's what it is, where these bitters are made, long since moved to Trinidad. The formula dates from the 1850s. They have been and deservedly remain the bitters everyone knows and uses. Angostura is 47.5 percent alcohol. Strong stuff in every way.

I'm in the Luggnuts (have I mentioned the Luggnuts? It is the band I play in) listening room here at the Bean, sipping my first Trinidad Sour, when Jenny, week's work done, comes in, ready to drink. Lucky man. She tastes, loves, the Trinidad Sour, but goes along with my plan for testing different drinks. I make a Japanese for her.

This is a classic, dates from 1860, and simple. It follows the original cocktail formula of spirit, sugar (here orgeat, perhaps a first in a cocktail), and bitters. The twist is essential in this one.

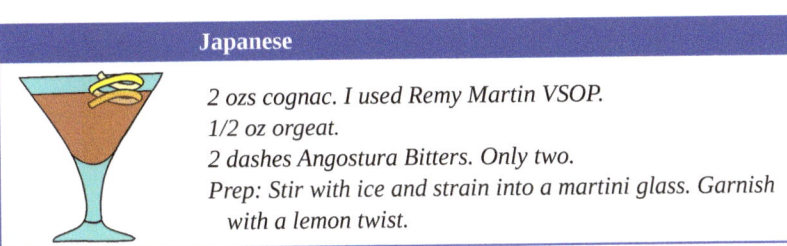

Japanese

2 ozs cognac. I used Remy Martin VSOP.
1/2 oz orgeat.
2 dashes Angostura Bitters. Only two.
Prep: Stir with ice and strain into a martini glass. Garnish
with a lemon twist.

She loved it. Cognac is under used and underrated these days as a spirit for cocktails. Note the similarity to a Sidecar. If you plan to visit both Japan and Trinidad of an evening, be sure to travel first to the Land of the Rising Sun.

Bitters and Hops

The Sawyer proved so impressive on Wednesday, my taste buds having been compromised by the Trinidad Sour, that I'd used only half the Angostura called for in the Tux2 recipe. A return was in order. Besides adding a quarter ounce of Angostura, used Tanqueray No. 10 as the gin, a good choice. And, having finished her Japanese, Jenny ordered up a Sawyer for herself. Three observations claimed our attention.

First, Jenny made a shrimp dish of heavy cream and spinach, served over excellent Carolina Basmati rice. In its own right the meal was outstanding, but it was made even better by the Sawyers. Drinking cocktails as aperitifs or post dinner is longstanding. But it has seemed they might accompany dinner as well, and this pairing was a strong proof of the concept.

Second, over the past five or more years, I've sampled dozens of craft beers all around New England, with particular emphasis and love for New England double IPAs. Jenny loves them as well, the more hops the better. And, of course, these wildly hopped beers have become a particular favorite all over the United States. Some breweries, such as the acclaimed Tree House in Massachusetts and the Alchemist in Vermont, have made their vast reputations and fortunes almost entirely on the backs of double IPAs. The attraction people have to hops is so strong that it has occurred to me often that they are like catnip for humans. Literally, it seems to me as if hops have a narcotic effect on many of us.

And here, so far as I know, is an original observation: hops are a bittering agent just as bitters. Adding enormous doses of bitters to cocktails seems no different from adding enormous doses of hops to ales. We will attend to this similarity moving ahead, looking for, perhaps even attempting to invent, bitters-based cocktails, the equivalent of New England double IPAs.

In closing, one last observation cannot be shunned as, in the interest of science and of accuracy, of truth and of beauty, the following must be said. A catnip-like narcotic effect occurred once both parties had consumed their Sawyers although, the effect was, ahem, specifically aphrodisiacal. Keeping in mind that bitters originally were medicine, is it possible that our ancestors were restored in ways they dared not report? You can be certain that we will dutifully throw ourselves into the cause of science and will not neglect further cause and effect on this subject!

With that, we draw the curtain on the evening.

16 May Saturday

Yes, too much Friday left me slow to think about Saturday, and at the last minute, not really needing a cocktail, chose a Fog Cutter, about which we could make small talk, but it is enough to say that the day felt like summer weather had at last arrived, and a Tiki drink topped with ice seemed just the thing. Besides, I had near empty bottles of cognac, sweet vermouth, and gin—all ingredients in this powerhouse—and was not feeling particular. In they went.

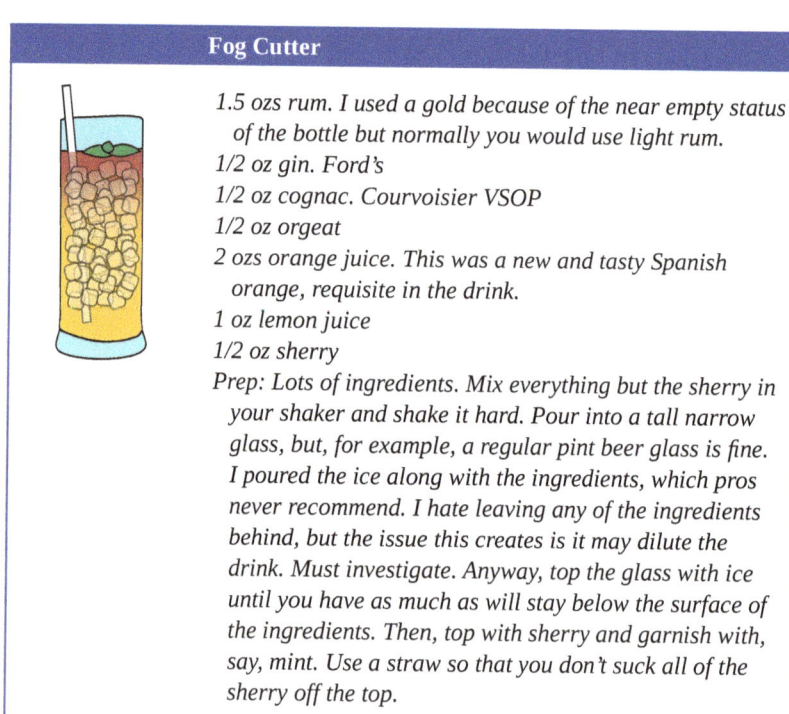

Fog Cutter
1.5 ozs rum. I used a gold because of the near empty status of the bottle but normally you would use light rum. *1/2 oz gin. Ford's* *1/2 oz cognac. Courvoisier VSOP* *1/2 oz orgeat* *2 ozs orange juice. This was a new and tasty Spanish orange, requisite in the drink.* *1 oz lemon juice* *1/2 oz sherry* *Prep: Lots of ingredients. Mix everything but the sherry in your shaker and shake it hard. Pour into a tall narrow glass, but, for example, a regular pint beer glass is fine. I poured the ice along with the ingredients, which pros never recommend. I hate leaving any of the ingredients behind, but the issue this creates is it may dilute the drink. Must investigate. Anyway, top the glass with ice until you have as much as will stay below the surface of the ingredients. Then, top with sherry and garnish with, say, mint. Use a straw so that you don't suck all of the sherry off the top.*

The famous Tiki Guru, Trader Vic, probably invented the Fog Cutter. With so many ingredients it strikes me as a cocktail that takes practice and probably a better regimen of spirits than the "ones almost gone" approach. But this one was not bad, felt like summer, and I'll try it again.

The evening was young, several bottles empty, and I could easily have called it a night. On the other hand, the Vieux Carré had always felt as if it might be the choice if I were marooned and could have only one cocktail's makings. Besides, it had been a while, March 29 to be exact.

This New Orleans classic, possibly my favorite, blended with the right selection of rye, cognac, and vermouth, tasted thin! Yes, thin. I was cheap with the ice, pouring the cubes from the mixing glass into my rocks glass, so perhaps it arrived diluted. Again, it is time to be serious about ice. It could have been, however, the intensities of the Trinidad Sour and Sawyer from Friday have set a new standard for spice. Once you have had gumbo, chicken soup is not going to be on your menu.

17 May Sunday

Our first dinner guest in more than two months, my brother Denis. Perfect for my cocktail aims because we like the same food and drink, disagree on most other things. Here was the cocktail menu: Alaska, Creole, Sawyer.

What Alaska? Perhaps because Harry Craddock says it was invented in South Carolina and is the favorite drink of Esquimaux? It is a classic cocktail in the "old fashioned sense"; spirit (gin), sugar (Yellow Chartreuse); bitters (orange). Simplicity itself and really, a little-known classic.

Alaska

1 1/2 ozs. gin. Used Fords (again, nearing the end of a bottle) and Tanqueray No 10. Both good, appropriate.
1/2 oz Yellow Chartreuse. Our dad kept Green but never Yellow, and he sipped it after dinner, never mixed it. Here, Yellow Chartreuse makes the drink a bit syrupy, because it is thick, but also makes it mysterious, bringing complexity to the dead simple.
2 dashes orange bitters. Not sure of the effect, or what to call the effect, but I tasted before and after adding bitters, and they make a big difference.
Prep: Mix and stir, strain into a cold coupe.

The three of us (Jenny had one too) liked the Alaska, but I'd say we did not love it. Still, it might be a good aperitif or even a cocktail to replace white wine over a dinner of fish, chicken, or musk ox.

We, or at least I, loved this one and along with Denis had two. Like the Alaska, the recipe for the Creole as you see it here, or as nearly as our house ingredients allow, appeared first in *The Savoy Cocktail Book*, and its recipe is very much like both the Manhattan and the Brooklyn. Louisiana comes to New York by way of London.

1 1/2 ozs rye. Old Overholt 100 Proof Bonded is what we used, our house rye.

1 1/2 ozs sweet vermouth. Tried both Antica Formula and a newly bought craft version from Vermont. Both were excellent with, perhaps, the edge going to Vermont. If this proves true, goodness, quite the shock.

1/2 bar-spoon Amaro Montenegro. The Savoy recipe calls for Amer Picon, another amaro of course, but one unavailable at the NH Liquor Outlet. Have had good luck substituting Amaro Montenegro for other amari, and sure enough, here I think it made the drink. It will be worthwhile to try Aperol (as recommended by Tux2) and probably others. I guess Amer Picon is bitter orange, which opens many possibilities. Also, the Brooklyn calls for Amer Picon in The Savoy Cocktail Book.

1/2 barspoon Benedictine. I really need droppers as pouring Benedictine into the barspoon is not easy. It is the sweetener, so add to your taste.

Prep: Sir with ice and strain into a cold coupe.

Compared with a Manhattan, the amaro replaces bitters, the Benedictine replaces (in the Savoy) Maraschino, but the vermouth and rye are identical. Compared with the Brooklyn, which weirdly calls for Canadian whisky and a 2:1 whisky to vermouth ratio, with maraschino as the sweetener, but both include the same 2 dashes of Amer Picon. I've been eager to try a Brooklyn for months. But at any rate, the similarities are impressive… to me.

And Denis did not say much, for which he is locally famous. I loved the Creole and am eager to try it beside a Manhattan and a Brooklyn. And now what I am calling another Louisiana drink, perhaps the best of them though little known, has come calling. Thank you, Tux2.

Home Business in a Pandemic

The pandemic poses special problems for inns, and Denis has given his soul to the Follansbee Inn for years. He can't have guests as the big season begins, and even if he is allowed to have them, they may not come. In New Hampshire, inns must do well in summer because the winter season for them is bleak. He has good reason to worry.

Jenny and I have promoted the idea of selling food, and the night seemed like a good time to bring up the notion of food paired with cocktails. Denis and I, thanks to his son Collins, have long explored the emerging New England craft beers, and the Sawyer seemed like the place to offer my comparison to double IPAs.

But again, Denis doesn't say much. I think he got the comparison and theoretically approves matching cocktails to food. I'm pretty sure he liked the Sawyer. Will any of this go anywhere? Doubtful. But that doesn't diminish the fun of imagining.

18 May Monday

At sea. But what about tomorrow? Brooklyn? Creole, Manhattan comparison? Need more rye.

19 May Tuesday

A couple things. Bought Evan Williams 100 proof Bottled in Bond Bourbon at, I think, $15 or $16. It is very good and at that price and proof will be our house bourbon for now. An email from Kari Paulson describes Caperitif, which turns out to be a South African vermouth that dates back to the 19th Century, is an ingredient in several cocktails in *The Savoy Cocktail Book*, but was lost in the 1960s. Now it is reborn in the 21st Century, though not at the New Hampshire Liquor Store. And finally, *Bitters* by Brad Thomas Parsons arrived, and I've read it. Learned some useful things and helped me to spend some money. Meanwhile, to the business of the evening.

More on Home Business and the Pandemic

The pandemic is causing many small business owners to surrender. Today we learned that our coffee shop here in Warner, Schoodac's, is closed for good, at least as now run by its owner Darryl Parker. Of greater note than our local loss, in New York City, the Pegu Club, perhaps the first of the cocktail bars to arrive in Manhattan during this cocktail renaissance, is closed forever. Let's drink a Pegu Club, which dates to 19th Century Burma of the British Empire, in memoriam. The first recipe for it appears in *The Savoy Cocktail Book*; the one here is from *Bitters*:

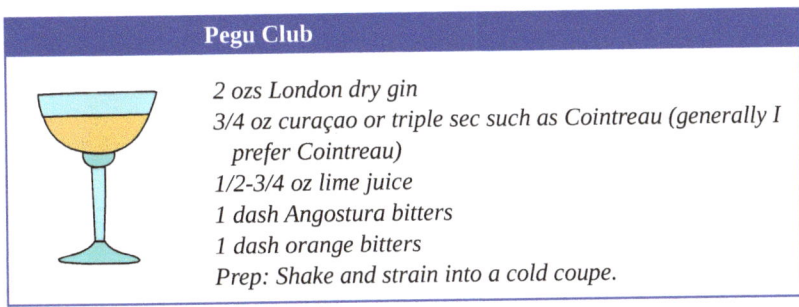

Pegu Club
2 ozs London dry gin 3/4 oz curaçao or triple sec such as Cointreau (generally I prefer Cointreau) 1/2-3/4 oz lime juice 1 dash Angostura bitters 1 dash orange bitters Prep: Shake and strain into a cold coupe.

It's not unlike a Gimlet and is a type of sour. Very nice.

What's in a Dash?

But the recipe and the book, Bitters *that is, raise another issue: what's in a dash? Or more exactly, how much is in a dash? Generally it is not the indifferent, or perhaps I should say quick, shake of a hurried bartender. A dash is six to eight drops or one-eighth of a tsp. Let's not disappear too far into the weeds here, but a scientific test makes the problem clear.*

I took a bottle of Angostura bitters and a bottle of Angostura orange bitters. To get a dash—1/8 tsp—of the first takes two modest shakes. A dash of the second takes only one shake. I'm guessing the plastic with a hole in it through which you shake the bitters is made in the same place in the same way since the bitters are from the same company, the bottles the same size. Why the difference? Probably the regular Angostura, which has more ingredients, is a bit thicker.

Some artisanal bitters come in bottles with eye droppers making it possible to release the fluid drop by drop into a cocktail, an approach a busy bartender can be forgiven for ignoring.

But at home… a real stickler might buy a set of bottles with droppers and pour all of his or her bitters into them. Or, you can buy matching shaker bottles and use them for your bitters. They are attractive and should ensure that different brands of bitters dispense more evenly although, if I'm right about differences in viscosity, who knows?

Anyway, we're deep enough in the weeds to stop, though perhaps not forever.

20 May Wednesday

Jennifer, still at her desk for a meeting, asked for a drink she likes. She seldom makes specific cocktail requests and knowing her preferences well I asked whether she would prefer a Manhattan or a Swanky Panky.

And she chose the latter, a richly rewarding moment because for the first time I had to use this Cocktail Diary to summon the recipe (13 May). I followed the recipe exactly, but the particular drink seemed better than ever. Practicing a cocktail somehow improves it or us. She was very pleased.

For months I've wanted to try this old standard that, apparently, originates in Barbados, is a proto-Tiki drink, and is built, normally, to cool you down on a hot day. New Hampshire is rarely hot, and while I love smashing ice with a mallet in a Lewis bag as much as the next person, I prefer my drinks, with rare exceptions, served up. But sometimes habits get in the way of the Good:

Corn 'n Oil
1/2 oz falernum (Taylor's Velvet Falernum)
1/4-1/2 oz lime juice
2-3 dashes Angostura bitters (at this point I'm thinking 2 shakes = 1 dash from a regular Angostura bottle)
2 ozs dark rum
Prep: Fill a double-rocks glass with smashed ice. Add the falernum, lime juice, and bitters. Stir. Then float the rum by pouring it into the drink over the back of your barspoon.

Lovely to see, lovely to drink.

21 May Thursday

Here's another bitters-heavy cocktail that is great, the Seelbach. My kind of drink. Not dainty. Rich. And strange.

Tux2 notes that he/she lists the recipe backwards compared with what you'd expect. And, for different reasons, I'd say we usually build cocktails backwards when we begin with the base spirit which (1) usually is the most expensive ingredient and (2) tends to make me, anyway, forget the dash of this or that at the end. Here's another way to build:

> ### Seelbach
>
> *1/2 oz orange liqueur. Used Cointreau.*
> *7 dashes Peychaud's Bitters (remember 2 shakes per dash)*
> *7 dashes Angostura Bitters (ditto)*
> *1 oz bourbon. Evan Williams 100 Bottled in Bond, which works great.*
> *Prep: Stir, strain into a chilled flute if you're making a single, or into a chilled coupe for the double. Top with champagne, which you are unlikely to forget.*

And another way, especially if you're using a largish coupe, double everything. I mean, 28 shakes of bitters!

Finding an Order in Mixing

It's not a bad practice to begin with your least expensive ingredients in case something goes wrong. If you pour too much Cointreau (which is not cheap but you use less of it) it's easy to adjust the other parts.

But back to the main point which is that the Seelbach is to my taste. Indeed, after a Brooklyn, I capped the night with a second double Seelbach. Mistake.

Like the Hanky Panky and the Creole, this is another long-time riff on a Manhattan.

> ### Brooklyn
>
>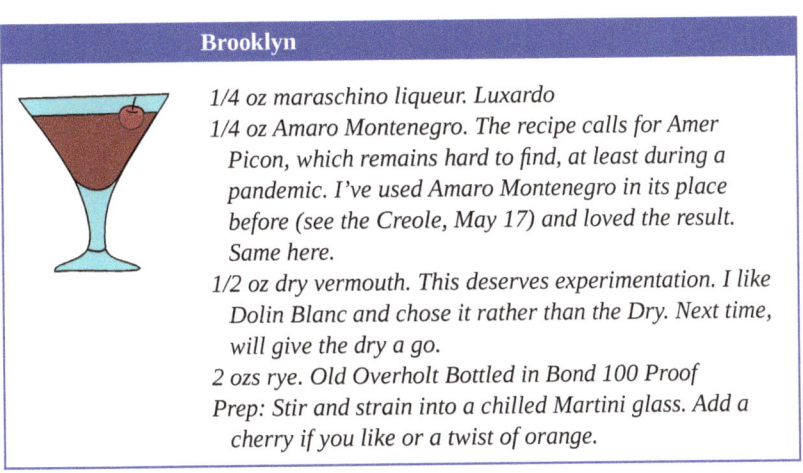
>
> *1/4 oz maraschino liqueur. Luxardo*
> *1/4 oz Amaro Montenegro. The recipe calls for Amer Picon, which remains hard to find, at least during a pandemic. I've used Amaro Montenegro in its place before (see the Creole, May 17) and loved the result. Same here.*
> *1/2 oz dry vermouth. This deserves experimentation. I like Dolin Blanc and chose it rather than the Dry. Next time, will give the dry a go.*
> *2 ozs rye. Old Overholt Bottled in Bond 100 Proof*
> *Prep: Stir and strain into a chilled Martini glass. Add a cherry if you like or a twist of orange.*

This is a cocktail that deserves reverent attention and will likely take a few attempts to get right.

22 May Friday

Deck drinks at Rick and Ruth's with the core of the Luggnuts. We're a big core. Rick Lugg, our leader; Ruth Fischer, his wife; Ann Saunderson, and sometimes her husband George, a former blacksmith and NH State Representative; and me are the frontline. Rick Pollok, an MD, plays keyboards; Mitch Simon, retired law professor from UNH, is the drummer; and Dan Morrissey, a hydrologist, is the bass player. Our wives are equally part of the group, including Jennifer, Ricky Piano's wife Doreen, Mitch's wife Susan, and Dan's wife Laurie. Quite the list. All like to drink.

Lively conversation, some about what we're doing differently, some about how we can emerge from sequestration, how we might "Live Free or Die." Who would have guessed the world had made a Live Free or Die Cocktail? Well, not the world; *Death & Company.* Why the name? No clue. But it is a fine cocktail, dark, complex, delicious.

Traveling Cocktails, Observation 1

It also travels. That is, we sat out, appropriately distanced, on the deck, did not go inside. Beforehand I made enough for several drinks that Jenny and I would share and had put them in a thermos. Brought along a couple of flutes and a decent bottle of prosecco. Simply poured the cocktail from the thermos, about 2/3 of a glass, then filled with the prosecco. Excellent system. The recipe below uses proportions in case you want to make this one by the batch.

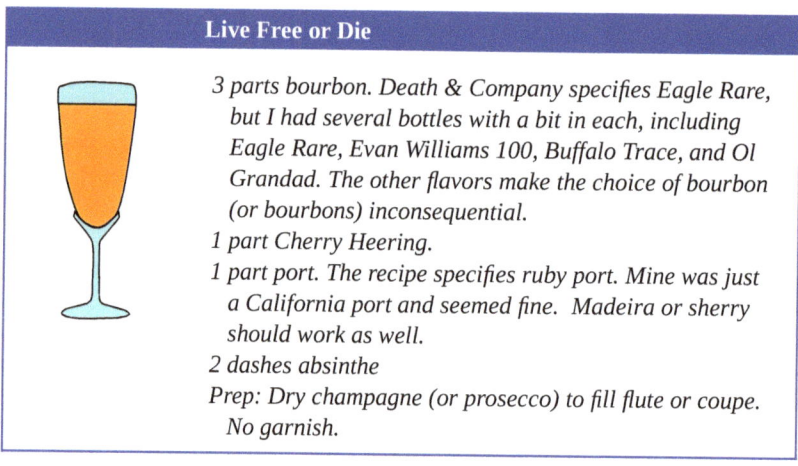

Live Free or Die

3 parts bourbon. Death & Company specifies Eagle Rare, but I had several bottles with a bit in each, including Eagle Rare, Evan Williams 100, Buffalo Trace, and Ol Grandad. The other flavors make the choice of bourbon (or bourbons) inconsequential.

1 part Cherry Heering.

1 part port. The recipe specifies ruby port. Mine was just a California port and seemed fine. Madeira or sherry should work as well.

2 dashes absinthe

Prep: Dry champagne (or prosecco) to fill flute or coupe. No garnish.

Feared that the port and Cherry Heering would make the drink too sweet, but the dry prosecco perfectly counteracted the sweetness without making the cocktail watery. I found it intense, and its deep garnet color lovely to look at. Should probably be New Hampshire's state cocktail, drunk always with my song, "Live Free or Die" (what else?) playing in the foreground, no talking allowed or needed. (Lyrics below with subject-suitable emendations.)

"Live Free or Die"

The silver sun is sinking low deep snow all around
We'll need a cup of kindness to get by
We could leave this cold and dark old place for something warm or fine
But I guess we'd rather live free or die [alternatively: But we'd rather drink a . . .]

April is the cruelest month, things only last a while
Old people like old mountains must let go
We've no hope or strength to hold onto by and by
So carpe diem, *live free or die.*

Chorus:
Take me to New Hampshire when I'm far away or tired
To some hard old Yankee who stands his ground
Take me to her granite walls to her fleeting endless nights
To her lakes and to her little towns

The summer sun rules the land, rain parches every tongue
Green days we never want to end
We celebrate freedom's birth and mourn her passing by
Knowing we'll never live free or die

The air begins to shiver, the leaves grow old and bright
A world so lovely it makes me want to cry
We've stacked our wood, picked our fruit, labored into the night
That's how we live free or die

Chorus:
Take me to New Hampshire when I'm far away or tired
To some hard old Yankee who stands his ground
Take me to her granite walls to her fleeting endless nights
To her lakes and to her little towns

And when we're done lay our bones with those who piled these stones
Our graves will read like. . . license plates
"New Hampshire, beneath your hallowed ground
Lies one who [drank,] lived free, and died."

23 May Saturday

A second evening of outdoor drinking seemed to call for a summery cocktail. But this is New Hampshire. And the weather turned chilly, which may have chilled my feelings toward the Daiquiri I brought along in a thermos.

Two things: The Haitian Barbancourt white rum seemed too intense for the drink, and the agave wasn't a good choice for the sweetener. And, the ratios I used were wrong. See 4 April for a much better version than the recipe I will not bother you with here. I guess the choice of rum and sweetener and the proportions all matter. Go figure.

24 May Sunday

Had a hard bike ride in the morning and worked in the yard moving dirt all day, so pretty done at the end. I'd bought some exotic bitters by mail, a couple of them from New Orleans, and this seemed a good night to check them out.

Old Fashioned (see 6 May for recipe)

I like Eagle Rare (the bourbon does matter here, of course) and maple syrup. Replaced Angostura with the Chickory Pecan Bitters from El Guapo of New Orleans. The flavor of the bitters comes through, subtle but distinctive. I'd say this will be my Old Fashioned of the future. But who knows?

For sentimental reasons I love the idea of this cocktail, and the Creole Bitters seemed a perfect choice, which they were. On 29 March reported the first, delightful encounter with Cocktail de la Louisiane at 10 Castle Street in Great Barrington, Massachusetts. Oh, to be able to return!

But the recipe I used here from Tux2 was far too sweet thanks to the overrepresentation of Benedictine. On a second try, used the following:

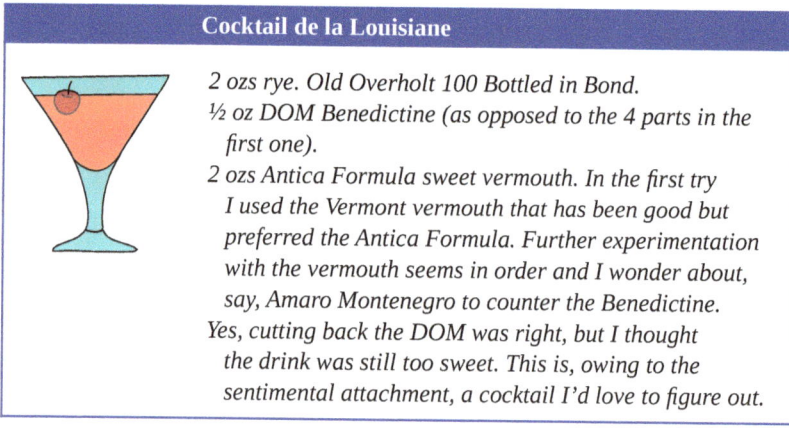

Cocktail de la Louisiane

2 ozs rye. Old Overholt 100 Bottled in Bond.
½ oz DOM Benedictine (as opposed to the 4 parts in the first one).
2 ozs Antica Formula sweet vermouth. In the first try I used the Vermont vermouth that has been good but preferred the Antica Formula. Further experimentation with the vermouth seems in order and I wonder about, say, Amaro Montenegro to counter the Benedictine.
Yes, cutting back the DOM was right, but I thought the drink was still too sweet. This is, owing to the sentimental attachment, a cocktail I'd love to figure out.

[Note: One reason this failed was I forgot the bitters. It happens. This version is rye, not cognac. And I omitted absinthe. Altogether a hash.]

25 May Monday—Memorial Day

Drank beer for the first time in a great while. And they were high-end beers from Tree House. But I'm now a cocktail guy, it seems, almost exclusively.

26 May Tuesday

A moral dwells in this story. Last week Jenny and I drank the Live Free or Die cocktail and loved it (them, really) while back in early April I reported unfavorably on the Scofflaw. The moral is that your choice of ingredients can make all the difference.

Live Free or Die

Last Friday I reported using the dregs of various bottles of bourbon, finishing them and building a thermos full of Live Free or Die. Worked fine. Indeed, the amalgamated bourbons seemed better than the Eagle Rare specified by *Death & Company* with which I began. The right bourbon, however, is not the key to this drink. Ruby port is the recommended wine for a Live Free or Die, but I'd read that madeira is also excellent and probably sherry as well. Not so!

Madeira takes over the drink, does not blend well with bourbon or champagne. Worse, the cocktail looks like a glass of madeira, in itself not a bad thing, but a catastrophic fall from the deep purple, philosophic hues of port. So yeah, season the cocktail as you would season a soup. But don't be perverse.

Scofflaw

In Central Park Monday a White woman who was letting her dog run loose called the cops when a Black man asked her to leash the creature in what was a bird habitat. Claiming that he was threatening her, though a video he took proves he was calm, not at all threatening, she phoned 911. Both the woman and gent had Cooper as their last name, but they were not married or related. In an interview Mr. Cooper referred to Ms. Cooper as a "scofflaw," the first time I have seen the term used outside the cocktail world.

The word was coined in 1924 as part of a contest instituted by a prohibitionist who officially declared "scofflaw" the winner as a term referring to undesirables who broke the law, choosing to drink alcohol during Prohibition. But check this out. In New York the term has somehow joined the quotidian vocabulary, at least in Central Park, where a scofflaw is, nearly one hundred years along, a person who flouts the signs that direct them to leash their dog. One can be certain that Ms. Cooper is privy neither to the application of the word to her and her dog nor to its origins. Mr. Cooper, on the other hand, surely knows the origin and history of scofflaw, its probably wide application in Central Park, and how to behave when confronted with such a witless criminal.

But the irony, of course, is that the Prohibition scofflaw deserves our approval as one who flouted the law for all the right reasons. The modern-day scofflaw, by contrast, probably won't wear a mask in a grocery store, leash her dog in the park, or leave her AK47 at home when she asserts her rights to behave badly. All that said, the Scofflaw, made as it should be, is a very rich drink:

Scofflaw

1.5 ozs rye. (As usual, Old Overholt 100 Proof bottled in Bond)

1/2 oz Dolin Blanc vermouth

1/2 oz Dolin Dry vermouth. Before proceeding I should say the vermouth makes this cocktail work. The deux Dolins perfectly bring together the other flavors and the sweet-sour tension

1/2 oz lemon Juice

1 or 2 dashes grenadine

1 or 2 dashes orange bitters

Prep: Shake and strain into a cold coupe.

So built, the sour-sweet tension seems about perfect, the cocktail living up to its heretical origin. Here's to Mr. Cooper and to calm in the face of hypocrisy.

27 May Wednesday

Good but familiar and not a drink for a hot day:

Remember the Maine
2 ozs rye 3/4 oz Antica Formula 2 tsp Cherry Heering 1/2 tsp absinthe Prep: Stir, strain into a chilled cocktail glass, cherry garnish.

Thought it good to try the Maine not long after the New Hampshire (Live Free or Die) cocktail. But the day had been hot, and in NH we lack air conditioning. The drink is too sweet and too complex for warm weather. I mean, anything with Maine in the title really should not be considered during a heat wave. Another time…

Collins versus Cocktail

The Tom Collins, by contrast, is perfect for a hot night, a summer highball if ever there was one. And it introduces several important topics: David Embury (who I've mentioned before without introducing), the Collins family, and sours, to which the lovely Collins are all related. First, the cocktail, although technically, owing to the addition of carbonated water, it is no longer a cocktail and is, specifically because of how it is served in a tall glass with ice and soda, a Collins:

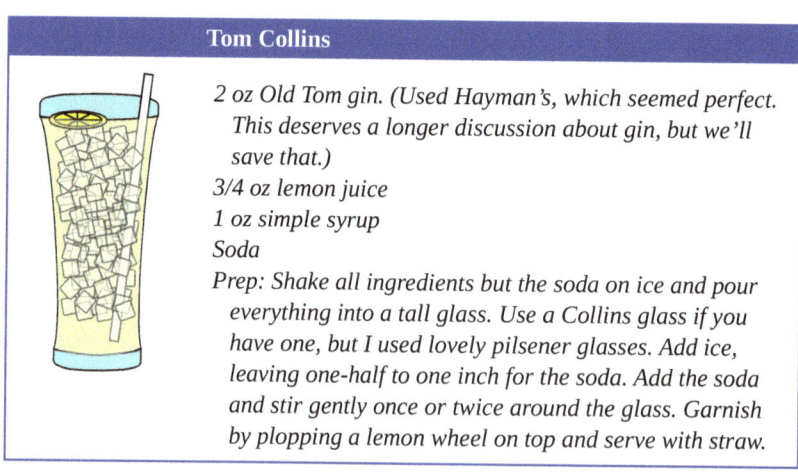

Tom Collins
2 oz Old Tom gin. (Used Hayman's, which seemed perfect. This deserves a longer discussion about gin, but we'll save that.) 3/4 oz lemon juice 1 oz simple syrup Soda Prep: Shake all ingredients but the soda on ice and pour everything into a tall glass. Use a Collins glass if you have one, but I used lovely pilsener glasses. Add ice, leaving one-half to one inch for the soda. Add the soda and stir gently once or twice around the glass. Garnish by plopping a lemon wheel on top and serve with straw.

David Embury: The Cocktail Lawyer

About David Embury, his 1948 book, The Fine Art of Mixing Drinks. *Any serious cocktail lover should own this book; it stands with the great* Savoy Cocktail Book *as seminal. But it is seminal largely because Embury had encyclopedic knowledge of mixing spirits and is especially good at delineating groups of cocktails that really amount to the same supporting cast with different spirits as the main actor. As a result, Embury makes it practical for any home bartender to have a significant repertoire at his or her fingertips. Unlike David Wondrich, Embury is not a fine prose stylist; he was a lawyer first, so imagine what he had to overcome to write a readable book. But Embury had opinions, strongly held.*

He generally considered cocktails to be aperitifs, and to whet the appetite, they could never be sweet. A sour, to Embury, really was sour. Drinks need to be strong, at least 50 percent and usually much more of the volume is the base spirit or spirits. He prints hundreds of recipes but by dividing into categories, he makes it possible to remember more than one could without such organization, and he makes clear that no recipe is prescriptive. Embury sees the proportions as a place to start; beyond that, the drinker decides, provided that "for the aperitif cocktail the final blend with the liquor base will produce a drink that is dry, not sweet. . . let it never be sweet. This is a matter not of ruining the drink but of ruining the appetite and the digestion" (page 139). The man had principles.

Here, then, is Embury's magic ratio: 1 sweet, 2 sour, 8 parts spirit. He liked them strong, make that STRONG. Today our tastes generally are more like 1 sweet, 1 sour, 2 parts spirit. Gin, rum, whisk[e]y (rye, bourbon, Irish, Scotch), cognac, applejack, tequila, vodka (though he hardly mentions, and despised the stuff) are all the same. Some can be improved with bitters; some with one sweetener or another (simple syrup, grenadine, raspberry syrup, orgeat, agave, triple sec, curaçao, Benedictine, maraschino, etc.); lemon or lime may be optional.

Finally, as noted above, Embury was a lawyer. Like you and me, he was no professional bartender. But his contribution, thanks to what must have been a powerful love of drink, was considerable.

28 May Thursday

Colonel Collins

Pedro Collins del Bean = a Presidente over ice
The entry, which stands as written on May 28, was clearly a placeholder that was never placed. Will leave it to the reader to infer what it would have been. If you do, send your answer, and I'll owe you a Pedro Collins del Bean on the house.

29 May Friday

Launched my dad's old, now refurbished, Bell canoe in the Warner River for a twilight cruise with Brick and Laura. The highlight was a serenade by a thrush, specifically a Veery, that sings like an angel. He is plain, brown, small, and high up, but sure can sing.

I had, and have been, during a May heat wave, searching for a hot-weather cocktail, but on this evening for one that traveled by paddle-propelled vessel. The Improved Whiskey Cocktail, which meets some criteria such as being mixed by the batch, poured into a thermos that can be put in a freezer, and that therefore will stay cold aboard canoe, proved too boozy for our clientele and too sweet for me. Poor choice, but here is the recipe:

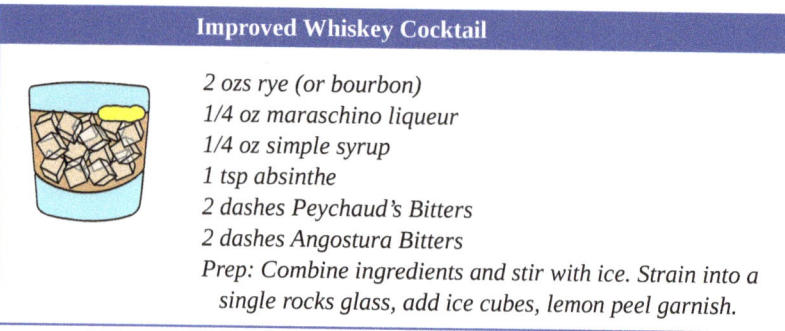

Improved Whiskey Cocktail

2 ozs rye (or bourbon)
1/4 oz maraschino liqueur
1/4 oz simple syrup
1 tsp absinthe
2 dashes Peychaud's Bitters
2 dashes Angostura Bitters
Prep: Combine ingredients and stir with ice. Strain into a
single rocks glass, add ice cubes, lemon peel garnish.

Really, not far from a Sazerac, and so, surely, better than the version I made. Practice. Practice. Practice.

30 May Saturday

Jenny was grumpy Saturday morning, and when yet another book for me arrived, handed it over disapprovingly. Despite the spousal condemnation, I was delighted, but being a mature old fellow, mostly resisted its perusal over breakfast and put in a very hard day pulling stumps with our John Deere ("Nothing runs like a Deere") tractor, which mollified and ultimately calmed her. By the time the cocktail hour arrived, she was ready for whatever turned up.

Happily, Jamie Boudreau.

Jamie Boudreau is blessed with smell and taste, drive, and knowledge, that enable him to turn the toasts of years, or centuries, past into modern pleasures. And so the Champs Elysees, a mostly forgotten cocktail that I'd tried but found disappointing, turns into golden cheer for the evening. Here is Boudreau's recipe:

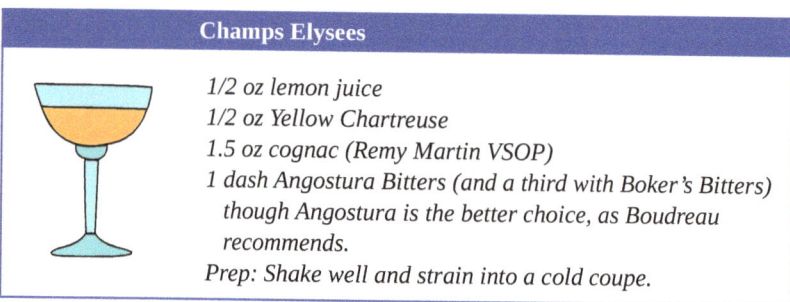

Champs Elysees

1/2 oz lemon juice
1/2 oz Yellow Chartreuse
1.5 oz cognac (Remy Martin VSOP)
1 dash Angostura Bitters (and a third with Boker's Bitters)
though Angostura is the better choice, as Boudreau
recommends.
Prep: Shake well and strain into a cold coupe.

The heat wave has passed. We had a strong north wind all day, and the State is back to its natural condition. We didn't need a tall cooler, one of the Collins family members. But when we do, on the river, listening to any Veery who wants to serenade a girl, the Champs Elysees will be our perfect travel companion.

31 May Sunday

At sea (for the first time in quite a while).

1 June Monday

<table>
<tr><td colspan="2" align="center">Cubed Old Fashioned (Jamie Boudreau) Modified</td></tr>
</table>

1 oz rye
1 oz cognac
1 oz rum (Cuban 7 year, Barbancourt 15 yr, or St James)
2 dashes Boker's or Angostura
1-2 dashes pecan bitters
1 dash orange bitters
Maple syrup (and cherry juice). NOT the 1/4 oz old fashioned syrup Boudreau's recipe calls for. Start with a barspoon.
Prep: Pour all ingredients into your mixing glass with ice. Stir. Serve up in a cold coupe or on the rock in a double rocks glass.

Old Fashioned

Boudreau, Wondrich, all the way back to Embury, and I'd guess further, cocktail aficionados love an Old Fashioned. It is spiritually pure in some ways, lacking any adulterants, so if you love booze, an Old Fashioned is a good way to get a heavy fix.

My Cubed Old Fashioned, which I like a lot, was not Boudreau's cocktail because one ingredient, his Old Fashioned Syrup, is way, way over the top.

Lots of cocktail writers would have you make up any number of mixing ingredients rather than buy them; lots of high-end cocktail bars make their own versions of ingredients, such as Peychaud's Bitters, grenadine, etc. To mix Boudreau's Cubed Old Fashioned with his Old Fashioned syrup you'll need, (1) a liter of rye, (2) 4 cups of white sugar, (3) 4 cups of Demerara sugar or muscovado sugar (what can that be?) (4) allspice berries, (5) whole cloves, and (6) star anise. (By the way, if you were to substitute dark rum for rye in this confection you'd be pretty close to Allspice Dram. More on that another day.) If you use 1/4 oz per Cubed Old Fashioned, the recipe will enable you to mix about 152. Unless the Cubed Old Fashioned becomes your daily drink of choice, and it could, that's pretty much a lifetime supply. In other words, why not stick with maple syrup, which is damned good?

A bit of a rant, but I'll add that confecting your own ingredients can be fun and useful, as in grenadine and simple syrup. But the bar manuals fail to take into account that you are not serving hundreds of drinks, and most of what they suggest has few applications. So… either skip the cocktail or make-do. The latter works surprisingly well most times.

2 June Tuesday

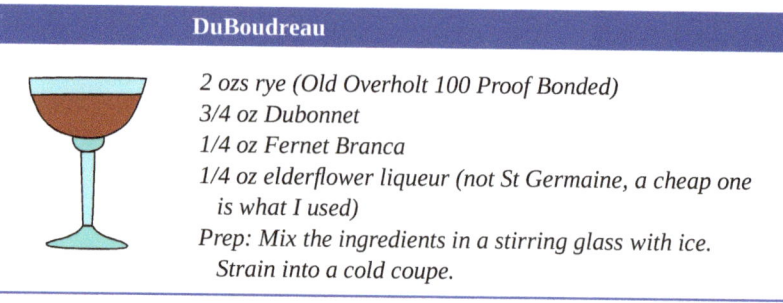

DuBoudreau
2 ozs rye (Old Overholt 100 Proof Bonded) 3/4 oz Dubonnet 1/4 oz Fernet Branca 1/4 oz elderflower liqueur (not St Germaine, a cheap one is what I used) Prep: Mix the ingredients in a stirring glass with ice. Strain into a cold coupe.

Why is it that many cocktails at first are okay, but not great, perhaps too sweet, maybe just like other cocktails? And then after a few sips, get better. Jaimie Boudreau wouldn't name a cocktail for himself if he weren't happy with it. And sure enough, give this one time.

3 June Wednesday

Political Rant

The implications of our Dear President's last name swim across my sense that the Universe may be a Jokester from time to time. But it's all coming clear. For example, the Second Amendment TRUMPS the First Amendment. Thus, those right-wing creeps who carried their AR-15s to the Michigan State House last month because their "rights" were deeply offended by a temporary stay-at-home order meant to prevent them from freely infecting the near and the far with coronavirus had it right. The George Floyd protesters, complaining as they are about how people of color have been treated in the New World since 1492 should be exercising their Second Amendment Rights. If they did, we'd be treated to a televised war on our own soil. How much fun! Or, on another subject, "drain the swamp" means that defying Congress and using one's office any way you like TRUMPS the need for inspectors general to question nefarious doings among the lowlifes our Dear President appoints every chance he gets. If, as in the case of, say, Jeff Sessions, the appointee is not a low enough form of swamp life, there is always a William Barr in the mire to remind us that draining the swamp really means clearing out anyone who stands in the way of undermining the law. Or take environmental regulation. In pursuit of ever rising portfolios, the needs of corporations to make big profits TRUMP the need for breathable air or potable water. Ah Universe, you are a funny one.

For quite a while I've ignored tequila. When Cinco de Mayo rolled past, I thought hard about Margaritas and moved on without ever mixing one. We have tequila at the Bean, a lovely bottle from El Rey De Los Gatos in Monterey, Mexico, though I can't say whether the tequila itself is any good. But at least one book in our cocktail library recommends Milagro Reposado, which is middle-shelf reasonable, and so I bought a lovely bottle. Plus, today our grandson Jon is seven, and he's a Texan, so we're going to try Canon's Remember the Alamo.

Remember the Alamo

2 ozs tequila. Milagro Reposado for a start, and a second with El Rey de los Gatos, a third back to Milagro. In fact, the tequila seems to matter little because the vermouth is so intense.

1 1/4 oz Punt e Mes, an Italian sweet vermouth that is famously intense. Not many recipes call for it, mostly because it takes over, as it did here, but who minds when the drink is so grand.

3/8 oz Cherry Heering, a ridiculous measure I know, but this version is a bit bigger (why not?) than the Canon version, yet not so big that a 1/2 oz would make it too sweet. You can find 3/8 oz in a properly graduated jigger.

2 dashes Angostura Bitters. Yet, this drink seemed to call for bitters experimentation. In number 2, I mixed Angostura and Chocolate bitters equally. In version 3, I used Chocolate and Boker's. Take your pick, they're all good, but I was partial to the chocolate.

Prep: Serve in a coupe than has been misted or swirled with absinthe. If you swirl, drink the extra rather than tossing it, I say. Garnish with a cherry.

Surely you could use mescal or perhaps pisco (which I've never tried) in place of tequila. And you might even try whisky, maybe rum. Indeed, I just might give some dark rum a go. Or how about a less forceful amaro, say Amaro Nonino? On the other hand, why mess with something already delicious? The drink is rich, mysterious, unlike anything else I've had.

If war breaks out we may need a Remember the Alamo behind the pocket shutters (I think we'll need to call them Republican shutters in the way they were once called Indian shutters) in our living room. Purportedly designed for arrows, I suppose, in 1792 or 93, ours may prove ineffective against assault rifle rounds. If so, Remember the Bean!

4 June Thursday

At sea

5 June Friday

This, is the drink of summer:

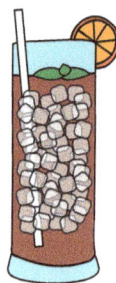

> **Planter's Punch**
>
> *3 oz dark rum. Myers's is a good choice as some evidence, or at least some claims, suggest the drink originated in Jamaica. As many recipes as bars exist, but here's one to begin with. From here, if you like it, use ingredients you have in mind or to hand to dial this one in.*
> *1 oz lime juice*
> *1/2 oz lemon juice*
> *1/2 oz grenadine*
> *1 tsp simple syrup*
> *3 dashes Angostura Bitters. Don't forget the bitters, which I sometimes do. Many recipes for this do not use bitters. I think they're great here, and you could try others besides Angostura.*
> *Prep: Stir this one, even though most recipes call for shaking (owing to the citrus). Pour ice and all into a tall glass. Add more ice to fill. Garnish with whatever fruit is handy (mint, not a fruit I guess, is also nice). Serve with a straw if you have one.*

Pretty good? I should say. Other iterations included 1 oz each of St James *rhum*, Barbancourt 15-year-old *rhum*, and Goslings 151, replacing the simple syrup with agave, and various bitters, including the spicy Creole, and a mix of Boker's with Peychaud's. All terrific, this punch is built for experiments.

It's Friday, and by starting on this too early, I face a painful, hard bike ride tomorrow. Oh well, the drink is worth it. That said, "Planter's Punch," whether originally from Charleston (which has a hotel claiming to have invented the drink) or Jamaica, suggests privileged white people on their veranda, looking out over hot cane fields, slaves at work—and the leaves of sugar cane plants, if they do not cut like knives, hurt like hell—drinking a cooling libation, the uplifting rum resulting from that slave work. A few tastes and one can imagine the drink helping planters to justify and celebrate their elevated lives. As part of its alchemical power, alcohol can transform a cruel idea into a sanctified one, enabling those planters under its heavy sway to imagine they had brought order, civilization, and God into the benighted world of their lucky slaves.

6 June Saturday

Spent the afternoon at the Black Lives Matter march in Concord—sweet, powerful, and hopeful, run by students who knew how to make an impression. Planter's Punch, which I'll pursue in due course, was a poor symbolic choice for the evening cocktail. Instead, we chose *Death & Co's.* excellent Naked and Famous, at least in proportions and some ingredients, which is a Last Word inspired delight.

And the choice proved inspiring because of its possibilities. After a nap, as we each sipped the first Naked and Famous of the evening, I told Jenny about how it seemed to me a cocktail book could be useful. And someday, it is unlikely but not forlorn, this diary could prove to have been the beginning of a successful, published book about cocktails. News Item: Here's the idea; you are the first to know.

Why a Cocktail Book Resulted from a Pandemic? *The Descriptive, the Prescriptive, and the Experimental*

Old and new books about cocktails sell well; interest in the drinks is keen; dozens of Internet sources with information are at our fingertips for free; and knowledgeable, smart people apply themselves to writing about cocktails as a labor of love, an excuse for drinking, and an exploratory adventure. Why not?

In that flowering environment, what is left to say, especially by one who has never been a bartender and until recently knew little about cocktails? Really it is thanks only to the Pandemic of 2020 and the need to chemically improve our stay-at-home-every-evening plight that, compared with many, I've gained a measure, so to speak, of expertise. And through it, I've looked for the niche where a new outlook could be useful. Here it is.

Books about how to make cocktails and which cocktails to make fall into camps. The traditional ones name ingredients and proportions, but do not prescribe specific brands or varieties of spirit. In this camp, a typical Manhattan will be 2 ozs bourbon or rye, 1 oz sweet vermouth, 2 dashes Angostura Bitters, cherry garnish. As with most general cookbooks, which do not tell us which brand of flour, kind of butter or milk, or type of salt to use in making biscuits, cocktail recipes give us the choice, or responsibility, for choosing the brand of bourbon and vermouth, offering no guidance at all.

Without guidance, we miss possibilities or make mistakes. For example, confusion exists about Canadian whisky: it is not rye. Why bourbon or why rye? Between them, which brands are good choices? Which vermouth, since many with vastly different flavors, none terribly expensive, are possible? Sure, Angostura bitters are standard, have been for a century, but suddenly an array of bitters can turn a Manhattan into THE Manhattan for you.

By contrast, a more current species of cocktail book will be very precise about ingredients:

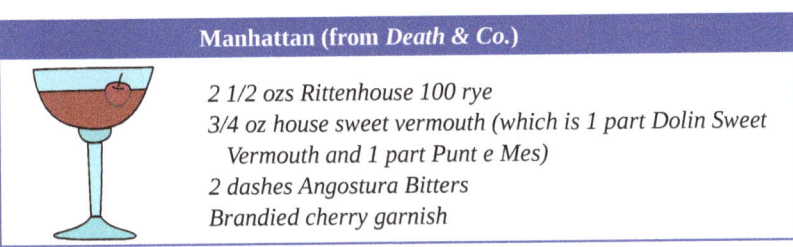

Manhattan (from *Death & Co.*)

2 1/2 ozs Rittenhouse 100 rye
3/4 oz house sweet vermouth (which is 1 part Dolin Sweet
    Vermouth and 1 part Punt e Mes)
2 dashes Angostura Bitters
Brandied cherry garnish

In Manhattan, everything is readily available. In the rest of the world, Rittenhouse Rye may not be (it is not in New Hampshire). Do you have Dolin Sweet Vermouth? The Dolin vermouths are excellent, but we're more likely to have Martini and Rossi Rosso. Will it do? And if you have it, is the opened bottle refrigerated? What about Punt e Mes? Ever heard of it? Are you ready to make up your own supply of Death and Co's house vermouth? And are there choices of bitters that might complement (you can use more than one bitter in a glass) or replace Angostura? If so, what are the possibilities? A fundamental, classic three-ingredient cocktail, yet so many questions.

In short, cocktail recipe books usually are either descriptive (rye, sweet vermouth, bitters) or prescriptive (this rye, that vermouth, Angostura Bitters). A detour to cooking can help explain what we're trying to do here.

My favorite chef is Paul Prudhomme, and his Chef *Paul Prudhomme's Louisiana Kitchen* is the book I begin with for many dishes. Prudhomme's recipe for Dirty Rice (Rice Dressing to me) calls for ground pork, chicken gizzards, and chicken livers. I use ground pork and ground beef, no gizzards or livers. His spice list specifies at least twice the cayenne pepper that people in the frozen north can tolerate. My resulting amended dish is in demand around here, where livers and especially gizzards are mostly disdained and where spice at least used to be embargoed at the Massachusetts/New Hampshire border. Despite some basic differences, no one would fail to recognize that each version of the dish is rice dressing (or, errr, dirty rice).

In the world of cocktail recipes, a similar approach might work as follows. The cocktail below is a *Death & Co.* original, not actually famous, but really good:

Naked and Famous (from *Death & Co.*)

3/4 oz Del Maguey Chichicapa Mezcal (How about
*   another mezcal or perhaps tequila?)*
3/4 oz Yellow Chartreuse (is Green an alternative?)
3/4 oz Aperol (could Campari work?)
3/4 oz lime juice (is lemon juice a substitute?)
Prep: Shake the ingredients and strain into a cold coupe.

Note also the equal measure of each ingredient, a formula borrowed from the vastly better known Last Word (equal portions of gin, Green Chartreuse, maraschino liqueur, and lime juice). But at home, where being pulled over and breathalyzed is unlikely and where making a buck on a drink is not the point, wouldn't we rather use 1 oz, not the 3/4 oz, that the original recipe specifies? Would not change a thing about the taste. As to the ingredients themselves, I tried all of the parenthetical possibilities, all are good, each having either large or subtle effects, but none spoiling the essence of the original *Death & Company* cocktail, which I have never in fact had. Del Maguey Chichicapa Mezcal is locally unobtainable, though the mezcal I used was excellent, and replacing it with Milagro Reposado Tequila made a lighter, less intense cocktail, but then, that is what many people prefer, just as some want less cayenne or, good heavens, lite beer.

In each recipe you'll find variations on the theme. As when a musician plays a song, today's version may be slower than yesterday's, in a different key, emphasize particular phrasing. In your bar, you'll sometimes have several nearly empty bottles of gin whose combined contents will, it turns out, yield a delightful riff on an old favorite.

It's taken a pandemic and taken a while, but this ship now has a course.

7 June Sunday

At sea.

8 June Monday

Dialing in Planter's Punch is today's business. We start with data from Friday: lemon without lime is fine, or lemon and lime. We have not tried lime without lemon. Simple syrup should be replaced by agave. Bitters are essential and Angostura alone fine. But the drink seems to yearn for others and for combinations. Similarly, a Jamaican dark rum such as Myers's is good. But other rums in combination are richer.

We're short on limes and so began with the lemon-lime combination then moved to lemon only. Either approach works without, to me, discernible improvement from one to the other. A combination of Angostura and Peychaud's Bitters is better than Angostura alone. But in subsequent iterations the combination of Creole Bitters (2 droppers) and Peychaud's Bitters (1 dash) was better, richer. Will stick with that formula.

As to the rum, because the recipe calls for 3 ozs, I've decided three rums. If 3, at least one must be 151 proof, and Goslings Black Seal is all I have, so it is number one in the mix. Black Seal is so black that

I thought why not try an ounce of white rum. Both Barbancourt (Haiti) and Diplomatico (Venezuela) are excellent. I tried each and probably lean toward Diplomatico. Finally, for the last rum I tried Havana Club 7 year with the Diplomatico and St James with Barbancourt (both Haitian). The last was a little deeper, more complicated (or something) and probably will taste muddled to many people. The cleaner combination of Havana Club (if you can get it) and Diplomatico seems more likely to find general appeal. So here's the recipe I'm going with

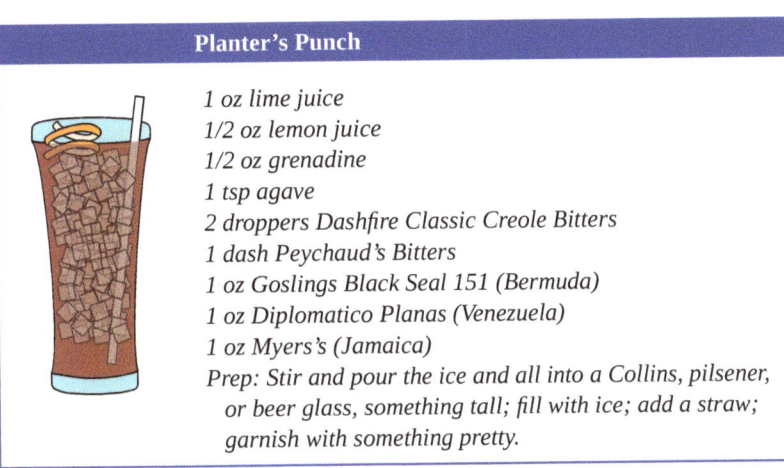

Planter's Punch

1 oz lime juice
1/2 oz lemon juice
1/2 oz grenadine
1 tsp agave
2 droppers Dashfire Classic Creole Bitters
1 dash Peychaud's Bitters
1 oz Goslings Black Seal 151 (Bermuda)
1 oz Diplomatico Planas (Venezuela)
1 oz Myers's (Jamaica)
Prep: Stir and pour the ice and all into a Collins, pilsener, or beer glass, something tall; fill with ice; add a straw; garnish with something pretty.

No, I have not tried the rum combination. But how can it be anything but great? And, indeed, I may need a bottle of Appleton, a finer Jamaican rum, as the coup de gras in place of Myers's.

Dialing in. How is it we have so many rum choices? How close to perfect does a cocktail need to be?

9 June Tuesday

At sea

10 June Wednesday

Mai Tai (from the Schofield Brothers)

1 oz Jamaican rum (e.g. Myers's or Appleton)
1 oz aged rhum agricole (e.g. Barbancourt 15 year old)
1 1/4 oz lime juice
1/3 oz orange curaçao
1/3 oz orgeat
1 dash Angostura Bitters
Prep: Shake and pour into an ice-filled rocks glass. Mint sprig and lime wheel garnish

A similar but less fussy recipe from Tux2:

Mai Tai (Certified Bean Mai Tai)

1 oz gold rum (used the ubiquitous Bacardi Gold, which is cheap and Puerto Rican, not Jamaican)

1 oz dark rum (15-year-old Barbancourt Rhum from Haiti, St James from Martinique, White Diplomatico from Venezuela)

1 oz lime juice (no need to be exact here. A little less or more doesn't matter.)

1/2 oz curaçao

1/4 oz orgeat

1/4 oz simple syrup (I used agave, now standard here for rum and tequila drinks)

Prep: Shake and pour everything into rocks glass. First, though, put the lime you squeezed into the bottom of the glass. Mint sprig garnish.

Ice in the Shaker versus Ice in the Glass

Every recipe I read calls for straining to keep the ice in the shaker rather than pouring it into the glass, making it part of the drink. I'm guessing shaking could warm the ice enough to turn the drink watery. On the other hand, using the original ice is like licking the bowl when your mama mixes a batch of brownies. I can't stand to let it go to waste.

Into the rocks glass went the entire contents of the shaker, and I wish to report it had no bad effects whatsoever. These drinks were all excellent. The Bacardi Gold is cheap but it is the perfect backbone for this drink, not too light or dark. Most recipes call for Jamaican rum, say Appleton, but it is far more expensive, and I doubt it would improve what is a nearly perfect cocktail.

Yes, nearly perfect. Usually, I feel the need to try alternative spirits or measures of ingredients. Here, I'm sticking to the Tux2 recipe above, noting that the 15-year-old Barbancourt *Rhum Agricole* is the best of my choices as the second rum. We have others here, such as Havana Club, but the Mai Tai presented is so good I'll find other drinks to toy with. The only issue this Mai Tai presents is whether it should replace Planter's Punch as the drink of summer. Naahhh! We'll drink them both.

11 June Thursday

Was to be at sea but became fascinated by Tux2's description of a Maiden's Blush (and how could one not be?). The thing is, Tux2's recipe is quite the outlier among Internet versions, but once you go to Harry Craddock's *The Savoy Cocktail Book*, things begin to clear. Craddock gives us not only two Maiden's Blush(es?) but immediately after, two Maiden's Prayers. Most recipes, indeed all that I've found, amount to the Blush No.1. Tux2, however, combines the two, taking lemon from No.1 and absinthe from No. 2, then adding his or her own touch of raspberry cordial, replacing grenadine in the other recipes, and prescribing Old Tom gin rather than dry gin.

Turns out, Tux2 relied on history, went farther back, to 1912, and uses the exact recipe from *Recipes of American and Other Iced Drinks*. It is brilliant. The absinthe and lemon kind of hold one another at bay, the one sweet, the other sour. The licorice in the absinthe can thereby (I never use this word, but here it has a religious connotation) rise up and out. I bought something called Metcalfe's Raspberry Liqueur for this drink and have no clue if it resembles raspberry cordial. But it causes the maiden to blush heavily and delivers, well, fruitiness. Finally, I'll try another with, say, Plymouth Gin, but the Old Tom is very fine here. And just a warning: This maiden is dangerously captivating.

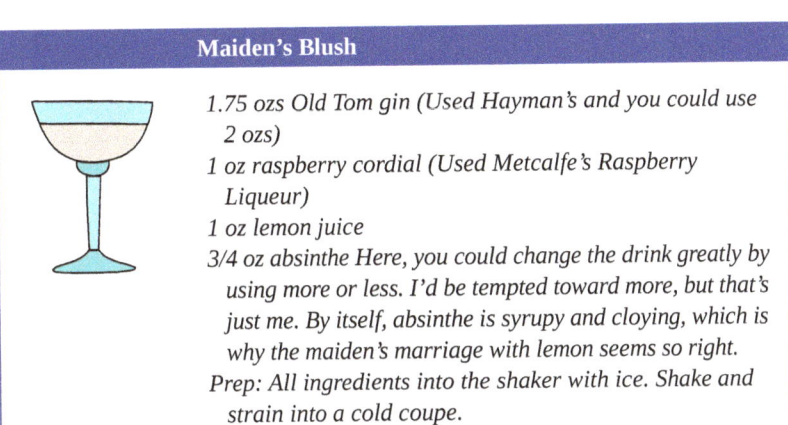

Maiden's Blush

1.75 ozs Old Tom gin (Used Hayman's and you could use 2 ozs)

1 oz raspberry cordial (Used Metcalfe's Raspberry Liqueur)

1 oz lemon juice

3/4 oz absinthe Here, you could change the drink greatly by using more or less. I'd be tempted toward more, but that's just me. By itself, absinthe is syrupy and cloying, which is why the maiden's marriage with lemon seems so right.

Prep: All ingredients into the shaker with ice. Shake and strain into a cold coupe.

Cocktails Awakening the Senses

Many cocktails on first sip do not measure up to what one expects. It seems to me that the subtleties of these concoctions require our senses of taste; smell; sight; and on occasion, touch, as on the tongue, to awaken, sharpen, understand what is on offer. More often than not, at first I feel disappointed with a new cocktail, especially if the description that has captured me is well done. But then, a few sips in, almost as if a warm-up is required, the tastes become sharper, more delineated, and more evenly spread across the plane of the tongue. Of course, with the higher awareness comes, or perhaps is brought on by, the delightful effects of alcohol in the brain, the lifting of cares, the transportation to another realm, an easy, graceful paring away of murky reality in favor of a less troubled space. The Maiden's Blush, perhaps so aptly named for her effect as well as her complexion, is just such a cocktail, helped surely by the dangerous qualities of the wormwood in absinthe. If this is madness, I'll swear to banish sanity every evening! If this is madness, let's have another round!

12 June Friday

Our first dinner out since the plague. The Tavern on the Lake, more a pond, in Hopkinton. They have a basic bar so, I thought, let's try a basic cocktail, and as it's been among my recent trials, the Mai Tai seemed a good place to understand homemade against bar made.

Run-of-the Mill Bars

Next time we go, I may order another Mai Tai just to get a photograph. Or better, perhaps someone else will order one. The word Abomination comes to mind. Seating is outside because of the pandemic, so I didn't see this monster's creation but suspect it involved a pre-made package. The most apparent fruit juice, color and taste, was orange, though not fresh orange, and I'm guessing canned pineapple juice. I've seen Internet versions that call for these and grenadine, spiced rum and coconut rum, though I doubt any of those found its way here. I'm guessing a cheap Bacardi and the mix. They added a slice of orange and a maraschino cherry; the massive dose of red dye by itself could have proved fatal. The drink was so bad, and weak besides, that I ordered a second just in case the first was an error, being careful both times to pass the cherry along to Jennifer, who is younger and stronger than me. No improvement.

The point is not to ask for pity but to warn you against run-of-the-mill bars. A Mai Tai is not hard. Its ingredients seem commonplace or should be in any bar that dares to charge $12 for a lousy cocktail. Apparently, if you're going to do your drinking outside the home and outside establishments with bona fides, choices will be limited, very limited. Save your money for a bottle of good rum.

[Post-Covid Note: Absence sharpens awareness, helps you see things that blend into the background of the commonplace. This first visit to a bar in months showed and clarified what I could not see at all. The result was a long-standing perspective that helps explain how different bars operate, especially their limitations, and the rarity of good bars. The experience also proved fundamental in shaping my understanding that the home bartender will, except on destination vacations to fine cocktail bars in great cities, be the best source of his or her own cocktails. It is also worth adding that being a home bartender prepares you to take advantage of the best cocktails when you visit a great bar and to understand the limitations of how to order in the less-than-great but perfectly respectable establishments that you will find in good hotels and fine restaurants. Thank goodness for that abominable Mai Tai.]

13 June Saturday

Our first sail of the year was about perfect, with our friend Stephanie Fox, always an interesting conversationalist and worldly savant.

Once home, I needed to go back to a Mai Tai just to be clear about the real thing versus the Abomination. The one difference in my first Mai Tai tonight and those of the past week was the use of Pirat as the dark rum. Really, it is more a golden rum and lacks the character of the Barbancourt 15 year old, though it is as expensive. It seemed time to put a cap on this cocktail. Made one last iteration of what I believe to be The Ol' Bean Mai Tai, as described on June 10. Yes, that version now has official Bean Certification.

14 June Sunday

Rick and Meg Stewart visited in the backyard. Made them a version of the Stiggins' Daiquiri #2 from Canon while Jenny and I drank Cobbler's Dreams. No real report on the daiquiri; Rick liked it. But the Cobbler's Dream is the best Manhattan I've ever had, even if its inventor, Jamie Boudreau, calls it a variation of a Martinez. What we've got here is Plato against Aristotle, the concept of Forms versus forms, at work.

If there is an ideal Martinez, a Platonic Martinez that is an abstract changeless ideal, outside time and space it would consist of:

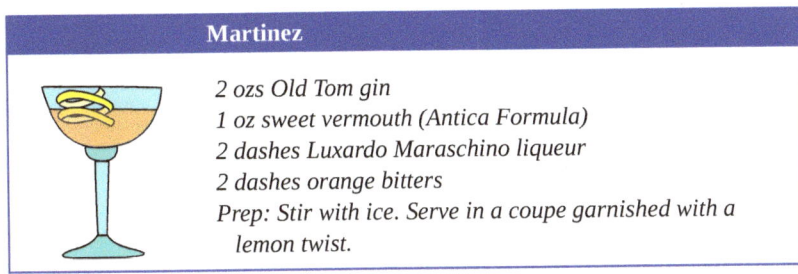

Martinez

2 ozs Old Tom gin
1 oz sweet vermouth (Antica Formula)
2 dashes Luxardo Maraschino liqueur
2 dashes orange bitters
Prep: Stir with ice. Serve in a coupe garnished with a
    lemon twist.

And a Platonic Manhattan would be

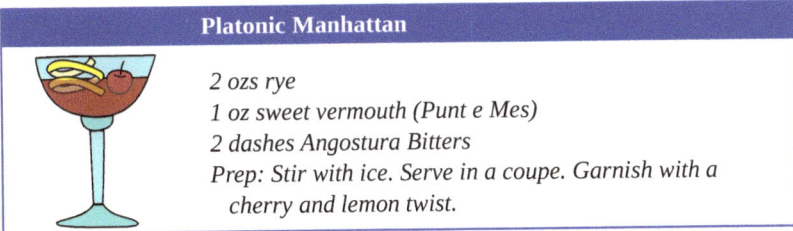

Platonic Manhattan

2 ozs rye
1 oz sweet vermouth (Punt e Mes)
2 dashes Angostura Bitters
Prep: Stir with ice. Serve in a coupe. Garnish with a
    cherry and lemon twist.

An Aristotelian Cobbler's Dream, a form of it as opposed to its Form is

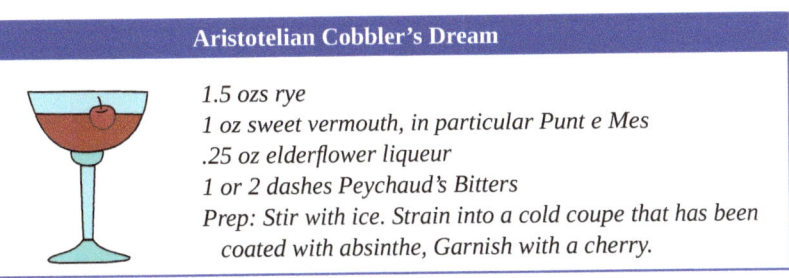

Aristotelian Cobbler's Dream

1.5 ozs rye
1 oz sweet vermouth, in particular Punt e Mes
.25 oz elderflower liqueur
1 or 2 dashes Peychaud's Bitters
Prep: Stir with ice. Strain into a cold coupe that has been
    coated with absinthe, Garnish with a cherry.

My argument is that the Cobbler's Dream is no Martinez at all, largely because the base spirit is rye, not gin. The alchemy of cocktails often is subtle, and it is in the Cobbler's Dream, but the base spirit is fundamental to identity, so that going from gin to rye is more than a variation. Additionally, the Cobbler's Dream includes all of the other elements of a Manhattan—bitters and sweet vermouth. The addition of elderflower and absinthe enriches but does not a form of Martinez make. Were we to stir up a Martinez, a Manhattan, and a Cobbler's Dream everyone would call the last a form of Manhattan rather than of Martinez. (Don't I have anything more momentous to argue about?)

Meanwhile, the brilliant improvement on a standard Manhattan is Punt e Mes. I've tried various sweet vermouths, but none has the presence of this one. Certainly, it will be worth testing, say, Antica Formula, with the additions of absinthe and elderflower. But right now I am betting the Platonic Form of a Manhattan includes Punt e Mes.

15 and 16 June Monday and Tuesday

At sea. The two days is for me a pandemic first.

17 June Wednesday

At last, the sacrifice is about to end. Denis is coming to dinner, and I am planning three drinks:
1. **Planter's Punch** (82)
2. **Perra Por Favor** (Canon, 63)
3. **Cobbler's Dream** (Canon, 91)

All were delicious with Planter's Punch a good place to begin on a hot day. Followed my own recipe (see 82) and am sticking with it.

Perra Por Favor

This will not be to everyone's liking; at least, it wasn't to Al's and maybe not to Denis's. Al's comment was insightful, suggesting the boy has sensitive tastebuds, which his childhood diet supports, since he ate only frozen waffles with maple syrup, without butter. He said the drink had many flavors he loved but there was one, a smoky one, that he did not care for. That one, I'm certain, was the main ingredient, mezcal.

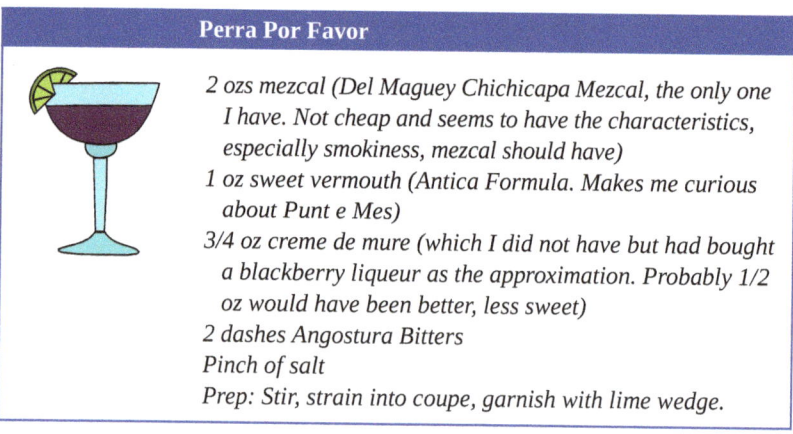

Perra Por Favor
2 ozs mezcal (Del Maguey Chichicapa Mezcal, the only one I have. Not cheap and seems to have the characteristics, especially smokiness, mezcal should have)
1 oz sweet vermouth (Antica Formula. Makes me curious about Punt e Mes)
3/4 oz creme de mure (which I did not have but had bought a blackberry liqueur as the approximation. Probably 1/2 oz would have been better, less sweet)
2 dashes Angostura Bitters
Pinch of salt
Prep: Stir, strain into coupe, garnish with lime wedge.

As usual, took a few sips, but I loved this cocktail, though as suggested above, it apparently is not to everyone's taste. I could also see trying it with an amaro such as Amaro Montenegro and as mentioned, the vermouth Punt e Mes. The Canon recipe calls for Cocchi Vermouth di Torino.

The Order of Cocktails in an Evening

The order of the cocktails was important. Planter's Punch on a hot early evening, tall, cool, pretty in its pilsener glass, seemed a good beginning and proved to be so. The Perra Por Favor was the night's experiment, so I thought just before dinner might be about right. Given the dark, smoky, complex nature of this cocktail, later in the evening would suit it on a regular basis, but early was fine as an experiment. The Cobbled Together Dream was meant for later in the evening, but Denis and I had ours with a dinner of lamb burgers and corn on the cob. Delicious. I really like a sweet drink with a salty dinner. And I concluded the evening with a second Cobbled Together Dream, which was in actuality one too many, but mighty fine.

18 June Thursday

At sea.

19 June Friday

Seemed a good day to try something new and from a relatively new source, Brad Thomas Parsons's book *Bitters*. Besides, I like bitters. Sent Steve Poore a recipe for a Sidecar, to which he responded with a vivid description of the perils he and Rochelle have encountered making cocktails, such as using inferior grenadine, using key limes rather than Persian limes. But in a return email tried to reassure him, based on my Mai Tai encounter last weekend, that bars can't be trusted to make a good cocktail. But back to tonight's choice, the Allegheny Cocktail. I'd planned to make one then move along to a Pisco Sour, having never tried Pisco, but the Allegheny was just too good.

As with so many cocktails, the first few sips seemed undistinguished. But further along, the cocktail was irresistible. Here's the recipe, which by the way, I present as made, by that I mean, doubled:

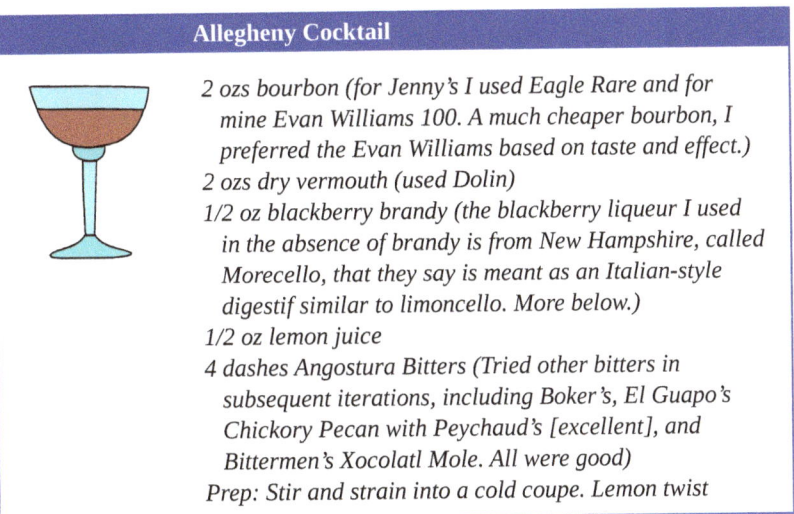

Allegheny Cocktail

2 ozs bourbon (for Jenny's I used Eagle Rare and for
    mine Evan Williams 100. A much cheaper bourbon, I
    preferred the Evan Williams based on taste and effect.)
2 ozs dry vermouth (used Dolin)
1/2 oz blackberry brandy (the blackberry liqueur I used
    in the absence of brandy is from New Hampshire, called
    Morecello, that they say is meant as an Italian-style
    digestif similar to limoncello. More below.)
1/2 oz lemon juice
4 dashes Angostura Bitters (Tried other bitters in
    subsequent iterations, including Boker's, El Guapo's
    Chickory Pecan with Peychaud's [excellent], and
    Bittermen's Xocolatl Mole. All were good)
Prep: Stir and strain into a cold coupe. Lemon twist

I drank three, Jennifer two, and we were both very happy. The key seems to have been the blackberry liqueur, which turned the cocktail darker and added a sweet spiciness that nestled with the lemon. I'm guessing most any blackberry spirit would serve. And if blackberry works, raspberry would as well, along with many other fruit-based spirits, say apricot or peach, and perhaps a little farther afield, elderflower.

Inventing Cocktails: A Start

Bourbon is under-represented in cocktails and doesn't, perhaps, deserve the fate. Now, I'm unsure of the role played by the dry vermouth in the Allegheny but love the idea. It seems, then, with the list of ingredients amended to (1) bourbon, (2) dry vermouth or even amaro, (3) fruit liqueur, (4) lemon juice, and (5) bitters, you could invent many another delicious cocktail and call it or them whatever you fancy.

By the way, we ate frozen pizza with the cocktails, and it was a fine combination.

20 June Saturday

To prepare for a socially distanced dinner at our friends Brick and Laura's, I tried to improve the Allegheny Cocktail in ways noted yesterday. As I've done before, putting several of the cocktails in a thermos and the thermos in the freezer for an hour or so makes a nice way to drink outdoors. But I thought the cocktail itself could have been better.

> ### Inventing Cocktails: Continued
> *Tried various things such as Amaro Montenegro, raspberry liqueur, Cherry Heering, Boker's and Peychaud's bitters and ultimately an equal mix of the original blackberry liqueur and Dubonnet. None improved the cocktail, but the trials got me fairly drunk. By the time we reached Brick and Laura's, with the thermos loaded and cold, I was on the edge of too much, or way too much. This cocktail improvement notion can be a dangerous game. A fellow who too enthusiastically seeks the Platonic version of a cocktail may find himself with no version, no sense, no memory, no tongue.*

21 June Sunday—Father's Day

Jenny's family came to dinner. I smoked ribs and barbecued salmon. But I didn't drink; had too much Saturday. However, I got three women real drunk—my two mothers in law, Jean, Jenny's mother; and Beth, her stepmother; and sister-in-law, Wendy—and felt quite good about it. The medicine: Planter's Punch. Three rums for three women: Myers's, Diplomatico, and Goslings Black Seal 151, did good work. They loved the drink, as a deserved summertime stalwart. Tasty, lots of ice, large, pretty, cooling.

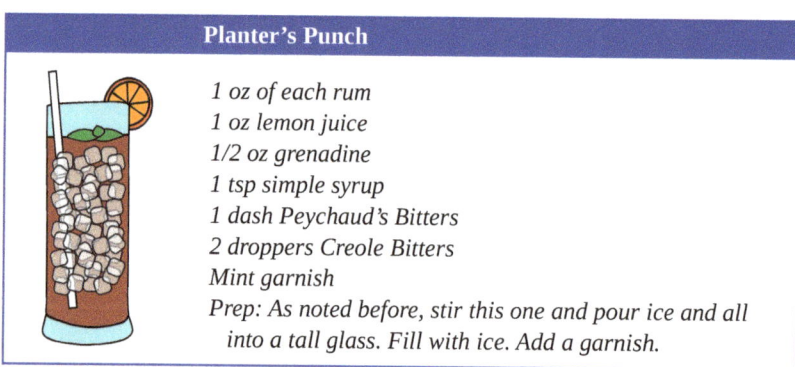

Planter's Punch
1 oz of each rum
1 oz lemon juice
1/2 oz grenadine
1 tsp simple syrup
1 dash Peychaud's Bitters
2 droppers Creole Bitters
Mint garnish
Prep: As noted before, stir this one and pour ice and all into a tall glass. Fill with ice. Add a garnish.

Should be easy to recall. Well, we'll see about that.

Tim Goodrich

A few words about Jenny's father, Tim Goodrich, who stuck with his usual Long Trail Ale. Tim is a kind, cheerful, optimistic character despite sudden, near total blindness that afflicted him only a few years ago; longstanding profound deafness; and well-advanced dementia. Last year they decided to spend summer months here in a boxcar replica, really an RV, adjacent to the Ol' Bean and built by local carpenters. The idea is that they escape the Florida heat; this year, the Covid-19 epidemic that is raging in Florida; and we can help Beth in her care of Tim. Jennifer, a natural caregiver, loves the chance to spend time with her old dad. The boxcar isn't quite ready for them yet, but we've had a pad built for it. Expected to arrive from Contoocook in a couple of weeks. Meanwhile they're staying with us.

I had maybe two glasses of wine over a long day and evening, so this counts as time at sea in my book, and I'll need to test something new tomorrow.

22 June Monday

A hot afternoon. The cocktail of the night, one I'd never heard of, from Tux2, is the Puerto Rican Racer.

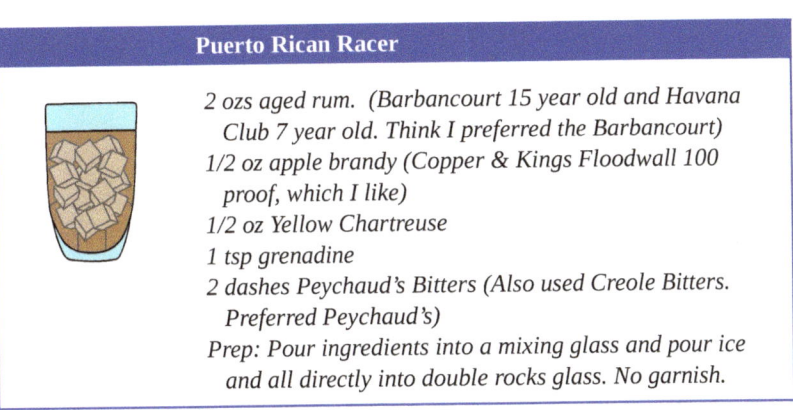

Puerto Rican Racer
2 ozs aged rum. (Barbancourt 15 year old and Havana Club 7 year old. Think I preferred the Barbancourt)   1/2 oz apple brandy (Copper & Kings Floodwall 100 proof, which I like)   1/2 oz Yellow Chartreuse   1 tsp grenadine   2 dashes Peychaud's Bitters (Also used Creole Bitters. Preferred Peychaud's)   Prep: Pour ingredients into a mixing glass and pour ice and all directly into double rocks glass. No garnish.

For the first time in this long quarantine, woke in the night with a sick headache. Fumbled around in the dark for Tylenol and Excedrin, found one of each, gradually took effect. Could blame the three Racers, but a bigger contributor was a salad-only dinner. Still the sweetness of the drink, dominance of Yellow Chartreuse, must have contributed. I'd try lighter on the Chartreuse, perhaps a 1/4 oz and a 1/2 tsp of grenadine, maybe 3/4 oz apple brandy. But I'm not sure. The cocktail has a lot going on, and I wonder if, say, Amaro Montenegro in place of the Chartreuse would be worth a test. This is a very boozy cocktail, a bit oily, probably not a great choice on a warm evening. One last thing is that the apple brandy to my palate gets lost. This seems to me to happen with the spirit. Its taste is relatively light, making me wonder if it is the right choice to stand up to the rum and Chartreuse?

23 June Tuesday

At sea.

Not drinking but diligently researching. On Friday April 24 I wrote Between the Sheets in the Diary… but nothing more. One hopes the gap was for good reasons. And if so, perhaps they can be rediscovered. We're going to dine at Rick and Ruth's Thursday, a brought-in meal from our favorite Concord restaurant of many years, Hermanos. Normally, when we go to Hermanos, all of us drink Margaritas on the rocks, which are very good there. But I made Margaritas for the four of us just before the pandemic, on Leap Day, so it seems good, after so many cocktails, so much writing, to offer something different. Daiquiris came to mind, but then I re-stumbled on Between the Sheets. In preparation for Thursday, tomorrow's fare will be the best Daiquiri I can make and then at least one Between the Sheets. Whichever proves more promising, by Jenny's lights, will be Thursday's drink.

One reason for the choice of Between the Sheets is Steve Poore. He finds the Daiquiri to be his summer drink so far, but last week I sent along a recipe for a Sidecar. And really, the two are classic sours, the one made from rum, lime, and sugar, the other from cognac, lemon, orange liqueur, and sugar. A Between the Sheets, appropriately I suppose, marries the two:

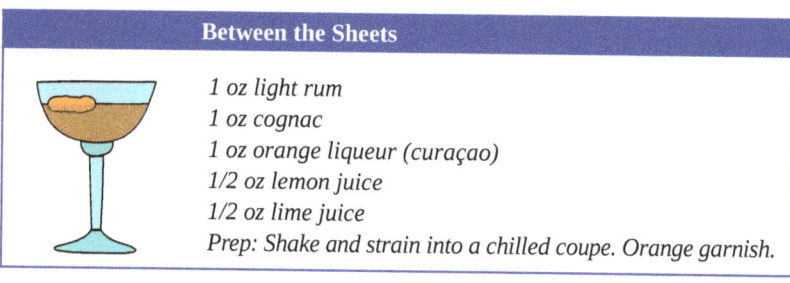

Between the Sheets

1 oz light rum
1 oz cognac
1 oz orange liqueur (curaçao)
1/2 oz lemon juice
1/2 oz lime juice
Prep: Shake and strain into a chilled coupe. Orange garnish.

24 June Wednesday

But then, there is the Hemingway Daiquiri and the Maggie Smith.

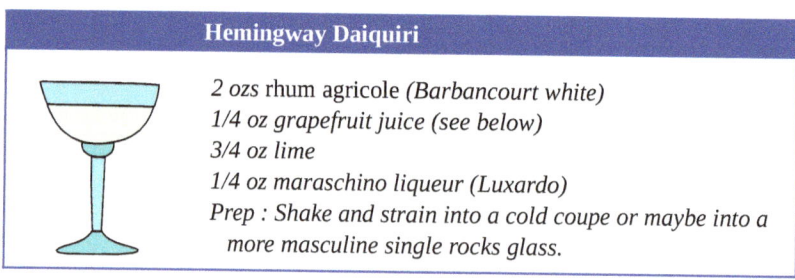

Hemingway Daiquiri

2 ozs rhum agricole *(Barbancourt white)*
1/4 oz grapefruit juice (see below)
3/4 oz lime
1/4 oz maraschino liqueur (Luxardo)
Prep : Shake and strain into a cold coupe or maybe into a more masculine single rocks glass.

These proportions can be infinitely adjusted, except, for example, you'd not want less rum, since Hemingway was a died-in-the-wool alcoholic who loved the stuff. We must be true to history. Second, if 1/4 oz grapefruit is enough by some lights, I'm thinking we could forget history and do without. Besides, I take some cholesterol-reducing medicine, and the doctor says drinking grapefruit juice with it could be fatal. I do not want to die being historically correct about Hemingway's preferred form of Daiquiri.

And then we have…

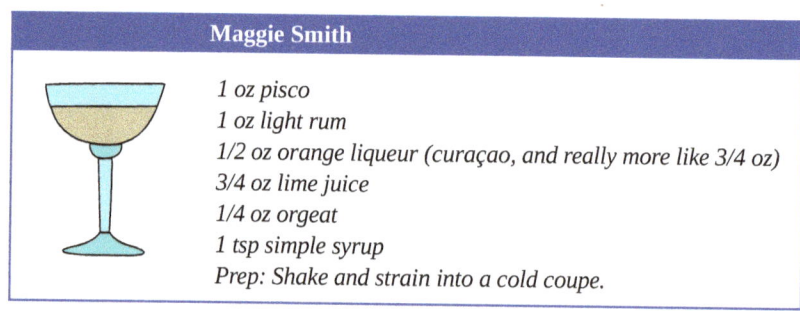

Maggie Smith

1 oz pisco
1 oz light rum
1/2 oz orange liqueur (curaçao, and really more like 3/4 oz)
3/4 oz lime juice
1/4 oz orgeat
1 tsp simple syrup
Prep: Shake and strain into a cold coupe.

Here we have adumbrations of the Daiquiri, of course, but also of the Mai Tai (that is lime juice, rum, orange liqueur, orgeat). Indeed, swap the pisco for a dark rum and you have a Mai Tai.

We tried them all. The first, a straight-up regular Daiquiri (2 ozs Bacardi white rum, 3/4 oz lime juice, 3 barspoons superfine sugar) in its simplicity, its refreshing clarity, its cold-sweet-sour cleanness, was in some ways the best. Or if not the best, perfect for a hot afternoon.

At the same time, I had a straight-up Daiquiri made with Haitian Barbancourt white which had that "funky" *rhum agricole* taste. Jenny hated it, or at least pronounced it not a patch on the ass of her drink. I, by contrast, sort of preferred the funkiness to the clarity.

She then moved to a Between the Sheets, following my own recipe of half lemon, half lime, which was fine, and she drank it happily. I didn't see a real improvement over the original, however. Meanwhile, I went along to the Hemingway Daiquiri, sans any toxic grapefruit, continuing with the Barbancourt. In effect, maraschino replaces sugar, and a bit heavier on the maraschino than Papa apparently liked. I'll call it good but no better than the original, and so perhaps the real difference lies in the grapefruit.

Finally, the drink I'd aimed for, Maggie Smith, came on deck. And I was probably too booze-headed to taste much except that it was good. I wonder if a 1:1:1:1 ratio of pisco: rum: curaçao: lime juice and 1/2 oz orgeat or even 3/4 oz, eliminating the simple syrup would work? And what about superfine sugar instead of simple syrup?

Ah well, so many variations, so little capacity.

25 June Thursday

Big Rocks and the ClearlyFrozen Icemaker

For two days I've been experimenting with a clear-ice maker called ClearlyFrozen. This is an ice cube tray that makes clear cubes. I love it.

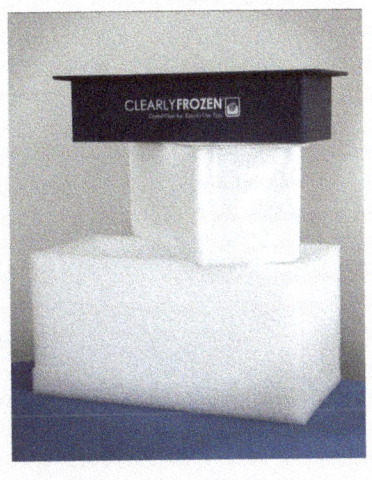

To be at their best, cocktails need clear ice. For years, I've been buying ice, cocktail cubes, at the grocery, usually a bag every time I go, because I hate to run out and so keep the freezer a bit overstocked. They're fine, but they are small cubes and melt quickly. We've just been through a heatwave and putting them in the ice bucket and the ice bucket on the bar means that they begin to get watery almost immediately. A better approach, by the way, is to keep your ice bucket in a refrigerator, pull it out to make drinks, then put it back in—if you use an ice bucket rather than going directly to the freezer.

Lots of products for making clear ice at home are on the market. Some are freezers and expensive; plus, the reviews I've seen lead me to doubt their ice, which is to say, some cloudiness can occur. Preferring to try a cheap experiment, at random I ordered a ClearlyFrozen set-up, which consists of three parts: the blue silicon rubber tray, a white rectangular plastic liner into which the tray fits, and a styrofoam box into which the whole thing loads. About $30 from Amazon.

I'll spare you the details, but you use tap water, and the process is simple. The ice is crystal clear, the cubes large (2 inches), made 10 at a time. What I like best, however, is that this lends to a process perfect for a retired fellow. Here's what I mean.

The cubes take something like 16-20 hours to freeze. I've only made two batches, and my timing is still being worked out, but it looks like 19-20 hours is right for our freezer. My plan is to release the cubes in the morning, at 7:00 am. Thus, I'll start freezing tomorrow's batch at 11:00 AM. If this proves right, I'll make it a daily practice. Once the cubes are frozen, you move them to a plastic bag in the freezer until you're ready to use them, which frees the ClearlyFrozen system for the next batch.

Daiquiris, Rum, and Parentage: A Speculation

Hermanos on deck at Rick and Ruth's. Served Daiquiris from a "portable bar" (an ice chest with shaker, various rums, pre-made sugar-lime mix). Served Ruth and Jenny a Daiquiri with Bacardi white, Rick and me with Barbancourt white. In round two, Rick and I had Pirat gold, which was very good, I thought. It wasn't as if we lingered over differences and flavors as way too much in the world, including Donald Trump's ignorance, incompetence, lack of integrity, and cruelty, was on our minds. Doesn't Trump always come up? Isn't he exhausting?

But some points about spirits came clear thanks mostly to the Daiquiri's simplicity. First, more than in any other cocktail I know, with the possible exceptions of the Martini or Old Fashioned, the Daiquiri allows the flavor of its base spirit to come through. Rum is perhaps the most diverse liquor, made in different ways and places; some aged, some not; can be black to clear; can be 151 to 80 proof; distilled in different machinery; made directly from sugar cane or from by-products of sugar making, creating quite different flavors. As a result, if your goal is to explore what seems best to you, even if simply on a day, at a time, the Daiquiri is a powerful enabler. You could drink rum neat, of course, but that is hardly a refreshing summer treat. The Daiquiri, by contrast lets any rum you like, poised between the sour of lime and sweetness of sugar, stand out and be savored. Which brings up a philosophical-chemical question.

Combining Spirits or Genes: What Do You Get?

It is popular to combine two, even three versions of the same spirit in a cocktail (I use three different dark rums in a Planter's Punch); has long been common to use two different spirits (cognac and rum or bourbon and applejack) in a cocktail and recently even three or more; and obviously the presence of vermouth, amari, or even bitters, each with its own alcohol, creates hundreds or thousands of different taste experiences, most of them at least interesting, and many divine. But when you shake or stir two rums together along with only lime and sugar, can you taste both? Or, in fact, do their molecules so mingle that they create a third rum that is neither, just as a child has characteristics of both parents but is not one or the other?

If you know both parents, it is likely to be easier to say this or that characteristic comes from mother or father. But you also might simply see the child as resembling only one parent, though not at all the same. A child also could look quite unlike either or both. Similarly, two varieties of the same spirit in a cocktail may blend into something that tastes like neither, or one spirit or the other could dominate. I think it is the rare aficionado who can say he or she tastes this rum here, that rum there in the same glass.

All of this is to suggest that the simplicity of a Daiquiri deserves attention and respect as a means of understanding the taste and feel of various rums in the cocktail environment. But by being conscious of what we could, or might not, taste, perhaps we'll get some answers, or at least hypotheses, about what tastes to expect when we mix certain spirits.

Did that make sense?

26 June Friday

A Gin Sour could serve a similar function for gin as the Daiquiri serves for rum. Gin Sour? Much as I've read about cocktails, with the exceptions of the two Davids, Embury and Wondrich, I don't think anyone mentions a Gin Sour. Before looking at what they say, let's consider the Gin Sour on its own terms.

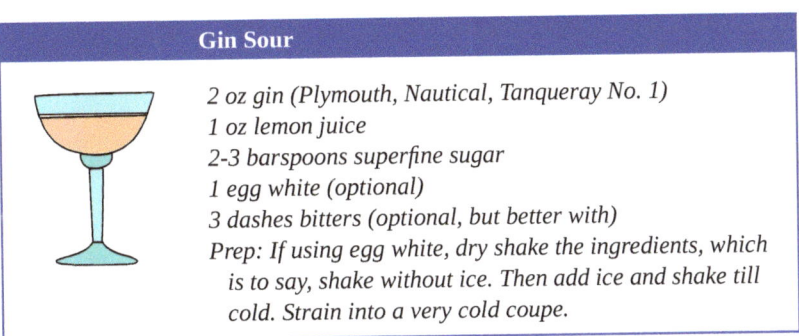

Gin Sour

2 oz gin (Plymouth, Nautical, Tanqueray No. 1)
1 oz lemon juice
2-3 barspoons superfine sugar
1 egg white (optional)
3 dashes bitters (optional, but better with)
Prep: If using egg white, dry shake the ingredients, which
*   is to say, shake without ice. Then add ice and shake till*
*   cold. Strain into a very cold coupe.*

There are other gins to try, but one taste of the Plymouth Gin Sour, first without and then with Angostura Bitters, was enough for me to revere this as a Platonic Cocktail. How is it that something so good gets so little notice? How can I have gone through life, many of us gone through life, without this drink? Gin is not as forward as rum, perhaps, in standing apart from its surroundings. But each gin blends with the lemon and sugar in its own way, a different experience from the Daiquiri, but no less satisfying. The Angostura Bitters, and I love to try different bitters but this was so good I did not, give a charming pink hue and the bitter flavor comes through beautifully. Thus, I'll always add those three dashes. Dr. Cocktail includes Pink Gin in *Forgotten Cocktails*, which is Plymouth Gin (he insists it must be Plymouth) and Angostura Bitters. He rightly notes that some transubstantiation occurs between this very particular combination that results in a legitimate cocktail deserving of its own name. Thus, it's no real wonder that the bitters are so perfect in our Gin Sour.

But where has the Gin Sour been, where did it go? The expansive *Ultimate Bar Book*, which claims to be a "comprehensive guide," and that indeed includes thousands of cocktails, with gin versions numbering in the hundreds, presents what I'd call near gin sours, but none so named and no recipe that is the one we used. For example, Hemingway's hangover cure,

Death in the Gulf Stream

2 ozs gin
1.5 ozs lime juice
Pinch of superfine sugar
3 to 4 dashes Angostura Bitters
Prep: Shake and drink quickly right from the shaker.
*   Garnish by chewing a lime peel spiral.*

Hemingway meant this to be quite sour to jolt one back to a drinking frame of mind. It is close, but no Gin Sour.

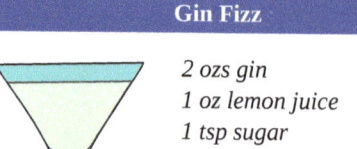

Gin Fizz
2 ozs gin 1 oz lemon juice 1 tsp sugar (and you could stop here and have a perfectly good gin sour) 2 to 3 ozs club soda Prep: Shake before adding soda.

And no bitters. Why the soda, I wonder? It's like preferring skim milk to whole.
In New Orleans you'd never drink a Gin fizz not preceded by Ramos:

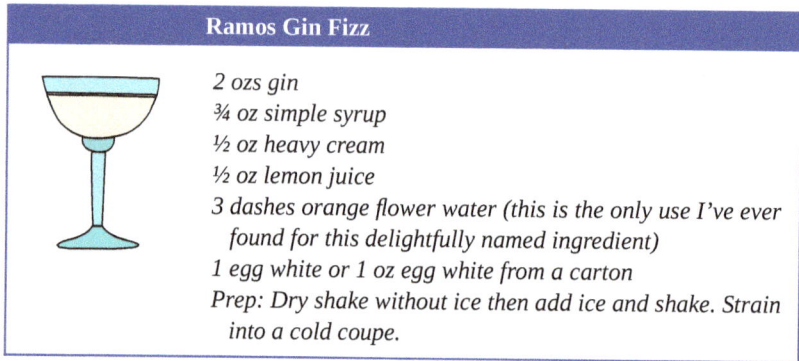

Ramos Gin Fizz
2 ozs gin ¾ oz simple syrup ½ oz heavy cream ½ oz lemon juice 3 dashes orange flower water (this is the only use I've ever found for this delightfully named ingredient) 1 egg white or 1 oz egg white from a carton Prep: Dry shake without ice then add ice and shake. Strain into a cold coupe.

As a youth in New Orleans the very occasional breakfast at Brennan's included many delicacies but none more welcome than a Ramos Gin fizz. Parents in attendance, no one checked an ID. To me this always will be a breakfast drink and, truly, the only Gin Fizz I care about.

Tom Collins
2 ozs gin 1 oz lemon juice 1/2 oz simple syrup 3 ozs chilled club soda Prep: Stirred where a Gin Fizz is shaken. Served on ice where the Gin Sour is served up.

That said, no reason in the world why a Gin Sour should not be shaken without soda, then ice and all poured into a Collins glass, and topped with soda. If so, make mine a double!

Yet, the absence of bitters…

27 June Saturday

Spent the night aboard *Sea Sisters* and took the "portable bar," leaving aboard tools and ingredients that could be spared from the Bean and that will be wanted on voyages. After all, mariners and spirits have a long history.

Seemed a good time to move away from sours and, since Jenny loves a Manhattan, we tried a new idea, the Black Manhattan.

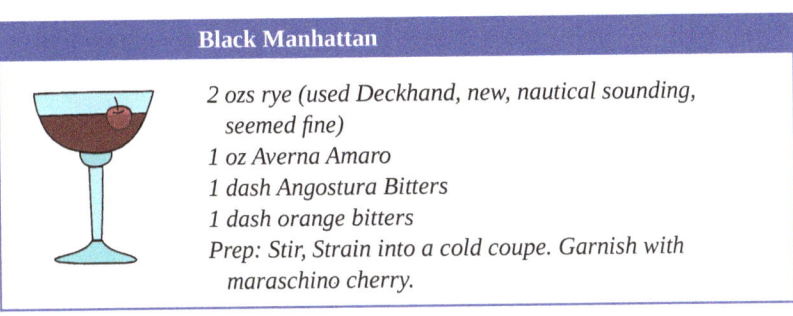

Black Manhattan
2 ozs rye (used Deckhand, new, nautical sounding, seemed fine) *1 oz Averna Amaro* *1 dash Angostura Bitters* *1 dash orange bitters* *Prep: Stir, Strain into a cold coupe. Garnish with maraschino cherry.*

People describe this as a brooding Manhattan. The source of brooding is the Amaro Averna in place of vermouth. I'm new to the possibilities of Amari, but we have a few of them now at the Bean and, indeed, replacing a vermouth with an Amaro makes perfect sense to me. We could spend at least a week trying various Amari (Montenegro, Nardini, and other dark, complex versions) and vermouths.

28 June Sunday

At sea.

29 June Monday

The Southside and the Bramble are both gin sours, both new to me. The one is a classic, though under reported. The other, from England in the 1980s, migrated to the US with changes, and is fantastic. Here's how they went.

Two, perhaps three weeks ago (when you live in Infinite Time keeping track of weeks is a muddle), I re-used the bow half of a dinghy I'd built about five years ago as a garden for mint. It is outside the window of the Bean Bar and looks great. My friend Brick brought over some spearmint (I think) and I bought several other varieties. We now have a mint tropical forest growing in that dinghy, all we can harvest, and lots of fresh variety.

I've been perplexed about the virtual absence of a Gin Sour and have begun to catalogue in a table, sours of all spirits. It was in preparing for this sour leg of our voyage that I stumbled on the Southside and the Bramble.

Southside

Some commentators call it a classic and some books exclude it altogether. For example, the *Essential Bar Guide* includes hundreds of gin-based sours but no Southside, perhaps because it is no more or less than a gin Mojito:

<table>
<tr><td colspan="2">**Southside**</td></tr>
</table>

	*2 ozs gin (Plymouth, Aviation, Ford's + Hayman's Old Tom). In some ways, Aviation was the best fit for this drink, seeming to let the mint speak more fully. But as always, Plymouth was lovely, and combining an Old Tom with a dry gin seems promising. Really, any gin will be fine.*

3/4 oz lemon juice (or half a lemon.) Some recipes specify lime, which would require a whole lime usually. Use what you've got.

3/4 oz simple syrup (or two to three barspoons superfine sugar)

6-12 mint leaves (depends on the mint you choose. Some leaves are much larger or more pungent than others. But really, you cannot have too much).

1 dash Angostura Bitters (if you like)

Prep: If you use superfine sugar, first combine it with the lemon and dry shake to dissolve, then add the mint, gin, ice, and shake. If simple syrup, put everything in the shaker and rattle it hard. No need to muddle the mint as its leaves are delicate and will bruise and fracture during the shake. If you like broken mint leaves in your glass, simply strain into a cold coupe. If you prefer no fractured floating leaves, double strain. Mint sprig for garnish.

Combining Gin and Other Spirits

Gin is easily the most companionable spirit, liking the company of most any ingredient. So I wonder, in an age when combining different spirits is popular, if anyone has ever combined gin and rum to create a Mojito South, or something? And in answer to my question, yes, Death & Company, self-identified as the originators of combining spirits, offer the City of Gold Sling, which comprises Hayman's Old Tom Gin and El Dorado 12-year Rum; the Night Watch, which includes Ransom Old Tom and Cruzan Black Strap Rum; and Hadley's Tears, with Appleton Estate Rum and Bols Genever. They've combined a couple of gins with bourbon, gin with calvados, gin with mezcal and tequila, and probably others.

So yeah, why not a SoMo? If it works, we'll cry "Gimme SoMo!"

Bramble

Here was the real star of the night, as much for the way it is served as for the flavor. I'm wary of drinks served over ice, fearing they will prove too dilute. Not the Bramble. And another thing to like is that gin, lemon, sugar, and blackberries are easy to assemble.

Bramble

2 ozs gin (take your pick; I used Plymouth)
1 oz lemon juice (or half a lemon)
1 oz simple syrup (or 2-3 barspoons superfine sugar)
5 blackberries
*Prep: If using superfine sugar, combine it with the
   lemon juice and stir or dry shake to dissolve. Add four
   blackberries and muddle. Pour or spoon about 1/3 of
   this mix into a double rocks glass. Top with crushed
   ice (see below for ideas about ice crushing). Add gin to
   the shaker (and you could try rum), stir, and pour into
   the crushed ice. Add ice to fill the glass. Garnish with a
   blackberry.*

Crushing Ice

The proper bartender's way is to put cubes in a Lewis bag and clobber it with a mallet. Lewis bags are canvas [Note: Not the Chimes@ Midnight Lewis bag, which is Dacron, available on our website for the bargain price of $25] and cheap on Amazon or a million other places. A wooden hammer is better than most other tools, and you'll see ice mallet + Lewis bag combinations for sale. As are many sailors, I'm a sewer (pronounced so er) and use a site called Sailrite for most of my supplies, including a mallet meant for setting grommets. If you want the ULTIMATE ice mallet, grommet setter, at $95.95, this beauty is the one (sailrite.com: Barry King Mallet Hammer Style 3#).

Obviously, lacking any of these tools or stand-ins, you can put ice in a dish towel and whack it on something hard.

Mostly, for certain summer cocktails—the Bramble and Planter's Punch are two I call essential—crushed ice is requisite, fun, and the results fabulous.

30 June Tuesday

At sea.

1 July Wednesday

Oh boy, a good day for a cocktail, two, three, or who knows? So many to choose. So many ingredients on the shelf. So little capacity.

I've been studying *Death & Company* more closely, and it really is very good. While studying, I found a recipe that resembles a Bramble, the Get Lucky, calling for blackberries (why waste them?) and crushed ice. Also, I just happened to buy Flor de Caña rum, which the recipe specifies, and to have made honey syrup. Serendipity at its most luxuriant. I've also got ginger syrup, orgeat, and—obviously—Peychaud's Bitters. But it's 3:40; must be patient.

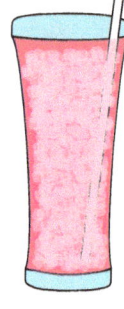

Get Lucky

2.5 ozs rum (Death & Co. calls for Flor de Caña dry white. I have Flor de Caña 7 year old, which is gold, looking like reposado tequila. A great rum and beautiful here)
1 oz lemon juice
1/3 oz orgeat
1/3 oz ginger syrup
1/3 oz honey syrup
Drizzled Peychaud's Bitters
Prep: Muddle the blackberries in the bottom of a pilsener glass and fill the glass with crushed ice. Use a little crushed ice to shake the rum, lemon, and syrups, then pour everything into the glass. Drizzle Peychaud's Bitters on top as garnish. You might want a straw.

The gold rum makes a gold drink with dark blackberries in the bottom and with the drizzled bitters on top this is altogether dramatic. The combination of three syrups with the rum is delicious. If the drink has a flaw, or even two, it is that the blackberries aren't truly integral, are mostly just a light show. They look great but don't much contribute to the taste. Could be better, as with the Bramble, to muddle them with the lemon and syrups then spoon some into the bottom.

The Add-a-Little-More-Booze Strategies

The ice lasted way longer than the cocktail, which was so good, so refreshing, I drank it (or, more precisely, them) right up. But why waste perfectly good homemade ice? I poured some of the delicious Flor de Caña and some honey syrup into the glass. And you know, this too was delicious, inspiring, novel, and made perfect use of the remaining ice. First, then, the Add-a-Little-More-Booze Strategy may prove a major contribution to cocktailers worldwide!

Second, it is worth pausing to say that the recipes you find in books and online are for drinks made in commercial bars. Also, the cocktail at its beginning was a small drink meant to be swallowed quickly, not lingered over. But at home on an evening, when driving is unnecessary, and when you are not trying to make a buck on the drinks you serve, cocktails can, in my view should, be bigger than those served in a bar. One pleasant effect is that you do not need to make as many, can spend more time drinking the ones you have prepared.

As a result, the recipes here are usually about a third larger than you'll find the same recipes from other sources. To do this, I've simply scaled them up, and you could scale them back down. But why would anyone do that?

This is another *Death & Co.* cocktail and is used as an example of how bartenders tailor something to the wishes of a customer. It is a good one:

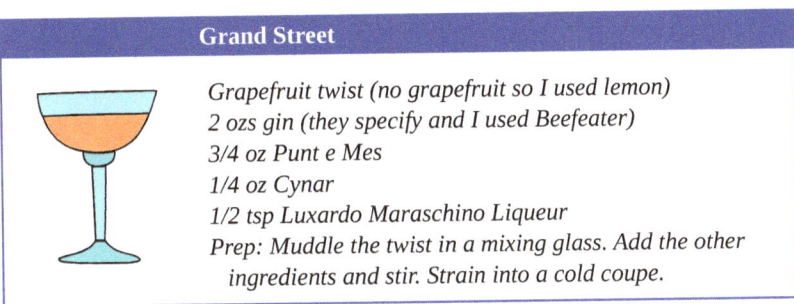

Grand Street

Grapefruit twist (no grapefruit so I used lemon)
2 ozs gin (they specify and I used Beefeater)
3/4 oz Punt e Mes
1/4 oz Cynar
1/2 tsp Luxardo Maraschino Liqueur
Prep: Muddle the twist in a mixing glass. Add the other
*   ingredients and stir. Strain into a cold coupe.*

A fine cocktail in every respect, mostly thanks to the vermouth (Punt e Mes) and amaro (Cynar). Either of those is pungent and can overpower a cocktail. Here, they somehow work together. I'd say the main job of the gin is to boost the alcohol content to a useful level. Liked this so well that after the first, when I thought Jenny wasn't looking, sneaked a second.

2 July Thursday

At sea.

3 July Friday

I am a part of all that I have met;
Yet all experience is an arch wherethro'
Gleams that untravell'd world whose margin fades
"Ulysses" (Tennyson, Alfred 131)

Join me. Any voyage of exploration is perilous. One cannot predict or avoid great storms that rise up suddenly, the miseries they inflict, the sleeplessness through dangerous nights at the helm, the horrors of a lee shore, or the possibility that having ventured too far we will plunge over the edge of the earth. What monsters, in our voyage, wearing beguiling forms, lurk? Yet, we cannot rest from travel if, as Ulysses says, we will "drink life to the lees." We will hear the chimes at midnight many times, and we will discover new lands whose beauties will captivate. Join me.

A Word of Caution: Observing Limits

For seafarers like us it is crucial to know and observe, mostly though not always, limits. For me it is best not to venture beyond three cocktails in a night. At that limit no slurring or falling or embarrassment eventuates; sleep comes fast and deep; and no medicine to ward off headaches and hangovers is required. Four, on the other hand, is a tipping point where, especially if drunk in quick succession, the tongue grows fat, the memory dim, and the aftermath sullen. Even lashed to the mast, however, the Siren call of a new discovery can be too much to overcome, and we may crash upon the rocks of Scylla and Charybdis. If together we "follow knowledge like a sinking star, /Beyond the utmost bound of human thought," let us pledge to enjoy the mystical effects of spirits, but like Jack Aubrey, through discipline, mostly drink to good and pleasurable effect rather than finding that alcohol is a Siren, a Circe,…

Okay, enough of that. Today's menu:

Had a call with Elise, Mark (a friendship from work past happily renewed in retirement), Ruth, and Rick, our third of the pandemic, and I'd sent them the Bramble recipe earlier in the week. In keeping with the Bramble, I tried a Lucky Bramble, based on *Death & Co.*'s Get Lucky.

The idea of the Lucky Bramble was to mull the blackberries in the three syrups and lemon juice called for by *Death & Co.* before putting, as in the Bramble, about a third in the bottom of the glass. And of course, we are changing from gin (Bramble) to rum (Get Lucky). Here you go:

Lucky Bramble

4 ozs rum (2 ozs Flor de Caña and 2 ozs Barbancourt White)
5 blackberries
1/2 oz lemon juice
1/2 oz orgeat
1/2 oz ginger syrup
1/2 oz honey syrup
Peychaud's Bitters on top
Prep: Lightly muddle the blackberries in the lemon juice and the three syrups then spoon about one-third of the mixture into the pilsener glass. Crush ice and fill the glass. Lightly shake the remaining mixture with rum and some ice, then pour everything into the glass. Bitters on top.

Only partly successful. The mixture at best permeated the drink better than in the Get Lucky. But mulled blackberries floating about were not beautiful, and I cannot say the drink itself was terrific. In short, of the two, I'll probably stick with the Bramble. Sigh.

From here it was on to the Flor de Jerez, but with proportions modified from the *Death & Co.* version which is heavy on sherry, light on rum:

Flor de Jerez

1 oz rum (Appleton Estate Aged)
2 ozs sherry (Lustau Solera)
1/2 oz apricot liqueur (All I have is a cheap version that needs to be replaced)
1 oz lemon juice
3/4 oz honey syrup
2-3 dashes Angostura bitters.
Prep: Shake with ice then strain into a coupe.

Very pleasant tasting, even with my poor apricot liqueur and the wrong sherry, but downright ugly. Sometimes shaking aerates a cocktail so much that it looks muddy. And this one, muddy yellow or maybe close to what my friend Jimmy Krefft used to call "baby-shit yellow," was unappealing. After sitting for a while, it clarified some. But I wonder whether grenadine or raspberry syrup might be an improvement over the honey syrup? And really, can't say I recall much else about this one, having drunk a fair bit, though not so much that I failed to move along to one more *Death & Co.* production, the:

Conference

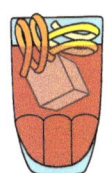

1 oz rye (used the new Old Overholt 86 proof)
1 oz bourbon (Wild Turkey 101 proof)
1 oz Calvados
1 oz Cognac (Remy Martin VSOP)
1 tsp simple syrup (maybe I used two. It was too sweet)
2 dashes Bittermens Chocolate Mole Bitters
3-4 dashes Angostura bitters
Prep: Stir and strain into double rocks glass with one large ice cube. Lemon twist (recipe calls for orange twist as well).

Obviously, I'd had too much to drink by this time. Even so, I have some lingering recollection. Often stirred drinks like this one—kind of an Old Fashioned on steroids—are boozy (nothing wrong with that) but too sweet. I should have used just a bit of simple syrup and perhaps it would have worked better or, more precisely, come close to working at all. The real problem for me, however, lacking a connoisseur's tongue, is that the combination of so many spirits in the Conference yielded no taste of any of them. It's back to that question: when you combine things do they chemically form some entirely new monster that submerges the identity of its separate parts?

4 July Saturday

Easily the least happy July 4th of my lifetime. The President, D Trump, gave a divisive speech to a mob of unmasked Trumpeters at Mt. Rushmore last night, barely mentioning the Coronavirus although deaths the past several days each have broken new records for all-time highs. We're humiliated in the world, not allowed, for example, to travel to England or Europe; have lost our generally understood position as a source for good internationally; and our racial hatred is exposed as a wound whose scab is ripped off. For the first time—and how can that be?—heard Frederick Douglas's July 5, 1852, speech given in Rochester, New York, about what Independence Day means to a Negro. I'd call it the most powerful speech I've ever read or heard. Listened to the Lincoln Project's recitation of the Gettysburg Address, which seemed political compared with Douglas's passion. How can we be so ignorant?

We need a drink, and I believe Cuba is the place to go. The Bean Boat Mint Garden is luxuriant, a tropical paradise. I've cut a pile of several different mint types and plan to use them along with our homemade ice to prepare lots of Mojito!

Success! I have not seen a recipe for a Mojito that includes Velvet Falernum. Why not? It must make the cocktail a bit more expensive, but at what cost? I mean, with Falernum, you'll want to drink a million of them. The bitters may, or may not, be useful. I say, add them.

<table>
<tr><th colspan="2" align="center">Falernum Mojito</th></tr>
<tr>
<td></td>
<td>

2 ozs rum (Bacardi white is all you need)
1 oz lime juice
1 oz Velvet Falernum (John D. Taylor's. This is my
  innovation, and it is a really, really good one)
2 barspoons superfine sugar (or whatever you like)
1 dash Angostura Bitters
An ounce or two (to taste) of soda water
Lots of mint
Prep: How you build this cocktail is critical. You do NOT
  want to smash the mint so that it is dark, limp, and
  broken. Rather, press a barspoon against the leaves,
  or clap hands with the leaves in them, but don't really
  "muddle" the mint. Also, this drink can, probably
  should, be made in bulk, not one off. Make it in a pitcher,
  not a glass. If you use a pitcher, each refill will be
  mintier than the one before.

</td>
</tr>
</table>

Multiply the ingredients based on the ratios above, say, to 16 ozs rum, 8 ozs lime juice, 8 ozs Falernum, but probably NOT 16 barspoons of sugar. The Falernum includes sugar, so go light initially, add more if you need it. Put all this stuff in a pitcher, swirl it until you're sure the sugar dissolves, press the mint, take a taste, and add more of whatever you think is needed.

Put a stem of mint in a pilsener, Collins, or any other tall narrow glass. Indeed, a red wine glass, not tall or narrow, would work fine, as would a pint glass or a flute. Maybe rub the mint a bit first to release its oils. Fill the glass most of the way with crushed ice or just use cubes. Pour the liquid, saving some room for the soda water. Give the whole a swirl, and you'll have a fabulous Mojito. With luck, you've made about eight, but if you're drinking with a partner who is self-restricting, or very self-restricting, enjoy the evening!

5 July Sunday

At sea, except for the Foundation beer at the pizza joint in Kittery where we ate, rather than cook aboard.

6 July Monday

Sailed to Biddeford, Maine, but never arrived. Left our mooring at 7:10 AM to allow ample time for the Memorial Bridge from Portsmouth to Kittery (or the other way around) to acknowledge, prepare, and lift for us. Tide on the Piscataqua, which has America's second largest tides after the Columbia river, was going out as we traveled downstream, but mostly, by now, we hang back far enough that the heartbeats and the blood pressure in old veins are sustainable.

A north wind made sailing directly to our destination impossible in *Sea Sisters*, so out to sea we went, toward Spain, until realizing sometime in the afternoon that the course I'd plotted was for Downeast, and… it is a longer story…so about we came and now, finally, have returned to where we began, our mooring in Eliot, Maine, dined, drunk Black Manhattans, to the point that now it is you and me. Tonight's Black Manhattan was much superior to the last. I'd thought about it all day, and we climbed the Piscataqua against a falling tide, which means slowly, though the engine was at near full power, through the Memorial Bridge, always nerve splitting, and along to the Great Cove Marina, where Jenny is a mooring expert. As foolish males have failed to do: Stand clear, mate!

She has been drinking very little (more for me) as the result of lack of sleep and anti-anxiety medicines (that apparently do no good). We ordered up two Black Manhattans:

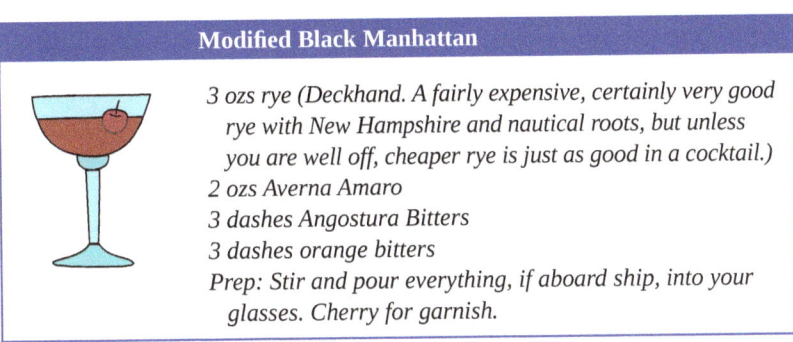

Modified Black Manhattan

3 ozs rye (Deckhand. A fairly expensive, certainly very good rye with New Hampshire and nautical roots, but unless you are well off, cheaper rye is just as good in a cocktail.)
2 ozs Averna Amaro
3 dashes Angostura Bitters
3 dashes orange bitters
Prep: Stir and pour everything, if aboard ship, into your glasses. Cherry for garnish.

Aboard ship you could lack a cocktail spoon. The business end of a butter knife works great for stirring. Used three cherries for J's cocktail because she needed and deserved them. The modification is my usual practice of enlarging a cocktail, to make fewer, drink more.

Sea Sisters has a black hull, and the black drink is now her ship's cocktail. No Pusser's Rum for us (though I like that too).

But, yes, we really have been at sea, which is a hard living.

7 July Tuesday

Al and his friends Carter and Xander joined us for a roaring sail. Wind was 10-23 knots and on all tacks we flew. To windward, the rail was often deep in the water. The two friends had never sailed, though all three work at a marina on Lake Sunapee and have been denizens of the lake their whole lives. The ocean, the hard wind, big waves (some I'd guess as high as 6 feet), the tide, the Isles of Shoals, heeling hard but in a wind for which *Sea Sisters* is made were about as grand an introduction to sailing as possible.

The boys were happy enough with the boat that they spent the night aboard, which sent J and me home for a needed night's sleep. Left the young men with directions for making their own Black Manhattans.

[Note on Guests and Quarantine: Teenage children can't bear to be without their peers. Al and his friends worked on the lake all summer, dealt with the public, all of it outdoors. My brother had guests at his inn and no mask requirement. Among our friends, who were very careful, Jenny and I stayed outdoors, wore masks. We took our chances with Al and his friends and to some degree with Denis, got lucky, and things worked out.]

8 July Wednesday

The Bean Mint Forest is flourishing, but even so, tonight's cocktail, one I've been waiting to try for a while, will include no mint. It is from Canon, the Petruchio (the anglicized spelling from *The Taming of the Shrew*), despite the Italian amaro Aperol.

Petruchio

2 ozs gin
2 ozs Aperol
1 oz lemon juice
4 dashes orange bitters
2 dashes simple syrup
1.5 oz egg white (2 egg whites; one reason for this cocktail is to try store-bought egg whites in a pint container. Sure enough, I'll never discard another orphaned yoke, which is to say, these container whites were great.)
Prep: Froth with a frother if you have one (they're cheap on Amazon) after combining the ingredients. Otherwise, dry shake to whip air into the egg white. Then, shake with ice and strain into a chilled coupe. Garnish with, well, why not mint?

This cocktail adorned with mint is gorgeous. When frothed or dry shaken, air whipped into the egg white, a gradual realization in the shaken drink in which pink (or is it orange pink?) materializes below, while the frothy head rides above, is lovely. The cocktail is neither sweet nor sour, tastes in a mild way like a dessert, though not full of calories. I drank two, made one for Al, who pretended not to like it as much as he did.

It is dangerous. You can easily drink more than you need.

Green Glacier

Probably a mistake. This cognac-based stirred cocktail from Jamie Boudreau, comprising cognac, Green Chartreuse, creme de cacao and Boker's Bitters, was undistinguished. The cognac was not at all assertive; the main spirit could have been anything. Nor did the Chartreuse power the drink with its long list of botanicals. I suppose it was there, but exactly in what way could not tell. The creme de cacao came through as a slight chocolate backdrop. Mine is a cheap version of that spirit, not Marie Brizzard, which is unavailable in New Hampshire. Would a better version have made the difference? Who knows? And finally Boker's Bitters, re-made in Scotland, give a cocktail no identifiable flavor. I'm tempted to walk down three flights of stairs to try a taste but, well, that can be reported tomorrow. For now, however, I will not tempt you with the recipe.

And the evening? I'd call Petruchio a success, a lovely, tasty confection to be served especially to those who appreciate a colorful, frothy drink.

9 July Thursday

At sea. But, landed at Total Wine and Liquor in Danvers, Massachusetts, which has a more extensive stock of liquors than the New Hampshire Liquor Store. I'm here, now, christening the place: Totally Liquored. And may God have mercy on our souls.

Totally Liquored Aka Total Wine

It had been six months since a last visit, making it easy to spend $300. They had Rittenhouse 100 Rye, which is cheap and the go-to brand in many cocktail books, and Amaro Nardini, which I have no immediate ideas for, but, while expensive, if our good friend Bob Nardini shows up, he'll know we keep him in mind. Many years ago, on a dull night in Wooster, Ohio, Bob and I spotted a drive-through beer dispensary in our rearview mirror, wheeled round in the middle of the main street, and as we drove through pointed to what we wanted as some fellow heaved bottles, cans, and cases into our trunk. We returned to the hotel and sat on the ground out back drinking and telling old tales till the dawn.

Peach liqueur, Falernum, Flor de Caña extra dry white rum, Unterberg, Pierre Ferrand Curaçao, Plymouth Sloe Gin, Lillet Rosé, St. Elizabeth Allspice Dram. Oh, the treasures!

Tasting Amari

This new cargo led me to think it would be smart to try a liqueur glass of amari, vermouths, and liqueurs in general, to get a sense of what they're like and how they can be expected to affect a mix. Began with Amaro Montenegro, a favorite mixer when I lack a particular ingredient. It manages to be sweet and bitter at the same time. A bit like the Sour Table, I'm beginning a list of these many, many ingredients. It will try to describe their flavor, name some cocktails where they can be used, and suggest how they would influence a combination. A Table could go something like the following:

Amaro Montenegro *"The bartender's best friend"*
Category: Amaro. An herbal liqueur
Bitter and sweet.
40 botanicals.
Drinks: Amaro Sidecar (replace the Cointreau with Amaro Montenegro).
Black Manhattan (replace the vermouth with Amaro Montenegro).
And so on. . .

10 July Friday

Tonight will test the Mojito recipe, with a few alterations to prepare for tomorrow's debut. One change will be to mix it in the glass and to begin with mint and sugar, lightly muddling them before adding lemon juice and rum. The ice regime will be a combination of, first, cubes, and then crushed. Also, will compare the Flor de Caña white with Bacardi white.

And all was okay. Beth and Al liked them quite a bit. But the Saturday event was postponed by weather. That is, we're meeting people only outdoors, and the weather is looking wet.

11 July Saturday

The Canon Cocktail Book is a good one, and I'll often find something by just opening it. Tonight, the Novara. It relies on passion fruit syrup and many are bad, the way many grenadines are bad. But I happened on one that looks promising, made by Small Hands Foods, and will give it a try. If it proves usable, who knows? A Hurricane could be in the works!

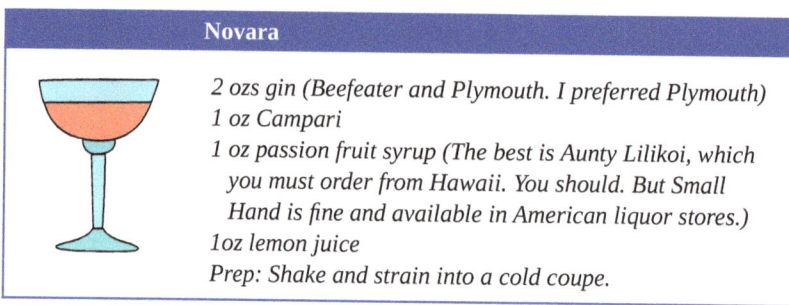

Novara

2 ozs gin (Beefeater and Plymouth. I preferred Plymouth)
1 oz Campari
1 oz passion fruit syrup (The best is Aunty Lilikoi, which
* you must order from Hawaii. You should. But Small*
* Hand is fine and available in American liquor stores.)*
1oz lemon juice
Prep: Shake and strain into a cold coupe.

Delicious and beautiful. More than that, a descendant of the Negroni and the clear serendipitous mate of a Petruchio, which, to remind you, includes gin, Aperol, and lemon juice. The main difference is that the Novara is sour, and I'd say much more assertive, reflecting the power of Campari compared with its less dominating mate Aperol. And, the Novara includes no egg white, making it less, far less, frothy. I'd imagine one could substitute the two Amari, one for the other, call the resulting cocktails by another name, and find happiness. And the passion fruit was quite good.

12 July Sunday

At sea. However, considering going ashore for a Millionaire. This is a cocktail from *Ted Haigh's Forgotten Cocktails* that I tried way back in March and liked so well that I stayed away fearing we'd run short of Plymouth Sloe Gin. But the supply has been replenished, and last time the only rum, and it was plenty good enough, was Myers's. Still, this Millionaire can afford other, pricier rum, so why not experiment?

And we did, using 8-year-old Appleton Estate Rum, and in place of the apricot liqueur, a fine peach liqueur. Was this better than the March version? Probably not, but it is/was very fine, made me very happy.

Meanwhile, taste tested Dolin Red Vermouth against Punt e Mes, and they are strikingly different, each delicious in its own way, but for its strength and dark bitterness, the Punt e Mes deserves to be drunk alone as, I'd say, an after-dinner drink. It would stand up to any cigar. (For more, see the note on "Amari, Vermouth, and Fortified Wines" on May 10th.)

13 July Monday

A return visit to the Hemingway Daiquiri, largely to be clear that the recipe my friends Steve and Rochelle requested works. And, indeed, getting the drink right took three tries. Neither Diplomatico nor Bacardi rum added anything to what seemed a bland drink to have been named for so famous a drunk. As before, Barbancourt White was just right for me because you could taste it. More important, however, mixing the grapefruit and lime juice with a large barspoon of sugar and stirring before adding ice, then adding between 3/4 and 1 oz of Maraschino, stirring, and finally adding the ice and 2 ozs of rum was the right chemistry. Served in a cold coupe with a sprig of mint.

After working at the Hemingway, the genius of Cuba's bartenders, and the sadness that we cannot visit, perhaps made more poignant by pandemic sequestration and that Cuba, with its fine medical system handled Covid as perfectly controllable (maybe one Covid death), was on my mind. A little-known Cuban cocktail, La Chaparra, is brilliant, a kind of rum Manhattan with muddled lime peel standing in for bitters.

La Chaparra

1 lime peel. Skin a lime peel in the latitudinal direction getting a fair bit of it.

1 tsp simple syrup or a little less

2 ozs rum (I used Cruzan aged from St Croix, which was great. If you can get Havana Club 3 year old, that is where to start. Lots of experimentation possible)

1 oz red vermouth (Dolin Red. But I'd love to try this with Antica Formula, Punt e Mes, or an Amaro. Again, possibilities)

Prep: Put the lime peel in your stir glass with the simple syrup and muddle, not hard, but assertively. You want to break the lime oils and essence free. Add ice, vermouth, and rum. Stir until frosty cold and then strain into a cold coupe. Once the drink is in the glass, discard the ice and use the muddled lime peel as garnish.

I'd say the use of lime peel in this is inspired. Its freshness, aroma, and sourness permeate the drink at every level, making it the rare, stirred summer cocktail. This fine, vanishing alchemical triumph deserves to be called a Havana, taking its place alongside the Manhattan as the signature drink of its native city. And yes, the lime peel as bitters is wonderful, but I'm tempted to add a bit of bitters as well.

Oh, and going back to the grapefruit, I'm forsaking the cholesterol medicine that could kill me should more grapefruit cocktails come my way. Prudent, don't you think?

Part II: Life in a Fishbowl

14 July Tuesday

The Boxcar Arrives and with It, Trouble

Tim and Beth's boxcar RV arrived early, and setting it up took the day, even for a low-level helper (that's me). I was too tired to mix a cocktail and too tired not to have a beer.

Tim and Beth live in Florida, but are New Englanders and hate the southern summer, though not as much as many of us southerners hate it. In a story that began last summer, they will live in the boxcar, a sort of RV tiny house, in our big yard until autumn, when they will go back to Vero Beach. They hate their native winter even more than the Florida summer.

Besides the southern heat, Jenny's dad is here because Covid in Florida is uncontrolled and especially lethal to the very old (he will be 87 next month). His loss of sight makes even slow, small moves from one place to another fraught. The boxcar should help; he can't get lost in it.

Tim also has what I'd call advanced dementia. He was diagnosed three years or so ago and has done all a person who can't hear or see can do to stave it off, short of giving up the beer he loves every evening, which would, of course, have been a fool's solution. Being here, we hope, gives Beth a break because Tim needs constant help, as a child might. He can entertain himself for periods, but lots of routines baffle him.

We, Jenny in particular, do what we can, and the presence of relatively unfamiliar company (us) is a useful difference, so they come to dinner often. From the time they arrived this evening after the short walk from the boxcar, Tim seemed lively. He had problems with his hearing aids, but Beth installed new batteries that helped, and then he followed me outside to offer company while I barbecued the burgers, and soon Jenny and Beth also came along.

Aquavit

Post dinner, a bit revived, guests gone to their early beds, a tasting seemed in order, and I chose Linie Aquavit. Initially it made little impression, but in time, I grew to like it considerably and would welcome it as an after-dinner drink.

Several kinds of aquavit are commercially available, with Linie seemingly the most common and a good one. It is a strong Scandinavian spirit, that includes alcohol, caraway, and dill but is used in only a few cocktails. At some point we'll try out the Gefion. (See 27 August).

15 July Wednesday

The town health officer arrived in his pickup truck today. He said neighbors had called him to in to inspect, believing that the boxcar with people living in it might violate zoning laws. The neighbor who sent the inspector is the one who is on the town Zoning Board. The toilet in the boxcar composts and so needs no septic. But the pad we'd had built included a buried barrel for gray water. The inspector advised us that we'd need a holding tank for the gray water and could then pump it into the septic system for the house. This is a setback, perhaps, but we can solve it. Tomorrow, Beth and I are going to an RV store to see about a holding tank.

The boxcar is technically an RV rather than a tiny house, which would have been illegal, and is movable and licensed to be towed on the road. The inspector acknowledged the difference. The photo shows the boxcar, which we think is an adornment, not an eyesore. Some neighbors, I take it, disagree.

Off to Marge's for cocktails with Lisa, Susan, and Christine. I've made Falernum Mojitos. Lots of mint, falernum, bitters, the whole deal. I think they'll be a major success and will report.

Yes, good work. In particular, Susan was happy they were not muddled so much as to be full of leafy parts. But to my taste they were too sweet because I failed to follow my own advice and limit the sugar, owing to the presence of falernum. I feel done with these for a while and am announcing a change of plans for the Friday muffuletta dinner at Rick and Ruth's: Planter's Punch.

16 July Thursday

At sea, definitely and entirely. No grog ration at all. Have been drinking too often and last night too much.

Beth bought a holding tank for the gray water. Once it is full (holds 40 gallons, I think), we'll use the tractor to pull it to a first-floor bathroom window and pump the water into the toilet. From there it will flow into our septic system. The inspector returned and declared us legal though he pointed out that the town limits living in an RV to 90 days a year. In 90 days, someone may need to remind me to love my neighbor.

Outdoor dinners with friends are occasions now for trying out the recipes for cocktails we've discovered. I'd assumed Mojito, but we had these Wednesday, and so Planter's Punch seemed a good outside-on-the-deck replacement. Yet, as happens, in looking down the list of cocktails I've enjoyed, others looked promising. For example, the Naked and Famous. What to do? How about a pitcher of the one and a thermos of the other?

17 July Friday

Planter's Punch in bulk for the muffuletta dinner. Made enough for roughly 16 drinks to serve six people. Besides being strong (3 cups of rum, one cup 151 proof) the mix is heavy, perhaps too heavy, on Creole and Peychaud's Bitters. I've crushed the ice and wrapped up fine bar glasses to take along. Garnish will be both mint and lime wheels.

The rum is a cup of Goslings 151 proof; a cup of Appleton 8 year old; and the last cup is Barbancourt, Diplomatico, and Bacardi white. The three bottles were nearly empty, so I used them up. Two cups lime, one cup lemon. Half a cup of grenadine and 12 or so teaspoons of agave. And, again, a lot of Creole Bitters and a fair bit of Peychaud's. Oh my. Dangerous.

Additionally, crushed ice beforehand, brought glasses, and for garnish, sliced lime and mint sprigs. Took along Q soda water to lighten the cocktail for anyone who found it too strong.

Rick drank three and so did Ruth. I guess I did too, Mark one less and Elise and Jenny only one, as expected, for they were to drive. Apparently, the overload of Creole Bitters wasn't too much.

18 July Saturday

Against her wishes, my mother reached 89 years today, locked in her room in a nursing home in New Orleans.

At our house, unexpected company, who brought beer as an offering, led to drinking three beers, led to getting up to piss about four times last night. This is too much information, I guess, but cocktails have no such effect. As a result, I sleep undisturbed until the sun appears. Advantage, cocktail.

Before moving to beer, I was able to choke down two new cocktails, both from Tux2, both based on allspice dram. Odd name, and what is it?

> **Allspice Dram**
>
> *A product of Jamaica, allspice dram is made from allspice berries, which grow on Pimenta dioica trees. I found some made by St. Elizabeth, apparently a good choice, at Total Wine and Liquor (i.e., known in these pages as Totally Liquored), and because it appears from time to time in cocktails, thought it best to have some on hand. For a while, its slender bottle was a bit lost on the shelf, but rediscovered, the time was right for a try. [Turned out, I learned you can make your own allspice dram. See 10 April 2021.]*

Sherpa is a cocktail invented only in 2016 by the founder of one of NYC's new, great cocktail bars, Milk and Honey. It is the rare bourbon cocktail, built like an Old Fashioned in a double rocks glass, and is, in fact, a very good substitute for that classic. I slavishly followed Tux2's recipe because all of its ingredients appeal to me. But I'm guessing the curaçao here at the Bean is sweeter than his/hers, or maybe she/he just likes sweet drinks, because this was good but too sweet for me. Here's the recipe:

<table>
<tr><td colspan="2" align="center">**Sherpa**</td></tr>
<tr><td></td><td>
2 ozs bourbon (I used Eagle Rare)
1/4 oz allspice dram (St. Elizabeth)
1/4 oz curaçao (Bold is what we have, which accounted
for my drink being too sweet. I'd like to find a drier
curaçao, such as Pierre Ferrand Dry Orange Curaçao.)
2-4 dashes orange bitters (but others are, as always,
worth trying)
Prep: Build the cocktail in a double rocks glass without
ice. Add a large clear cube. stir, garnish with a lemon
twist (which I forgot to do).
</td></tr>
</table>

Despite the tiny amount of allspice, its flavor comes through, especially with licorice notes. In describing the Sherpa, Tux2 mentions the venerable Lion's Tail, so why not?

<table>
<tr><td colspan="2" align="center">**Lion's Tail**</td></tr>
<tr><td></td><td>
2 ozs bourbon (Eagle Rare)
1/2 oz St. Elizabeth Allspice Dram
1/2 oz lime juice
1 barspoon simple syrup
1-3 dashes Angostura Bitters
Prep: Combine in a shaker and strain into a chilled coupe.
</td></tr>
</table>

Delicious! More allspice means more flavor. The combination of ingredients would never have occurred to me, but the lime suits it perfectly. I'll try this as a stirred cocktail, just because I prefer stirring and don't have enough of those. You could use different bitters and might try agave in place of the simple syrup or even a barspoon of sugar, which makes a difference in rum cocktails. Anyway, this is a stop you'll be pleased to have made.

19 July Sunday

We were, in fact, at sea, sailing our boat *Sea Sisters* out of Portsmouth, but on reaching home a cocktail seemed the right way to celebrate a fine sail. We had Pierre Ferrand Dry Orange Curaçao, another surprise from the vastly productive visit to Totally Liquored two weeks ago, so obviously we'd want a revised Sherpa. One look at the Pierre Ferrand label showed that this is a top shelf curaçao, and so it proved. And the day had been very, very hot, so a cooling, slightly altered Lion's Tail, also was appropriate.

Made one for Jennifer and one for me. Hers was the original recipe with lime and so forth. Mine was larger and different.

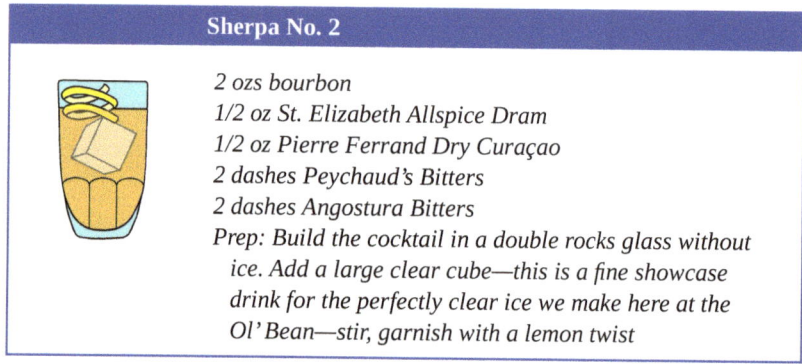

Lion's Tail No. 2
3 ozs bourbon (finishing off the Eagle Rare) *1 oz St. Elizabeth Allspice Dram* *1 oz lemon juice* *2 dashes Peychaud's Bitters* *2 dashes Creole Bitters* *Prep: Combine in a shaker and strain into a chilled coupe.*

Omitted the simple syrup and this could have used another half ounce of allspice dram. A bit sour, it was complex, thanks at least in part to the bitters, and we both preferred this version to the basic recipe.

Sherpa No. 2
2 ozs bourbon *1/2 oz St. Elizabeth Allspice Dram* *1/2 oz Pierre Ferrand Dry Curaçao* *2 dashes Peychaud's Bitters* *2 dashes Angostura Bitters* *Prep: Build the cocktail in a double rocks glass without ice. Add a large clear cube—this is a fine showcase drink for the perfectly clear ice we make here at the Ol' Bean—stir, garnish with a lemon twist*

More allspice dram and the dry curaçao make this a better drink, less sweet, lovely with our clear cubes. A brilliant evening sipper.

20 July Monday

For a while I've been making grenadine using POM. It's easy and the result is as good as grenadine gets, or at least as good as it needs to be. I still resist making simple syrup, though that's about to change, and for some reason, making allspice dram has become a necessity. Except that Market Basket has no allspice berries, so we're delayed, not on hold.

Today was a hard one, and I'd expected to be at sea, but needed a lift. As you know, I prefer stirred drinks to shaken ones. Shaking is an effort, and you have to keep a supply of citrus, so could be laziness. Could be the clarity of stirred drinks; they often are like looking through glass, through jewels, as opposed to the cloudiness shaking imparts by aeration. Often *Jamie Boudreau's Canon* is the book I'll go to when in doubt. It's not too much (*Death & Co.* requires more searching), and the drinks have ingredients for which, while I might lack the specifics, substitutes work well. Tonight's cocktail is exactly such a find.

<table>
<tr><td colspan="2">Zim Zala Bim</td></tr>
<tr><td>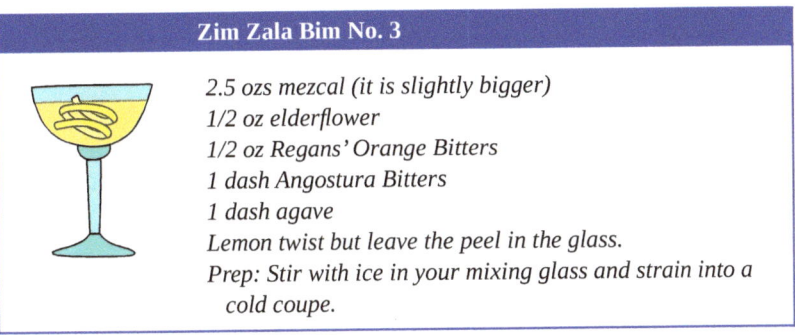</td><td>2 ozs tequila
1/4 oz elderflower liqueur
1/4 oz agave
1/4 oz Regans' Orange Bitters
Prep: Stir with ice and strain into a cold coupe.</td></tr>
</table>

I liked this one immediately. No delayed reaction. But it is sweet. The agave, rather than simple syrup, is my normal sweetener for tequila. But then it struck me that this can be assembled and tasted before adding sweetener. And indeed, iteration two has a mere dash, perhaps a bit more, of agave, and it is perfect. But I made another serious change, moving from tequila (Milagro Reposado) to mezcal (Xicaru Silver).

Jennifer hated it. The mezcal is smoky and, I'd say, bitter. The elderflower and dash of agave leave a sweetness on the front of the tongue, but it is quickly overcome by the smokiness of the mezcal, which apparently you like or do not like. I'm calling this a very interesting variation on the Zim Zala Bim and will stick with it for one more tonight.

Feeling expansive for undecipherable reasons, I made this final Zim Zala Bim-like cocktail that has these variations:

<table>
<tr><td colspan="2">Zim Zala Bim No. 3</td></tr>
<tr><td></td><td>2.5 ozs mezcal (it is slightly bigger)
1/2 oz elderflower
1/2 oz Regans' Orange Bitters
1 dash Angostura Bitters
1 dash agave
Lemon twist but leave the peel in the glass.
Prep: Stir with ice in your mixing glass and strain into a
    cold coupe.</td></tr>
</table>

Best yet, I'd say, though a bit drunk. The Angostura improves the color and helps the bitters take over the sweet almost completely, though with enough sweetness left.

The Manly Love of Smoke

Could be there is some cave dweller left, mostly in men, many of us, that when we taste smoke causes us to reckon the flavor satisfying and overpowering. Years ago, I visited Chiapas, not Oaxaca where mezcal is made, but a neighboring southern Mexican state. The tribes of indigenous people were still discrete; the Zinacantans, Chamulas, and San Martins, lived apart in their own villages, dressed their own way. A smoky Chamula church, dark and more cave than structure, was far more pagan than Christian. My companion, an anthropologist, spoke Spanish, but she might as well have spoken Arabic. The San Martins nearly flayed me for photographing a ritual Easter parade that included flagellating an acting Christ figure. Mezcal has that ancient, pagan, smoky character.

21 July Tuesday

The Neowise Comet

At sea and from here, the dark, mostly clear night sky showed us the new comet Neowise in the northwest. As the sky darkened, it was visible with the naked eye but much better through binoculars. The tail is grand. Neowise will be visible another three nights or so before moving off for 6,800 years. Was the most monumental celestial sight I've seen in probably 60 years, or perhaps 51, when Neil Armstrong stepped onto the moon.

22 July Wednesday

Felt like time for new things, probably some by-product of our renewed fear of the virus and that we'll be distanced indefinitely. Anyway, began with

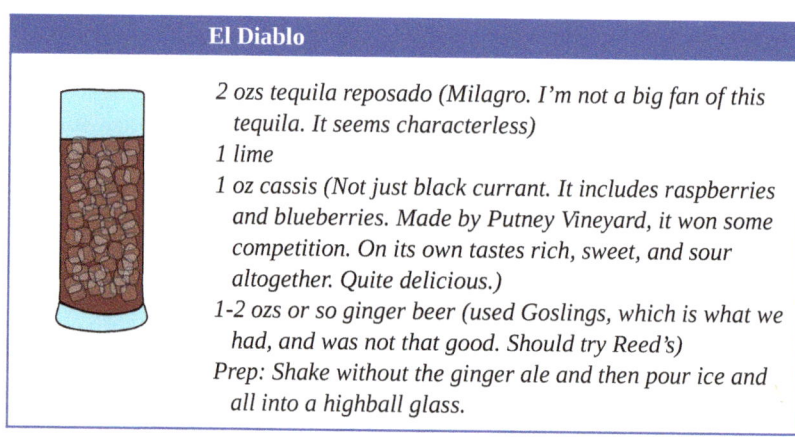

El Diablo

2 ozs tequila reposado (Milagro. I'm not a big fan of this tequila. It seems characterless)
1 lime
1 oz cassis (Not just black currant. It includes raspberries and blueberries. Made by Putney Vineyard, it won some competition. On its own tastes rich, sweet, and sour altogether. Quite delicious.)
1-2 ozs or so ginger beer (used Goslings, which is what we had, and was not that good. Should try Reed's)
Prep: Shake without the ginger ale and then pour ice and all into a highball glass.

Beautiful deep red thanks to the cassis. And tasty. Made a second with a bit of grenadine but was better without. This is an overlooked Mexican cocktail that deserves more attention. Could be a fine one for those summer deck parties we're seeing this year.

Experimented with the Brooklyn back in April and vowed to refine it. Here's the current recipe

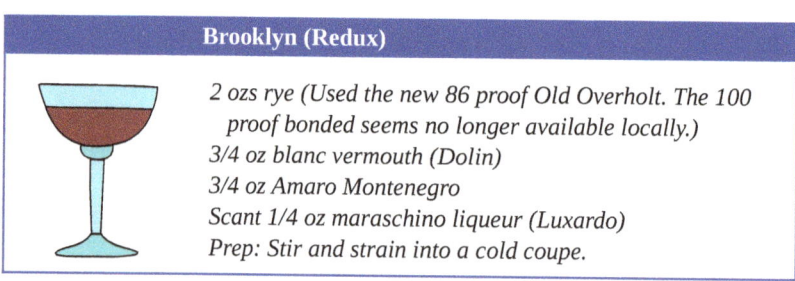

Brooklyn (Redux)

2 ozs rye (Used the new 86 proof Old Overholt. The 100 proof bonded seems no longer available locally.)
3/4 oz blanc vermouth (Dolin)
3/4 oz Amaro Montenegro
Scant 1/4 oz maraschino liqueur (Luxardo)
Prep: Stir and strain into a cold coupe.

The vermouth and going easy on the Luxardo improve this cocktail. But I think there is more to it.

Somehow, I believed I'd had a Boulevardier, a fine classic, but no. And it is excellent, a big improvement over its brother, the Negroni, thanks to the unlikely marriage of Campari and bourbon. If bourbon is on the sweet side, Campari's complex bitterness offsets it nicely.

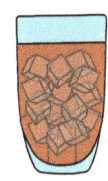

Boulevardier
2 ozs high-proof bourbon (Wild Turkey101)
1 oz Campari
1 oz sweet vermouth (Dolin Rouge; just as good with Rosso. Need to try Antica Formula)
Prep: Stir with ice. Serve up in a cold coupe. But you can drink this with ice in a double rocks glass, and in July, it is mighty fine, as my daddy would say.

Wonderful. I'm calling this the cocktail of the week. The Boulevardier easily replaces a Negroni for me, and I think it could substitute for a Vieux Carré. It's a great classic.

23 July Thursday

Thinking that with more attention I could settle El Diablo and get it right. But no. The correct mix remains elusive. Not that the cocktail isn't good; it is. But the taste disappoints where the color is superb.

El Diablo Redux
2 ozs tequila (Jose Cuervo Reposado this time, and I like it better than the more expensive Milagro, I think)
1 oz cassis
1/2 lemon (made a total of four of these with lemon the last and, I think, best. The half lemon is not quite as sour as the whole lime that I used till then)
Dash of agave sweetener
2 ozs ginger beer (Reed's, which is a spicy choice)
Prep: Shake without the ginger ale and then pour ice and all into a highball glass.

But as I say, this cocktail, much as I wish it would, doesn't quite live up to expectations. One thought is that the cassis, which is quite lovely on its own, may not be suited to this use. It has a distinct sourness to go with sweetness, and perhaps with the citrus, it is too much sour.

24 July Friday

First thing this morning watched Alexandria Ocasio-Cortez's brilliant reply to the odious Ted Yoho's non-apology for the vulgar way he abused her on the capitol steps. Her restraint and poignancy were brilliant.

Plan was to try out the El Diablo at a band rehearsal, but because it isn't ready, will substitute the Boulevardier. Results should be interesting. Drinking going into practice, I'm guessing, after a long layoff, leads to no good. So, decided against taking anything but beer. Ruth served up a Gin & Tonic; drank only one, and it was enough. Had a beer with dinner. Practice went well.

Back home we ate the chocolate cake Ruth made for J's birthday and looked for the comet, but without binoculars, saw nothing. Al and Skylar then showed up and everyone ate cake, Al and Jenny opened presents, and we proved you could have a party without alcohol. Who knew?

This morning I found a leftover cocktail, a Petruchio (?) in the bar's refrigerator.

25 July Saturday

Jenny and Al's Shared Birthday

Dining at the Sunapee Country Club to celebrate Jenny and Al's (the latter *in absentia*) birthday. Will drink that Petruchio left over from Al and friends' debauchery, and then think I'll have a Get Lucky made with our own homegrown blueberries. We planted the bushes but do nothing toward their cultivation, yet they are determined to produce, and this cocktail could prove the best way not to waste them.

Turns out we have an alchemical miracle, blueberries into gold. Oh my, the color is indescribable. And just to say, we drank the leftover Petruchio, which was good as new, and the first Blueberry Birthday ever made. Then, off to dinner.

At our table, I hoped to order a Boulevardier, but our inexperienced waitress knew they lack Campari. So, I ordered a Manhattan, and like the Mai Tai at the Lakeside Tavern, it was awful. What I got was a glass of cheap rye with one of those horrible, dangerous, red-dye cherries, no vermouth, no bitters, and really, no cocktail that could be called a Manhattan.

Again, bars in restaurants out here in rural America cannot be trusted. In some cities, perhaps many cities, and surely in New York City, a Manhattan would be a Manhattan. But, you know, we'll have to see. Meanwhile if your nearby bar lacks Campari, order wine. Trust only your own bar at home to deliver a Boulevardier unless the bartender asks what bourbon and vermouth you would like, or at least offers a plausible recommendation.

This cocktail is not an invention; it is based on the Get Lucky from *Death & Company*. Blueberries replace blackberries, and in our case, blueberries we've grown (though, in truth, that is insignificant). The real difference is in how the drink is built. Let's begin at the beginning:

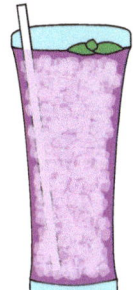

3 ozs rum (Flor de Caña Dry White is best, as Death & Co. *says for their Get Lucky. But I'm guessing any white rum will serve because it will let the color from the berries through)*

1 oz lemon juice (that is, 1/2 lemon. If you prefer tart, use the whole lemon)

1/2 oz orgeat

1/2 oz ginger syrup

1/2 oz honey syrup

Prep: Put maybe six or eight blueberries into your shaker. Ultimately, I think, the number doesn't much affect the taste but does matter to the color, which I hope you'll see is important. Squash these blueberries with your muddler. Do NOT muddle them. All you really want to do is break the flesh open. Add the other ingredients. Here's the novel part. If you have large cubes of ice like we make here at the Bean, put three in a Lewis bag and strike them once each with your 3-lb hammer, rolling pin, or whatever whacker you use. That is, break, but do not crush, the ice. Pour the ice into your shaker. Shake, but not too long or hard. You'll feel the cold and condensation on the outside of the steel vessel. Pour everything, including the ice, into something like a Pilsener, Tom Collins, or even pint glass. The idea is to fill the glass with cocktail and ice. Drizzle Peychaud's Bitters on top, insert straw, perhaps garnish with mint, and serve.

But before drinking, admire the color. Rose? Grapefruit? Airy blue? Depends on the berries. Experiment with number and how crushed you want them. And the taste!

26 July Sunday

Mel's 40th birthday

At sea. Had we been near Mel, in New Orleans, we would have celebrated. As it is, sent her Simon Pearce double rocks glasses so that she and Commander CJ, her husband, could celebrate together.

27 July Monday

The hottest day of the hottest summer I've lived through in NH. Not great at all as we are inadequately equipped to deal with heat. A Georgia Mint Julep, as described by Dr. Cocktail, seemed a good choice. This is not the standard, Kentucky Mint Julep, which calls for bourbon and powdered sugar; I like this version much better, especially for its many possibilities.

Pick a lot of mint; you will not want to attempt this cocktail without your own supply or a supply that you could, under cover of night, steal from your neighbor's yard, along with a chicken if they've got any.

Recipes call for a barspoon or so of sugar, but the drink is already quite sweet. After a couple tries, I settled on putting a lot of mint leaves in a glass or shaker. As to the style of glass, we have quite a few stolen beer glasses with stems. These are a good choice, although if you have stolen silver goblets, prefer them.

Georgia Mint Julep

2 ozs cognac (which is what the Dr. Cocktail recipe calls for, not bourbon, or rye. I tried all three and preferred rye, cognac, bourbon in that heretical order. You could probably use rum or tequila, but I haven't tried them.)

1 oz peach brandy (I used Montbisou Peche Liqueur, an intensely sweet, French product that accounts for why sugar was superfluous. I read somewhere it is available at Trader Joe's, and it is not expensive. Seems a good choice here.)

Dash agave syrup (kind of an afterthought that I preferred to sugar. But, for example, honey syrup or orgeat might be better still. It's 8:41 AM and I am ready to try some of these mods!)

Dash or two of bitters (I like bitters, and in this sweet drink, they seemed, and were, a good idea. I used Angostura and then Pecan Chickory Bitters, preferring, of course, the latter)

Prep: A dozen or so mint leaves. Put in the glass and press them with your muddler, spoon, anything that applies pressure to release the mint oils. Stir to mix then add crushed ice and stir again. Put enough ice so that it just covers the spirits. Mount a bouquet of fresh mint stems down into the glass. No straw. You want the tippler's face buried in the mint as she/he tipples. Added benefit: she/he will smell like mint perfume when under the dazzling influence you kiss her/him.

Excellent for a hot day, at least if you or your neighbor have mint that needs using. You can drink quickly, so that it doesn't go watery, or sip slowly. And it'll have some flavor and lots of aroma to the end. The flavors of the liquors are not distinct, and the cocktail does not seem boozy. I'll probably use 3 ozs of the base spirit and 1.5 ozs of peche liqueur from here on. This is a treat to look at, festive, and as such should be an at-least-once-a-summer tradition for a hot, miserable day.

28 July Tuesday

The Boxcar Case (continued)

At sea. Except, as it turned out, needed lots of medicine. As mentioned earlier, Jenny's dad and his wife Beth are living in a lovely RV next to our house for the summer, as the pandemic rages in Florida, where they live the rest of the year. Some of the neighbors don't like the trailer, which is built like one of the boxcars of the Concord to Claremont Railroad that used to run and for which a station still exists, right below our house. I walked over to our nearest neighbor who had been giving me the cold shoulder to hear how he felt. Lots of anger because he felt betrayed that, as an abutter, I had not told him this was coming. Although a died-in-the-wool laconic Yankee, he went on for a while. By the end, a drink was inevitable.

You know how sometimes the Universe seems to be listening? Earlier in the day I'd opened *The Canon Cocktail Book* to pages 114-115, where Nirvana was waiting. Jamie Boudreau says, "You'll finish content in the knowledge that whichever of life's issues is getting you down at the moment, you'll always have light on the path to your own private Nirvana." So it proved.

Nirvana

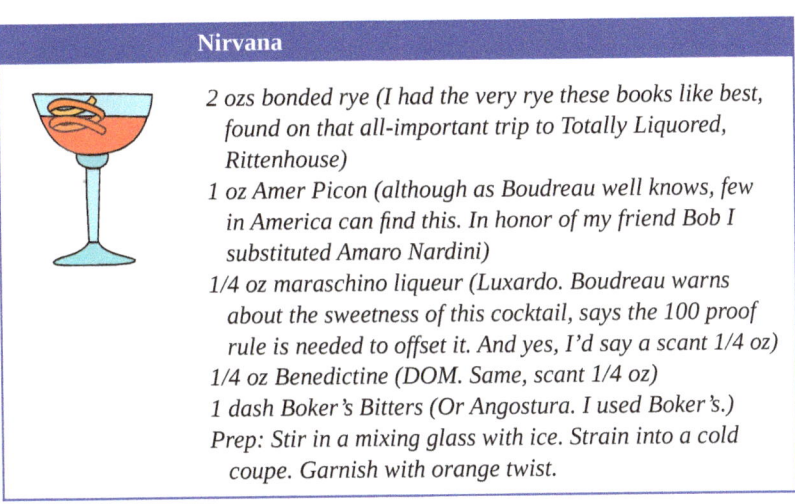

2 ozs bonded rye (I had the very rye these books like best, found on that all-important trip to Totally Liquored, Rittenhouse)

1 oz Amer Picon (although as Boudreau well knows, few in America can find this. In honor of my friend Bob I substituted Amaro Nardini)

1/4 oz maraschino liqueur (Luxardo. Boudreau warns about the sweetness of this cocktail, says the 100 proof rule is needed to offset it. And yes, I'd say a scant 1/4 oz)

1/4 oz Benedictine (DOM. Same, scant 1/4 oz)

1 dash Boker's Bitters (Or Angostura. I used Boker's.)

Prep: Stir in a mixing glass with ice. Strain into a cold coupe. Garnish with orange twist.

Halfway through, I'd found Nirvana. Boudreau thinks of it as a Negroni substitute, which surprises me, as it seems much more in the (ever growing) Manhattan family. Who cares? Once you have reached(?), achieved(?), discovered(?)—who cares?—Nirvana, especially this early in an evening, why stop seeking?

Nirvana #2

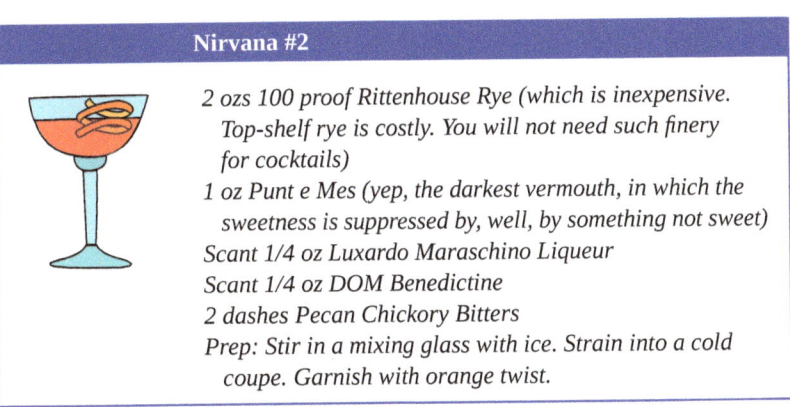

2 ozs 100 proof Rittenhouse Rye (which is inexpensive. Top-shelf rye is costly. You will not need such finery for cocktails)

1 oz Punt e Mes (yep, the darkest vermouth, in which the sweetness is suppressed by, well, by something not sweet)

Scant 1/4 oz Luxardo Maraschino Liqueur

Scant 1/4 oz DOM Benedictine

2 dashes Pecan Chickory Bitters

Prep: Stir in a mixing glass with ice. Strain into a cold coupe. Garnish with orange twist.

Once you've found Nirvana I'm supposing everything is, at the least, nearly perfect, leaving us to inch toward the Absolutely Perfect, which I'm working at right now. The Pecan Chickory Bitters were possibly better than the Boker's, but they are a New Orleans product, and you know my bias there. Still, the idea means something. Getting there…

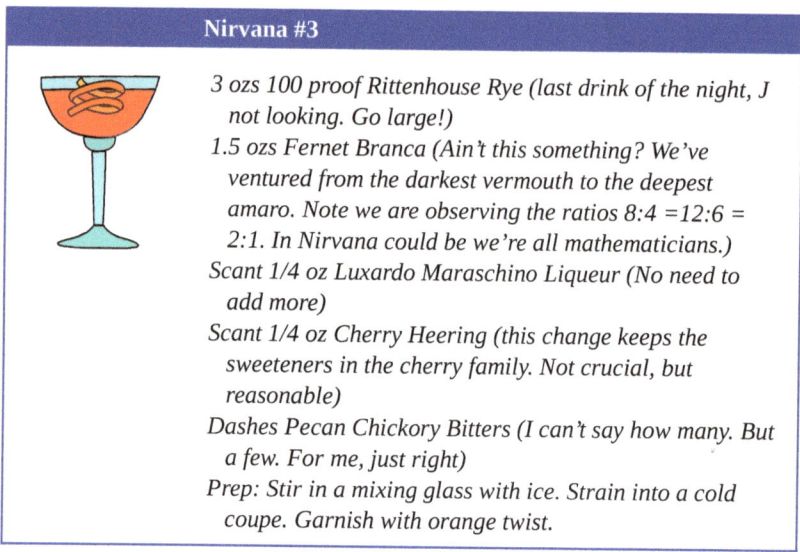

Nirvana #3

3 ozs 100 proof Rittenhouse Rye (last drink of the night, J not looking. Go large!)

1.5 ozs Fernet Branca (Ain't this something? We've ventured from the darkest vermouth to the deepest amaro. Note we are observing the ratios 8:4 =12:6 = 2:1. In Nirvana could be we're all mathematicians.)

Scant 1/4 oz Luxardo Maraschino Liqueur (No need to add more)

Scant 1/4 oz Cherry Heering (this change keeps the sweeteners in the cherry family. Not crucial, but reasonable)

Dashes Pecan Chickory Bitters (I can't say how many. But a few. For me, just right)

Prep: Stir in a mixing glass with ice. Strain into a cold coupe. Garnish with orange twist.

Here we are, Perfect Nirvana. Sir Galahad himself would have toasted the moment. The Fernet Branca is a deep mystery. Someday, Amer Picon may travel to NH. Meanwhile, Nirvana is how, when, where you find it.

29 July Wednesday

Aboard *Sea Sisters*, where a seagoing bar, in this now long, extended, at-sea metaphor, is essential, or hypocrisy will overwhelm the whole idea of showing you the glories of your own bar wherever you hang your hat or toss your duffel. If you can build a respectable bar aboard a 36-foot seagoing sailboat, where heeling at ridiculous angles that often fling cabinets open, tossing the contents will-he, nil-he everywhere, then you can build your own bar pretty much anywhere.

The drink of the night while pondering the seagoing bar was Black Manhattan, pretty refined and simple, but I'll replay its contents:

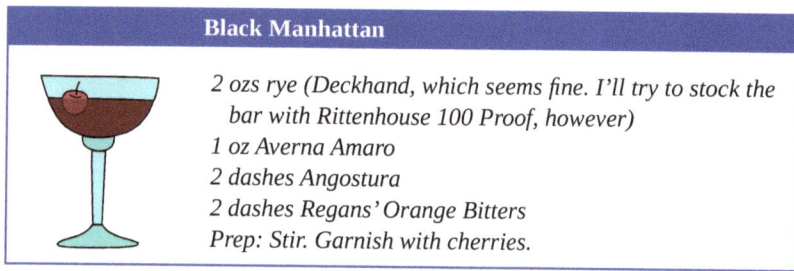

Black Manhattan

2 ozs rye (Deckhand, which seems fine. I'll try to stock the bar with Rittenhouse 100 Proof, however)

1 oz Averna Amaro

2 dashes Angostura

2 dashes Regans' Orange Bitters

Prep: Stir. Garnish with cherries.

Cooling any cocktail is trickier out here. We have a refrigerator with a small freezer and bring ice. But I'm always trying to save ice. So, I stirred the drink with a big Bean cube and got it cold. Late in the cocktail I poured what was left of the ice and water into my glass and drank it up, then made another. Waste not.

A Seagoing Bar

Until now the bar was in a port-side cabinet. Pretty big, but hard to reach around the seating area in the main salon. I've now moved it to a cabinet above the sink in the galley, where it is close to spoons, ingredients, ice, and glasses. Not roomy but will serve us well. And because the door opens aft, rather than to starboard or port, it won't fling open, the whiskey bottles fly out, on a steep heel.

30 July Thursday

Will sail with my girlfriends (as Jenny calls them) then try out the bar once returned to the mooring. Plans call for Gimlets and Dark and Stormies.

And a fine sail the five of us enjoyed. At the end, while we awaited the opening of the Memorial Bridge that connects Portsmouth, NH, and Kittery, ME, across the Piscataqua River, I went below to make drinks.

Began with one Gimlet to give everyone a chance to see whether they liked it.

The Gimlet and Rose's Lime Juice

An old story, the Gimlet was invented to overcome the deadly effects of scurvy on sailors. In 1867 a Scotsman, Lauchian Rose, patented his formula for preserving lime juice with sugar rather than alcohol. Today Rose's Lime Juice is familiar in grocery stores, so I suppose more than a few people drink Gimlets. Otherwise, what do you do with the stuff?

Years ago, I'd mistakenly ordered a Gimlet in Montreal, when what I meant was a Gibson, and was unhappily surprised by the electric yellow-green cocktail that arrived, though I drank it. Yesterday's Gimlet was my second.

The original ratio, at least as described in Raymond Chandler's novel *The Long Goodbye*, and in *The Savoy Cocktail Book*, was 1:1 gin to Rose's Lime Juice. This is where we started yesterday, but the three crew who tried it elected instead Dark and Stormies. I drank the Gimlet. And a second try proved better:

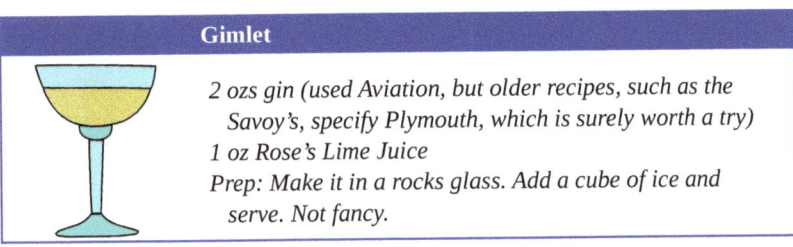

Gimlet

2 ozs gin (used Aviation, but older recipes, such as the Savoy's, specify Plymouth, which is surely worth a try)
1 oz Rose's Lime Juice
Prep: Make it in a rocks glass. Add a cube of ice and serve. Not fancy.

This 2:1 ratio worked better. The drink is intense enough, and Rose's Lime Juice retains just enough of the recipe of the original—compared with Rose's horrible grenadine—that it is fine. You can, however, make your own version of the lime juice, which I may yet try based on a recipe that seems doable, and get even better results.

Additionally, you'll find recipes that specify fresh lime juice, sugar, and gin. These are Gin Daiquiris; they are NOT Gimlets.

Dark and Stormy

Meanwhile, the Dark and Stormy was preferred among *Sea Sisters'* sailors. And I'll add that making these cocktails amounted to the debut of the Sea Sisters Bar, which proved just fine. To be honest, the Dark and Stormy drinks I produced were based on no recipe but were 2 ozs dark rum (a choice of Goslings or Pusser's), in a glass with ice, Reed's Ginger Beer, and a slice of lime squeezed in the glass. I'm not presenting it as a recipe because I believe down the road we can do better. On the other hand, all glasses came back empty with requests for a refill.

No one aboard developed symptoms of scurvy, but symptoms of drunkenness were evident.

31 July Friday

Hmm. Off to band practice this evening. On turning 60, I decided to see if anyone so old could learn anything at all and started playing guitar. A couple years later this led to forming a band with friends, all of whom are much more accomplished than I am. The Luggnuts write a fair number of our own songs, and have played quite a bit around New Hampshire, losing money almost every time. We've been derailed from practice by the pandemic but are planning to play an outdoor concert in late summer. It isn't easy, but we think it is possible to practice safely outdoors.

Cocktails, naturally, improve our playing. But which? Nirvana #3 or Blueberry Birthday? The latter to use our blueberries, of which we have many.

Made in quantity, and to save the Flor de Caña, which requires travel to Totally Liquored, used Bacardi. Tried to buy orgeat at the NH Liquor Store and the grocery. No luck. Used what we had and then made the rookie mistake of completing that part of the sweetener with agave when I should have used simple syrup. Why? Agave is brown. The best thing about this cocktail is its color, and I can't know yet whether the brown from the agave will degrade it. Fingers crossed.

Blueberry Birthday in Quantity

36 ozs rum (Bacardi white, which should be enough for
   12 cocktails, probably more)
16 ozs lemon juice (which puts us between the sweeter
   and more sour versions, I think)
6 ozs honey syrup (enough for 12)
3 ozs orgeat
3 ozs agave
6 ozs ginger syrup.
Prep: Will take mostly cubed ice and see if it needs to
   be smashed. Not much smashing required. Put the
   blueberries in the bottom of each glass. Smash them
   slightly. Added ice, pour. Dash Peychaud's Bitters on top
   and stir slightly with a straw. Beautiful color, smashing
   cocktail.

Rust and all, of course we sounded just fine.

1 August Saturday

Lashed to the Mast: A Week of Abstinence Begins

Passing near the isle of the Sirens, and already in danger of becoming a Lotus Eater, I've asked the crew, Jenny, to tie me to the mast. Will be here, according to the plan, for a week. Listen for my cries!

Yet, day one of almost any punishment can be endured. After sailing with Jenny's dad, we didn't reach home until 8:00 PM or so, well past cocktail time, thoroughly beat, and so the bindings were not too tight.

A few words about sailing with Tim: he has courage. He's blind and needs to step from dock to dinghy and then from dinghy to sailboat. Aboard he hardly moves, but he drinks beer, which in due course leads to its own problem. Out on the water he hallucinates, thinking, for example, we're in a parking lot, that waves are trees, or that we're following a bear. With all of that, he loves the sail. I'm guessing, it is partly the motion, partly the release from land where each step is a challenge, partly the memory of days on Lake Champlain with his young children. And partly sailing is something, given that so much is lost to him forever, he can still do.

2 August Sunday

The Benefits of Alcohol

Already I can make out the Sirens' song across the waters of the hours. If you use the Internet to self-diagnose you've seen that most any malady can be improved by avoiding (at best) or minimizing (at least) your intake of alcohol. We know better, and celebrate the blandishments of alcohol, that in cocktail form start with tastes, smells, arrangements, and colors; before long become a feeling of, say, elevation, in the brain; migrate to the fulfillment of a desire for more; along the way may animate conversation or deepen contemplation, truly or imagined; and lead to a sense of placidity or well-being, calm perhaps otherwise unavailable.

If alcohol does all those things, others as well, it is easy to understand how it becomes a habit with the potential to do us more harm than all of that good. I've maintained along the diary that no ill effects disturb my sleep or hang over to the next day so long as I hold fast at a generous three cocktails in a night. It's probably only honest to add that five or six days each week I exercise by either spinning on a stationary bike in a class where the rhythm of music, commands of the instructor, and sweat of other riders push us on; riding a bike outdoors; or by lifting weights, all enough that during the pandemic I've lost weight and am in good condition as old men go. In other words, one can drink and exercise heavily, benefitting, I believe, from both.

Yet, always one who loves a nap, I have found this summer that naps themselves have become a habit. By early afternoon I am overcome by fatigue. It has seemed recently that my naps are longer, as much as two hours, a time I do not try to regulate. Is it possible, then, that the fatigue is a lingering result of alcohol most nights, especially if my liver is working hard and energy is further depleted by exercise?

And so, here we are, tied to the mast!

Jennifer and I just had words because, having had no drink since Friday night, I just had a long nap and reported the fatigue felt the same as if I'd been drinking as usual. She fired back that it's too soon, I'd been sailing two of three days, had cut the grass today, and had ridden hard yesterday. I'm telling you this only as a matter of science. So far, after a night of abstinence, I feel and behave (well, Jenny says I'm grumpy) no different from after a night of routine drinking.

And on we sail…

3 August Monday

It is right to say that the decision to be lashed to the mast, to hear the Siren song of Alcohol but not act on it, was driven by a failure of energy. Last week it dawned on me that days I go to the gym, lift weights for an hour and then go to spinning class for another hour, invariably lead to a quick retreat to our bedroom on returning home, reading for a few minutes, and then falling into a dead sleep. Is this pattern the result of asking too much of an old body that is processing alcohol along with exercise?

Yesterday I reported feeling no better than after nights of drinking. Today, having worked unusually hard at the gym both with weights and spinning, having come home and de-veined kale along with other chores, and then gone upstairs without eating, I read, placed an order with the Boston Shaker, paid boat insurance, showered, changed, and came downstairs for lunch. Having eaten, at 2:21 PM I'm writing and have very little hint of fatigue.

The plot, as we say, thickens…Jennifer continues to believe I'm grumpy.

4 August Tuesday

The Evil Effects of Abstinence on Behavior

Unpredicted consequences are everywhere in human life. We think that laying a plan will lead to results we want, yet often catastrophe ensues. Such unforeseeable results occur in large scale—say the Vietnam and Iraq wars where our might was supposed to win quick victories, or the Trump economy that encountered a pandemic, a pandemic that was supposed to amount to nothing more than a foolish liberal plot but that persists—or in our little lives, which is where I'm bemused by the raging effects of forswearing alcohol. Am I grumpy? Undeniably. Am I more energetic? Could be, but that may prove an emerging disaster.

The grumpiness seems as if it truly could be chemical. A body and mind used to the stimulus of alcohol and suddenly deprived of it, may well react with withdrawal that shows up as unpleasant behavior. I seem—okay, am—critical, disengaged, irritable. The condition is not unlike suddenly stopping exercise; the endorphins disappear, and depression results, or so it has seemed to me down the years. Unlooked for consequence number one of being lashed to the mast: an unpleasant disposition. Or as Jennifer said it, "Who knew I'd be married to one of the Seven Dwarfs?" Or, a more famous grump, Tennyson's Ulysses aptly describes his version of how I feel,

> It little profits that an idle king,
> By this still hearth, among these barren crags,
> Match'd with an aged wife, I mete and dole
> Unequal laws unto a savage race,
> That hoard, and sleep, and feed, and know not me.

Critical. Disengaged. Irritable. And (I'd better add) Jenny is not aged.

Yesterday, as reported, I returned from the gym and did not crash into a nap, felt pretty good, did stuff. But I did not report that at the gym I was stronger than usual, more energetic and probably as a result, tweaked my lower back, which stiffened, and soon had me listing to starboard. Could it be that like other sedatives alcohol in its way constrains our physicality? As a bicycle racer and before that as a runner, I thought so and did not drink for years, simply because in those tortuous competitions every joule of energy helps. But now that I've put on the mantles of age and retirement, could it be that stressing a worn heart beyond its powers or decaying muscles past their current abilities is dangerous? Unlooked for consequence two: more energy than is good for an old, easily broken body is an evil because, as Ulysses observed,

We are not now that strength which in old days
Moved earth and heaven, that which we are, we are;
One equal temper of heroic hearts,
Made weak by time and fate, but strong in will
To strive, to seek, to find, and not to yield.

And this test at the mast seems to be saying that the effects of alcohol offer hope for sustaining the will to continue that quest within the bodily constraints imposed by age.

5 August Wednesday

The Absurdity of Self Denial (At Least in a Pandemic)

As the pandemic drags on with no end foreseen, people are reporting that they feel a deepening depression. Infinite time has no demarcations; days, weeks, months flow indistinguishably, like water at different times or places in a river, all look alike. Heraclitus be damned; the river seems always the same.

But for me, the ritual 6:00 pm cocktail includes planning, preparation, effort, and reward, each cocktail having its own account in this diary as a further individuator, with the result that I've never been bored or desperately needed the pandemic to end because each day is, in fact, different, and with this diary, I can return to the most important particulars of any day.

Improved energy, better sleep, longer life, clearer thinking—all said to be benefits of throwing off alcohol—could improve a life under more normal circumstances, I suppose. During a pandemic, the anticipation of the brightening effects of alcohol and then the lightening itself are so profound that self-denial at the end of a day would be absurd.

6 August Thursday

Made two Witch Hunts, one for Jenny, one for Beth, and none for me last night. Looks fetching. Here's the recipe:

Witch Hunt

2 ozs scotch (A blended scotch is good here. I've been using Shackelton, simply as a matter of reverence, and the report is it worked well.)
3/4 oz dry vermouth (Dolin Dry)
1/2 oz Strega Liqueur (New to the Bean. Been seeing it in the cordial aisle at the NH Liquor Store and so bought some. An Amaro that, once past this damnable alcohol fast, I'll try and report on in the [fictional] Amari chapter. The Strega Prize is awarded every year for the best work of prose fiction in Italian.)
1 oz lemonade (Made this in the shaker with 2 ozs lemon, 2 ozs simple syrup, 4 ozs water. Plenty left after the cocktails, which I poured into a glass with clear cubes as my share. No alcohol, but the best lemonade I ever drank.)
Prep: Stir this one and drink with ice.

Will I quit drinking? Jennifer asked if I feel lost without the cocktail to plan and look forward to at the end of the day. In other words, it is not only the alchemical virtues of alcohol that improve a day but the anticipation of them. But more than just that, during the pandemic, rather than isolated, unnatural, depressed, I feel busy, content, alive.

7 August Friday

Dangers of the Mast or Wagon

Never, ever, under any circumstances put yourself on the wagon, which I say, still drunk, I think, at 9:15 the next day (that is, Saturday), because when you leap off that moving conveyance, you're likely to embarrass yourself (you might, for example, fall into a swimming pool) and, more important, it could be deadly. Jenny untied the bonds that held me to the mast, and the Siren call that had rung in my ears all week wrapped its rhythm about my brain and over roughly five hours, pulled body and soul into a spinning vortex of inebriation that continued through the night, as I woke in the dark, stumbled to the toilet, no less drunk and disoriented than when the last drink of the evening found its way down the hatch.

To make matters worse, and we've all been here, this was a gathering outdoors at the house of a couple, our first invitation, people whose thinking and values we admire. It's likely they don't really enjoy the company of a dedicated drunk, and so the chance for a new friendship may have been lost. Now, this may sound self-pitying, but during a pandemic, at an advanced age, how often can you make new friends? How often do you find new people who are generous spirited, aware, uncalculating, and not judgmental? And then, owing to a self-imposed experiment of a bad idea, you stamp yourself as a fool who could fall into their pool, drown yourself, and leave them with a memory that spoils their very home. But enough of that.

Naturally, when you've tied yourself to the mast for a week, your body has excreted its stores of alcohol, making you surely more vulnerable to its effects than you would expect. I began the evening with a strong beer from Treehouse (8%. Scott, the host, had 11 cases) and felt no real jolt from it. But then, having made a LOT of Planter's Punch with many rums, including St James, Barbancourt, Bacardi, Appleton, Flor de Caña, and most devastating, Goslings151, I began the descent into some Dantesque Circle of Hell to which drunks are consigned, possibly, since I cannot sober up even at 9:50 the next day, forever.

Sorry. Let's get to the point,

Being tied to the mast is, number one, dangerous. Once unfettered, your celebration may be so extreme that in far too many ways, you'll probably do lasting damage—to friendships, health, memory, time itself. Your body, no longer used to the daily ministrations of controlled amounts of spirits, no longer disciplined to the limits beyond which a mariner cannot travel, is vulnerable to both excess and intensity. Rather than enjoying the freeing spirits of a day, you're likely to suck in the lost ghosts of the week-of-torment all at once with disastrous results. Rather than rendered sublime, mild, easy, happy for the night, you'll be degraded, wild, intense, miserable into (and it is past 10:00 AM now) the next day, wrestling with regrets, dizziness, caught in a moment when looking back cannot change the thick-tongued speech, the unbalanced steps, and looking ahead—especially to the cocktail of the evening—holds no joy. Horrible.

Sleep, moralizers say, improves once you stop drinking, but is in fact ruined by the absence of alcohol and then by its powerful return. Clearly these moralizers extrapolate from piety, not experience. I've written that cocktails improve sleep compared with beer because you don't need to urinate during the night, can usually sleep hard right through. Jumping off the wagon, by contrast, leads to a bladder that refills as if fed by some Niagara, causing you to wake (one hopes) in the dark; fall out of bed disoriented, drunk, with a sick headache; weave to the bathroom and then weakly, haltingly find your way back to bed and to sleep; only to repeat this absurd tangle again, again, and who can say how many agains, through your broken night. And I will add, nor does sleep improve during abstinence. My normal drinking pattern results in deep, untroubled, dreamless sleep. Abstinence led to vivid, long, troubling dreams, made it vastly less restful than after a night of joyous drinking. Horrible.

It is 10:30. When have I ever lingered abed till 10:30? Is this some reversion to the teenage years? Again, heedless consumption, as the inexperienced prove, leads to unwanted consequences. I am entirely persuaded that the drinker must practice his craft daily or suffer the fate of the unpracticed. Drinking must not be casual. Indeed, it requires exercise, or we lose the ability to control it, and instead, it controls us.

Finally, the last, least desired consequence of this exile from alcohol, is that one could turn away from alcohol altogether. What then? **Would such a life be worth living?**

8 August Saturday

Being no rookie, I had some sense that such a drunk could happen. Still, I am surprised, especially that through the morning I felt drunk, which has happened only once that I can recall, way back in my twenties. Nonetheless, at dinner time, fixed myself and Jenny Swearengens.

Al Swearengen, saloon owner in *Deadwood*, is one of the great TV characters, and I think one of the great fictional characters period, with more than a little likeness to a character Shakespeare might have created. A drink with his name on it, from *Death & Co.*, even in my weakened state, was irresistible.

Swearengen Sling

2 ozs bourbon (used Wild Turkey 101)
1/2 oz amaro (the recipe calls for Amaro Nonino, which I don't have. In mine, used Amaro Nardini; in Jenny's, used Liquor Strega. Both excellent. I'd hoped the Strega would lend its yellow color to the cocktail, but it did not. I'm not quite sure whether I like its look, its color.)
1/2 oz Cherry Heering
1/2 oz lemon juice
1/2 oz simple syrup
2 cherries (the recipe calls for brandied but I had only Luxardo Maraschino, which were fine. You can easily make brandied cherries, and it could be worth doing as well as inexpensive.)
Prep: Muddle the two cherries in a shaker. Add ice and the other ingredients. Shake. Strain into a rocks glass with ice. Add a cherry for garnish and serve with a straw.

What is a Sling?

But what is a sling? It is a predecessor to the cocktail from the late 18th Century made with spirits, water, sugar, and often nutmeg, that by mid-19th Century included ice. Slings did not include amaro or Cherry Heering or lemon juice, at least, that is, until the cocktail slipped out of America, made its way across the Atlantic, and by late 19th Century came all the way round to the Raffles Hotel in Singapore, where the Singapore Sling was not invented but became famous (Wondrich, 151-152). By then, the English had included citrus and liqueurs in slings, sometimes with awful results. But the Singapore Sling is far from awful and deserves attention. So, also, the Swearengen.

9 August Sunday

Slings (continued)

The Swearengen Sling is taking us to unanticipated places, including for me, back to *Deadwood*, which I may re-watch with our upgraded WIFI, once the TV works again. Meanwhile, the TV is in no hurry for improvement, so let's return to slings. Before that, I'll warn you, that we may be walking into the cocktail (or, uh, sling) weeds. Skip if this looks boring, though you might want to go directly to the recipe for the Straits Sling and give it a go.

Among the prototypical books about cocktails, the Belgian Robert Vermeire's *Cocktails: How to Mix Them* from 1922 has an air of seriousness and simplicity that makes him a good source. He was a traveled bartender, unpretentious, but clearly cared about his work. His book is organized based on principles we've long put aside, which is to say alphabetically, except for cocktails, which come first, and then by type of drink, from cobblers, coolers, crustas, and cups through slings, smashes, sours, and toddies, all types that in our less precise age we'd simply call cocktails, or even less descriptively, drinks.

Here is Vermeire's description of slings: "All slings are made the same way; one has only to substitute the base liquor. When desired cold, use water and ice; when hot, use boiling water."

Not very helpful, except the first of his two sling recipes, for a Hot Apple Jack Sling, is traditional:

Fill a tumbler half full of boiling water and sugar syrup to sweeten, 3/4 gill of Apple Jack Brandy or Calvados and stir up gently. Squeeze the peel of a lemon into the glass and add grated nutmeg. Some people prefer a tablespoonful of fresh lemon juice also in it.

Water, sugar, spirit, nutmeg, and in this case, some citrus. Simple and close to the original idea of a sling. And medicinally, relief from the common cold or flu.

But his other recipe, the Straits Sling, is far more worldly. The residents of Singapore still call their island the "Straits," and the Straits Sling predates the Singapore. This well-known Singapore drink, well iced and shaken contains:

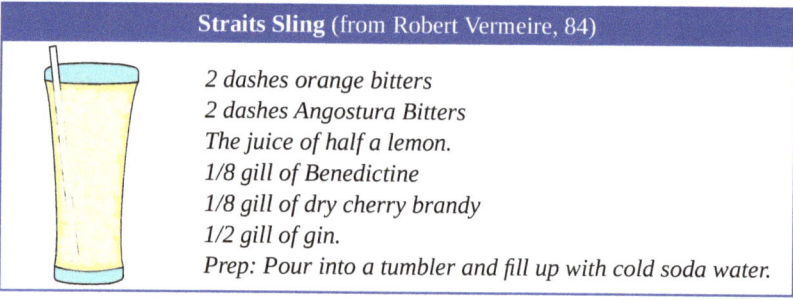

Straits Sling (from Robert Vermeire, 84)

2 dashes orange bitters
2 dashes Angostura Bitters
The juice of half a lemon.
1/8 gill of Benedictine
1/8 gill of dry cherry brandy
1/2 gill of gin.
Prep: Pour into a tumbler and fill up with cold soda water.

According to Dr. Cocktail (266), the dry cherry brandy Vermeire had in mind was not Cherry Heering or Luxardo Maraschino, which in fact are very sweet. Instead, he meant an eau de vie, a distillate of cherries that would be very dry. Returning to the Swearengen Sling, specifying Cherry Heering leads to a variation of the Singapore Sling. You would need kirschwasser, which I cannot find here, to have something like a Straits Sling. Are you following?

So, here's the plan. Pierre Ferrand Dry Orange Curaçao is not the least bit sweet and amounts to an orange version of kirschwasser. Let's give Vermeire's recipe a try, but substitute the curaçao for the cherry as follows:

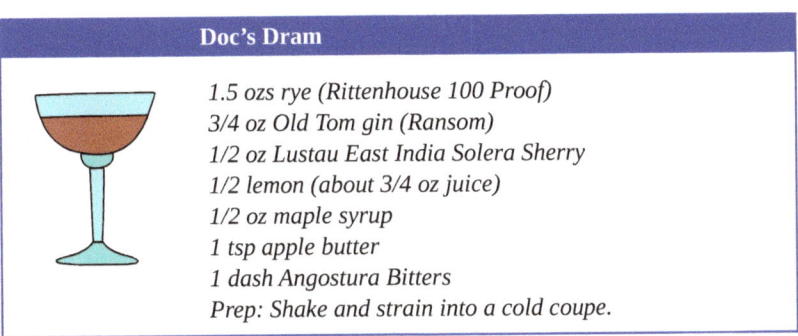

Singapore Sling
2 ozs gin (Plymouth)

2 ozs gin (Plymouth)
1/2 half lemon
1/2 oz Benedictine (DOM)
1/2 oz dry orange curaçao (Pierre Ferrand)
2 dashes orange bitters (and doesn't this seem to suit the curaçao?)
2 dashes Angostura Bitters
Prep: Measure ingredients into a shaker, shake with ice. Strain into a cold coupe. And for tradition's sake, grate a bit of nutmeg on top. Note that I've omitted the soda water and ice in favor of serving the Straits Sling up, a suggestion of Dr. Cocktail.

Umm. I don't hear Robert Vermeire turning over in his grave.

Dozens of recipes for the Singapore Sling exist, but they have in common with each other, and with the Swearengen, sweet liqueurs such as Cherry Heering, Benedictine, and Cointreau. They often have a variety of fruit juices. For my money, however, the drier, nearly forgotten Straits Sling is more interesting.

Whew! Like you, I've slung enough for one day. Let's move on to something else: from *Death & Co.*, Doc's Dram:

Doc's Dram

1.5 ozs rye (Rittenhouse 100 Proof)
3/4 oz Old Tom gin (Ransom)
1/2 oz Lustau East India Solera Sherry
1/2 lemon (about 3/4 oz juice)
1/2 oz maple syrup
1 tsp apple butter
1 dash Angostura Bitters
Prep: Shake and strain into a cold coupe.

My sister-in-law Wendy, no real fan of mine, called this the best drink she's ever had. My mother-in-law Beth, who has had many cocktails here, particularly liked this one, as did Jenny and I. It has the right amount of sweet and sour, with ingredients that add their particular flavors. I'm especially happy to find a second cocktail (don't even recall the first, but it is from Dr. Cocktail) that makes use of the enormous jar of apple butter taking up space in the pub fridge. If a balanced taste with many interesting flavors, profound but not sparkly, suits, you could hardly do better than Doc's Dram. The only thing to hold against it is the pretty large number of ingredients.

10 August Monday

Denouement

At the gym this morning, was strong and energetic with weights and in an especially hard spinning class, a so-called ladder, was in the red and yellow district of my heart rate monitor for a considerable time. In other words, Friday's colossal drunk followed by more moderate, but customary drinking Saturday and Sunday, had no bad physical effect, after the Saturday hangover. Moreover, I'm upstairs typing on our bed and feel no fatigue. Were the naps that led me to the week of misery and abstinence merely a habit?

Won't say much or anything about this as we sail ahead but will monitor it to report signs of creeping weakness possibly caused by drinking. Right now, I see nothing but bright cocktails in my future, and in yours!

Aboard *Sea Sisters*, and have been reading a grand translation of *The Odyssey*, the best possible place for such reading. The translator, Emily Wilson, seems brilliant to me. Entirely speculative, but I think she lets ancient Greeks be who they are. The men, for example, moan and cry considerably over lost comrades, wives, parents. These misty heroes seem especially unmanly by our cultural lights. And then, for example, during Odysseus' visit to Hades, he recounts lots of the myths we still know and gods and heroes whose names have lasted, but they often sound like insincere acquaintances looking for a conversation, though in this context, about life and death rather than shopping. Are they "primitive" or sophisticated in ways so strange to us that we cannot follow? And with all of that, the tale resonates here, today, aboard *Sea Sisters*.

I'm writing on deck as the sun goes down. Third Manhattan, a black one made so by Averna Amaro, is superb. Having established a bar aboard ship, and thinking ahead as we must do, if I've got too much of an ingredient at home, it'll get good use here. We have ample Old Overholt and a new bottle of Fernet Branca at the Bean, so the dregs of the first bottle are aboard. Fearing we'd run short of the Averna Amaro we had in the *Sea Sisters* bar, Manhattan number one of the evening was the 86 proof Old Overholt (the new Old Overholt) that in our liquor store has, apparently, replaced the bonded 100 proof Old Overholt, and an ounce of Fernet Branca.

This was terrible, should not be repeated, although it did not get tossed overboard. Let's revisit the condemnation. The Fernet Branca, dark-as-night-in-Hades Manhattan was way too bitter, completely controlling, which is the cocktail equivalent in this drink of a boorish husband. No need to go into the details of its composition; avoid 2 ozs of rye and 1 oz of Fernet Branca together.

Yet, it is important to say that the drink was not vile. That is, if your motivations are economical, to drink up dregs in combination with other dregs in an unlikely maritime, or another, setting, as we say in the 21st Century vernacular, "Go for it."

And good luck to you, pal!

11 August Tuesday

After a pleasantly cool night aboard *Sea Sisters*, relief from a broiling day ashore, had a fine conversation with my friend Steve Poore; did some normal maintenance, including varnishing the toe-rail; bought lobsters; then drove home for a dinner with J's mother. Meanwhile, my brother Danny called, offering Alex his 2010 Prius with 131,000 miles, half the number on Al's car. I've found a place in Houston that will replace the battery for $800—as opposed to dealer cost of $4,000—and so may go there on my way back to New Hampshire ("on my way" if going west from New Orleans to Houston to travel north isn't out of my way).

But you need a drink. For tonight, a long story, about the Mother-in-Law, a pre-prohibition, New Orleans cocktail that not only is fabulous, but that can, should, be made by the quart for serving immediately when you're not up to mixing. The recipe appears in Ted Haigh's *Forgotten Cocktails* but comes from the New Orleans grandmother of a fellow in New York, Brooks Baldwin, by way of his friend Chuck Taggart. Confusing, but hang on.

Baldwin's grandmother got the recipe from her mother-in-law before World War I, and one of these women seems to have modified what was called a "Zazarac" (search me???), omitting its absinthe, to suit her own taste. Baldwin's grandmother made it a quart at a time and kept it in a lead decanter for pouring.

Based on a trial run, I'm considering doing the same, minus the lead. But here's a problem. The original called for a small amount of Amer Picon, which is not distributed in the United States any longer. Good substitutes are available in some states, Torani Amer and Amer Boudreau, but not here, and as far as I can tell, not nearby.

A common substitute, the one I used, though apparently less rich and lacking the distinctive orange flavor of Amer Picon or its substitutes, is Amaro Montenegro. I added orange bitters to the recipe, and dry orange curaçao, which look helpful. Other amari, however, may deserve a go. I'm thinking, for example, of Liqueur Strega.

Here is a link and the base recipe as boiled down by Chuck Taggart of *Gumbo Pages*

https://www.gumbopages.com

Mother-in-Law

2.5 ozs bourbon (he likes Buffalo Trace; nothing wrong with that. I'm going with the much cheaper Evan Williams 100 proof bonded)

1 tsp Cointreau (I'm using Pierre Ferrand Dry Orange Curaçao, which is not at all sweet. The drink, I believe, should be less sweet than the Cointreau makes it)

1 tsp Luxardo Maraschino

1 tsp simple syrup (I prefer agave)

2 dashes Peychaud's Bitters

2 dashes Angostura Bitters

2 dashes Regans' Orange Bitters

2 dashes Amaro Montenegro (or another Amer Picon stand-in. I'm now betting on Campari)

Prep: Put the ingredients into a mixing glass with cracked ice, stir, then strain into a cold coupe. Cherry for garnish.

And to scale it up to a quart for keeping handy in a non-leaded, or leaded, bottle:

740 ml bourbon

2.5 tsp Peychaud's Bitters

2.5 tsp Angostura Bitters

2.5 tsp Regans' Orange Bitters

2.5 tsp Amaro Montenegro (or whatever we finally decide)

1.5 ozs Pierre Ferrand Dry Orange Curaçao (or Cointreau)

1.5 ozs agave or simple syrup

Keep in a fine decanter. When you need a drink immediately, simply pour 3 ozs (or more) into a mixing glass with cracked ice, stir. Strain into a cold coupe. Cherry for garnish. Or serve it on the rock with a big clear cube.

Now, officially, the Bean House Cocktail.

12 August Wednesday

We continue to explore the Mother-in-Law with dry orange curaçao, Liquor Strega, and Campari. Fernet Branca is probably worth a shot, but do not hold me to it. Meanwhile, one more point about abstaining from alcohol.

One Last Note About the Virtues of Drinking (I promise)

We often see conflicting "medical" reports about the dangers and benefits of alcohol, though I'd say far more of the former. But it's worth noting that every civilization and some species of proto humans have drunk alcohol, mostly a lot of it. Indian elephants like alcohol and, apparently, are respectable drunks, if sometimes unwanted guests, when their long noses lead them to barge into home bars, which is unlikely to prove a problem for most of us.

It's not improbable that natural selection has favored drinkers as many of us are around, and these days, anyway, we last well past our child-bearing years. It's not impossible, for example, that a slightly drunk fellow, or elephant, is more charming than a teetotaler, gets the genetically favored females, and has superior children. As Robert Dunn, the Penny Poet of Portsmouth, wrote:

> Lift the dark wine to the light
> whether cheap or dearly bought
> Abstainers are a grumbly lot—
> nothing in the world moves right
> or stands still the way it ought
> Gently then with all your might
> lift this darkness to the light
> and leave the world to move or not.

And maybe, by lifting, you will move the world through natural selection.

13 August Thursday

Life After Our Expiration Date

Jenny's father Tim is at the stage where many, most even, of us might want to allow assisted suicide to carry us over the bar, and I've thought more than once that he was wrong not to look for an end rather than demand to keep going. He repeats himself a lot; can be tedious, I guess mostly without knowing it; and cannot see or hear but a fraction of any dialogue. He is a burden to Beth, constricting her life after she spent 40 or 50 years in the traces and is at last released from work…only to be mother to an ancient man.

Sadly, the Republican neighbors (it's true as far as I know that only Republicans hate it) have described their boxcar as a "gypsy wagon," an "ice cream stand," or a "hot dog shack." In fact, it is lovely and finely crafted, painted as a replica of a real railroad car on the Concord to Claremont line that ran along the Warner River not more than a few hundred feet from us.

I'm guessing we have not seen the last of the cabal of three households who want the boxcar out of the neighborhood. When Jennifer and her blind father walk down the street for exercise in the mornings, if these neighbors are out, they don't say hello, they literally turn away. Tim, at least, doesn't know. I suppose it is a double irony that all of them are his age and that he is a lifelong Republican. So much for empathy.

Anyway, tonight, with little vision, less hearing, and myriad hallucinations that too often take the place of anything real he might see, Tim used himself as the butt of a running joke about his maladies. The joke was self-aware in ways that made us laugh hard, that delivered us an evening of joy and some pathos, and that helped me see that hanging on past our expiration date can—for one who overcomes the humiliations and limitations—even be fulfilling.

But enough. The Mother-in-Law Cocktail was again much loved. Tonight's version used Campari, as a bitter, if not orange, substitute for Amer Picon. While I sampled the drink only through a bartender's straw, it struck me that with dry orange curaçao, Campari could be the finishing touch.

Meanwhile, I made Jenny and me each a St Charles gin and tonic, hers with Tanqueray (our least favorite) and mine with Plymouth Gin (better); followed by another with Tanqueray 10 (improving); Beefeater, and this one, my favorite of the night, was sweetest in a cocktail that needed more sweet (see below); and last, irresistibly, Hayman's Old Tom Gin (also excellent). Here is how to make a St Charles, which as far as I know, is the definitive New Orleans G&T. When in the city, get one at The Columns.

St Charles Gin & Tonic (from Chuck Taggart, *Gumbopages*)

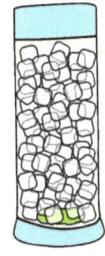

Lime: Peel as much skin off one lime as you can with a potato peeler. Do not be obsessive. If you leave half the skin, the world will not fall over. Put the skin in a Collins, highball, or pint beer glass. Almost any glass that allows room for your drink and for ice will work.

2 ozs gin (Try ones you like. This drink lets the flavor of the gin dominate and brings it out. I think it can help you understand why you prefer one gin to another. Again, we tried Tanqueray, Plymouth, Tanqueray No. 10, Beefeater, Hayman's Old Tom. My least favorite was Tanqueray because it is London Dry and made the drinks too bitter. Tanqueray No. 10 was sweeter and much better. And who knew Beefeater was really very sweet? I'd better do this again.)

4 dashes Peychaud's Bitters

Prep: Pour the gin into the glass with the lime peel and muddle them aggressively, if not destructively. Add the juice of the lime, ice till the glass is nearly filled, and the bitters. No need to be gentle here. Stir. Add Fever Tree or another premium tonic to fill the glass. Do not be cheap, using inferior tonic (Polar, Canada Dry, Schweppes). Rub the rim with one part of the spent lime. Stir and fill the glass as needed.

The effect is a gin version of the old New Orleans cocktail, Brandy Crusta. I'd like it for that alone. But certainly, here's a G&T that is more than a highball, as St. Charles Avenue is more than a street, that has class.

14 August Friday

Last night, enthusiasm for St Charles trials got the better of my judgment, drank a fourth, and as night follows day, feel desperately bad. The Luggnuts are rehearsing for an outdoor concert in nearby Contoocook next month. At practice, I served up the St Charles G&T, not very successfully really, and had one myself, adding a quarter ounce of Maraschino Liqueur that did not really change the bitterness of the drink. It may be time to accept that the St Charles is better as an idea than a reality. Still, its creator, Chuck Taggart, has good ideas, including one with allspice dram called Reveillon, that sounds interesting. This, then, is a note to self to give that Christmas-inspired cocktail a try…before Christmas.

15 August Saturday

Had lunch at Simon Pearce with J and her dad. We're daddy-sitting today, a term someone else must have coined, but that came to me in the face of the many people in my age group, Brick for example, who are doing some form of it. Irritatingly, Tim keeps saying, "Just you wait, Henry Higgins," for my turn. He'll join us tonight for Senie Hunt, a young man who grew up next door and is a terrific percussion guitarist, in an outdoor Covid concert, which, I'm guessing, Tim will neither see nor hear.

He heard well enough and tapped his foot. Back home, I sorely needed a cocktail and chose the modified Mother-in-Law. The chief modification was Campari in place of Amer Picon and its other surrogates, and it was great. But then, in the night, replacing simple syrup with maple syrup, which works for bourbon in an Old Fashioned, seemed another mine with potential. Sunday, I plan to clean and organize the bar and look for the decanter I have in mind for all future Mothers-in-Law, whose whereabouts escapes us tonight. As a result, I'm thinking one more trial with maple syrup and then on to the final recipe.

16 August Sunday

Not that it comes to mind every anniversary, but on this day 51 years ago, at age 19, I got married for the first time. Married at 19 was obviously a terrible idea for me, as it generally is for boys, which I was, and then a horrible husband, though we had a daughter, Juliet, who is a good person and has made her way in life very well despite my deficiencies as a father. Luckily, her mother moved on to a better husband.

Jenny and I watched *I Am Legend*, a Will Smith film about another pandemic, one that now seems a thousand times more plausible than it could have before our pandemic. A tense and powerful film, in which, as is true now, Vermont offers hope against the virus, or its spawn, such as an illegitimate takeover of our government by Trump and his Myrmidons.

But more important, the Mother-in-Law is now, I think, resolved. Here is the recipe for one of mine:

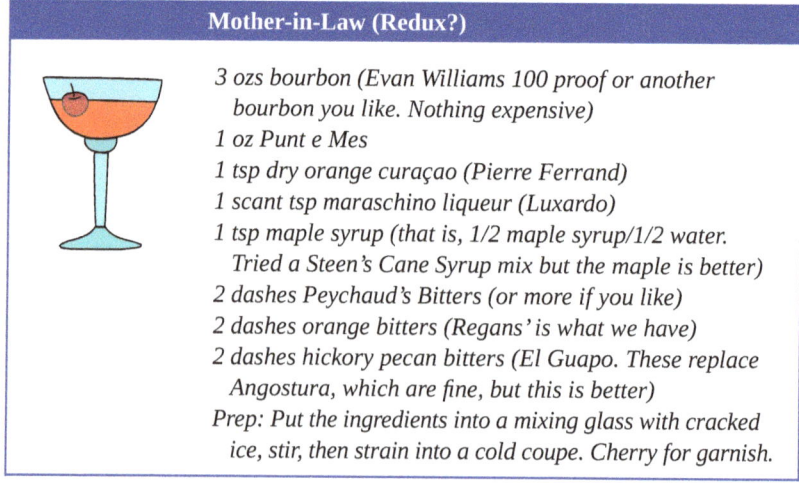

Mother-in-Law (Redux?)
3 ozs bourbon (Evan Williams 100 proof or another bourbon you like. Nothing expensive)
1 oz Punt e Mes
1 tsp dry orange curaçao (Pierre Ferrand)
1 scant tsp maraschino liqueur (Luxardo)
1 tsp maple syrup (that is, 1/2 maple syrup/1/2 water. Tried a Steen's Cane Syrup mix but the maple is better)
2 dashes Peychaud's Bitters (or more if you like)
2 dashes orange bitters (Regans' is what we have)
2 dashes hickory pecan bitters (El Guapo. These replace Angostura, which are fine, but this is better)
Prep: Put the ingredients into a mixing glass with cracked ice, stir, then strain into a cold coupe. Cherry for garnish.

The long search for the best version preparatory to making and decanting a quart is over... or almost over. I guess Fernet Branca in place of Punt e Mes deserves a try before closing the case. But after that one last try, we will have the Bean's Official Cocktail.

Reimagining the Bar

Now to the big event of the day, reimagining of the Bean Bar. Over time, since before the pandemic, we've expanded our stores until the bar had become a mess, disorganized, everything in the wrong place, or at least enough things. But today, somehow, a better system emerged, and the bar is clean, sensible, streamlined for cocktail making. The main spirits are on shelves to the right of the sink, and the complementary enhancers are across from the sink with me in between.

No surprise but making a cocktail when you're not shoehorned into a space disorganized and poorly built for the task, is a far greater pleasure than bending, stooping, searching. Among our friends, home bars usually are, well, not bars at all. The liquor hides away somewhere, emerging only for an evening with guests. Most stick with one cocktail, say a simple one such as a Gin & Tonic, and then stick with one gin and one brand of tonic. In the dim past I've found myself doing the unforgiveable, buying pre-mixed Margaritas or more recently Old Fashioneds. Yikes. But, thanks to the pandemic, the Bean has a great home bar—at least I think it is—and who's to judge?

17 August Monday

Tonight we have a band rehearsal, but I can't wait to get home to mix up a Fernet Branca Mother-in-Law. The practice reminded me that our friends Rick and Ruth used the Green Glass, a cocktail they had tried at the Bean, as the name for an app used in their now sold business. We'll be giving that one and Phil's Dorflinger rehearsals of their own this week.

As to the Fernet Branca Mother-in-Law: Excellent. I guess Punt e Mes or Fernet Branca work equally well. Give each a Ten. I'll be mixing the quart batch this week, choosing the one that finds its way into other cocktails less of the time and will again give the recipe when we get there.

18 August Tuesday

The Green Glass is the signature drink for Scrappy's Celery Bitters, and as such, it is almost unknown. I doubt that Rick and Ruth have had one of the cocktails since their app-naming inspiration.

Nor had we until last night. With high hopes, we gave the Green Glass a try, gave it a few shots of absinthe and different bitters, tried the recommended Plymouth Gin and Tanqueray No.10, all to no avail. This drink is not tasty, and the taste it has isn't very good.

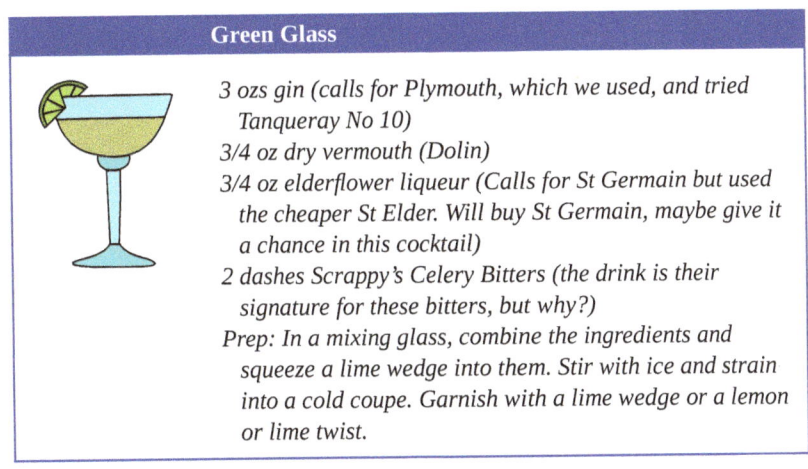

Green Glass

3 ozs gin (calls for Plymouth, which we used, and tried
    Tanqueray No 10)
3/4 oz dry vermouth (Dolin)
3/4 oz elderflower liqueur (Calls for St Germain but used
    the cheaper St Elder. Will buy St Germain, maybe give it
    a chance in this cocktail)
2 dashes Scrappy's Celery Bitters (the drink is their
    signature for these bitters, but why?)
Prep: In a mixing glass, combine the ingredients and
    squeeze a lime wedge into them. Stir with ice and strain
    into a cold coupe. Garnish with a lime wedge or a lemon
    or lime twist.

First taste lacked sparkle. Often a cocktail improves as the tongue adjusts. Not this one. I added absinthe and later Peychaud's and Boker's Bitters to no avail. And Jenny agreed that she was unimpressed. My tongue is not very sensitive, and I was never able to taste the celery bitters.

Seldom does a cocktail fall so short. Plymouth Gin is my favorite, and, for example Pink Gin, which is nothing but Plymouth Gin and Angostura Bitters, perhaps with some lemon rind, a mid-nineteenth century drink, is quite good. And perhaps a dash of Angostura would have improved the Green Glass. Okay, so maybe one more try, with St Germain and Angostura Bitters. Sheesh, a fellow should know when to give up. The world has far too many great cocktails to follow bad ones over the cliff of never-ending possibility. But here we are.

On the other hand, the name works quite well for an app.

19 August Wednesday

The mornings have been low 50s and even high 40s. Along the way to Portsmouth for a sail, many more trees than I expected were strikingly golden. It's time to bring out the last drinks of summer before moving to the darker shades of autumn.

Here is a tiki drink from Don the Beachcomber, dated around 1940. I love the *rhum agricole*, falernum, and allspice dram, so how could this go wrong?

Three Dots and a Dash

1/2 oz lime juice
1/2 oz orange juice (Used Valencia oranges, and they were great. I've had poor luck in cocktails with navel oranges and so it seemed worth trying other varieties.)
1/2 oz honey syrup
1/4 oz falernum (John D Taylor Velvet Falernum)
1/4 oz allspice dram (St. Elizabeth)
1.5 oz rhum agricole (Barbancourt)
1/2 oz aged rum (I used aged Flor de Caña for one and Cruzan for the other. Any good golden, or even not so good, should work)
1 dash Angostura Bitters
Prep: Shake hard with crushed ice. Pour everything into a footed pilsener glass or a regular pint glass and add ice to fill. Garnish with three cherries. Straw.

Wonderful, the first better than the second. For the second, rather than put a cut lime in the fridge, I used all of it, making the drink tarter. Mistake. One thing that makes this cocktail, and I've found this in others, is the flavor of the honey syrup, which extra lime overcomes. Also, I still have not made allspice dram, but have collected the ingredients and hope to make it soon. I love the stuff, and with Taylor's Velvet Falernum and fine Barbancourt Haitian rhum, what could be better? Finally, Pecan Chickory Bitters deserve a try in this fine cocktail.

We're not done with summer, though as Bob Dylan wrote, "It's not dark yet, but it's gettin' there."

20 August Thursday

At sea (literally was sailing) for a change. This is as good a time as any to bring up Jenny the sailor. When children, she and her brother sailed with their dad, Tim, on Lake Champlain in an old Lightning. He'd take them out in foul weather, and while it isn't a Great Lake, Champlain is big enough, seas rough enough, water cold enough that such a boat could find itself in trouble. Neighbors told Tim he was crazy for endangering his children.

The children wouldn't hear of it. And now when she is aboard a sailboat, Jenny is as intrepid as any sailor I've known, never afraid, always lighthearted and at ease. If she's had a hard day or week, raise a sail and she is herself again, cares left ashore. Her brother is the same. And in his dotage, where Tim cannot be at the helm, the feel of a boat, and the chance to sail with those brave children, keep him eager for any chance to put to sea.

21 August Friday

About 5:30 PM a thunderstorm, rare this summer, raged through. Wind and rain whipped into a frenzy, putting me in mind of a hurricane, which, in its New Orleans cocktail form, I'd been thinking about for a while.

The Original Hurricane

You'll recall the Mother-in-Law, which I yet have to make in its quart form. The original letter that revived that lost cocktail was sent from a New Orleans refugee in New York to his friend at home, Chuck Taggart, author of the gumbopages.com blog (I think it qualifies as a blog but could be just a website). At any rate, Taggart's account of the Mother-in-Law led me to look more closely at his cocktail work (he does food and other consulting as well in helping visitors to discover New Orleans), where I stumbled onto the Hurricane.

You can look for yourself at his history of the drink, which appropriately originated in a surfeit of rum at Pat O'Brien's as Prohibition ended (though some would dispute that Prohibition ever took hold in the Crescent City, where reports are that a stranger during that pandemic could at any time find a cocktail within minutes of arrival). More important, to me, than the history, is Taggart's description of the devolution of the Hurricane into a bright red, entirely artificial, sickly *sweet confection that only a tourist would drink.*

But Taggart, realizing that lemon wasn't always artificial, doggedly sought out the Original Hurricane, which is what we'll explore. The surprise is that this cocktail began as one of the relatively few holy grails of its kind, the three-ingredient cocktail. In its simplicity, absence of show, modest strength, and revelatory tastes, you get, to my way of thinking, an undervalued classic.

But here's the thing; to reach this holy grail you'll need passion fruit syrup. You can find it locally (at Shaw's grocery, for example) or remotely but nearby (the Boston Shaker), and it will be fine, better than fine. But Taggart makes the case that you can also go online to Aunty Lilikoi's and order the finest passion fruit syrup in the world, which I had done a few days ago, and which arrived from Hawaii surprisingly rapidly, sometime before the thunderstorm struck today.

Original Hurricane

2 ozs dark rum (Take your pick. I began with favorites, the Haitian rhums agricole, Barbancourt 15 year old and St James 7 year old. But any dark rum will shine. You could try Jamaican, such as Myers's or Appleton Estates. Flor de Caña from Nicaragua is a great one. Goslings Black Seal of Bermuda is favored among Taggart's friends. In short, you can't go wrong if you choose one you already like.)

1 oz passion fruit syrup (Aunty Lilikoi!)

1 oz lemon juice (or 1 oz lime juice. The original calls for lemon, but Taggart prefers lime, and he is right)

Prep: Measure the ingredients into a cocktail shaker. Add crushed ice. Shake until cold…cold in your grasping hands. Pour everything into a double-rocks glass. Top with crushed ice to fill the glass. Garnish with a flag of orange wedge and Luxardo cherry.

This storm will blow you all the way to Paradise.

22 August Saturday

The Goodriches joined us here to celebrate Tim's 87th birthday.

The Boxcar War Widens

Three households of Republican neighbors want the boxcar gone. It offends their sense that trailers are for the hoi polloi and inappropriate in a "historic neighborhood." Today, recalling the Health Inspector's caution that 90 days is the legal limit for living in an RV in our town, I wrote the town fathers explaining the situation and suggested it is time for Warner's very restrictive implementation of the Accessory Dwelling Units Law to be reconsidered. How can people fail to understand that offering a separate space for family members to live comfortably, safely, and inexpensively is a deep, humane necessity for the future?

Here we have our New England version of Donald Trump's objection to affordable housing in suburbs translated as a very appropriate-looking RV (we and the preponderance of our neighbors think) for old, debilitated relatives. Republicans love to criticize liberals for our nimby attitudes towards, say, power plants. But that, of course, is so long as neither power plants, people of color, nor the elderly in trailers move into their neighborhood.

Which all means it is time for a drink, and why not Three Dots and a Dash (see August 19), the Morse Code signal for victory.

23 August Sunday

At 4:00 expected for a patio dinner at the Kendall's exquisite house along with Rick and Ruth. The drink of the day, described in Friday's entry, is the original Hurricane. Luckily, we have bottles of Aunty Lilikoi's Passion Fruit Syrup to leave behind for both families. For the drink-of-the-night Hurricane, used 15-year-old Barbancourt as the rum, perhaps my favorite. But it is too dominating for this cocktail. An Appleton Estate or gold Flor de Caña would work better, I believe. Still, pretty darn good.

The Bungling Home Bartender

And then, starting tomorrow, with luck, we hope to spend much of the week aboard *Sea Sisters*, where we will shake down our seagoing bar in a most serious way. To that end, here at last is the Mother-in-Law by the quart:

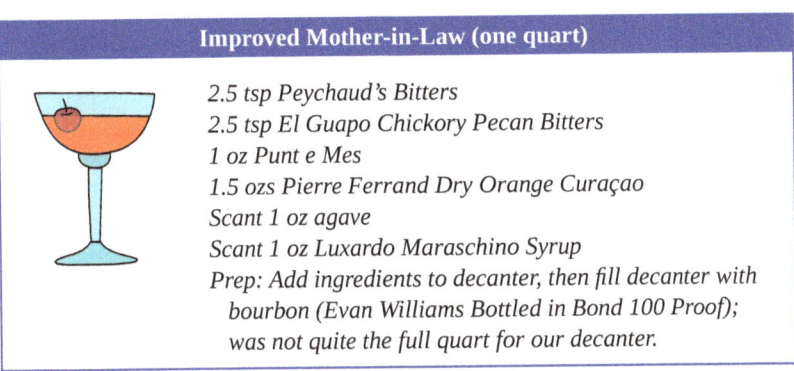

Improved Mother-in-Law (one quart)
2.5 tsp Peychaud's Bitters *2.5 tsp El Guapo Chickory Pecan Bitters* *1 oz Punt e Mes* *1.5 ozs Pierre Ferrand Dry Orange Curaçao* *Scant 1 oz agave* *Scant 1 oz Luxardo Maraschino Syrup* *Prep: Add ingredients to decanter, then fill decanter with* *   bourbon (Evan Williams Bottled in Bond 100 Proof);* *   was not quite the full quart for our decanter.*

Wait! What happened? Al says too sweet. He's right. Does not work in a rocks glass with one big cube. Too diluted. Lord, a mess. Proportions are wrong. Ingredients wrong.

Damn.

A conscientious bartender can bungle. But by no means should we throw out booze that remains perfectly suited for inebriating, even if it doesn't taste great. Just don't serve it to anyone but yourself.

And do not drink it as penance. Drink it after a hard day when a bad taste in your mouth deserves to be remembered for the lessons it can teach. I'm betting that after a few sips the taste will not matter, and the alcohol will have soothed whatever hurts.

24 August Monday

When you're preparing to go offshore, really on the sea, or maybe to go camping, it's critical to take stock of needs and supplies. Always begin with the cocktails you'll serve; that way, the rest of your tiny world will revolve around those decisions.

Traveling with Cocktails

To begin: Avoid the complicated. Ingredients take space, and because it's laborious to calculate which ingredient will run short first, make do with a few. I stick with the three-ingredient classic cocktails: Manhattans (for me Black Manhattans), Dark and Stormy, and Old Fashioned, Last Word, or, say, a Bees Knees. Over several days, even beyond one day, ice is not easy to keep. Unless you're a billionaire with a 100-foot yacht, ice-intensive, Tiki-style cocktails are pretty much out of the question. That said, citrus can be left out of the refrigerator or cooler with no ill effects for a few days; lemon trees in Florida are not air-conditioned. As a result, sours, citrus based, simple, and able to save many a mariner from the ravages of scurvy are a first-rate choice for a voyager or a camper. You'll not want to return from a weekend voyage with gums receding, teeth spontaneously evacuating your jaws, skin bruised and erupted in rash, hair follicles bleeding. Sours are a delicious way to avoid such an ugly fate.

When you think about cocktails, or just randomly turn to a page in your favorite book about them, the right one, as if conjured, often presents itself. I've never had a Bees Knees but have inadvertently been laying the groundwork for months. And so, the cocktail for the trip:

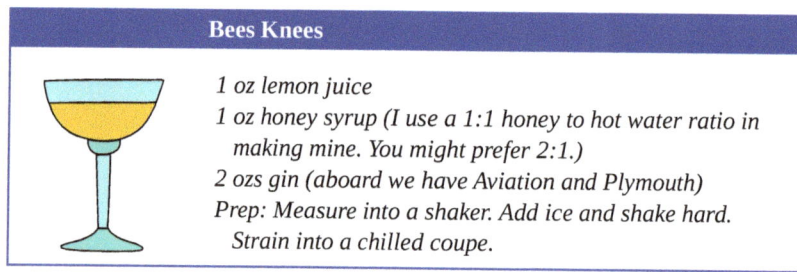

Bees Knees

1 oz lemon juice
1 oz honey syrup (I use a 1:1 honey to hot water ratio in making mine. You might prefer 2:1.)
2 ozs gin (aboard we have Aviation and Plymouth)
Prep: Measure into a shaker. Add ice and shake hard. Strain into a chilled coupe.

Pretty great. The Bees Knees is like high-test lemonade, but better. This slightly post-Prohibition cocktail should survive virtually any gin, if London dry. Old Tom would be too sweet. And it is easy. A relatively little-known classic. Not too heavy or boozy. Festive.

25 August Tuesday

A Strategic Turn in the Boxcar War

Today the Town Administrator in Warner replied to the letter I sent Sunday as follows:

Dear David and Jennifer,

I am writing to respond to your request for an extension for your relatives staying in Warner from Florida. The Board feels this is a hardship and has approved a 30 day extension. If that needs to be extended, the Board will review again as you get closer to the end of the 30 day extension.

Best regards,
Diane

Considerate as far as it goes, and we're pleased with the quick, kind response. Still, owing to weather and curiosity about Maine, Jenny and I spent the day traveling roads and asking town clerks about their implementation of Maine's ADU (Accessory Dwelling Unit) law. Warner's restrictiveness to housing old people on their children's property outside the big house led us here. And for most of the day we found Maine's townships and clerks little better than our slice of New Hampshire.

But we spotted a small house built in 1720 or 1730, with a big barn at 162 Old Road in Eliot, Maine, the town where we keep our sailboat, just over the border from New Hampshire. The house and property looked perfect, so we went to the town clerk in Eliot who helped us talk to the Officer in Charge of Municipal Enforcement, not her real title, but in majesty, close enough. And this young woman looked up the property, listened, and when we told her we came with a trailer for an 87-year-old man, and his care-taking wife, she waved away any difficulties, said if a neighbor questions their presence, she would tell them it's not permanent, "it is a trailer." Meanwhile, we can't raise the real estate agent. The house may well be under contract as any property is moving quickly, and we could be denied this dream house.

BREAKING NEWS: Kimberly Wade, the agent, just texted. House has knob and tube wiring. No insulation. Sold "As Is." Another Work House. Just what I want! Reading the reports now.

And deep into the night the reports intimidated me (Jenny was asleep; no need to wake her). The inspector was thorough, seemed to identify every defect, including more than a few I'll need to fix at the Bean unless we sell our house "as is." To give you a flavor of the scope of work this nearly $300,000 house requires in an absolute seller's market: insulation; plumbing; every appliance a modern house has; kitchen cabinets, sink, floor; a new sill; drip edges (which is to say, some things you may not have heard of); vermin riddance; and a bar.

Naturally, I couldn't sleep. And of course, by morning light, I'd persuaded myself this is a job for me. Sober, in a way.

26 August Wednesday

The agent is out of town, so no chance to see the house, and a cold front came through last night. Cool enough to require long pants, socks, a sweatshirt, and five layers for Jenny, with a wind in at least the teens, so we sailed.

An enormous gulf exists between day sailing and passage making. If you aim to go anywhere, think about Columbus, Magellan, Drake, Hudson, Lasalle, Vikings, and voyagers back a couple of thousand years. Today we watched in dread as waves broke over rocks a couple miles offshore in a place we've been past many, many times and even with our highly accurate, up-to-date electronic charts, had never seen before. We were within sight of a light on Boon's Island, where a ship broke up in the Eighteenth Century, before the light, and the marooned sailors, within easy eyeshot of the someday-to-be Maine Coast, resorted to cannibalism, as food and hope ran short.

A daysail, on the other hand, uses any wind from whatever direction to bend the canvas on a tack that suits you. And so today we sailed at length, no destination in mind, aware that places we might go—Biddeford Pool to the north, Gloucester to the south—would be easily reached, but of course the return tomorrow might be entirely different. After one of the best tacks of my life into the mouth of the Piscataqua River, we're at our mooring, have dined in a princely way, watching I-95 traffic and a ribbed sunset.

No Bees Knees either. One Black Manhattan for Jenny, two for me. A day at the helm in 20-knot winds, lee rail buried, tires a sailor. Jupiter is up, chaperoned by Saturn. Do we daysail, do what we've been happily doing? Or do we set a course, "To sail beyond the sunset"?

27 August Thursday

A complicated day, one when saying anything might be the worst thing possible under the influence, late at night. J and I slept till seven-thirty aboard *Sea Sisters*, had a fine breakfast (cooked by me), together repaired a helm-to-rudder connection. And later, we looked at the house in Eliot on a fine lot where the Town Regulator of Ordinance Administration said she (and the town) would gladly accept the in-laws in their boxcar trailer.

The 1720 house, on which I'd pinned my hopes, lay on a beautiful lot, had a fine barn and was a disaster, not updated, possibly ever, with beams turned to powder by beetles, little charm, and a maw ready to swallow every last dime of our savings.

We drove home and Al, who goes to UNH Saturday, requested a dinner of grilled salmon, baked potatoes, and strawberry salad. Jenny was happy to say "of course" and invited Tim and Beth to join us.

Somehow the evening came together, and Al took himself behind the bar, which he likes much more now that I've organized it. Indeed, I'd made Gefions (from Tux2) for Beth and me, which were okay but nothing Special:

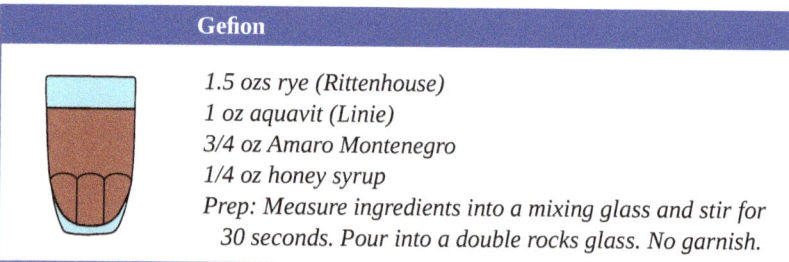

Gefion
1.5 ozs rye (Rittenhouse)
1 oz aquavit (Linie)
3/4 oz Amaro Montenegro
1/4 oz honey syrup
Prep: Measure ingredients into a mixing glass and stir for 30 seconds. Pour into a double rocks glass. No garnish.

As I say, these were undistinguished, tasting to my unrefined tongue like too many other, similar cocktails.

But then Al put himself behind the bar, rearranged the glasses so that our crystal from Denmark stands out. But he wanted a cocktail, like the apparently popular Mother-in-Law, that comes already made. We agreed a Black Manhattan in a leaded crystal decanter I've been around my whole life might answer. And it did.

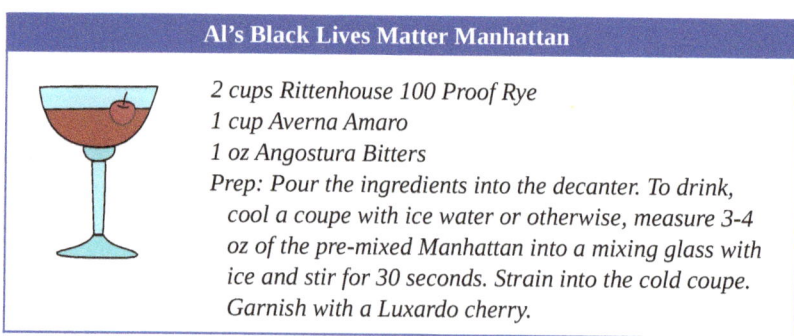

Al's Black Lives Matter Manhattan
2 cups Rittenhouse 100 Proof Rye
1 cup Averna Amaro
1 oz Angostura Bitters
Prep: Pour the ingredients into the decanter. To drink, cool a coupe with ice water or otherwise, measure 3-4 oz of the pre-mixed Manhattan into a mixing glass with ice and stir for 30 seconds. Strain into the cold coupe. Garnish with a Luxardo cherry.

This was so good that I drank a short Defective Mother-in-Law and discovered, measured out from the decanter, it wasn't bad. (Again, never throw booze away!) Indeed, I would have had more but could feel the territory was dangerously close to shameful drunkenness. Good sense, or at least some sense, prevailed.

28 August Friday

These pre-mixed cocktails awaiting our pleasure at the end of a hard day are beckoning, but I'm going to be restrained tonight. Still, they could be trouble and are surely a sight to behold in their beautiful containers, a labor saver, and sirens to be feared. I'm considering trying to find five or six that, like soldiers, stand ready to be deployed. I wonder if some of my unusual favorites, a Black Betty or Sawyer, for example, are candidates?

"We'll have to see," my psychoanalyst Cliff Hall used to say.

29 August Saturday

Selling the Ol' Bean Tavern

We're listing the Ol' Bean for sale, a life-changing move to what could well be my last home. We're hoping to find property in Eliot, Maine, where *Sea Sisters* lives. At best we'll buy a lot and put a log cabin kit on it. The town already has said it's okay to have the boxcar/trailer on our property, should we buy one, with Tim and Beth living in it. And I've explained to Jennifer that the log cabin must have a bar.

Those new things led to the pretty rare decision to make two brand new cocktails. First, the Bensonhearst, one in a large group of NYC cocktails that I happened upon in the very fine book *101 Cocktails* by Francois Monti. Here's the recipe

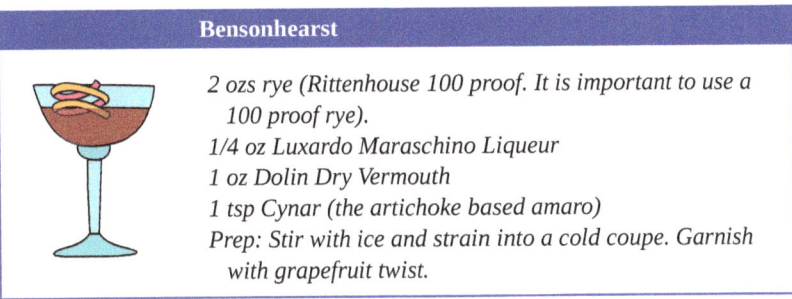

Bensonhearst

2 ozs rye (Rittenhouse 100 proof. It is important to use a
   100 proof rye).
1/4 oz Luxardo Maraschino Liqueur
1 oz Dolin Dry Vermouth
1 tsp Cynar (the artichoke based amaro)
Prep: Stir with ice and strain into a cold coupe. Garnish
   with grapefruit twist.

Loved it. Somehow that drop of Cynar shines through and gives this cocktail a complexity that makes it a drink to relish.

At the same time as I made the Bensonhearst for Jenny, I made a Greenpoint, named for another Brooklyn neighborhood, for me:

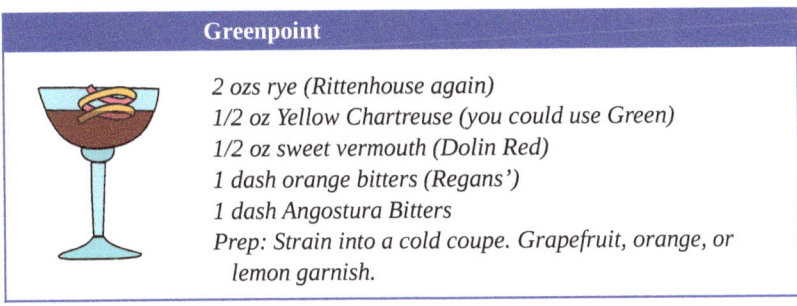

Greenpoint

2 ozs rye (Rittenhouse again)
1/2 oz Yellow Chartreuse (you could use Green)
1/2 oz sweet vermouth (Dolin Red)
1 dash orange bitters (Regans')
1 dash Angostura Bitters
Prep: Strain into a cold coupe. Grapefruit, orange, or
   lemon garnish.

The problem immediately became which we liked better, and tonight, Jenny liked mine, I hers.

We switched, and then I preferred hers and she mine.

But we loved them both, and both seem candidates for decanting, once we get more decanters. Why the grapefruit garnish? Mostly to keep a grapefruit from being wasted. It was, however, a fine garnish, adding aroma and flavor that blended with both drinks and overwhelmed neither.

30 August Sunday

We sailed with Jenny's brother Timmy, his wife Lidieth, their son Theo, and a terrified Papa Tim. Sustained winds of mid 20s with gusts to 34 knots, one reef in the main, and a partial jib. *Sea Sisters* showed herself off as the weatherly boat she is.

As I've noted, normally Tim enjoys boats and sailing despite his limitations. He likes to drink beer underway even if doing so leads inevitably to the need to take a leak, which turns into a complicated step-by-step process and at least once proved wet, embarrassing. His hallucinations, which a doctor friend said mostly result because without sight or hearing, his brain invents replacements for the stimuli that used to inform it, are especially lively aboard ship. He sees trees where there is water and parking lots or buildings where there are waves. He gets cold at about 75 degrees, on the North Atlantic it is never that warm, and wears everything he can to avoid sunburn. Yet, on he goes…at least until we scared him out of his wits today.

Once back at the mooring, I served Bees Knees and Black Manhattans from *Sea Sisters'* nautical bar to the huge satisfaction of all customers, including Papa Tim, who most of all, needed a drink stronger than beer.

31 August Monday

At sea.

*2025: our new bar. That's right, we survived the events you'll find in the coming pages.
And Chimes is in Williamsburg, Virginia...we hope for a long time.*

1 September Monday

Lifted weights, went spinning. Drove to Eliot to walk a lot we could buy. Band practice. Microwave dinner. Worry about Al at UNH. Needed a drink. But lordy, I was exhausted. On the Bean Bar sit two decanters, one with a bit of Mother-in-Law remaining and a second filled with Black Manhattan.

Oh my, this is dangerous. Down went the Mother-in-Law. On came the Black Manhattan. You might normally measure these into a cold coupe, but a double rocks glass with one cube of clear ice was so easy, so lovely, and jiggers so unnecessary, that I'd gone from cold sober to happily lit in a matter of minutes.

What are we going to do? Replenish the Mother-in-Law right away, perhaps vary it a bit. More important, get more decanters and find more cocktails served from them at any moment's notice! Here at last is the explosion I sought all those years ago: the Decantered Cocktail!

2 September Tuesday

With Jim Greason, brewed one of the red ales we've been making since 2010. Joined by my father-in-law, Tim, we drank beer along the way, enough that I'm afraid I forgot to pitch the yeast. Luckily, we discovered our error and pitched it.

Cocktail versus Beer

After a lifetime as a beer drinker, and an especially exciting few years as dozens of great breweries have opened all over New England, I've gotten clear that cocktails are my preference. For one thing, in the age of the New England double IPA, too many beers taste "chewy and fruity." The differentiation, as with wine, is so fine that my palate misses the point. To me, the many ways to make a Manhattan present a far wider range of tastes than the gamut of New England IPAs. But the Manhattan is one among a million cocktails, while IPAs are among only a relative handful of beer styles that I'd put past my lips, preferring nothing to bad beer.

And then with beer you have the matter of peeing in the night and a heaviness in the belly that play no part in cocktails. So yeah, let me find that Mother-in-Law by the quart recipe and see how it can be tweaked to be even better.

3 September Wednesday

Here, after a trip to the liquor store, is

> **Decantered Cocktail:**
> **Improved, Improved Mother-in-Law (one quart)**
>
> *2.5 tsp Peychaud's Bitters (ultimately used more like 1/2 oz)*
> *2.5 tsp El Guapo Chickory Pecan Bitters (same)*
> *1 oz Campari (Except, this time I am leaving out the Campari. That way, we can try Campari, Punt e Mes, Fernet Branca, and so forth with individual glasses of the cocktail)*
> *1.5 ozs Pierre Ferrand Dry Orange Curaçao*
> *Scant 1 oz agave*
> *Scant 1 oz Luxardo Maraschino syrup (from the cherry jar, that is)*
> *Prep: Fill decanter with bourbon (Evan Williams Bottled in Bond 100 proof. Some was left in the bottle for other uses).*

4 September Thursday

Decantering Minus One Ingredient: Why?

All we need is a dash of the amaro for an individual cocktail. I love to try slight changes in cocktail recipes and having all the other ingredients made up seems a perfect way. We may find other virtues of the Decantered Cocktail, besides that it's easy when you're weary. With that as the basis for perfection, we have a good beginning.

Leaving the Amer Picon substitute out of the decantered Mother-in-Law was a good idea. I made one with Campari, another with Antica Formula Vermouth, and a third with the gold Strega Liqueur, and would say that I liked them in that order, with the last too sweet. Lots more, such as Amaro Nardini, Aperol, and Fernet Branca on the amari side and Punt e Mes and Dolin red vermouths are possible. Adding the ingredient couldn't be easier and makes refinement straightforward.

Is this original? Could be. Never heard of it in any book.

5 September Friday

Off to frontline practice at Rick and Ruth's, with food brought in from our favorite Concord "Mexican" restaurant, Hermanos. All four of us have long loved Hermanos' Margaritas on the rocks, but this time I'll make the drinks.

Lots of Margarita recipes exist, but really, simple is better. I like orange curaçao in place of Cointreau or another triple sec, and this time will try a high-end version, the Pierre Ferrand Dry Orange Curaçao. Also spied a Margarita in Difford's Guide made with falernum, so I think that too deserves a try, though it violates the "simple is better" maxim. Because I'll mix these in bulk beforehand and then shake them before serving, here are the ratios, rather than amounts:

> **Falernum Margarita**
>
> *1 part Pierre Ferrand Dry Orange Curaçao*
> *1 part lime juice*
> *1/4 part Taylor's Velvet Falernum*
> *2 parts reposado tequila*
> *Prep: Shake hard and strain into ice-filled, salt-rimmed glass. To rim, use a spent lime or a wedge to wet the outside, not the inside, dummy, of the glass. Diamond Crystal Kosher Salt, which does not melt as easily as Morton's owing to the way it is dried, adheres and won't melt away. Garnish with a lime wedge.*

Besides Margaritas, this seems like the time to try a Pisco Sour. I bought pisco on the last trip to Totally Liquored and haven't opened the bottle, have never tried the stuff. Lidieth, our Costa Rican sister in law who travels Latin America, was talking about Pisco Sours on the sailboat last weekend with great reverence.

Pisco

Pisco is a grape-based brandy, the national spirit of Chile and Peru, and the Pisco Sour is the beloved national drink of both. That said, in 1948 David Embury, the Wallace Stevens of cocktail writers, in that he was a lawyer, not a bartender (many would point out Stevens was an insurance executive and argue he really was not a poet) is regarded by many as the best cocktail writer of his era. Of pisco he said, "Another grape brandy that definitely I do not recommend comes from Peru and is known as Pisco. Such aging as it receives (and to judge by its flavor, that is very little) is done in unglazed crocks or jars and not in wood. I am told it is quite popular in Peru—which is one reason I am satisfied to remain in the United States" (Embury 70). By its clear look we can say that pisco still is not aged in wood, but we hope it has improved. If not, we can be in concert with Embury, since Americans are now pariahs in Peru, as we are everywhere.

I'll not make these in bulk, however, and may use some lemon (calls for lime).

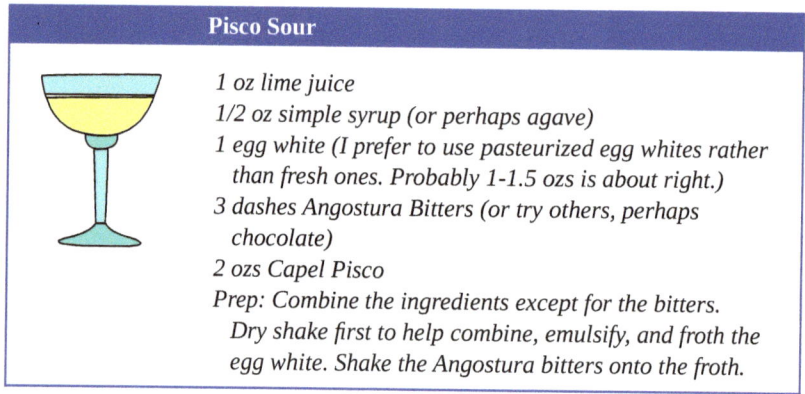

Pisco Sour

1 oz lime juice

1/2 oz simple syrup (or perhaps agave)

1 egg white (I prefer to use pasteurized egg whites rather than fresh ones. Probably 1-1.5 ozs is about right.)

3 dashes Angostura Bitters (or try others, perhaps chocolate)

2 ozs Capel Pisco

Prep: Combine the ingredients except for the bitters. Dry shake first to help combine, emulsify, and froth the egg white. Shake the Angostura bitters onto the froth.

Dry Shaking

Clap the parts of your shaker together extra firmly, or the pressure from the dry shake may blast them apart, a messy, irritating, wasteful annoyance. Then, shake with ice. The result should be a creamy head.

Despite Embury's reputation and his cavils, these were fabulous. Embury may well be the Wallace Stevens of bartending.

6 September Saturday

The Pisco Sour was the hit of last evening (Friday), which felt more like "the old days" than any since the pandemic began. We even, briefly, went indoors to look at the video about the Luggnuts and the Ol' Bean. Rick seemed amusedly interested in a decantered cocktails business.

Tonight, I'm writing at the bar, Tim and Beth coming to dinner. It's cool out. Perhaps it is time for a Sawyer, which I have been looking forward to all summer.

No Sawyer, rather, a Trinidad Sour, or two. And for Beth a Pisco Sour. And a couple of Mothers-in-

Law, to be discussed. And finished off yesterday's batched Margaritas. Yikes!

The Trinidad Sour could be the best drink ever, certainly for aroma. The powerful smell of the ounce of Angostura Bitters is better than hops in a New England double IPA. Be sure to pry the plastic off the top of the bitters so that they will pour. But the next time you use the bottle, don't forget that the bitters will pour, not dash their way out.

And the flavor matches the smell. Orgeat. But where recipes call for rye, I used rum, particularly Barbancourt 15-year-old. And although the recipe, or a different recipe with rye, appears earlier in the Diary, here it is again:

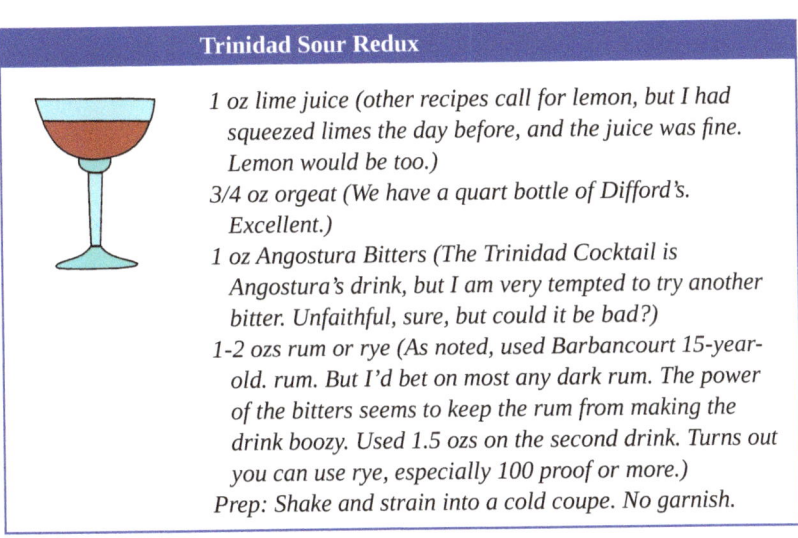

Trinidad Sour Redux

1 oz lime juice (other recipes call for lemon, but I had squeezed limes the day before, and the juice was fine. Lemon would be too.)

3/4 oz orgeat (We have a quart bottle of Difford's. Excellent.)

1 oz Angostura Bitters (The Trinidad Cocktail is Angostura's drink, but I am very tempted to try another bitter. Unfaithful, sure, but could it be bad?)

1-2 ozs rum or rye (As noted, used Barbancourt 15-year-old. rum. But I'd bet on most any dark rum. The power of the bitters seems to keep the rum from making the drink boozy. Used 1.5 ozs on the second drink. Turns out you can use rye, especially 100 proof or more.)

Prep: Shake and strain into a cold coupe. No garnish.

Keep in mind that Angostura Bitters are just shy of 90 proof. That, with the rum, makes for a properly powerful drink, and, if I'm right about the power of the bitters to suppress the taste of booziness, this could become a devil of a drink.

From the two Trinidad Sours, moved along to Mothers-in-Law. Remember, in making up the decantered version we left out the Amer Picon substitute to try different possibilities, such as Campari. Tonight, after pouring the Mother-in-Law into a double rocks glass with one big cube of clear ice, I added Punt e Mes. The amount was not specific, perhaps just short of an ounce, and used color to tell me when to stop. I think this will prove the best Amer Picon substitute. It helped the drink gather, oh, let's call it, majesty. For a second go—as you see, anything for science—used Fernet Branca, which I did not like quite as much, but which also is mighty fine.

Finished the evening by downing the Margaritas, taking a half-full glass up to bed. I must have been disagreeable, and drunk, as J gathered up her blanket and slept in another room. Got to be careful, folks.

7 September Sunday

A needed break.

8 September Labor Day

Is there a working person's drink to celebrate this holiday? Lite Beer? "Beer keeps the workingman strong," Brits used to say, I think. What about a cocktail? A Martini? Something with vodka? I see the Paloma (a Margarita) and the Boilermaker (whiskey and beer), but both sound awful to me. Yet, years ago a Scotsman showed me that scotch and beer are fine together and go right to your head. You can sip slowly and chase a good malt whiskey with a beer.

Whether it is a working person's drink or not, a Whiskey Smash looks appropriate to the day and to the time of year.

Whiskey Smash

2 ozs bourbon (Evan Williams 100 proof)
2 lemon wedges (halve the lemon longitudinally, then
   halve that at the equator. Cut the quarter lemon in half
   along its pole-to-pole axis. Follow that?)
3/4 oz simple syrup
6-8 mint leaves
Prep: In the shaker, muddle two of the lemon wedges that
   resulted from your geography lesson. Add the other
   ingredients (don't forget the mint) and ice. Shake hard.
   Double strain into a double rocks glass with one large
   clear cube. Mint sprig for garnish.

Let's begin with the mint. It's late summer, and the mint in our boat garden is lush and lively. This cocktail is a good way to make use of some of it before frost kills everything. And I like that it isn't muddled or overpowering but fresh and present.

When you shake, the ice will break up the mint leaves. About ice, I've recently come to believe that one large cube and a few smaller ones in the shaker is a valuable practice. The weight of the large cube seems to power mixing of the ingredients, especially with help from the rattling smaller ones.

Double Straining

In this cocktail, the ice breaks up the mint leaves, so if you strain as usual with a Hawthorne strainer (pictured), parts will fall into the drink and aren't pretty. By pouring through the Hawthorne into a mesh strainer and into the glass, you'll get a clean drink. It's kind of fun to do.

The drink, and I had a second made with Canadian whisky, is lightweight. I'm guessing people who don't care much for the flavor of spirits, who like vodka, will find this an agreeable use of Canadian whisky. You'll find recipes for it on sites for Seagram's and Crown Royal, which are, I'd say, the vodka of whiskys. I tried bitters, but they didn't help and work against the natural character of the drink. The Whiskey Smash is refreshing and easy to make, puts mint to good use, is not fussy. It would be a nice surprise cocktail to serve someone you suspect is not much of a drinker and asks you to make up something they'll like.

Made with bourbon the cocktail we're considering is a Whiskey Smash; made with any Canadian grain spirit, it is a Whisky Smash. Why? Somehow, to make the world more confusing, lexicographers have agreed that made in the United States or Ireland you have whiskey. Made in Scotland, Canada, or Japan, you get whisky. Sheesh!

The lightweight nature of the Whiskey Smash was driven home forcefully when I poured a taster of Mother-in-Law and added a bit of Amaro Nardini and shard of ice to it. Our friend Rick Lugg's birthday is next week, and because he showed interest in the Decantered Cocktail, I'm going to give him a quart of Mother-in-Law. Our pal Bob Nardini is a legend of braininess, who, in giving me a book written by a poet who loves Martinis, probably did more to propel me toward cocktails than anyone else. By mixing a Mother-in-Law with Amaro Nardini as the Amer Picon replacement, I think Rick—like Bob and me an ex-Catholic—will find the Nardini transubstantiation the best way to achieve a Nardini-like glow, even if imagined.

Whether it is the contrast to the Whiskey Smash or the fit of the Amaro Nardini, this version of the Mother-in-Law seemed the best yet. It has a deep, warm, full character all its own that few cocktails achieve. I can't wait to try a full double-rocks glass of it!

9 September Tuesday

Tomorrow is my brother Denis's 65th birthday. I'm thinking a quart of Mother-in-Law will help ease him through this marker of old age. Used Punt e Mes as the mystery ingredient.

10 September Thursday

Somehow Wednesday got lost. Wonder where it went? (Turns out August has 31 days. I've been a day ahead for a third of a month. Call me Early.)

We're off (Jenny, Tim, and Beth) to look at a small house on a nice lot in Kittery. Move to Maine? The Ol' Bean is too big, and in Maine we'd be near *Sea Sisters*, plus we like the coast. If we move there, it'll be a big deal, and I'm nervous about it. This is when you need a drink.

I'm thinking of the Dorflinger, Phil's favorite, a classic that I've never tried: gin, absinthe, orange bitters. The gins I see recommended are Plymouth, St George, and Tanqueray 10. But I'm guessing the absinthe is key. For one, real absinthe should be high test, make that HIGH test, between 120 and 140 proof. The best we can do here at the moment is 110 proof. Here's the beginning recipe:

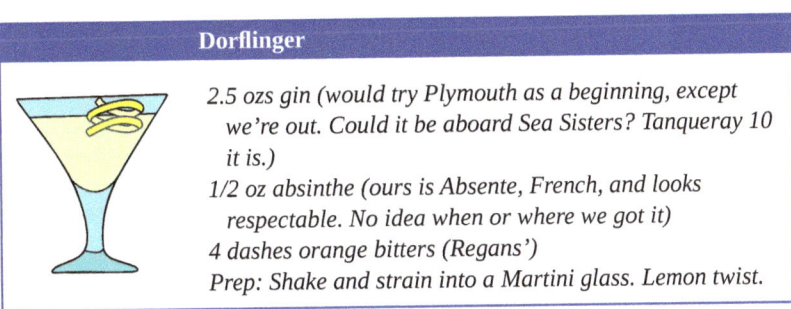

Dorflinger

2.5 ozs gin (would try Plymouth as a beginning, except we're out. Could it be aboard Sea Sisters? Tanqueray 10 it is.)
1/2 oz absinthe (ours is Absente, French, and looks respectable. No idea when or where we got it)
4 dashes orange bitters (Regans')
Prep: Shake and strain into a Martini glass. Lemon twist.

This is pretty much an old-style Martini with absinthe in place of the much weaker vermouth and with more bitters, mostly to offset the strange taste of the absinthe. It should knock your head off. No wonder

Phil likes it.

But it's only 4:30, and we're off to the coast. With luck, we'll return early enough to try this one, though not a day early.

11 September Friday

The luck was a restaurant in Portsmouth called the Black Trumpet that charmed us in every respect, so much so that we bought the owner-chef's cookbook.

Manhattan: Another Test of a Restaurant Cocktail (continued)

I began by ordering a Manhattan, part of the series of trying cocktails at restaurants, proving they fall far short of what we can make for ourselves. Not the first one at the Black Trumpet, nor the second one.

The cherry: Luxardo Maraschino, so right away you know the bartender is serious. Served in a cold Martini glass. The vermouth: Antica Formula, which the waiter, when asked, knew it to be. Among the choices of rye, I picked Woodford Reserve, much more expensive than any rye I buy. Well, it could be worth the price.

The success of this cocktail (and we're not going to go on about the food, which was fabulous) leads me to wonder if I should be trying other amari, besides the Averna, in the Black Manhattan?

Dorflinger at Last

We got to the cocktail hour, and I mixed up a Dorflinger as described. Drank three, the second with Beefeater, which did not suit as well as the Tanqueray 10. Used closer to three ozs of gin and 3/4 oz of absinthe, a proportion that seemed just right.

My friend Phil, turns out, drinks his on the rocks, a great surprise. This is a Martini, rather than a glass of cold gin; it's got flavor, body, depth, character. Why dilute it with ice?

The Plymouth Gin is aboard *Sea Sisters*, so will need to try it later. But you could decant Dorflingers by mixing them, then putting the bottle into the freezer. I'm guessing that they would be better than immediately mixed and could survive temperatures near absolute zero, especially with a 140-proof absinthe.

And with that, we'll leave you to dream of frozen decantered cocktails.

12 September Saturday

We found ourselves, along with Jennifer's family, dining outdoors at a Mexican restaurant in Portsmouth, ordering house Margaritas as soon as we could strip off our masks. Lidieth, told the Venezuelan waitress which members of our party spoke Spanish (including me, a gigantic exaggeration), but who knows, perhaps our cocktails appeared faster as a result. And I faked understanding just fine.

Margarita: When a Mexican Restaurant Goes Wrong (continued)

Faster, maybe. Better, I hope not. Once again, we have restaurants making cocktails on the cheap from ingredients that never drew breath, or sucked water from soil, rendered in imaginary colors, this one an other-worldly green, that tasted bad, and weak, but—true to the reportorial calling—I had two.

Sadly, because even if the tequila contained agave, which I doubt, it was virtually impotent. We left the restaurant barely transformed from the dismal figures we were on arrival, despite that the food was acceptable.

I think what galls me most about such on-the-cheap, though very expensive (they cost $12 apiece or more) cocktails is that they forgo lime juice, even frozen, for something made in a lab, replacing real citrus with syrup that could never spoil, rendered in a color that could only be poison. Mostly we must be resigned to doing our best drinking at home.

13 September Sunday

Lidieth travels Central and South America. She has educated taste and mentioned while sailing a couple of weeks ago that she'd seen pisco in the Bean Bar and loves a Pisco Sour. I believe in Lidieth for many reasons and, you may recall, soon made these fine cocktails. They were delicious. But Lidieth has not been able to find pisco, so I brought along our bottle together with the other ingredients needed for sours.

The awful Margaritas intruded, and no Pisco Sours were made in Portsmouth yesterday. But a lot of them were made in Warner beginning at 6 pm tonight. A major reason, beyond the need to taste real, freshly squeezed citrus, was that I thought the Pisco Sour might nicely offset the smoky, savory flavor of Goody Cole's takeout barbecue. Goody Cole was a witch, and apparently through a spell, this is New Hampshire barbecue good enough to eat in Texas.

Of course, I was right about the suitability of the Pisco Sour.

14 September Monday

Made Rick Lugg the latest version of a Mother-in-Law, which by now is different enough from where it began that the reconstructed cocktail deserves a name of its own. Here you go:

Bob Nardini and I have sat on the ground till sunrise and told sad tales of former lives many times. No one loves a strong cocktail more than him. My hope is that, by drinking quantities of the Mother-in-Law Nardini, patrons of the Bean will be persuaded they're as smart and worthy as Bob.

I've tried many amari and vermouths as replacements for Amer Picon, and fittingly, none bests Amaro Nardini. The other measures of ingredients are the result of extended trials.

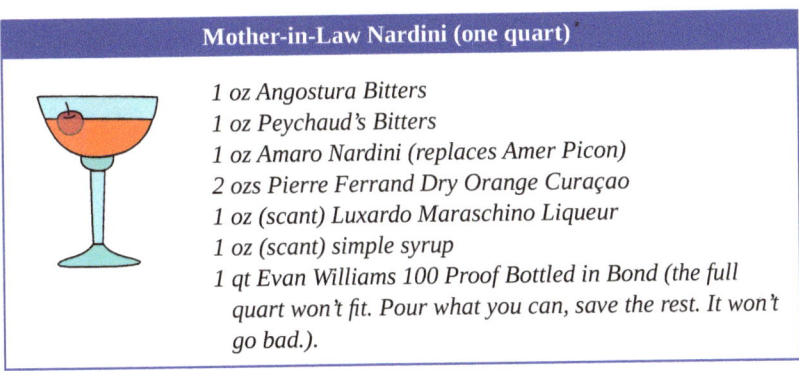

Mother-in-Law Nardini (one quart)*
1 oz Angostura Bitters
1 oz Peychaud's Bitters
1 oz Amaro Nardini (replaces Amer Picon)
2 ozs Pierre Ferrand Dry Orange Curaçao
1 oz (scant) Luxardo Maraschino Liqueur
1 oz (scant) simple syrup
1 qt Evan Williams 100 Proof Bottled in Bond (the full quart won't fit. Pour what you can, save the rest. It won't go bad.).

The first quart to leave the Bean was prepared for the 65th birthday of Rick Lugg, one of Bob's greatest admirers and best friends. Nothing can make turning 65 easier than a dose of the Nardini. Nothing but a double dose.

15 September Tuesday

A tremendously stressful day. J and I rarely fight but today came down to yelling and declaring. I'd found the "ideal house" for us about two minutes from our boat in Eliot, Maine; Jennifer had not. (In the light of another morning she was more right than I was.) But we'd left home at 6:30 am and by the time we returned, fought, and realized Tim and Beth were coming to dinner, we were wretches.

Luckily, enough Mother-in-Law was in its decanter for both of us, and we were saved, saved by cocktails. I went on to Black Manhattan, which put every care in the rearview mirror.

16 September Wednesday

Woke next morning to the idea that we should think about two sailboats: one, maybe a catamaran, in the south for winter, and *Sea Sisters* up here. To hell with a house. What it comes down to is that those inventors of bitters and cocktails who understood their medicinal qualities were right, the effects more widely valuable than penicillin, quinine, or the polio vaccine, and never mind Covid.

Yes, so I woke up thinking we should buy a sailing catamaran, keep it in Florida, live on it over winter. We'd keep *Sea Sisters* in Maine and get an apartment in Ipswich. Figured Jenny would think two sailboats was nuts, but, surprising woman, she liked the idea. We're ready for something different. And a different cocktail symbolically sealed the deal, though not till evening

Had apple-pear brandy I bought in Berlin years ago. Chuck Taggart, the New Orleanian who did more than anyone else to reinvigorate both the Mother-in-Law and the Original Hurricane, has a drink called the Réveillon that uses pear brandy, and here it is:

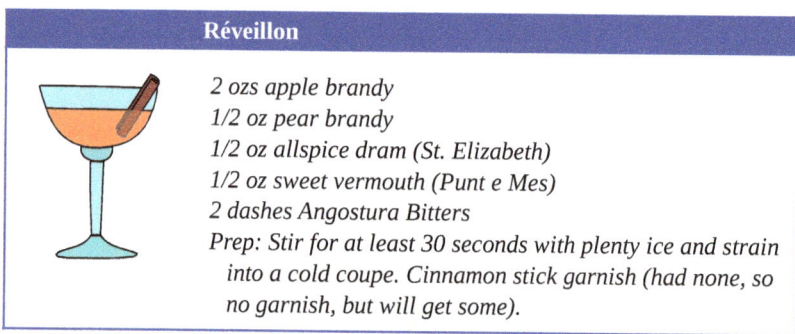

Réveillon
2 ozs apple brandy
1/2 oz pear brandy
1/2 oz allspice dram (St. Elizabeth)
1/2 oz sweet vermouth (Punt e Mes)
2 dashes Angostura Bitters
Prep: Stir for at least 30 seconds with plenty ice and strain into a cold coupe. Cinnamon stick garnish (had none, so no garnish, but will get some).

This drink is wonderful. The aroma by itself is so good and powerful that you'll want to inhale with each sip. And I sipped slowly, unusually so for me, and made a total of five for Jenny, Beth, and me. I wasn't tempted to change anything but would love to get real pear brandy and perhaps try Antica Formula or Dolin Rouge in place of Punt e Mes. But really, it is hard to imagine that any change would improve this fine, dark, late-night cocktail.

Here's to something new!

17 September Thursday

The Luggnuts played our first concert since February. Getting ready has been a grind for me, but the concert was fun, being on stage enlivening. Afterward, the band sat around the bandstand in Contoocook, dined, drank beer, talked. Except for a beer, I did no drinking.

18 September Friday

Made a new batch of Mother-in-Law Nardini, which, because Jenny's mom, Jean, is here, could be tonight's cocktail, at least for Jean. For Jenny, me, perhaps not. I'm about to investigate *Liquid Intelligence* for recipes. It is probably the most scientific book about cocktails.

Oh, and now I'm thinking one sailboat, a larger monohull than *Sea Sisters* or a catamaran, is the better idea as it requires sailing to and from Florida every year. A few monohulls in the 40-foot range have a cockpit in the center rather than the stern and as a result can have an aft cabin, typically for the owners. That's us. *Sea Sisters* is a fine cruising ship, but her v-berth in the bow is poorly suited for living aboard.

Catamarans, on the other hand, are expensive, and while fast, do not really look like my idea of a sailboat.

Anyway, the cocktail of the evening is a Spruce Goose.

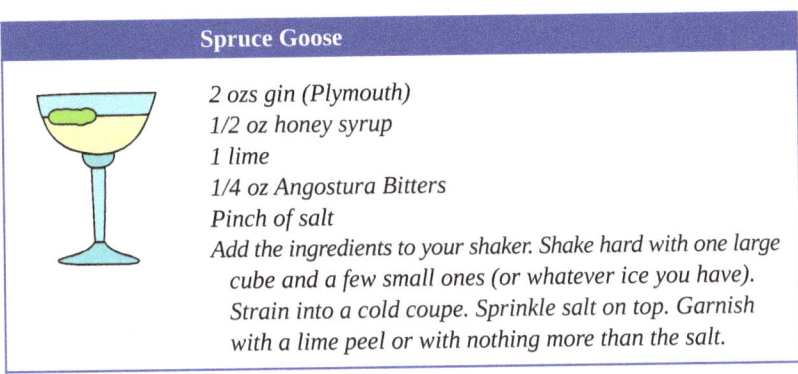

Spruce Goose

2 ozs gin (Plymouth)
1/2 oz honey syrup
1 lime
1/4 oz Angostura Bitters
Pinch of salt
Add the ingredients to your shaker. Shake hard with one large
*   cube and a few small ones (or whatever ice you have).*
*   Strain into a cold coupe. Sprinkle salt on top. Garnish*
*   with a lime peel or with nothing more than the salt.*

This cocktail is terrific, simple, and the ingredients are ones you should have. The sweet and sour of the honey-lime, the poignance of the gin-Angostura, stand together and separately. But it is the large dose of Angostura that transforms the cocktail into something special. But why Spruce Goose? Because it's one of a kind?

Meanwhile, Grandma Jean irritated me and made Jennifer murderous. The rule is, always has been during our marriage, that Jenny can take no more than a few minutes of her smart, but highly opinionated, mother before boiling over. Jean likes the idea of being a good mother and grandmother but generally finds the reality, say, taking care of the needs of children, especially boring. And of course, none of us, by her lights, are much good at the disciplinary routines parents should practice.

19 September Saturday

We worked hard outdoors preparing the house to sell. Jennifer is, I believe, obsessed. At the end of the hard-working day, she asked for a Black Manhattan. I poured hers from the decanter and made another using the more expensive Woodford Rye and Amaro Nardini. Can't say the latter was much, or any, better. They're both damn good.

20 September Sunday

Al and Skylar were here, so made a Spruce Goose for him, and he made a terrible Réveillon. Maxim: Any drink, except at a bad bar, is better than none.

21 September Monday

In the search for something new, I went, as is often the case, to *Death & Company*. I'd marked page 218 some time back because, apparently, it had several cocktails that were makable with ingredients on hand. Yet, this is a brandy section of the book, cognac and apple, and really, I'm not crazy about those two, except, I guess, cognac in a Sidecar.

But here's how it went. Made two Lilywhackers to begin, one for J.

Lilywhacker

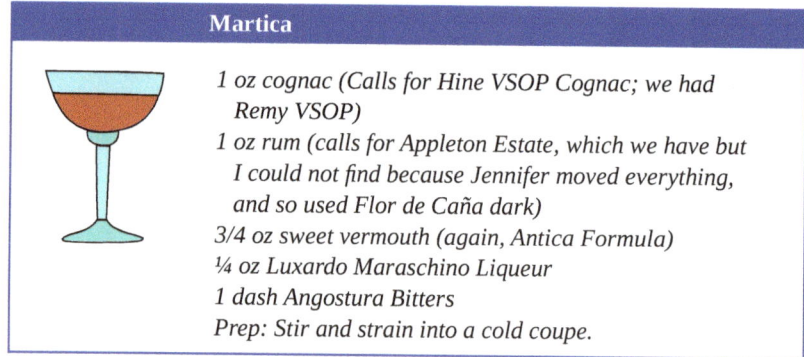

2 ozs applejack (the recipe calls for Laird's Bonded Apple Brandy, which you cannot get here, so made do)
3/4 oz Carpano Antica Formula (you can normally get this at Totally Liquored in Danvers, but not last time I visited. That said, it is easy to find. Don't be fooled by "Carpano Antica Formula" and "Antica Formula"; they are one and the same.)
1/2 oz Cointreau
1 dash Bittermens Xocolatl Mole Bitters (we had it so I used a couple dashes)
Prep: Stir everything over ice and strain into a cold coupe. No garnish.

This was okay, but on a second try I added an extra ounce of VSOP Calvados, and switched to Dubonnet Rouge, added more bitters and a quarter ounce of Cointreau. This was much better, perhaps even good enough to try again, though I'm fuzzy about that. But it was dark, mysterious, and more bitter than sweet.

Should have stopped with that second Lilywhacker, but a restless spirit, I moved on to

Martica

1 oz cognac (Calls for Hine VSOP Cognac; we had Remy VSOP)
1 oz rum (calls for Appleton Estate, which we have but I could not find because Jennifer moved everything, and so used Flor de Caña dark)
3/4 oz sweet vermouth (again, Antica Formula)
¼ oz Luxardo Maraschino Liqueur
1 dash Angostura Bitters
Prep: Stir and strain into a cold coupe.

Sounded promising but left me flat. That is, this tasted like a lot of other boozy but indistinct cocktails that seem especially common when stirring is called for. Sipped it in bed but, and to say truth, was not really in the mood for a drink, though willing to perform due diligence, and was never impressed. Unlikely to return, even if all the recommended ingredients appear.

22 September Tuesday

Back to the Spruce Goose. Have been thinking and saying to anyone who might care that Plymouth is my favored gin but tried Beefeater on the second round and believe it was better. Maybe I like Plymouth because commentators (Dr. Cocktail comes to mind) praise Plymouth rather than because I really prefer Plymouth. This would be a flaw in a person who aims to guide taste. More than that, I'll now have to try different gins, ryes, rums, and so forth in cocktails, which means more to drink. Damn, how lucky can you get!

23 September Wednesday

The liver took a well-earned break from alcohol today. I worry about this, about drinking every day.

Daily Cocktail Drinking

Medical guidelines discourage it. Yet, I normally feel none the worse for drinking, so long as I don't wander too deeply into the broken ground, or should I say, choppy seas, of too much or way too much. It could be that the results are insidious, creeping all the time without your knowing until, like a corroding drain or clogging artery, all at once when it is too late, your liver, brain, or some other part has eroded to the point that it bursts. (Sorry for that ugly image.) Meanwhile, the occasional break can't hurt anything but my disposition.

24 September Thursday

For the first time in a long while, the Last Word. A classic that has come up many times in this account but only once before as a cocktail in its own right. Here it is:

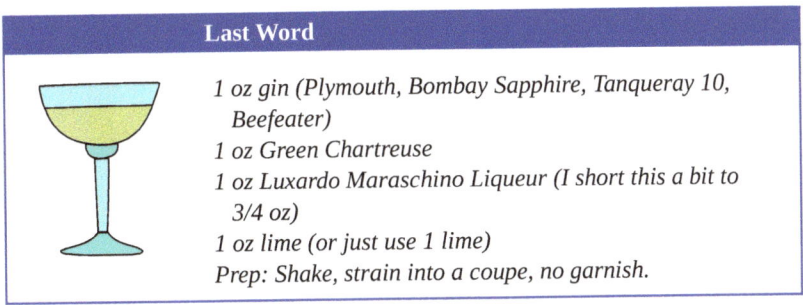

Last Word
1 oz gin (Plymouth, Bombay Sapphire, Tanqueray 10, Beefeater) 1 oz Green Chartreuse 1 oz Luxardo Maraschino Liqueur (I short this a bit to 3/4 oz) 1 oz lime (or just use 1 lime) Prep: Shake, strain into a coupe, no garnish.

The gin doesn't seem to matter; they're all good. This powerful cocktail is delicious, deserves to be drunk more often. Best of all, perhaps, is that there is almost nothing to remember, unless you short the Maraschino. That is, the amounts of ingredients are all the same (most recipes say 1 oz lime juice; 1 lime works just as well). If you're out of lime, use half a lemon (usually, because, at least where we buy lemons, they're much bigger than limes.). Easy, delicious, strong. Sounds like an advertisement.

25 September Friday

Sitting early morning in the Manchester, NH, airport on the way to New Orleans and, among many other fascinating adventures, a visit to the Cocktail Museum. Seeing everyone, or almost everyone, in masks is surreal, like something from a B movie. But this, after 6 months, is what we've come to.

Chicago Midway, busy if not crowded, felt dangerous, like I should come out of here and quarantine. Over the years I've always thought of air travel as submitting to being swallowed by a beast. It does what it likes until spitting you out the other end. Once, a woman sneezed hard on me walking through the Denver airport, and I soon came down with the worst case of flu I've ever had. Seems a real possibility inside this Covid beast.

Arrived New Orleans. The Prius Danny turned over to me is great, and already I like it. In the afternoon Danny and I sailed in a light breeze, and Dom, my oldest grandson, and his dad CJ came from Belle Chasse to join us for the evening. CJ and I had a pretty good beer from a brewpub near Danny's, and we ate dinner outdoors at the center of the Tammany Trace Bicycle Path because the Navy won't let any sailor (CJ is a Commander in the Navy) dine in a restaurant. Later, Dom came upstairs with me, in Danny's apartment, which by the way, he keeps only for his cat Grizz while he lives on his sailboat, *Solitude*. Dom and I talked, I told him a "Shaggy Man story," and he slept on the floor in his sleeping bag. Sweet.

26 September Saturday

Sailed with Dom, who did not want much of it, but saw a bald eagle. Dom wanted only to play games on my phone, and finally we sent him home with CJ. Danny and I sailed, a nice one, in the evening. Left him to sleep aboard (his usual practice) and went to the brewpub for a beer before sleeping with Grizz in his feline apartment. The evening sail had a pleasant breeze and the sun going down.

27 September Sunday

Breakfast at the Donut King (for me a huge sweet roll, chocolate covered and glazed donuts). Ran errands, tried and failed at an experiment spinning clothes dry with a mop spinner, which now goes to Jennifer, and picked up Tony, Mel's other father, for dinner in Belle Chasse at the new house Mel and CJ have bought. The guests included Julie, my older daughter, and her man David, a Jefferson Parish sheriff. He's a burly, powerful guy, a died-in-the-wool cop, who talked a lot, and who would be officially scary to miscreants.

Drank wine with dinner, but after dropping Danny at the boat, went to Barley Oak on the Mandeville lakefront for a couple of Belgian beers. Saints playing loudly inside, I sat on the veranda overlooking the lake, watching the moon with Jupiter and Saturn close by, wondering how the ancients, the Greek ones, came to make them their chief gods.

28 September Monday

Left Danny and drove first to Martin Wine Cellar, on to Totally Liquored, the New Orleans Cocktail Museum, and to Mel's. Spent LOTS of money on liquor, which felt good after making do with beer and wine for a few days.

Martin Wine Cellar was a disappointment. A New Orleans institution, its store of liquor was far smaller than I'd imagined. Found a few things, but not that many. Totally Liquored, on the other hand, laid out almost identically to the store I love in Danvers, a box store for booze, was well stocked, and I spent the usual over-the-top amount that promises to trouble Jennifer. But I've got the car to haul it, and a visit was past due.

The Cocktail Museum
A work in progress. The managers could use a museum consultant to help them configure the place, as I think they're missing lots of chances for presenting the history and value of cocktails. Covid is holding them back, of course; I was the sole visitor and only the third for all of Sunday and Monday. Bought a couple of books, including a second one from Death & Co., to help keep them going. The place seems likely to become one of those eccentric little museums that are a curiosity in their own right, never mind their subject. My favorite in that genre is the Florida Sponge Museum. I hope it still lives. The Pierce Arrow Museum in Buffalo is another.

On to Mel's and the boys where I'm staying now. Made Réveillons and Manhattans for Mel, CJ, and me, stopping at three. All ingredients came from the two liquor stores, and some will remain with Mel. The downstairs room where I'm staying would make a terrific bar (includes a fireplace), which I've advocated.

Just to say, this long cocktail voyage is now paying off in introducing new and old ones to friends and family. They are a conversation in themselves and open the way for other conversations, last night about the declining, imperiled state of the nation. Woke in the night with a bad headache.

And finally, heard from Bucky Jordan, and the Taswell 43, the boat I've now set my sights (unseen) on, is still for sale! Found this boat in Sailboats for Sale by Owner. She looks to be a fine specimen of the center cockpit/aft cabin monohull, well built in Taiwan. Bucky, his wife, and their two boys lived on her for several years, travelling the west coast from Seattle to Alaska to Mexico. They now live near Tampa, which is where the boat is docked. Built in 1989, she could be tired but is intriguing, worth a look.

29 September Tuesday

Spent much of the day with Mel, first at the gym, and prepared, with my plunder from Totally Liquored New Orleans, what I thought was a Sherpa for Mel and CJ as I left for Michael and Marianne's, friends for many years, to watch what turned out to be the Horrid Non-Debate. However, because I'd accidentally substituted pear brandy for curaçao, the Sherpa turned into what we're calling the Perfectly Acceptable Joyce. CJ drank every drop, and I was off.

Perfectly Acceptable Joyce

2 ozs bourbon (Used Evan Williams 100 proof Bottled in Bond)
1/2 oz St. Elizabeth Allspice Dram
1/2 oz pear brandy
2 dashes Peychaud's Bitters
2 dashes Angostura Bitters
Prep: Stir and serve over ice in a double rocks glass.

Michael and Marianne are as always: creatures of long-built structure who are delightful and needy in the sweetest ways. Michael bought a takeout dinner of, god love him, turtle soup and pecan encrusted redfish from Commander's Palace (whoever heard of takeout from this fabled restaurant? Michael, of course.). We ate in time to watch the debate begin, though Marianne adjourned upstairs to sleep. We, apparently, were too quiet, and she required us to holler "Asshole" frequently, which, subsequently, we did.

30 September Wednesday

Off today with Mel to Totally Liquored in Jefferson Parish next to New Orleans. We've bought the goods to make her a real home bar in a house that already has a bar sink and a cabinet with glass doors that should work perfectly.

Creating a Home Bar

Now that I think of it, this is my first chance to advise anyone about both the structure and pandemic-transcending glories of a home bar. And who could be better suited to the revelations than my daughter and her husband, who love a drink as much as I do.

Mel has most of the implements needed: a decent shaker, barspoon, muddler; Angostura, Peychaud's, orange, and even El Guapo Chickory Pecan Bitters (made in the town of Gretna, adjacent to her on the West Bank of New Orleans); Luxardo cherries; and some vermouth (Antica Formula and Noilly Pratt Extra Dry), gin (Tanqueray 10), rye (Rittenhouse 100), and bourbon (Evan Williams and the pricey Heaven's Door).

As inauguration tonight, we're having real Martinis and Older Old Fashioneds, as we're calling them, to go with New Orleans' best roast beef po' boys, shrimp remoulade, and Italian salad (sans olives) from R&O Restaurant. Ain't life something? And for some of us even a pandemic is endurable.

Older Old Fashioned

But the immediately important question is, what is an "older old fashioned"? The term belongs to Mel. Cocktail books persuaded me that today's minimalist Old Fashioned was purer, and so better, than the 50s version that began with muddled fruit. I'm now thinking, similar to the glass-of-cold-gin martini, the minimalist Old Fashioned aims to be mostly a glass of sweetened bourbon with bitters.

For a few years, from time to time, several friends and I have sojourned in Buffalo under the tutelage of Bob Nardini, a native of that underrated city. Buffalo has a native sandwich, the beef on weck (a salted bun), of German origin, at least I guess Germans invented it, but they could easily have been Buffalo Germans in 1837. That year, Schwalby's opened its doors and even today (well, perhaps not today) makes the best beef on weck, which I, a native of the po' boy, believe could be the best sandwich ever invented.

Can't say when, but somewhere along the trail, Schwalby's started to offer cocktails. I'm guessing the 50s, partly based on their Old Fashioned, which is muddled. They use a single rocks glass, and Maker's Mark, not a favorite of mine, is their only bourbon. Here's my take on their version, which unlike any other I've had, replaces orange with lemon. And what a difference!

Ultimate Older Old Fashioned

In a double rocks glass, muddle a wheel of lemon that is about 1/4 inch thick, with a Luxardo cherry, a half teaspoon of sugar, and a bit of bourbon. Be sure to push and twist on the lemon peel to release its oils.
Add 2-3 dashes Angostura and perhaps Peychaud's bitters. Stir. Add one large rock and fill the glass with bourbon to within 3/8 inch of its lip.
Stir again to cool.

Drink with beef on weck. Or a roast beef po'boy. Platonic.

And wasn't the combination of po' boys and cocktails terrific! That is not a question. A great evening with the boys and without. Told them their first "3Ds story" (David, Danny, and Denis), in which Danny heroically does not rat me out for beating him up after he and Tommy Swayze whipped me in basketball. Next morning, Thursday as I left, Travis asked for another "David, Danny, and Denis story." A genre is born.

1 October Thursday

Have been traveling for a week and spent the day on the road driving from Mel's in Belle Chase (and New Orleans) to Tampa, a brutally long way. The Danny-gifted Prius drove splendidly and logged more than 50 mpg for the entire day. Think about a small can of gasoline pushing a 1,000-lb plus car and its occupant along with 100 pounds or so of spirits on highways at 70 miles per hour for 11 hours, using fewer than 15 gallons to travel 700 miles, and you see that the human mind has done remarkable things.

Travel, however, even in a good cause, is not well suited to a sequestered cocktail diary. You might think, even hope, I'd quit writing. Don't hold your breath.

2 October Friday

Admittedly, this day is in many respects the point of this trip. After driving from Tampa to Vero Beach, it's evening, and I'm alone in Tim and Beth's condominium in the all-houses-no-matter-how-rich section of Vero Beach, where landscaping, driveway, and roofline define your relative success in life.

That said, it is comfortable here alone in a lovely room with no windows but plenty of light on what I expect will be a momentous day. After a tasty but Covid-fraught meal soon after everyone learned the President has the disease, the Florida restaurant where I had dinner was full of unmasked "citizens," the quotes meant to suggest that because we share a country, a government, in many ways a fate, fighting any war should be something we do together. Covid, surely, is a war; masks, a weapon.

I ate good food but felt filthy. Came home to the condo, showered, poured an Older Old Fashioned, which is going down as both tasty and strong, and here we are. Back to the momentous day.

A Journey Begins

Remarked or unremarked in this long outpouring, Jenny and I found that after deciding to sell our old house, a grand old house with a bejeweled tavern, another house would not suit us. We agreed, so easily as if to think there never really was another appropriate choice, that we'd use money from the sale of the Ol' Bean to buy a bigger boat. *Sea Sisters* is strong, trustworthy, beguiling, but she is too small for an old man, and his Vermont crunchy wife, to live on. Two problems, the berth and the head.

The berth, in the bow, known as a V-berth, is hard to slide into, hard to slide out of, and in the wee hours can be death to either of us when a piss is vital. The head is a complexity of anatomical and physical limitations, but worst of all, lacks a self-contained shower. The first, and last, shower anyone tried in this wet-head (on a boat, a washroom whose shower is not in its own stall. Pretty messy) was one Alex attempted after our first night out from Charleston when moving the boat to New Hampshire. He steamed up the whole boat and used pretty much the 100 gallons we expected to last the voyage. Perhaps I digress.

J and I know that we (speaking for no one else) can't really live aboard *Sea Sisters*. And, we thought only catamarans would accommodate our showering, toilet, and galley expectations to the point that we felt as if a catamaran was the alternative. So, we (I) looked for a cat and found a fast Australian version much improved by a blogging, Patreonic couple. I inquired, only to learn in their videos that they had forsaken her for a bigger, far more comfortable cat. Well, we think catamarans, for all their speed and creature comforts, do not look like boats. Looks count.

I found my way to a website called "Boats for Sale by Owners," inside Facebook, joined; early in the search landed luckily on a Taswell 43, *Lea Scotia*, owned by Bucky Jordan. The e-conversation led to yesterday's long drive to Tampa and today's agreement that, if we can find a slip near Vero Beach tomorrow, J and I are ready to pay 401K cash, far more than either of us had imagined, for a monohull of beauty and creature comforts. She has a queen-sized, custom-made bed with a comfortable mattress in the aft master cabin, which also has a head and separate shower with one of those showerheads I thought were available only in Dubai hotels, and a water temperature that is fixed to your preference (okay, roughing it is not the lifestyle we have in mind). Do long sentences in themselves suggest enthusiasm?

But for now, the very fine rye I bought in New Orleans stayed with Mel, and I drank the bourbon. The Older Old Fashioned is done… so I'll have another, bartender. But just to say, late in life, hoping the body and mind hold together for a while, nearly praying I didn't contract Covid tonight in the maskless restaurant, this boat has promise, and requires devotion, that could take us, well, around Florida, through the Keys from west to east, and in summer to New Hampshire and Maine. Then I'd guess, in 2021, back to Florida for winter.

But ahead? Her hull is insulated. She can be heated or cooled detached from any grid. She is unafraid of a sea, fast and conspiratorial if adventure is in your soul.

Will we find a slip tomorrow? One way or another, an Older Old Fashioned—now.

3 October Saturday

Yes, we have a slip at a yacht club in Stuart, Florida, called The Harborage. Destroyed by Hurricane Irma (a little worrisome that), the harbor has been newly rebuilt. It's a short trip to the Atlantic with no bridges needing to be raised, and Stuart's interesting downtown is easily pedaled. The marina is expensive, but it has a bar, restaurants, pool, hot tub, gym, and is attractive in its "I have made it" way.

We've put down a considerable earnest payment on the boat, have work to do, but *Lea Scotia* looks likely to be our home. I'm drinking a second Older Old Fashioned of the night to celebrate. One last revelation is that during today's long drives I thought the Harborage, I mean, The Harborage, might want to employ me from time to time as a bartender, help pay for the slip. Such a life.

Watched one of the greatest films, *The Big Lebowski*, and, well, it is about our End Times.

Which explains today's problems, somehow, and drank some odd Kind-of-Manhattan made with Amaro Nonino and Jerry Thomas Bitters in the rye. Amaro Nonino is not "bittersweet." It's sweet. Can't these tasters tell the difference? I'm going to have another Kind-of-Manhattan, to verify.

This is a diary about cocktails, but… today I discovered that to get to the posh marina where I've billeted us, we need to go under a 65-foot bridge (Hwy A1A) with a mast somewhere between 62.5 and 64 feet.

This is an old story for us. *Sea Sisters* used to need to go under the Sullivan Bridge in New Hampshire, at low tide, 50 to 55 feet. Terrifying. You look up, see the clearance is, well you cannot see the clearance. With *Lea Scotia*, we might need to wait for low tides, going in, going out, to reach this posh marina. Never a good thing. It is, what, marketing? These guys "have one slip left." I show up and lots, I mean lots, of slips are empty. They say they are rented, but the boats have not arrived. Okay, hurricane season isn't over.

Yet, no one asks, "How tall is your mast?" At 43-feet horizontal, *Lea Scotia* could easily have a 65-foot, maybe a 70-foot, mast if a racer. And, shockingly to me, they took a credit card number but will not charge against it until we arrive. One slip left? If berths are scarce, why not charge beginning now?

I'm no businessman, not looking for an I win/you lose fight. But apparently, if we can squeeze under the 65-foot AIA bridge, they will happily take our money. And we'll happily give it. . . Supposing that we have a mast.

If we do, an Amaro Nonino Kind-of-Manhattan will be fine.

4 and 5 October Sunday and Monday

Drank too much last night and need a day off. Tomorrow may be able to sail *Lea Scotia*, which would be fantastic. Ate Popeye's chicken, originally from New Orleans, for dinner. Awful, really. Once every 25 years should be enough.

Drinking Too Much

About drinking too much. Alone here in Florida, working on a manual for the new boat, pouring drinks improves the evening. I've stuck with three, but heavy pours, and in three nights finished a bottle of Rittenhouse 100 proof rye. The worrisome thing is I did not recall a whole lot about those evenings. For example, Sunday watched The Big Lebowski *and then an old debate between James Baldwin and William F. Buckley. Until I ran across another Baldwin clip on YouTube, I had forgotten the intensely moving debate.*

Blackouts, which I think these episodes are, signal alcoholism. Or if somewhat short of it, at least signal drinking too heavily, and yesterday I felt awful. Was easy, by the way, not to drink last night.

6 October Tuesday

Drove to Ruskin, sailed *Lea Scotia,* and she is a beauty on the wing. Elegant, powerful. Learned a lot from Bucky then drove to Tampa, dined at Outback (bad but short of awful), and spent the night in a Ramada near the Tampa airport. Drank a couple of Newport Brown Ales with dinner but needed a night of low (or no) alcohol.

7 October Wednesday

Woke about 3:10 in a panic over the boat. So much to do; little time and less knowledge to do it. But got to the airport early and used the flight back home to compose most of a letter detailing what needs Bucky's help. Beth picked me up in Manchester in her new Volvo SUV. Nice car.

To prepare for the vice-presidential debate, and to escape my weary, troubled mind, drank two Dark Horses from the newly bought *Cocktail Codex* (Day, Fauchald, Kaplan, 280. More on this essential book in due course):

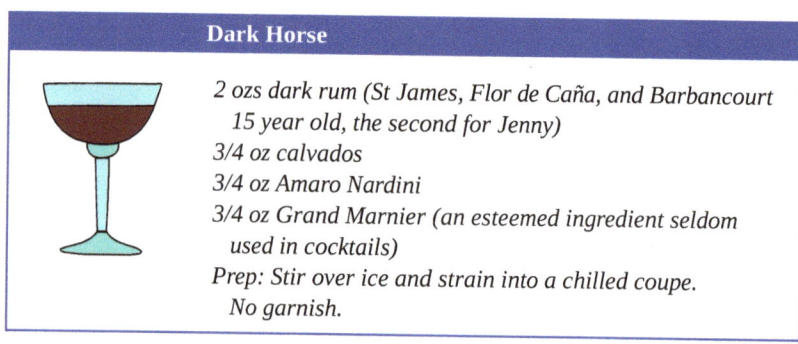

Dark Horse
2 ozs dark rum (St James, Flor de Caña, and Barbancourt 15 year old, the second for Jenny) 3/4 oz calvados 3/4 oz Amaro Nardini 3/4 oz Grand Marnier (an esteemed ingredient seldom used in cocktails) Prep: Stir over ice and strain into a chilled coupe. No garnish.

I especially liked the Barbancourt, whose distinctive rum flavor came right through. Jenny liked the milder Flor de Caña.

But not finished, though drunk, the debate approaching, needing courage…

Dave Fernie's Old Fashioned (Day, Fauchald, Kaplan, 18)

3 ozs bourbon (he calls for Evan Williams Black Label.
I used lower proof Eagle Rare)
1 tsp maple syrup (he calls for demerara gum syrup)
2 dashes Angostura Bitters (I used four. But, I am
re-examining what a dash really is. More on that in
another entry)
Prep: Stir over ice, strain into a double-rocks glass with a
big cube, of course. He calls for an orange and a lemon
twist. I had only the latter but did, as he says, rub it
around the rim.

An excellent Old Fashioned. The Older Old Fashioned, however, is more to my taste (and in truth, this is sort of that). The cocktail kept me lively through the entire debate, in which, no matter what anyone says, Kamala Harris beat Mike Pence like the dog he is.

8 October Thursday

A very satisfactory reply from Bucky, so I feel good again about *Lea Scotia*. Talked to CJ about our dates for the sail around Florida, which will be sometime in November. Tim and Beth came to dinner, chili I made. The drink of the night:

Martinez

2 ozs Hayman's Old Tom Gin (stay with this one)
2 ozs Antica Formula (same. Do not vary the recipe)
1 barspoon Luxardo Maraschino Liqueur
2 dashes orange bitters (I use Regans', but see below)
Prep: Stir with one large cube of ice and strain into a cold
coupe. Garnish with a lemon twist, expressed over the
drink, rim the edge, hang on the side.

The Scientific Dash

Here's the word on "dashes of bitters." I love bitters and wonder, what's in a dash? I do not now think it means just a quick ca-chunk. In each of tonight's Martinez's, the "2 dashes" I added came from 16 ca-chunks, eight per dash. Result: Jenny, Beth, and most of all Tim (who almost never drinks cocktails but insisted on two) loved this. I did too.

Indeed, whether the result of the 8-ca-chunk dash or the very fine blend of ingredients, this is easily among my favorite cocktails. I may try an amaro or two in place of the Antica Formula with the idea of making this by the decanter. And I may try a decanter using the Antica Formula, which should hold up because this won't last long. It is that good. And I had only one. I digress.

What's in a dash? One-eighth teaspoon is, more or less, official. Do "8 ca-chunks" equal 1/8 teaspoon? Search me.

9 October Friday

The Thursday Martinez was so good we went right back to it with Al home. Tim, who foreswore cocktails 50 years ago, asked for a Martinez Thursday, drank it, and after I'd made a second one for myself, drank that one too. I needed another.

But moving to the second one tonight, I thought it a good idea to try other ingredients, an Amaro, Averna, making a Black Martinez, in place of the vermouth, and DOM in place of the maraschino. Not nearly as good as the original.

10 October Saturday

Spent the night aboard *Sea Sisters* preparatory to our last sail aboard her for the season.

Bar Inventory

If you only casually monitor the ingredients in your bar, you'll find yourself lacking essential supplies, as I did. Thinking of a Black Manhattan, discovered we had neither rye nor bourbon. We had plenty of rum, but not a lot to mix with it and plenty of gin. We had Rose's Lime Water left from a sail in summer, and Gimlets (see 11 April and 30 July for the recipe) became the drink of the night with Nautical Gin. How sailor-like.

The Gimlet is not a bad drink either, and easy. It calls for lime juice, but lemon, which I had, works fine. Jenny drank one and I another, then she helped me, a bit, polish off two more.

11 October Sunday

A glass of Chardonnay or two, but nothing more than that to report. I count it a day off. The sail seemed especially tiring, and we both slept at home like the dead. Feel good today and am headed for a Covid test as the result of last week's flight from Florida.

Tonight, no matter what, the drink will be Sawyers (see tomorrow's entry for the recipe) I've been waiting all summer for this very autumnal cocktail, one of my favorites.

12 October Monday

Whether Columbus Day or Indigenous People's Day, it is Dom's birthday, our first grandson, and he'll be 9. We drank celebratory Sawyers, which we both loved, Jenny one, me three, though we also shared.

Here is the recipe, not changed, I'd guess, from earlier in the diary but made easier thanks to large bottles of Angostura and Regans' Orange Bitters from which I've removed the plastic dashers so that the liquid just pours.

> ### Ca-chunk Dashes versus 1/8 Tsp Dashes
> Meanwhile, the Peychaud's is in a dasher, and I still have no faith in how much it measures. That is, seems to me dashers usually deliver much less than a "dash." A dash should be about 10 single drops, which apparently comes to 1/8 of a tsp. Liking bitters as I do, as the world does or should, we might want to make the 1/8 tsp dash statutory.

But, then, here is the recipe, which in a Sawyer involves no dashes whatsoever.

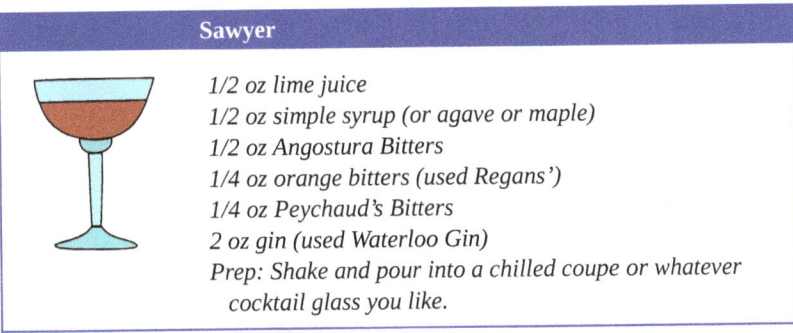

Sawyer

1/2 oz lime juice
1/2 oz simple syrup (or agave or maple)
1/2 oz Angostura Bitters
1/4 oz orange bitters (used Regans')
1/4 oz Peychaud's Bitters
2 oz gin (used Waterloo Gin)
Prep: Shake and pour into a chilled coupe or whatever
  cocktail glass you like.

In general we'll say, given that most cocktails using bitters call for 1 or 2 dashes, we need to know how many squirts from our dasher bottles come to 1/8 tsp. Dashing is highly mathematical.

13 October Tuesday

Three weeks till the November 3 election; one week till I go back and stay aboard *Lea Scotia*. Let's settle dashing once and for all time. But first…

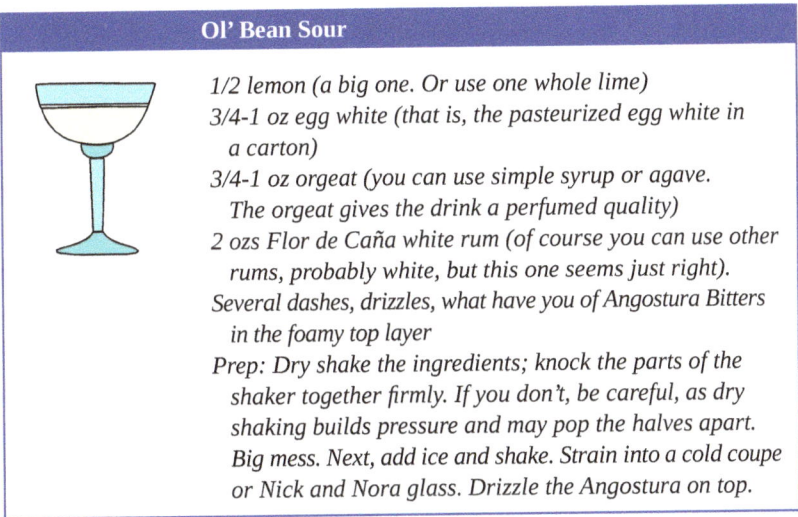

Ol' Bean Sour

1/2 lemon (a big one. Or use one whole lime)
3/4-1 oz egg white (that is, the pasteurized egg white in
  a carton)
3/4-1 oz orgeat (you can use simple syrup or agave.
  The orgeat gives the drink a perfumed quality)
2 ozs Flor de Caña white rum (of course you can use other
  rums, probably white, but this one seems just right).
Several dashes, drizzles, what have you of Angostura Bitters
  in the foamy top layer
Prep: Dry shake the ingredients; knock the parts of the
  shaker together firmly. If you don't, be careful, as dry
  shaking builds pressure and may pop the halves apart.
  Big mess. Next, add ice and shake. Strain into a cold coupe
  or Nick and Nora glass. Drizzle the Angostura on top.

Obviously, this is a Pisco Sour made with rum. And it may be better. In any event it is no sour bean but a delicious and dangerous drink.

Oh, dashes. Later.

14 October Wednesday

Started with an Old Fashioned, not intending to drink, but needed one, and the Perfect Old Fashioned made with Elijah Craig from the Cocktail Codex seemed worth another go (see recipe for Dave Fernie's Old Fashioned on 7 October). And it was.

Later, needed something more as Al announced he was moving from engineering to finance, dropping two classes, may not be going back to school in spring, and who knows what he didn't say? Poured a healthy dose of Mother-in-Law from the decanter.

Commentators go on about the perfection of the Old Fashioned and have pulled it, and my version of it, back from the pulpy, fruited drink of the past to a simple, clean one in the present. But you know, it is not—though for years I thought it was—my favorite drink. For example, give me a Sawyer or even an Ol' Bean Sour.

Heresy, I say, and a sublime realization. Having traveled this troubled sea these many months, it is good to know that so many cocktail confections are alchemical gold that it would be laziness to settle on one or even a few.

To the diverse joys of Diversity: May the unexpected always (or just now and again) delight.

15 October Thursday

Denis used the term "shit-faced" several times last night, referring to the effect of too grand a Mother-in-Law or the giant Black Manhattan I'd poured for him, and shit-faced is what he was, I was.

We started with the Autumn Old Fashioned from the *Cocktail Codex*. It's complicated:

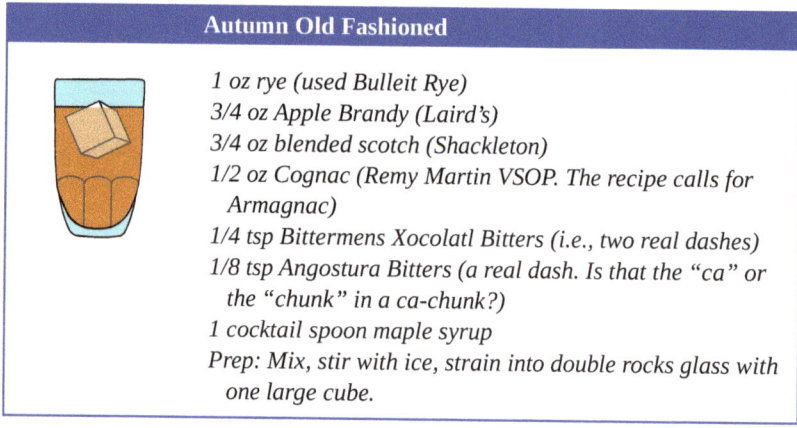

Autumn Old Fashioned
1 oz rye (used Bulleit Rye)
3/4 oz Apple Brandy (Laird's)
3/4 oz blended scotch (Shackleton)
1/2 oz Cognac (Remy Martin VSOP. The recipe calls for Armagnac)
1/4 tsp Bittermens Xocolatl Bitters (i.e., two real dashes)
1/8 tsp Angostura Bitters (a real dash. Is that the "ca" or the "chunk" in a ca-chunk?)
1 cocktail spoon maple syrup
Prep: Mix, stir with ice, strain into double rocks glass with one large cube.

Really good and just the beginning. Unable to mix a drink after two, poured the Mothers-in-Law and the Black Manhattans, resulting in the condition named above. My liver needs a break!

16 October Friday

The liver at rest.

17 October Saturday

After a busy day in which the realtors showed the Bean twice, and we tried to move ahead buying the new sailboat, Scott and Lisa Metzger came to dinner (they're the couple at whose house I got so blasted after the horrible week of abstinence), along with Al, who seems determined not to return to school, and Skylar. I'd made gumbo and pot de creme the night before, lit a fire and oil lamps. The house looked as good as it ever has.

Scott loves beer, especially Treehouse beer, which he always brings along in generous numbers of cans. I insisted he try a cocktail, to introduce my idea (I think it is mine) that bitters are to cocktails what hops are to beer. Made J and Lisa the Ol' Bean Sour, though with agave rather than simple syrup, which I don't think is quite as good, and made Sawyers for Scott and for me. His son in law had introduced him to the magic of bitters, so he wasn't surprised at the idea or the effect, and I think he liked the Sawyer quite a lot. But we moved along to the Treehouse, which was fine.

After Scott and Lisa left, Max arrived. He is a friend from Al's boyhood, introduced Al to hockey, resulting in years of cold rinks. A genuine athlete, who we agreed early in the pandemic, could come to our house. He and Al made a gym for lifting weights. Soon Max bought an expensive glass, from Simon Pearce, for his cocktails. The three of us drank a Rum Sour and a Black Betty. Betty, who I have not had in a while, tasted pretty darn good:

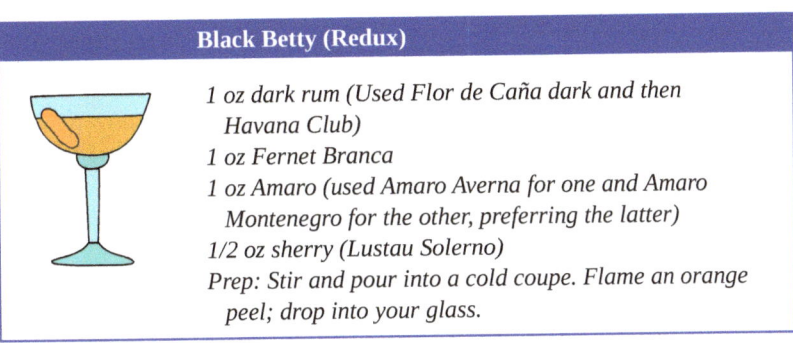

Black Betty (Redux)

1 oz dark rum (Used Flor de Caña dark and then
  Havana Club)
1 oz Fernet Branca
1 oz Amaro (used Amaro Averna for one and Amaro
  Montenegro for the other, preferring the latter)
1/2 oz sherry (Lustau Solerno)
Prep: Stir and pour into a cold coupe. Flame an orange
  peel; drop into your glass.

Pretty great drink the boys thought.

Flaming an Orange Peel

To flame the orange peel garnish, which you must do, light a kitchen match and once the sulfur dissipates, heat the peel till you can smell the oils.

A great evening for the cocktail without it being the center of things.

18 October Sunday

Looked for something new and in Tux2 discovered the Oaxaca Old Fashioned. Here's the recipe:

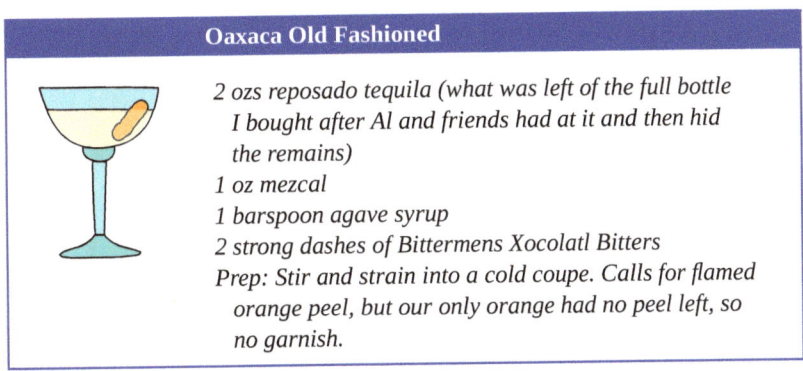

Oaxaca Old Fashioned

2 ozs reposado tequila (what was left of the full bottle
  I bought after Al and friends had at it and then hid
  the remains)
1 oz mezcal
1 barspoon agave syrup
2 strong dashes of Bittermens Xocolatl Bitters
Prep: Stir and strain into a cold coupe. Calls for flamed
  orange peel, but our only orange had no peel left, so
  no garnish.

Good, but I'm not sold. The orange would have helped. The flavor was not as strong as I'd hoped. Not giving up, but this is not on the magic list.

19 October Monday

A very busy day that began with a dream in which I realized the key I'd left at our marina, thinking it was for someone else's car and I had picked it up wrongly, was for Danny's/Al's/CJ's Prius, parked at the Marriott Hotel, Tampa Airport. This meant an unexpected trip back to Eliot, Maine. Got work done toward winterizing *Sea Sisters*, but the day was a sprint, and I need a tried, known-to-be delicious drink, especially as Jenny tried, unsuccessfully, to transfer money from BOA to a holding account for the new boat. She needed one too, so I made the drinks together, nearly filling the mixing glass.

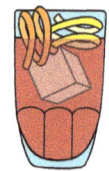

Conference (I doubled the numbers below)

1 oz rye (Woodford Rye)
1 oz bourbon (Elijah Craig Bourbon)
1 oz calvados (use a good one, or a good American apple brandy)
1 oz cognac (Remy Martin VSOP)
1 barspoon simple syrup
2 dashes Bittermen Chocolate Mole Bitters (REAL dashes, 8 -16 shakes)
3-4 dashes Angostura bitters (again, real dashes, 1/8 tsp each)
Prep: Stir and strain into double rocks glass with one large ice cube. Lemon twist (recipe calls for orange twist as well).

With the barspoon of sugar and the real dashes of bitters, the high-end spirits—especially the rye and bourbon—this was a complex, tasty, not-too-sweet, very powerful cocktail. We needed only one. I mean, 4 ozs of alcohol is a lot. Not sure which spirit dominated, but I think we knew they were all there. If you're looking to get someone drunk, especially yourself, here's a good way to do it. But many people will find this one too boozy for their taste. Not me.

It's interesting that I've now written so many entries, made so many new cocktails, that I don't remember lots of them, even the very good ones, and find searching this cocktail diary as fine a way to come up with something that feels new as looking at *Death & Company* or the *Canon Cocktail Book* or *The Savoy*. "Find" is a fine feature for a document like this.

On the other hand, a search that lets you describe what you have in mind and then produces a list of prospects would be better. I wonder if such a search is possible?

E.g.: Citrus/No citrus; Bitters/no bitters; Preferred spirit. Even that bit might help.

20 October Tuesday

We fly to Tampa, then drive to Vero Beach. Probably starting Thursday, J and I will spend our first week in Ruskin, on the new boat, *Lea Scotia*... It's nerve-wracking, really. Was this the right thing to do or an indulgence? Will it really cost less than to live in a house or much more? How hard will it prove to manage the boat's complex systems?

As I near the far shore, whose outlines are ever more evident than the one where I began, I feel some moral need to make right choices so that Jenny isn't left holding my bag. *Sea Sisters* was just a bit too small, with her lack of a real head and the V-berth as the main sleeping chamber, to live aboard. And this could prove to be Tim's last good season, or worse, making our help timely but the need short-lived. And Al is showing considerable interest in Florida, even saying last night he thinks he could be a professional skier. All rationalizations? We'll see.

Tim and Beth, who returned to Vero Beach October 8, expect a cocktail, so I need to find one Beth will enjoy this evening.

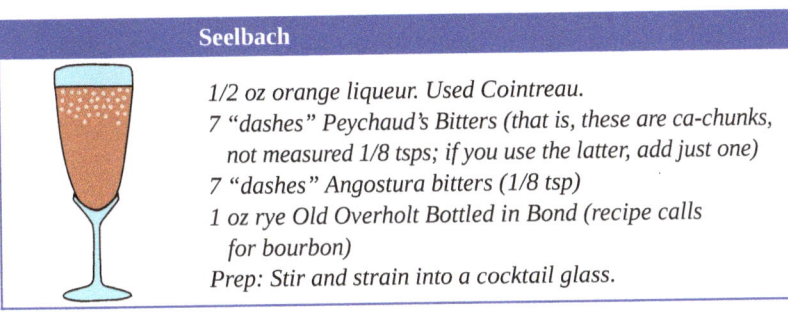

Seelbach

1/2 oz orange liqueur. Used Cointreau.
7 "dashes" Peychaud's Bitters (that is, these are ca-chunks,
  not measured 1/8 tsps; if you use the latter, add just one)
7 "dashes" Angostura bitters (1/8 tsp)
1 oz rye Old Overholt Bottled in Bond (recipe calls
  for bourbon)
Prep: Stir and strain into a cocktail glass.

I overdosed the bitters. Should have stuck with 8 shakes but used, maybe 24. Not bad. But unimpressive. Next tried a new one, the Pressure Drop, and it was much better.

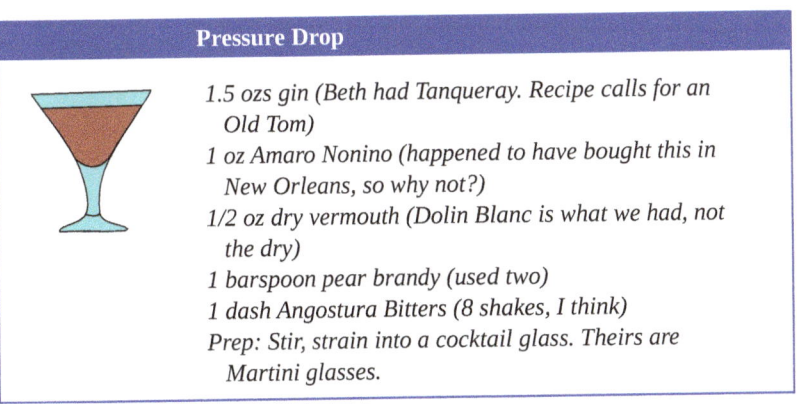

Pressure Drop

1.5 ozs gin (Beth had Tanqueray. Recipe calls for an
  Old Tom)
1 oz Amaro Nonino (happened to have bought this in
  New Orleans, so why not?)
1/2 oz dry vermouth (Dolin Blanc is what we had, not
  the dry)
1 barspoon pear brandy (used two)
1 dash Angostura Bitters (8 shakes, I think)
Prep: Stir, strain into a cocktail glass. Theirs are
  Martini glasses.

Better than the Seelbach, a *Death & Co.* original I got from Tux2. Tim was already drunk, and this one sealed his doom in the form of slurred speech. Ah well, he liked it considerably.

I'm seeing that the ingredients I've collected these many months (and must count them) are needed, or the number of possible cocktails is very few. It might be good to label cocktails with a searchable identifier indicating (1) anyone is likely to have the needed ingredients or (2) you can make a version but will probably need to substitute, and (3) unless you are dead serious, or make a trip to a big liquor store, forget this one. Something like that.

21 October Wednesday

Beth, Tim, and I are having Pisco Sours tonight by the book, no substitutions, err, well, maybe some rum... just to see.

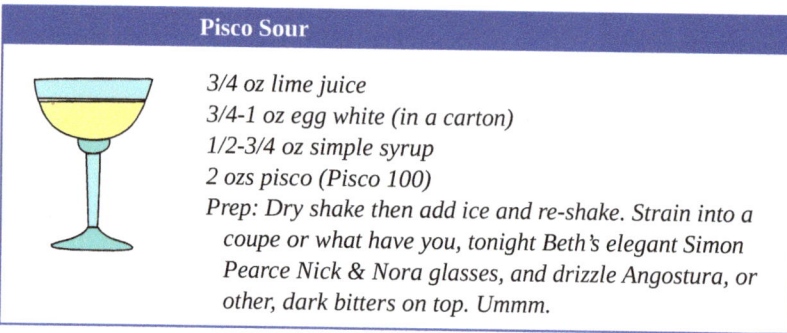

Pisco Sour

3/4 oz lime juice
3/4-1 oz egg white (in a carton)
1/2-3/4 oz simple syrup
2 ozs pisco (Pisco 100)
Prep: Dry shake then add ice and re-shake. Strain into a
coupe or what have you, tonight Beth's elegant Simon
Pearce Nick & Nora glasses, and drizzle Angostura, or
other, dark bitters on top. Ummm.

Which is what we did, except the carton of egg whites I'd bought was a carton of eggs. So we used real egg whites. And the drinks were a hit.

Turns out Beth and Tim have hoarded rum for years. Our generous Latina sister/daughter-in-law, Lidieth, brings them great rums from Nicaragua and Venezuela, and who knows where else, which they put in a cabinet. Beth broke out these bottles of aged, fine rum, along with a bottle of simple syrup that was pretty brown but showed no signs of mold. We shifted from pisco to rum as follows:

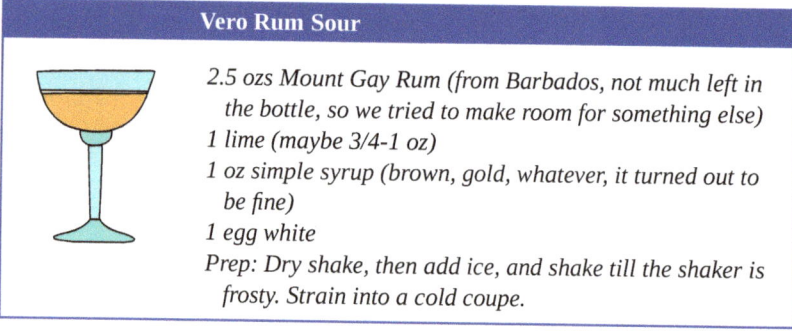

Vero Rum Sour

2.5 ozs Mount Gay Rum (from Barbados, not much left in
the bottle, so we tried to make room for something else)
1 lime (maybe 3/4-1 oz)
1 oz simple syrup (brown, gold, whatever, it turned out to
be fine)
1 egg white
Prep: Dry shake, then add ice, and shake till the shaker is
frosty. Strain into a cold coupe.

These—we made three, one for each of us—were fantastic, much better than the pisco version, declaring as we went that the drink was so good we might officially call it the drink of the winter of 2020-2021. It's hard to know whether a cocktail so named will live on, given the ignominy of a plague year or, perhaps, will contribute, as we have argued these many months, the alchemy of turning lead into a reason to live.

22 October Thursday

The *Lea Scotia*: Sailboat No. 2

The next, probably final, adventure begins. We buy the new sailboat, *Lea Scotia*, today. Jenny has not seen her, and is fully, monetarily, committed to living aboard. The money we made selling the Ol' Bean is now our boat. We don't know if the internet will work or the AC will drive enough air to keep her cool.

At least we know the earth isn't flat.

Okay then, Jenny trusts me. I pick her up at the Tampa airport, drive to *Lea Scotia* in Ruskin. And Jenny loves *Lea Scotia*! Thinks she is beautiful and fine, every detail well thought out. We celebrated with a small glass each of fine rum.

23 October Friday

Spent the day getting things in order aboard *Lea Scotia*, buying groceries, some equipment and other supplies, propane. Our first trip to a dollar store resulted in buying a tall green plastic bottle that will serve, perhaps, as a shaker. And surprise, it cost a dollar.

Ruskin is an odd town. Poor abuts rich, which seems uncomfortable for both. Restaurants generally are dives, and the marina is guarded. But a peninsula out into Tampa Bay is a modestly high-end vacation destination.

Tried to barbecue but the gas safety device broke a wire and then didn't work well, constricting flow, so we gave up on bbq and had grilled cheese, drinking Sherpas, modified as indicated below:

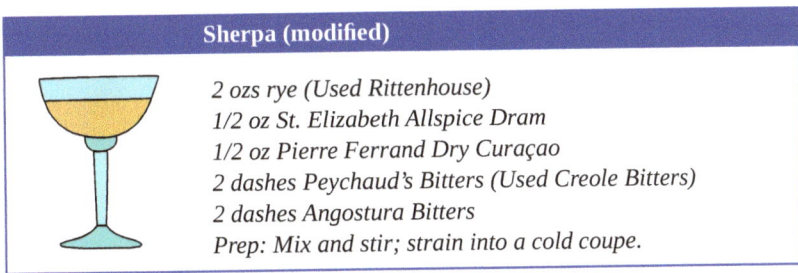

Sherpa (modified)

2 ozs rye (Used Rittenhouse)
1/2 oz St. Elizabeth Allspice Dram
1/2 oz Pierre Ferrand Dry Curaçao
2 dashes Peychaud's Bitters (Used Creole Bitters)
2 dashes Angostura Bitters
Prep: Mix and stir; strain into a cold coupe.

Delicious, indeed, too delicious. I drank three, and it is worth describing how we made the drinks.

Making Do with the Tools at Hand

That is, we have no bartools except a lime squeezer found in the supermarket. We used the tall green plastic bottle with a screw-on-top from the Ruskin dollar store to serve as the mixing glass/shaker. Had a small plastic storage container with concentric rings that served as our jigger. Now, whether the rings I used were ounces, or much more than ounces, they let us keep the relative proportions called for.

One of *Lea Scotia*'s finer points is that she has a genuine, or what I take to be genuine, liquor cabinet. And her galley's counter has a round part that is awfully fine for mixing drinks. The fridge and freezer are to hand. In short, this boat is built for cocktails, which surely were on the mind of her Canadian designer.

The three drinks I had to break in the bar may have been much more than any normal three, and certainly I was truly hungover all the next day, a price we gladly pay.

24 October Saturday

Our first sail, and everything went well. We left when the tide was high, meaning to return well before low tide. The former owner, Bucky Jordan, doesn't like to go out when the tide will be low. Well, we enjoyed the sail too much and got in only an hour before low tide, with some worrisome numbers appearing on the depth chart, down to 6.1 feet, where we draw 6.5 feet. But we never touched bottom and came smoothly into our slip with no drama whatsoever.

Got the bbq working and nearly blew myself up lighting it, singed hand and face. Drank milk.

25 October Sunday

A long day of errands that culminated at Columbia, a Spanish/Cuban restaurant in Ybor City begun in 1905 that was, really, spectacular. Among the best meals of both our lives. Jenny drank a Mojito that to me tasted of absinthe. I drank a Floridita Daiquiri that was delicious.

And in honor of this magnificent restaurant, where the staff was gracious, the pace perfect, the food astonishing, we drank Daiquiris aboard *Lea Scotia*. Our means are basic:

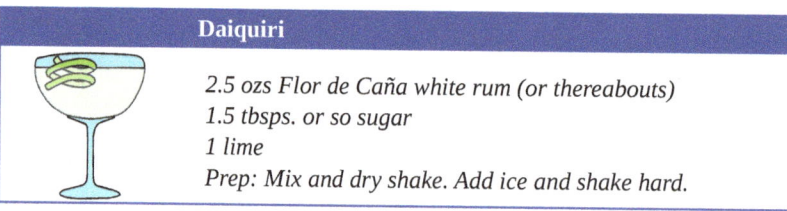

Daiquiri

2.5 ozs Flor de Caña white rum (or thereabouts)
1.5 tbsps. or so sugar
1 lime
Prep: Mix and dry shake. Add ice and shake hard.

The $1 Shaker

About that $1 green plastic bottle with a screw-on top. The cap has a small round spout, with a friction-fitting cover, so no strainer needed. Indeed, this could be the finest shaker I've seen, costs next to nothing. Lesson: You do not need high-end bar tools to make high-end cocktails.

26 October Monday

No chance to sail with Bucky today because too many questions, hot, and little wind. Made repairs to the propane system, and then cooked dinner… the main repair was getting the solenoid and the regulator working so the stove could cook. All of which called for a drink, a new one. I'd bought "Suze," which is made with gentian root (whatever that is) and have been eager to try it. Dr. Cocktail brings it up, but Tux2 has nothing to say about Suze. It is uncommon. I found it at the Totally Liquored store with Mel. We tried …

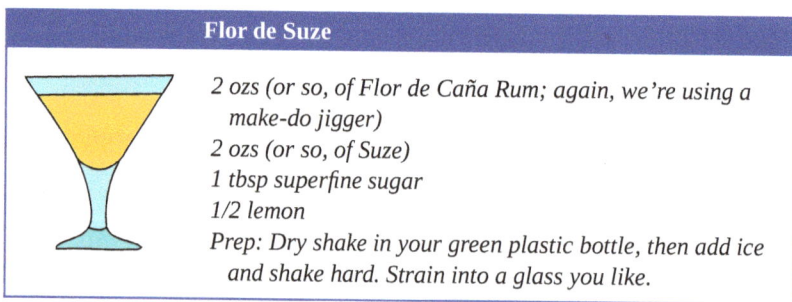

Flor de Suze

2 ozs (or so, of Flor de Caña Rum; again, we're using a
*   make-do jigger)*
2 ozs (or so, of Suze)
1 tbsp superfine sugar
1/2 lemon
Prep: Dry shake in your green plastic bottle, then add ice
*   and shake hard. Strain into a glass you like.*

Jenny proclaimed this is "good but not my favorite," which means she didn't like it, later describing it as "strong and flat." On the other hand, I liked its bitterness next to the sugary sweetness well enough to try the same recipe with the first real Laird's Apple Brandy (100 proof) I've found (again at the Totally Liquored store in New Orleans).

Suze

A bitter liqueur whose beauty may be its color above all, a sun yellow. With a light liquor, Suze glows in the glass like the sun beaming out.

EMERGENCY! EMERGENCY! As I typed the last sentence, smoke filled the main salon, evident even to me. Our new boat on fire!

We quickly traced the problem to the main AC, under the forward berth, and a given-up-the-ghost connection on top. It turns out that Marineaire, of Florida, made this thing. More tomorrow.

Meanwhile, the Apple Suze is needed (and quite good).

27 October Tuesday

Despair Begins

My fear that *Lea Scotia* would be tired felt realized. The forward AC perhaps spent, a new one costing above $3,000, and the aft AC freezing up after running for a short while, putting out barely any air from the blower. Yes, surely, no AC is a first-world problem. But we're in Florida!

Overnight I thought one of those in-the-room ACs could answer, but my brother Danny showed me otherwise. Led by the Internet to a local marine AC operation, turned out to be one guy in his house placing orders for equipment, but he sent me along to Steve Ward who is supposed to show up today less than one-half hour from now. Can he repair one or both? We'll see.

Meanwhile, Jenny and I spent a delightful evening in St Petersburg dining indoors at a bar, with only one other couple there and at the other end, out on a pier overlooking Tampa Bay. The food was good. Jennifer drank a Rosemary Manhattan made with Amaro Foro, which I had not heard of before. I drank two Hemingway Daiquiris made with canned grapefruit juice. Not ideal, but surprisingly acceptable. Under some conditions, say when grapefruit or pineapple juice is called for, canned is not inexcusable. (On the other hand, we are in Florida.)

Oh, and with the help of an AT&T SIM card, it appears we've gotten a "hotspot" connection to the Internet, through a modem I bought online, paired with the Pepwave router, and Jenny is working very well below on a video call that seems to be fine.

28 October Wednesday

According to Steve Ward, marine AC guy, she needs two new air conditioners at about $5 grand or so. Ordered them and he should install next week. Meanwhile Danny rides out a hurricane on his boat.

The worst thing about the day was my cowardice. Steve Ward, Trump license plate on the front of his truck, smoking, emaciated (reminding me of Eddie Higgins, famous for smoking with emphysema and drinking) came aboard and rather than insist we both wear masks, which he would have done, I waved them away. The rest of the day I imagined my lungs were corroding. Why am I such a coward about making other people uncomfortable?

Anyway, the day hot, AC barely functional, needed strong drink at the end. For Jenny I made an invented Allspice Manhattan.

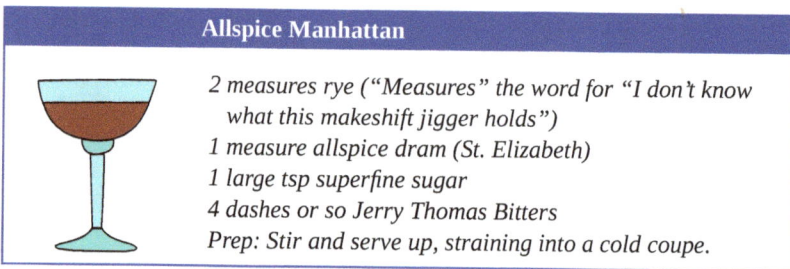

Allspice Manhattan

2 measures rye ("Measures" the word for "I don't know
  what this makeshift jigger holds")
1 measure allspice dram (St. Elizabeth)
1 large tsp superfine sugar
4 dashes or so Jerry Thomas Bitters
Prep: Stir and serve up, straining into a cold coupe.

Jenny declared she preferred it to the Rosemary Manhattan of the night before. Obviously, the allspice acts as a sweet vermouth or an amaro in the drink, but with its own delicious, complex flavor.

I had three Flors de Suze which I really believe are sunshine in a glass, but three left a little too much sunburn. Stuck right with the original formula.

29 October Thursday

Drove from Ruskin to Vero Beach where Beth had dinner for us, had found a bottle of pisco, and had most of a bottle I had left. We each drank a Pisco Sour and were glad for them.

30 October Friday

A mercifully easy day for me, and I took advantage of it to work out and to take a long nap. Drove to The Harborage Marina to show Jenny. She approved and *Lea Scotia* is inked in to her G99 dock space.

We hurriedly drove back to Vero for dinner at the house Jenny's cousin, Lisa, and her husband, Tim Swift, are leasing for a couple months. The only drinks on offer were scotch or some vodka concoction, no part of which I wanted.

Meanwhile, plans for the Last Waltz, the Luggnuts' farewell to their longtime practice space at the Bean next Saturday, move ahead with great anticipation by all parties. I'm planning to decanter Mother-in-Law, Black Manhattan, and Negroni, the last perhaps in some unusual form. The idea is to make everyone feel Covid safe. On this day in the United States, just shy of 100,000 people were diagnosed with Covid and nearly 1,000 died. The first is a record, the second could be close, even with better treatments.

31 October Saturday

Spurred to investigate the Negroni at 40,000 feet with only this Diary as a guide, I've found entries for the May Fair and for the Presidente, which I believe to be candidates for decantering. This week will be given over to experimentation in search of saving Luggnuts from the Covid Plague. Mother-in-Law, Black Manhattan, May Fair, Presidente. The Bean surely will be a star in the Cocktail Constellation. Tonight:

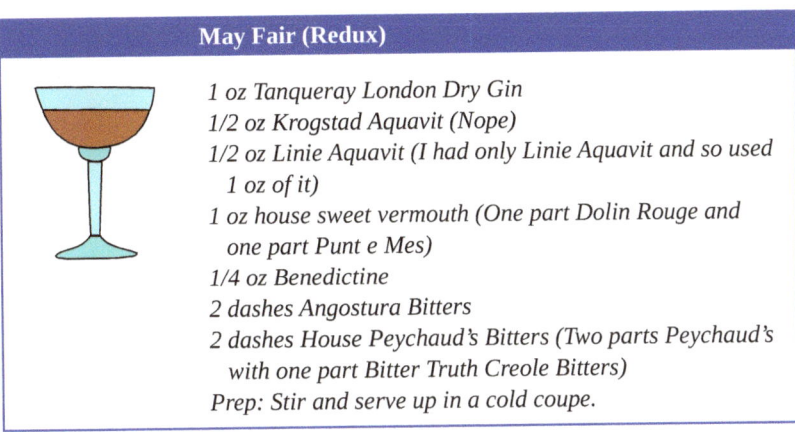

May Fair (Redux)

1 oz Tanqueray London Dry Gin
1/2 oz Krogstad Aquavit (Nope)
1/2 oz Linie Aquavit (I had only Linie Aquavit and so used
*   1 oz of it)*
1 oz house sweet vermouth (One part Dolin Rouge and
*   one part Punt e Mes)*
1/4 oz Benedictine
2 dashes Angostura Bitters
2 dashes House Peychaud's Bitters (Two parts Peychaud's
*   with one part Bitter Truth Creole Bitters)*
Prep: Stir and serve up in a cold coupe.

Made three, drank two, Jenny one, all much liked. Followed the recipe above but on my second inadvertently used Grand Marnier in place of Benedictine. Not much, though some not unpleasant, difference. This seems like a good choice as a decantered cocktail.

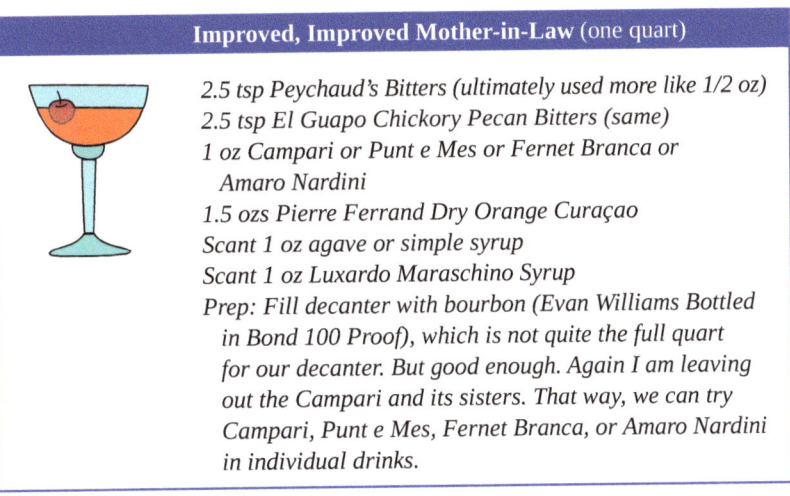

Improved, Improved Mother-in-Law (one quart)

2.5 tsp Peychaud's Bitters (ultimately used more like 1/2 oz)
2.5 tsp El Guapo Chickory Pecan Bitters (same)
1 oz Campari or Punt e Mes or Fernet Branca or
*   Amaro Nardini*
1.5 ozs Pierre Ferrand Dry Orange Curaçao
Scant 1 oz agave or simple syrup
Scant 1 oz Luxardo Maraschino Syrup
Prep: Fill decanter with bourbon (Evan Williams Bottled
*   in Bond 100 Proof), which is not quite the full quart*
*   for our decanter. But good enough. Again I am leaving*
*   out the Campari and its sisters. That way, we can try*
*   Campari, Punt e Mes, Fernet Branca, or Amaro Nardini*
*   in individual drinks.*

A hard month of many expensive twists. I'm pretty tired.

1 November Sunday

Back in New Hampshire, winter and this fateful month have arrived. Covid is rampaging, and post-air-travel from Florida, J and I are off to CVS for Covid tests at noon. My new iPhone 12 is activated, seems to work. Al kept the house in excellent shape. Feels good to be home.

But it won't be for long. Work on getting *Sea Sisters* readier for winter tomorrow. Vote Tuesday. Face and hands seared Wednesday. (The last, a dermatological treatment for my fair, sun-scarred, ancient skin.)

Found Natalie's Orange Juice at Can't Afford It, as Denis calls the Hannaford supermarkets, a juice we'd had in Florida and thought was excellent, fresh. Looked in Dr. Cocktail and found the

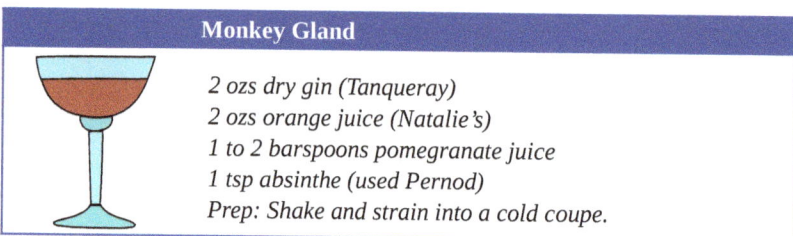

Monkey Gland

2 ozs dry gin (Tanqueray)
2 ozs orange juice (Natalie's)
1 to 2 barspoons pomegranate juice
1 tsp absinthe (used Pernod)
Prep: Shake and strain into a cold coupe.

A disappointment. None of us cared for this gland. I'd say the OJ was not as good as its Florida origin, which should be no surprise. But even at its best the OJ could not bring this drink up to anything likable. The parts never came together. You could taste each, but they didn't complement one another in the least. Word was this Monkey Gland improved a feller's virility. Let's hope there are other ways.

With the failure of the Monkey, was looking for something redemptive, and the Presidente seemed perfect... and was.

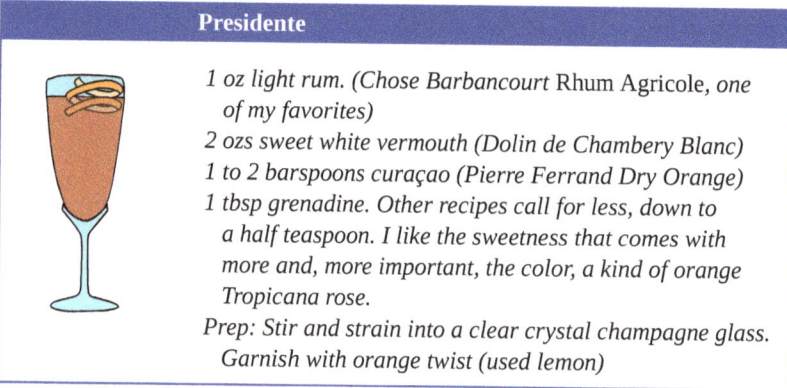

Presidente

1 oz light rum. (Chose Barbancourt Rhum Agricole, one
 of my favorites)
2 ozs sweet white vermouth (Dolin de Chambery Blanc)
1 to 2 barspoons curaçao (Pierre Ferrand Dry Orange)
1 tbsp grenadine. Other recipes call for less, down to
 a half teaspoon. I like the sweetness that comes with
 more and, more important, the color, a kind of orange
 Tropicana rose.
Prep: Stir and strain into a clear crystal champagne glass.
 Garnish with orange twist (used lemon)

The clarity of the glass lets light play through the Tropicana-rose-colored cocktail. And the shape of the flute makes this even lovelier. A treat.

2 November Monday

The election is tomorrow. Both sides are nervous, even scared. Certainly, the day is a culmination and the end of a weight we've all borne through the primaries, pandemic, conventions, and the campaign itself. Both sides are rather sure that if the other wins, the American experiment in democracy ends.

Tonight, then, let's try a classic, whose karma could help.

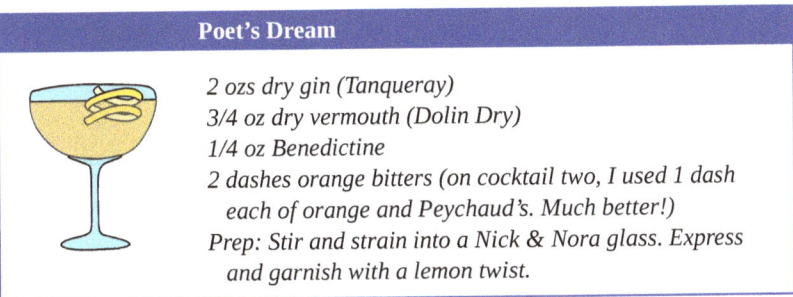

Poet's Dream

2 ozs dry gin (Tanqueray)
3/4 oz dry vermouth (Dolin Dry)
1/4 oz Benedictine
2 dashes orange bitters (on cocktail two, I used 1 dash
*   each of orange and Peychaud's. Much better!)*
Prep: Stir and strain into a Nick & Nora glass. Express
*   and garnish with a lemon twist.*

"2 dashes" here means 16 shakes. Thing is, I seem not to taste orange bitters. And, they had no effect on the color, leaving this a transparent cocktail. Okay, I guess, but a little color might help this Martini with Benedictine. On the second Dream, I used 8 shakes of orange and 8 shakes of Peychaud's. A revelation!

Maybe not a revelation, but for me a great improvement. You can taste the Peychaud's, and more than that, the Dream took on a rose hue, which, not that I'm an expert, should fire any poet's imagination. And improve Biden's chances tomorrow.

3 November Tuesday

Here at last. We voted in snow. Hopeful. Not much drinking come nightfall. Jim and Stephanie came with James's Christmas guitar, which is very nice, a Taylor mini with electronics that sound good.

Fixed the four of us a Rum Sour, with orgeat, and used too much. For drinking, that was it. Watched a couple episodes of Hap and Leonard to be distracted. Fell asleep about 10:30. Woke at 12:30; still no winner.

Managed to sleep uneasily till morning.

4 November Wednesday

Hard to weigh the difference between the hope of 2008, the dawn that greeted us next morning, and today's despair. No winner yet, though Trump declared victory at midnight, but even if Biden wins, that the election is close, a profound mystery and disappointment. How can a man so flawed be the choice of so many? How deeply decayed is our national character. And the pandemic, along with this diary, continues.

A dermatologist day, where I had PDT, photodynamic therapy, on my face. They begin by scrubbing your face with acetone and then a deep cleanser. Next, they cover it with acid (they really do this) and send you to sit for an hour and a half. All worse than it sounds.

When the acid has seeped deep into your skin a nurse takes you back and explains that this is about to feel like your face is on fire and, with the help of photos of former patients, shows you that you will come to look horribly burned for a week or two. She shows you an ice pack and a fan, along with cold wipes that she'll apply, explaining that the first 2 minutes of the 16-minute total under a laser are the worst.

She leans you back in the chair, puts blinders over your eyes, turns on the light, and AAAGGGHHHH, the searing is immediate, especially on the forehead and upper lip. You try to be brave. Reminded me of the story an old Irish priest told during mass about a barracks fire in New Jersey during World War II when he visited a burned sailor lying on his belly, dying, murmuring "Oh Lord, let me die. Please let me die." The priest went on to say that this pain, were we to make our way to Hell, would never stop. For me, it was 15 minutes of Hell. Will that mean 15 minutes taken off of forever in a Christian new world?

On this day, when now it appears Biden's chance of winning is growing, I feel as if PDT has burned away an old me, and with the country, maybe a new, better version will emerge. But make no mistake, such metamorphosis is painful, calls for a stiff drink, and soon.

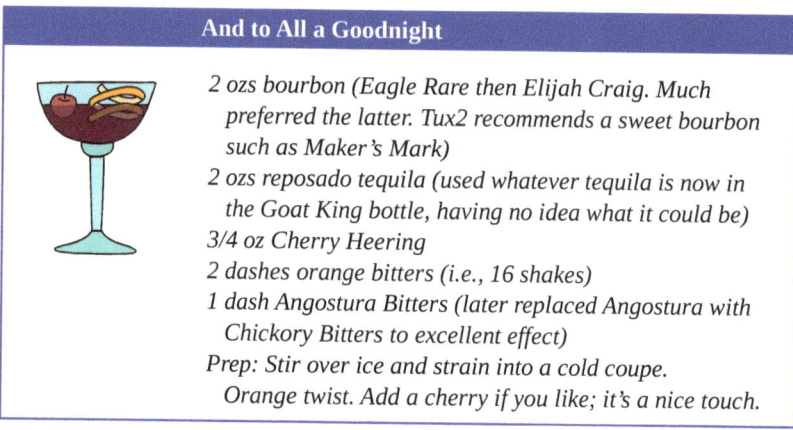

And to All a Goodnight

2 ozs bourbon (Eagle Rare then Elijah Craig. Much preferred the latter. Tux2 recommends a sweet bourbon such as Maker's Mark)
2 ozs reposado tequila (used whatever tequila is now in the Goat King bottle, having no idea what it could be)
3/4 oz Cherry Heering
2 dashes orange bitters (i.e., 16 shakes)
1 dash Angostura Bitters (later replaced Angostura with Chickory Bitters to excellent effect)
Prep: Stir over ice and strain into a cold coupe.
Orange twist. Add a cherry if you like; it's a nice touch.

A wonderful, unusual cocktail (bourbon and tequila? Never heard of the pairing before) that will surely work decantered. Intend to find out.

5 November Thursday

We go to our friends Ken and Kathy's for dinner tonight along with the Morrisseys. Not sure of masking protocol, but Kathy is a doctor. Our hope was to celebrate the great democratic victory. Could be that Biden will be called the winner sometime today, but then he may never be called the winner. Even if he is, we Democrats cannot be said to have won. The Senate remains in Republican hands; here in New Hampshire the State's House and Senate have flipped to Republicans. As a result, there will be no champagne.

But we'll have the much stronger And to All a Goodnight. Here is the decantered version I plan to prepare:

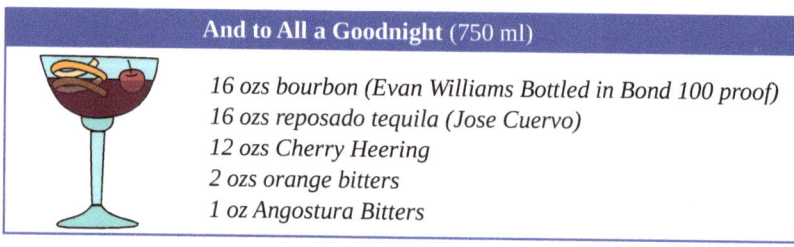

And to All a Goodnight (750 ml)

16 ozs bourbon (Evan Williams Bottled in Bond 100 proof)
16 ozs reposado tequila (Jose Cuervo)
12 ozs Cherry Heering
2 ozs orange bitters
1 oz Angostura Bitters

Will bring along orange twists, Luxardo cherries. Hope for the best… on all fronts.

Note that you cannot make this in a 750ml bottle; it won't all fit. I make it in a big glass pitcher, stir, then pour what will fit into my bottle, putting the rest either into a glass for "testing" or into another, smaller bottle for home use.

6 November Friday

A great time, great dinner, and the drink worked just fine. I avowed that it would put us all to sleep, and we'd wake when the nightmare is over. Okay, we didn't go to sleep, but the nightmare was more fun than it's been these eight months.

We're hosting a farewell to the Ol' Bean tomorrow night for the Luggnuts, setting up outdoors with a tent and heaters. Members of the band are mostly old, the health of several compromised, and all are trying to be very safe. But the Bean has been important enough in our lives that everyone is coming. Today, I'll make Perfect Manhattans, Mothers-in-Law, Poet's Dreams, and Presidentes to go along with leftover And to All a Goodnight, for tomorrow.

Which I did, the Mother-in-Law excluded, though not sure they're all really good. The Presidente seems okay, but the Poet's Dream is quite strong, boozy. Also, would like to make a pitcher of gin and tonic for Ruth with the Alpine syrup that has been here for a while. We'll see.

7 November. Saturday—Biden Wins!

And the Luggnuts, who've always been lucky about timing, celebrated outdoors at the Bean in 70-degree November temperatures. Hallelujah, Hallelujah!!

For the occasion we had Presidente, Mother-in-Law, And to All a Goodnight, Perfect Manhattans, Poet's Dream, and Ruth's G & No T, all good, up to our very high standards.

The last is as follows:

Ruth's G and No T

2 ozs gin (Tanqueray, which is what Ruth likes)
1/2 oz Alpine Tonic Syrup (this is the key ingredient, available online from the Boston Shaker)
4 ozs soda water (Canada Dry, and the 4 ozs is imprecise)
Prep: Mix in a Collins or other tall glass. Garnish with lime peel, serve, of course, over ice.

Oh blessed, blessed day. The Nightmare is lifted, the future bright, our friends joyous. Listened to old Luggnuts recordings with Rick and Ruth, Charles and Andi after everyone else left. My favorite is "Killer Bee," from Waterville Valley Post-Ride concert of about 2018 (I think). Good recording of what I believe to be the best cycling song yet written (it's a small genre): "Never gave up, never gave in/Held on like death, loved it like sin/You pedaled to Waterville Valley, Lord." By D. Swords.

8 November. Sunday.

No drinking. Jenny and I put *Sea Sisters* to bed for winter. Tropical storm Eta is beginning to menace the west coast of Florida, prompting me to think about leaving Monday, not Tuesday, for the long drive down, perhaps to prepare *Lea Scotia* for this storm.

9 November Monday—Leaving New Hampshire

No drinking. Left home at 11:00 and drove to the New Jersey/Delaware border. Listened to the radio a lot, NPR, where no one is noting that Trump's refusal to concede and contention that only well-choreographed fraud could account for his apparent loss is NOT about hoping to win the election or achieve relief from the courts. Rather, Trump is leading his Myrmidons into the ineradicable belief that he and they "was robbed." He wants to show them that he is fighting for the "Right," thwarted by the corrupt government he leads so that upon leaving office his base will be consolidated and a huge force. He'll lead a rump government that commands the Republicans in Congress making it impossible for the Biden administration to work with them. He'll lob grenades every day, gather attention, remain powerful—perhaps have greater power, with no responsibilities. It's his dream job.

10 November Tuesday

Drove to Charleston. Stayed at the Indigo Inn, an old favorite; dined at Hank's, another favorite. The city is replete with memories, including that this is where *Sea Sisters* was when we bought her. But let's talk about cocktails, since we've had enough of this rough abstinent period.

Hank's, a very fine seafood restaurant, has a good bar, and the bartender was my waitress. A signature cocktail is a Rum Old Fashioned, made with dark, I think 7-year-old Flor de Caña and cherry bitters. A bit bitter, but very good. Followed it with two Old Fashioneds made from Buffalo Trace that were much better, excellent. Bourbon is the stronger, more intense spirit. She muddled (lightly) some Luxardo cherries and a bit of orange, sweetened just a bit with Luxardo syrup.

I've adopted the fruitless Old Fashioned, but this is better. Will get the ingredients for *Lea Scotia*, if she survives this night, and try my hand at duplicating the cocktail aboard. If good, it'll be the New Older Old Fashioned.

11 November Wednesday

Long drive, the radio on again. Why is no one saying that Trump's game is not about a second term in office but about a second term out of office? It seems obvious to me that he isn't plotting a coup [Note: Was I ever wrong!] but simply bolstering his stock to become the bully that he loves being without the constraints of a job.

I'd add that his loss is likely soon to resemble the South's loss in the Civil War and to be ultimately judged a great victory. The South quickly beat back Reconstruction, implemented Jim Crow, recovered its lifestyle, and held sway for a hundred years and more. Trump's loss is likely to prove just such a win.

In Georgia the red will turn out and enable the Republicans to keep the Senate, probably helped by Trump. [Wrong again, thank goodness.] On January 20, Trump will muster his force with marching orders making it virtually impossible for Biden to govern. [Right, for a change, but with all the wrong ideas of what this meant.]

At Tim and Beth's while Hurricane Eta sits on our new boat, we drank Dark N Stormies.

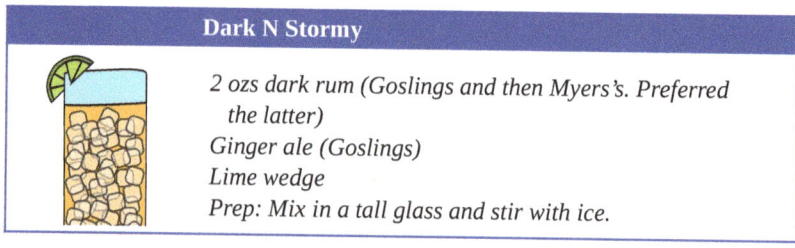

Dark N Stormy	
	2 ozs dark rum (Goslings and then Myers's. Preferred the latter) *Ginger ale (Goslings)* *Lime wedge* *Prep: Mix in a tall glass and stir with ice.*

Simple and good. Helped take my mind off this stormy, stormy day. Worth saying that Goslings holds some copyright or patent on the Dark N Stormy. When you use any rum but Goslings, the resulting cocktail may be a Dark & Stormy, or anything you care to call it, but will not be a Dark N Stormy. We must try to recover from the disappointment.

12 November Thursday

Drove to Ruskin and found *Lea Scotia* hale and hearty. Were almost no signs of the tropical storm. Worked hard moving things, mostly tools and parts from *Sea Sisters*, aboard. Went to the grocery and a Publix Liquor Store, where I found a bottle of Plymouth Gin, which led inevitably to a Plymouth Suze, or three, in celebration:

Plymouth Suze

 *2 ozs (or so, as I have no jigger) Plymouth Gin*
2 ozs or so Suze
1/2 lemon (and later one-half lime. Either works)
Prep: Shake in some sort of shaker and pour ice and all
into a double-rocks, or any, glass.

Suze controls the taste, whether rum or gin, which is fine with me. Have no amaro, no vermouth, limiting the scope of a cocktail.

A Basic, Sound Bar

What about *Lea Scotia's* bar? Space limits us, could limit you, so how about either bourbon or rye, not both, maybe Benedictine as a sweetener? We have superfine sugar as well. Also have Luxardo Cherries. Rum (light and dark), gin, rye; apple brandy; St. Elizabeth Allspice, curaçao, Suze; Jerry Thomas, Creole, and orange bitters; lemons and limes, maybe an orange; and an amaro and a vermouth. A basic, sound bar.

13 November Friday

Driving up the road doing errands, realized how uneasy I am in this red state. The giant fast-moving trucks; disregard for masks, though in this regard, Floridians seem to have improved; knowing that mostly any interlocutor will see me for a liberal. For example, when I invited the Trump-loving AC guy, chain-smoking Steve Ward, for a drink and to pay him, he's not interested.

On the long drive I thought about my reaction to Jenny's cousin Lisa. She is mightily privileged and has a way of saying pheromonally that she suffers us as relatives, though we inhabit a lower social stratum. It's just a feeling I have, of course, but I'll bet it is how Trumpkins feel around liberals. We people give off "I'm better than you" pheromones. It's the same as the racism we know so many people on the right feel without knowing they are racists. Probably no different from a big male gorilla signaling he is in charge.

After a fine dinner of barbecued pork chop, pasta, and a shredded iceberg salad, am drinking a Charleston (Hank's)-inspired Old Fashioned. Here's how to make one:

Hank's Old Fashioned

3 ozs (or so) rye (Rittenhouse. Again, it'll be either bourbon or rye aboard, and I'm choosing rye. The number of ozs depends on your glass, which should be double rocks, filled at the end to within 3/8 inch of the brim)

4 Luxardo cherries (not muddled, but lightly crushed against the side of the glass.)

A tsp or so of syrup from the cherries

Lemon wheel (muddle with the cherries. It is better than orange; use just a small wedge.)

Big dash of Creole Bitters (which is to say 8 shakes, and a fair bit comes out. Or use what bitters you've got.)

Prep: Stir all ingredients including at this point only an ounce or so of rye. Add ice to fill the glass, then add rye until you think you'd better stop, up to 3/8 inch from the rim.

Very dark in the glass, from the bitters, I think, and delicious.

Finally, one is tonight's limit. I've been worrying more than comfortable about drinking too much too often and have been waking up not feeling great. The moderation of old age? I hate it.

14 November Saturday

"The boat is starting to feel ship shape," a sentence I wrote while drinking last night's Old Fashioned. Next, inspired by the alcohol, I suppose, looking into the forward locker for the first time seemed a good idea. Bucky said it was big enough to climb in, only even a roach would have found it hard to fit because the locker was so crammed with gear, important things like a gizmo to keep the boat from rocking and a huge aluminum Fortress anchor. Never seen so much rope, and the canvas for covering the cockpit looked like an unsolvable puzzle. There was the spinnaker taking up a lot of the space. As I pulled things out, I could see there are shelves on either side, all full of STUFF.

Pulled out everything onto the floor of the forward cabin. Today's work has been to make the locker usable and to take off gear that seemed unnecessary. Done. And I am broken tired, but the boat is inching toward being organized. The tools are mostly in a space where I can find them. The gear is not well organized in that I can't lay hands on many things, but I know sort of where and what they are. As Danny suggested, soon I'll try to organize things as if this boat were a Lowe's. My car, on the other hand, looks like a seagoing homeless person is living in it.

Now for a cocktail. We have Allspice, so let's see… Planter's Punch!

This is an old (since summer) go-to cocktail that I usually make way too strong and so somewhere thought it best to discontinue. But limited ingredients call for compromise. Pay attention to this recipe:

> **Allspice Planter's Punch**
>
> *3 ozs (or thereabouts) dark rum (Beth gave me a fifth of Ron Zacapa that Lidieth gave her long ago. It starts out with 23 years of age and Beth had it so long the cork dried out and broke. But… well, more presently)*
> *1 oz St. Elizabeth Allspice Dram*
> *1 lime*
> *3/4 oz simple syrup*
> *10 shakes (= 2 dashes?) Jerry Thomas Bitters.*
> *Prep: Put ingredients in a shaker and shake brutally. Strain into a cold glass.*

Oh, my, my, my this is wonderful. It's like drinking the forest; I mean, the drink has this woody flavor that's unlike anything I've ever had. I'm not one who believes top-shelf liquors make a difference in cocktails. What I think we have here is a remarkable combination. That is, the Ron Zacapa, the allspice, and especially the Jerry Thomas Bitters have combined alchemically to make a cocktail that needs each ingredient as specified and no other.

Going down for the whale on this. No more lime, so drink two will be as before but with 1/2 a lemon. And if I'm able, drink three will use the other half lemon but dark Flor de Caña. You got to love a moment like this (which reminds me the world is burning from Covid… and here I sit).

Drink two was not quite as good, nor did I have another dark rum. Drink three, then, is apple brandy, half a lemon, half a lime (which, it turned out, was loafing in the refrigerator). Mighty good, if not as good as drink one. But not bad.

And, I tested all of the *Lea Scotia's* lights for night sailing. We're ready.

Addendum (very chatty today). VO brandy may not be as good as that beautiful rum, but it is easily better in this cocktail than in any I've made with apple spirits. Allspice Dram, Jerry Thomas Bitters may be the miracle we've spent these months hoping to find.

15 November Sunday

The Crew Arrives

CJ came to help me prepare for the journey from Ruskin, around Florida by way of Key West, and up to our destination, The Harborage Marina, in Stuart. A few words about this son in law. I love him, which is as we're supposed to feel, but after some soul searching, the feeling toward him has its own life. He is smart, brave, strong, and good to Mel and their boys. He's an enthusiast, a Navy pilot who also loves boats. And he loves a cocktail. CJ arranged for his high school friend Brian, an engineer, to join us on the trip. With three able fellows aboard, the voyage should be memorable and relatively straightforward. Three of us means one man can take a four-hour watch while the other two sleep; or, when it is time to eat, I'll cook while one of the others stands watch. The boat has a good autopilot, so "watch" will most often mean paying attention to our course, weather, and other vessels, not steering. We're thinking 48 hours at best to Key West, but more likely it could be 60 hours. I learned long ago that sailboats do not keep to schedules.

CJ and Brian are both on a schedule, the one imposed by the US Navy, the other by an infant whose mother needs help. Once in Key West, the two will go home, CJ driving the Prius, now at the Tampa airport. He has traded his beloved antique Bronco to Al for it. And speaking of the Devil, Al and Skylar are flying to West Palm Beach with Jenny and will drive to Key West to sail with me the rest of the journey to Stuart.

In St Petersburg, CJ and I stopped at my favorite store, Totally Liquored. Other stops were Trader Joe's and a fine lunch of black beans and a flight at a brewpub in St Petersburg. We came back to the boat, put goods away, and started drinking Planter's Punch, quickly finishing enough that CJ couldn't leave. He spent the night.

We used rum and rye, lemon and lime, but always, of course, Allspice Dram, which is the spice that makes this drink what it is.

16 November Monday

Spent the day hard at preparing to depart. CJ went scuba diving with his friend Brian in Brian's uncle Wayne's $200,000 open fisherman. Yes, the price is no typo. Has no head, cannot sleep on it, but $200K. The twin 300 HP engines burn hundreds of dollars in fuel while you travel at 55 mph.

Picked the boys up about 6:00 and dined at a restaurant on the channel where we depart. Not bad. Finished the evening with a Rye Old Fashioned, not my best version, but drinkable.

Part III: The Voyage

17 November Tuesday

The Voyage Begins

Back in about May, tentatively suggesting a voyage metaphor for what we were enduring, I had no clue that along the way we would go to sea. But we are about to cast off in a boat new to us. As every sailor must, we hope for the best... and as happens, the voyage begins problematically...

Aground

Departed the dock a little past 7:00 AM. Touched bottom in the channel, but nothing serious until we came to the entrance to Tampa Bay, at about 7:30. Aground, but backed off; aground again... and again... and again until it is now 3:10 on one of the best sailing days of all time, and we are, as mentioned, aground. Have tried every direction, every approach we could think of short of kedging off by taking the anchor ahead and using it along with the engine to try to pull ourselves to deep water. We launched the dinghy with the outboard and used it with a boathook to test the depth, find a channel, several times thinking we had. But no. And the head in our master cabin is not working. Really, this is disheartening, a terrible beginning.

At last, about 5:00 PM, we crossed the bar, made straight for the St Petersburg I-287 bridge under a good wind, passed through in the ship channel where ships and barges made us uneasy in the dark until we turned south, under a strengthening breeze, driving us onward.

18 November Wednesday

[Note: from this point until we reached Stuart on November 28, the entries are retrospective. That is, I was so beleaguered day and night that writing was impossible and was forced to reconstruct this part of the diary from memory.]

Screaming Along

We averaged 8 knots through the night, screaming along, dry, a following sea. Could have used less sail, but I screwed up reefing the main, though over-canvasing in a following sea was no problem for the boat.

Through the day, wind increased until approaching 30+ knots, seas rose to 10 feet. Before dark we hove to for a rest and dinner (a good one of pot roast in the pressure cooker with carrots, onion, celery served over rice), though all of us were queasy. I know we drank, maybe Planter's Punch, but can't say for sure.

Forty-Knot Gale

Then, we sailed through the night, gale wind up to 40 knots, seas to 12 feet. Sailed fast, too fast, for we feared reaching Key West before daybreak. Running aground there was a historical problem in the 1700s and 1800s that led to a large trade in salvage from reefed boats.

During my watch, the port-side porthole, in the guest cabin where CJ slept, shattered, broadsided by a wave, soaking CJ and everything in the cabin, drowning his cell phone, water streaming through as more waves crashed against the hull. CJ, always resourceful and with Brian's help, improvised something that kept out much of the water crashing against the hull as we sailed on.

Later, during CJ's watch toward morning, but still pitch dark, we began moving toward a shoal and decided to bring in the sails, start the engine. *Lea Scotia* has a mainsail that rolls into the mast, a nice idea that should make reefing easy. But the sail is old and stretched, the rolling machinery worn and cranky. Yet, thanks to CJ's strength and innovation, we doused the sails and went forward under power.

Running with the engine was fine until we began to see the corks that identify crab or lobster traps, hair-raising under power because their lines can easily wrap around a propeller shaft, stop the boat, and in a large sea make her vulnerable to being overwhelmed from the stern. I went forward and stood on deck before the mast to try to spot them and warn Brian at the helm. The seas were so fierce that the boat rolled to what felt like nearly 90-degree angles, but we hooked no traps.

19 November Thursday

Key West

And that's how we arrived in Key West: exhausted, relieved to be sheltered from the storm. Grabbing a mooring in the city field proved difficult, taking several tries in the rough sea while working to avoid being swept into other boats. But after five attempts or so, we hooked on and came to rest, shut the engine down, began in the light of day to see how boat and crew had fared.

Damage Assessment

Lea Scotia was beat up but proven seaworthy. Yet, with that simple, comforting observation, one of the worst, most deeply frustrating, ego-breaking periods of my life began. The proximate cause was the alternator on the boat's Yanmar diesel, which had shorted in the storm.

For all its ability to be propelled by wind, free from the constraints of fuels, a modern sailboat is an electric craft. Starting with the navigation system (who can use a sextant, who wants bulky printed charts?), depth sounder, and including lights, gas for the stove, fans, the windlass for dropping anchor, pump for fresh water, fuel and water gauges, refrigerator and freezer, batteries for starting the engine and generator, the modern sailboat requires both DC and AC power. *Lea Scotia* has a state-of-the art lithium-ion battery bank that stores up to 800 amp hours. With wind, solar, generator, and the engine alternator to replenish her batteries, she can be at a mooring or at sea for weeks or months without shore power.

To track the state of the batteries, we use a monitor that shows how many amps are coming in or going out, the amps stored, and SOC (state of charge) of the entire house and starting battery system. After motoring for several hours, as we had from well before first light until latching onto the mooring, SOC should be 100 percent. But it was not, was down to about 88 percent, reflecting a couple of days and nights at sea with the instruments on continually, solar at work but not fully able to keep up since, for example, we run the refrigerator and freezer (a significant power user) all the time. The alternator should have topped off our stored amp hours. Discovering it had not, we looked right away at the alternator, which Brian could see showed signs of having shorted out.

The aftermarket alternator on the boat, a brand called Balmor, is designed to deliver much more charge than conventional alternators and consequently is much more complex (of course). For example, the Balmor has an external voltage regulator with its own monitor and system of wiring. We had the boat's original Yanmar alternator on board as a spare; Brian's know-how and iPhone access to his dad, a diesel mechanic; tools such as a voltmeter; and even a lighted engine room. We weren't much worried.

Still, stripping out the Balmor wiring and reverting to the original wasn't simple, took much of the day. Once the job was done, we fired up the engine, and to our dismay… nothing. By then CJ and I had lowered the dinghy, strapped its outboard to the transom, and prepared to go ashore. Brian removed the backup alternator, while I fired up the genset, that is, the diesel generator used as another way to keep batteries charged, and CJ prepared to go ashore in the dinghy to find someplace to test both alternators and buy a replacement if necessary. CJ had also found a West Marine chandlery in Key West where we hoped to replace the shattered porthole.

Smoke Below as Impeller Follows the Alternator

While CJ began to load the dinghy with busted alternator and porthole, Brian emerged from the engine room saying smoke had filled the cabin. Simultaneously, from the stern, CJ could see the genset was not pumping water, and I immediately shut the system down.

The good news, maybe more a ray of hope than good news, is that when nothing comes from the raw-water outlet of a marine diesel the cause is obviously a broken water pump, called the impeller, a simple device that works like a fan spinning on a shaft. Thus, while CJ went ashore to investigate the alternator, Brian and I found the impeller housing and began to remove the old one.

Lea Scotia is just large enough to have a real engine room with access, through the removal of sound-proofing panels, on four sides. The one we needed for the genset impeller could be reached through about an 18-inch opening in the aft-cabin shower. Contorting to work on any engine part is difficult. With two diesels shoehorned into the space, a small contortionist with made-for-the-part tools is your best bet. We had neither. But we also had Brian, a smart, determined, experienced fellow who did most of the work to extract the screws from the housing, lost none in the bilge nor any of the tools, and then removed the impeller. One look proved the diagnosis. All of the blades were broken off and chewed up.

Meanwhile, as we went on deck and the day waned, CJ appeared on the horizon gunning the dinghy through white caps to announce that: one, he'd rented a golf cart ashore; two, we needed to check the boat in with the harbormaster; three, he had found at great cost a replacement porthole at West Marine, where they might have replacement alternators if the two we had were dead; and four, we should go ashore before everything closed. Having done our best only to discover the worst, we loaded ourselves into the dinghy and headed into the heart of Key West.

Key West, Land of Pirates

Ahhh, Key West. Home to Hemingway, six-toed cats, Truman's other White House; Jimmy Buffet, Duvall Street, America's southernmost point, dozens of bars, scores of musicians, great food, oddness. And pirates. Key West is like America's other most culturally unique cities, found mainly (Austin excepted) on the coast, such as both Portlands, San Francisco, New Orleans, Charleston, and Provincetown. Colorful; diverse; the result of historical forces, often mostly gone but their effects lingering.

One of the leftover forces in Key West is the pirate contingent, now old men in their withered seventies, drunk, drugged, teeth broken, skin leathered, eyes bloodshot, doing odd jobs, and prepared to take whatever they can get. It is common in Key West to return to your boat and find it has been boarded, perhaps still is boarded, by defiant old men stealing your expensive Raymarine gear. They are real pirates.

We checked in with the harbormaster, loaded into the golf cart, and with Brian as guide, pedal to the metal, lit out for Duvall Street. We went to Captain Tony's Bar, the Sunset Point (if that's what it's called), Sloppy Joe's, and finished the evening at a pretty good Cuban restaurant where the plantains were sweet, as recommended by Brian's uncle Wayne.

Along the way I tried a Hemingway Daiquiri at Sloppy Joe's and though made with canned grapefruit juice it was pretty good. Not on menus, surprisingly.

Later, as we dashed back out to the boat under a new moon, Brian awash on the floor of the dinghy, the day's blessings and curses felt about even, and Friday, the future, looked reasonably hopeful.

20 November Friday

Rising Anxiety

CJ delivered Brian to the fine little Key West airport at about 6:00 AM Friday and returned with a soaked breakfast sandwich as I was drinking a first cup of coffee. We were determined to overcome yesterday's deficiencies, beginning with the impeller if another could be found. To that end, asking the most recent owner, Bucky Jordan, seemed a place to start, as he was a man who believed above all in spares, so much so that I'd taken enough off the boat to fill my car, and a spare impeller could easily be among those parts left ashore. Anxiety, you see, was on the rise.

I texted Bucky to ask if he thought we had a spare and, knowing that an impeller could be almost anywhere and that Bucky's organizing seemed a thing of the moment more than a long-term plan, searching would likely use more of CJ's last day aboard than we'd like. Texting right back, Bucky said to try the upper drawer next to the settee on the port side of the aft cabin, where we found two impellers and a paper gasket.

Such relief, such exultation in something found. For once, perhaps things were not in the saddle.

CJ guided the installation, which took an hour or so and was not easy, especially delicately setting the gasket, but it wasn't long before we had the impeller in place. We fired up the genset; the batteries by now were somewhere around 70-79 percent charged. Water poured from the stern exhaust. But then, as we prepared to go ashore, the aft cabin again filled with smoke, the fire alarm sounded, and we shut down the generator.

Alongside the saltwater cooling system, marine diesels have a freshwater cooling side that, as in an automobile, uses a belt to turn pulleys that circulate the coolant. Because water was still coming from the stern, we knew the impeller was fine. The belt on the Onan genset was invisible behind a housing, and while CJ worked on the smashed porthole, I struggled to take the housing off, finally succeeding by the hardest. Once it reluctantly yielded to my labors, we found the belt had shredded.

Meanwhile, CJ discovered the porthole from West Marine would not fit and would be a more difficult installation. As a result, having done what we could through the morning, we loaded alternator, shredded v-belt, and unfit porthole replacement in the dinghy and went ashore. Once in the golfcart, we drove quickly to West Marine, where CJ returned the porthole and I went to the back, only to learn that they had no alternators.

At a nearby independent chandlery, which is where we went next, again no luck, except a phone number to call Marine Diesel on Stock Island, which I did, and where Mark assured me that he had the exact alternator we needed. But the day was no longer young, if not yet old, so we first tried an electrical supply store.

There, the owner took our shredded belt, quickly interpreted the letters and numbering on the side to mean it was a 360 mm belt, and soon produced 350mm and 370mm replacements of the same diameter, along with a much wider 360 mm belt that he claimed was the likely answer to our needs. The alternator expert had gone for the weekend, but a helpful new employee among this Trump-loving contingent (a sign behind the counter said "Making America Great Again") offered to test ours, reporting that it failed.

We gathered the belts; drove back to the marina, by way of a mail office that would receive the new porthole CJ had found in Connecticut and was having shipped overnight; called a Lyft; and headed off for Stock Island and Marine Diesel where Mark and his crew of pirates were poised to capture any treasure we might have. By now, the workday for regular businesses was over. Not for Mark when he had a mark in sight.

Victims of Piracy

Crew of pirates? Yes, In the early 70s when Jimmy Buffett wrote a "A Pirate Looks at Forty," Key West boys were smuggling weed, drinking heavily, getting laid, and fleecing tourists. In 2020 the extant aged pirates remain, teeth rotten, decades of drink and drugs having reduced them to remnants without hope of sex or much else except fleecing. They seem to get around on bicycles, survive mainly by cleaning parking lots, which apparently provides enough cash to drink through the evenings, so long as they are willing to sleep in a stolen or discarded kayak among the mangroves. Sometimes they run more sophisticated scams.

Mark fits the description entirely, right to the Marlboro between what's left of his front teeth, and announces he does not actually have the new Model 50 alternator he said he had but a rebuilt model 80, which is even better, a boy already taking this "brand new" alternator off an old engine in the shop. I waited with the pirates, them maskless and smoking, looking remarkably like characters from a Johnny Depp film, until Mark's pirate lady handed me the bill for $400.

I paid.

We left with the alternator and a new belt, generator belts from the electric shop, and had high hopes when the Lyft driver dropped us at the marina. Back aboard, CJ worked to install the alternator while I soon found that none of the belts fit the generator. At about 9:00, not knowing precisely how to connect the generator and having given up anyway, we started drinking, though I cannot recall what, cooked a frozen pizza, noted that the batteries were now in the low 60s, and slept.

21 November Saturday

CJ Departs; I Struggle

We sadly drove to the Key West airport in the golfcart, stopping for an excellent breakfast at a little Cuban street shop. CJ was worried about how things would go, felt terrible leaving, but had gone out of his way to find good instructions for installing the $400 new/used, 50/80 pirate alternator and had seen to the porthole that nearly drowned him. Jennifer, Al, and Skylar were due late in the evening, so I was eager to get things working.

On the way back to the marina I stopped at a Napa Auto Parts store to see if they had a belt to replace the 360mm on the genset. They did not have one on hand but had one in their Marathon store and could deliver it to Key West by 2:00 PM. A good start.

Once back at the boat, I installed the pirate alternator, but, before connecting anything, thought it best to ask Angie's help. She is a friend of my brother Danny, a marine electrician in Louisiana, and had worked on *Lea Scotia* in Ruskin. Coincidentally, she had been in Fort Lauderdale looking at a Tayana 40 or 42, which she ultimately bought and sailed back to Louisiana.

Toing and froing took time, but eventually we connected the wires in essentially the configuration CJ left me. Angie's next instruction was to turn the key to "ON" and see if the alternator light glowed. It did not. Angie said that meant the alternator wouldn't work. We decided I should have the pirate alternator tested, so off it came and went with me to the electrical shop in town that tested the Balmor and the Yanmar spare.

Upon reaching the marina in the dinghy, and just as I was ready to leave in the golfcart, a young man approached to ask what I had in mind for the Balmor alternator, which we'd left on the floor of the golf cart meaning to deposit it somewhere as trash. Told him it was junk. He asked if he could have it, and when I said yes, offered to sell me another Balmor he'd taken off a Pacific Seacraft. Offered it for $200. Said I'd think about it if he would install it and would get in touch later. He and another fellow were putting new brakes on an ancient ambulance in the marina parking lot. Pirates, young ones, surely.

$400 Dud

The $400 alternator? No go, said the electrical shop, it was a dud. But they had one that would do just fine and would order another if I wanted a spare. The replacement, this one truly new, cost about $138. I'd also removed the bulb for the alternator from the engine control panel in case it was burnt. They knew what it was, but had none, though they said an auto parts store might.

So, first, I went to Autozone thinking that if they had no bulb Napa would be a good fallback. But they did, and I bought a handful. By now it was close to 2:00, and I went to the Napa store where, hallelujah, the 360mm belt had arrived and looked like the shredded one it was to replace. Back to the boat, things beginning to look up.

All Gone Wrong

The batteries, of course were declining though bolstered by solar and some wind power. But with *Lea Scotia*'s full-time refrigerator and freezer, each night the power dropped a bit even if it was partly replenished by day. Seemed like job one was to get the genset going, and, indeed, installing the belt went surprisingly well. With high hopes, I soon started the genset and quickly raced up the companionway to see if she was pumping seawater. And she was. Only thing, our dinghy was gone.

Such a feeling. First, of being stranded. Second, of loss; the dinghy was worth about $3,000, and we needed it. Third, questions. Had it blown in the strong wind somewhere along the far shore? I couldn't see it. A pirate could find and declare it salvage, charging a lot for its return. Could a pirate have taken it? Sailboats are apparently often robbed in Key West. And most immediate, what to do? How was I to get ashore?

Called the marina, but the dockmaster was no help, offered no suggestions except to try US TowBoat, a service we subscribe to for unlimited towing and have never used. I called them, or tried to, except the call wouldn't go through, nor could I reach them by the Internet. A towing service for boats at sea that, when at sea, you cannot reach? Feeling desperate. The only soul I knew in Key West was Alex, the kid to whom I'd given the old Balmor alternator. Had his card and called him, asked if he could come for me in a dinghy. Must have seemed odd. I must have sounded ridiculous.

Saved by a Saint

He was still working on the brakes but said he could come when done. And I cannot say what I did next, but no more than 10 minutes later Alex sent a text saying he'd put a notice on the marina website about the lost dinghy, and some guy in another boat had responded. I should call him. Sure enough, this saint answered immediately, said I could see him a couple of boats over having a drink on deck, and he'd deliver the dinghy presently.

I knew the boat, *Steel Rules,* as an odd, dilapidated ship. Soon, its dinghy, mine in tow, headed over. I grabbed his dock line, and he handed me the line for our dinghy. Against vigorous protests, he finally accepted a $50 bill; said he always kept an eye open for stray dinghies; and showed no sign of disapproval, condescension, or sense that he must be dealing with a fool. And away he went. Never saw him again.

A Respite

I had shut down the genset to make talking easier (it is a bit loud) and did not turn it on when I went back down to install the new alternator. Also installed new bulbs in the engine control panel. Can't say how long it took, but by the end had no heart left to try the alternator. The day was old, and all I wanted was to leave the boat. Jenny had arranged for me to stay in the hotel where she would arrive much later. I gathered clothes and dop kit and was grateful not to have to return to *Lea Scotia* that night.

Checked into the hotel, looked online for a restaurant, and drove the golf cart downtown. Ate fried conch outdoors with French fries and coleslaw, delicious, along with some Swedish hard cider that was great. No cocktail, but the evening was pleasant.

I returned to the hotel, watched a bit of TV, including a show about pirates in the Keys, and eventually, at 1:00 AM or so, Jenny arrived after the long drive from West Palm Beach. Lying together, with Al and Skylar in the bed next to ours, felt grand.

22 November Sunday

Jenny and I woke first Sunday and went for the free breakfast poolside, where I briefed her on events and what had gone wrong, saying last that the new alternator was in place and I had high hopes it would work but needed last evening ashore in case it didn't because if not, I'd have been likely to throw myself overboard strapped to a cannonball, or to one of the alternators.

Al was especially eager to see the boat, and I'd managed to straighten it enough that he could be impressed, though it still felt damp and, to me, broken. Batteries were slowly depleting, now, I think, in the 50-percent-charged range, which is still okay for lithium ion.

Shoot the Diesel?

The time had come to try the new alternator, so I texted Angie. Al went up and turned the key to ON. Despite the new bulb, no alt light. Frustrated, and not really understanding why the light was important, I told him to start, then rev the engine. It ran, but I wasn't sure how to see if the alternator was delivering any charge and asked him to shut it down by pushing the red button next to the key. He pushed. Nothing happened. I jumped up the companionway, pushed the button. No response, the engine chugging along. How do you stop a diesel when the stop button doesn't work? Wait days for it to run out of fuel? Shoot it? I called Angie, who described a stop cable on the side of the engine accessed through the small door in the aft shower. Couldn't find it. More conversation with Angie. No luck. Al took a turn and suddenly the engine shut down. He'd found the cable.

Refuge in a Laundromat

Now we had another problem with the alternator probably still not working and no idea how this new issue had developed. Angie was off to a wedding or something, and I had no clue. The kids wanted to see Key West. We had wet blankets, sheets, and other laundry that needed washing.

Thus, our Sunday relief from the widening battle with boat systems was delivering ourselves to a laundromat followed later by a long, pleasant, expensive lunch with Al and Skylar along the waterfront. We drank pretty good, if weak, Mojitos made with actual fruit. In Florida, Key West, surely, they felt obligatory. Also, Jenny needed a place to work Monday for an important meeting that could only be accomplished in a hotel room, as it turned out, a nice one in a posh Marriott. That's where she and I spent the night, again, happily, away from the boat. Al and Skylar slept aboard.

23 November Monday

Jenny worked in the room while I returned to *Lea Scotia*. With Al and Angie's help, we began to look for the needle in the haystack of wires that was responsible for preventing the stop button from killing the engine. Torture, impossible, but somehow with the help of a note on an invoice from Cartagena, Colombia, in 2010, and with Al's intuition, we found and connected the blue wire near the yellow wire that controlled the stop button and, for once, the engine performed as hoped.

At some point I went ashore (details fuzzy) and picked up the porthole CJ ordered. Al easily installed it while I worked with Angie. But, by the time we figured out the stop button, the day had waned. We dined aboard and even drank, gin and tonics, I think.

To my chagrin, Jenny, democratic soul that she is, sent the children to the hotel for the evening. We slept well aboard and made way for a busy Tuesday.

24 November Tuesday

Jenny to the hotel, me to the boat by way of Starbucks and Napa where the latter had ordered in two other v-belts as spares for the genset. Worked with Angie and Al to figure out the alternator.

Alternators Everywhere and Not One Will Charge

Again, this alternator is new, non-piratical, that is, unless everyone and every business is a pirate operation here. The configuration is simple. One large red wire, the positive to the batteries, attaches to a post that reads BAT. The only other connections form a T, with the top for a wire that supplies power and the bottom that sends the signal to the ignition key, turning the ALT light on. These wires were attached to a T-connector, so identifying them was foolproof. Yet, we had no ALT light. I separated the two wires, disconnecting them from the T-connector, attaching the top one to the alternator, and with Al's help, strung a wire from the lower, signal wire, to the engine as a ground. And sure enough, the ALT light went on. But when we connected the wire to its terminal, nothing, and Angie said this positively meant the alternator was not charging. Nothing we could do changed this. Electricity may obey the laws of physics. To logic, it seems indifferent.

Ultimately, I decided to go back to the electrical shop to ask if they had an actual T-connector. Of course, they did not, but when I described the problem, they said they had a "self-exciting" alternator that enquired no t-connector at all. I bought it, now heavily invested in alternators that, so far, did not work. Back to the boat.

Removed the other new alternator and discovered that the self-exciting version had a bracket that kept the belt from aligning with its pullies, and nothing could make it fit. Briefly, I thought we'd found a cure, but we had not. I was done for the day.

We picked up Jenny at the hotel, and Jenny and I shopped for food for the voyage. Later, the four of us dined at the outdoor place where I'd had conch, only this time ate a very fine, if slightly tough, Florida lobster.

25 November Wednesday

Originally to be our departure date, we'd decided to stay another day. We needed more groceries for the voyage, had alternators to return, and required a strategy for sailing with no working alternator.

New Strategy: Who Needs an Alternator?

When sailboats are under sail, of course, the engine alternator has no role. Indeed, according to the many experts I'd consulted by now, they mainly top up batteries when under power. We had a working genset, although, since its repair on Saturday, I had not used it much because my head had mostly been in the engine room. But we could run the genset under sail. Angie thought we might need two hours a day, and that would be fine. We also have two solar panels and a wind generator to charge the batteries. In short, I was optimistic that we'd be fine without the engine alternator despite the current draw from refrigerator and freezer and from instruments and lights at night. What I had not counted on was that at some point, perhaps it had already happened, perhaps it happened later, the battery monitoring system that told us the state of charge (SOC) of the batteries, became confused. In effect, it told us we had more charge in the batteries, sometimes up to 100%, than was to prove true.

I installed the latest new alternator because the belt that turns it also turns the pump for the freshwater cooling system but knew it would not contribute to the batteries. We cleaned up the boat, and Jenny and I returned the golf cart, walked to Duvall Street, while the children went for an exhilarating ride on jet skis. We dined along the docks, a terrific lunch with some Waterfront Brewery beers that were good, and later saw the brewery itself. We found a dock for fuel and water and confirmed with the dockmaster that they would open at 7:00 AM Thanksgiving Day.

Then we walked back to the marina, stopping along the way at places that might have parts we needed. We met Al and Skylar and went out to the boat. Al and I hoisted the dinghy and put the outboard on the rail, started the engine and left our mooring. We slowly motored around the peninsula that separates the mooring field from the main waterway through Key West, found a good spot and deployed anchor and new anchor snubber to make the ride over night much more comfortable (and it did). We swam, noting a tremendous current that needed attention or someone could be swept away, and we used the showerhead on the stern to wash off salt with hot water. Felt great.

Cocktail of the night was the Hemingway Daiquiri made with real grapefruit. We slept peacefully. It seems time for a drink recipe, and what could be more fitting in Key West?

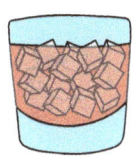

Hemingway Daiquiri (Redux)

2 ozs white rum (Flor de Caña)
1 oz grapefruit juice (fresh)
1 oz lime juice
3/4 oz Cherry Heering (we had no maraschino liqueur,
* which is what you normally use. But I liked the Cherry*
* Heering in this drink a lot!)*
Prep: Shake and pour ice and all into your cocktail glass,
* if aboard ship, probably plastic.*

The soul of tropical Florida, although invented, or at least sort of suggested, by Hemingway in Cuba. In all, the evening made me feel much more civilized.

26 November Thursday—Thanksgiving

Leaving Key West

Awoke and hauled in anchor early so that we had light but not yet sunrise. Easily found the marina with its fuel dock, but a big power boat beat us to the pumps and while motoring, another power boat almost jumped in front of us, except I yelled at the captain that we'd been first in line, and he yielded. Got a lot of water and not much fuel; cast off by 7:30 or 8:00.

Caught by a Crab Trap

We motored out of Key West, past the southernmost point in the US and found ourselves going directly into a stiff wind and rough seas. But it felt great to be underway, until…our prop smashed a marker and wrapped the rope of a lobster (or crab?) trap around the shaft. Skylar was the first to see we had hit it, and I was worried we'd damaged either prop or shaft.

We've sailed for six years in the pot-infested waters of Maine and New Hampshire, but we'd never wrapped one around the shaft. Far fewer of these dangers lurk in Florida, but I'd found one. Alex dove in holding a rope because of the current we'd felt last night. He confirmed the rope was around the prop, but before he tried to cut it out, the rope slipped off. And onward we went.

Day 1: Ten Miles

Not fast, not comfortably. We spent the day motoring into the wind and waves, making a mere 10 nautical miles rather than the 50 or even 75 we hope for, before dropping anchor behind a small key that we hoped would shield us a bit from the sea. It didn't really, but the anchor snubber, a bit of tackle that uses rubber as a shock absorber, helped.

Thanksgiving Dinner

Helped just enough that we barbecued potatoes and steaks on the grill for Thanksgiving dinner. Again, I don't really know what we drank, but we had some sort of probably not great cocktail. I'd gotten into the habit of overpouring, using way too much booze and including ingredients in inharmonious mixes. I'm pretty sure my lack of memory about the cocktails on the trip is less about blacking out than about how badly made they were.

27 November Friday

Up early, we pulled the anchor and again began motoring into wind and waves, slowly. After about an hour of this futility, Jenny called me into the cockpit for a meeting. The idea was to consider alternatives, and we quickly, if on Al's part a little reluctantly, decided to try sailing (imagine that!) by beating close hauled into the wind, shutting down the engine. We would go into the wind as close as we could on one tack, come about, and go into the wind as much as possible on the other. Our plan was to try a couple of short tacks, see how we did making-way north.

Under Sail!

Lea Scotia is a fine sailer, and soon we were going 6, 7, 8, and 9 knots with a much smoother ride. We came about, and the new tack was even better. We followed it pretty close to shore, then came about for a longer tack offshore. And now, we were progressing up the coast.

Near Marathon, we sailed into shallow water while passing divers and could easily see the bottom. The color was gorgeous. By late afternoon our tacks were long, and the wind had shifted enough that on the port tack we were making considerable gains north, the direction we hoped to travel. Near dark, still traveling at 7 knots, Alex noticed something that seemed to be jumping in our wake. Turned out, we'd hooked another trap, soon slowing our progress to a crawl. While I slowed the boat by luffing the sails, Al was able to hook the rope that anchored the trap and to cut us free. We decided then that at least for the night we would stay far enough offshore that there would be no traps. They seem to stop showing up at 150 to 200 feet of water. Worked like a charm.

As night fell, the wind picked up enough to scare Skylar, who, we learned later, was queasy for most of the trip. But we sailed into and through night at speeds of 8 and 9 knots, flying along.

We had decided to divide the watches, with me taking the first from 10 until midnight. Then Al joined me from midnight until 2:00, and during that watch we enjoyed one another's company and sailed beautifully. Al and Skylar had from 2:00 until 4:00 and then Jenny and Skylar from 4:00 until 6:00, when I joined Jenny until 8:00. We stayed far offshore to avoid traps and by morning were closing on Miami. The ride was fine for everyone but Skylar, who was still queasy. At 6 to 7 knots and making good headway north, sailing as well as we could have wished.

28 November Saturday

Progress Up the Coast

The wind quit before noon, so we turned on the engine. It's important to say that our battery meter was showing we had power and as a result I did not run the genset overnight, nor did we run it during the day, in part because the solar panels were going and in part because I was unwilling to run two engines together owing to the heat they would generate in the engine room. Put differently, my mistake, and a serious one. It seems plausible that more than a week of emergencies and failures had eroded my judgment.

The day moved slowly but progress was steady. By nightfall we calculated we'd easily make the St Lucie inlet before dawn, and, as the night was still with no sea at all, we decided to anchor outside the inlet until first light before attempting the circuitous route to the yacht club. I made cocktails for Jenny, Al, and for me... had two myself, thinking the tribulations were over. Used rum and Suze with lime and simple syrup. Strong. Fell asleep.

Everything Goes Dark, Including the Drunken Captain

About 10:30 the call came down from the cockpit that we'd lost all power—no charts, no depth, no lights. I drunkenly stumbled on deck, thinking we should drop anchor as we were near the inlet. But with our electric windlass, you can't anchor manually, or at least, I didn't know enough to know how. As I stumbled in a haze, we decided to keep flashlights handy, to go offshore where we'd be safe from traps, and to motor till dawn. And lucky we did because if the engine had been shut down, even the starter battery might have been so depleted that it would not have turned the engine over.

Jenny and I went below and slept till 2:00, then took our turn on watch. I was mostly sober. The night wore through ever so slowly. A couple of fast-moving boats nearby prompted us to shine flashlights on our mast, but none was dangerously close. And toward first light, we motored to the beacons that announce the inlet.

One Thing Worked: Backup Navigation

One thing we had done well was to have an iPad and a GPS called the Bad Elf for back-up navigation, in case the Raymarine system failed, which without electricity, it had. The standby aboard *Lea Scotia* is what we use as primary aboard *Sea Sisters*; the new 12-inch iPad has a great screen, the Aquamap software is very good, and the Bad Elf GPS picks up satellite signals anywhere in the world. At least I'd been careful to keep both fully charged. With this we identified the lights to the channel and steamed toward them. Much farther out than we'd imagined, by the time we could identify features on land and in the channel, daylight was full.

My last two, or really three, worries were that, first, our 6.5-foot draft would have us aground in the channel, which shoals badly. Fearing this, I'd called the Stuart US Towboat office the day before and asked what they thought. Woody, the gent on the phone, said we'd be fine but to stay on the northside of the channel. Second, Florida has lots of 65-foot bridges, and to get to the marina our 62.5-foot mast needed to pass beneath one of them that a couple of years before had been noted in Active Captain as only 64 feet and dubiously so at that. Third, as always, the landing, especially with a new boat in a new place in what could be narrow confines was a worry, not a huge one, but on my mind. Oh, the responsibilities of a captain, for crew, craft, and preservation of the ego in the presence of onlookers.

The Fishing Armada

Who would have known? As we entered the narrow, meandering channel replete with movable markers that were reset to follow its shoaling, a wave of enormous, fast-moving fishing boats came at us. In fact, not a wave, but wave after wave. These boats would have dwarfed Uncle Wayne's, and their wakes had us pounding sometimes at only 2 knots or so. Alex watched the iPad and kept me in the channel; Jenny and Skylar looked ahead to give us warning. Miraculously, given the record of this voyage, we never bumped bottom. Farther upriver we listened to a VHF conversation between two sailboats that soon passed us headed downriver, one of which had recently gone aground in the channel.

When the bridge came, with our harbor just around the bend, we easily sized up the span to go through, and a gauge said we had 64 feet clearance. The mast did not touch. On we went, soon identifying the outlines of our yacht club, The Harborage Marina, which we'd called. Turns out I knew where to go, and dockhands were waiting at our slip.

One last thing. The marina has filled up. Since we last visited, our part now shelters enormous, mostly 70 feet or more, motor yachts that take up a lot of space and that I did not want to hit. I went slowly, nervously, looking like a rookie and finally crashed a piling with our bow rail. Embarrassing, of course, but no damage. We tied up.

The voyage had ended.

29 November Sunday

Sunday, we found a good breakfast after failing to get any electrical power aboard even connected to shore power. I fired up the air conditioners, which worked briefly, and then everything shut down. Later, Beth picked us up and drove us to Vero Beach, where we had Thanksgiving dinner, a truly memorable one, with Beth, Tim, Timmy, Lidieth, and Theo. We drank wine. Drove back to Stuart. Found our weary way aboard and slept. No power.

30 November Monday

Help!

Early morning, Jenny and I are driving a rented Kia across the state to Ruskin to get my car. A few minutes past 8:00 I call the office of a marine electrician I've tried the day before, one recommended by our marina. His secretary, whom I'd spoken to, answers. She is sympathetic to our plight: no electricity even attached to shore power, no sign that the charger is going to bring up the batteries. But she reports that owing to a flurry of activity, they cannot look at our boat for 4 weeks. By then, without a bilge pump (electric of course) our boat may have sunk in place among the super yachts of the 0.1 percent. Despair, which by now, I'm growing used to.

Jenny recommends another electrician on the marina chart and disconsolately, without much hope, I call. He answers as Rich on his cell. I describe our situation. He says he's at our marina, will look later in the day.

After the long drive across Florida and back, Jenny and I dropped the $50 rental car and went to Tim and Beth's. Rich had visited the boat with Al aboard, and the report was he'd gotten the charger going. We were to touch nothing, and Rich would return for a look in the morning. Felt hopeful, and the beginnings of our land selves, our old selves, were starting to appear.

We stopped at Tim and Beth's, where a cocktail seemed in order, and at long last I set about the agreeable task of making not just one, but a decanter, based on ingredients in the house and the much loved Mother-in-Law recipe, which, owing to substitutions and to Beth's status, we hailed as the

Stepmother-in-Law
2 ozs Peychaud's bitters
2 ozs Angostura bitters (as I said, it's what they had, bought by me)
2 ozs Amaro Nonino
1 oz Mathilde Poire Liqueur
2 tsp Cherry Heering liqueur
750 ml Woodford Reserve bourbon.
Prep: You can use a measuring cup and a decanter, of course. Just stir or shake and pour over ice in a double-rocks glass.

It seemed too boozy for Beth, so I recommended drinking it over ice, with a splash of water. When we return, we'll see.

Jenny and I stopped to rent a storage unit and unloaded the gear I had taken from the boat and that could be sorted later. We found our way to *Lea Scotia*, and Al and Skylar had chosen a lovely restaurant, Sailor's Return, where the two of us dined, drinking inexcusably weak Margaritas, one lonely ounce of tequila in a 16-ounce beer glass. Still, I liked the place. And then, weary and in the dark, we slept.

1 December Tuesday

Good as his word, Rich returned. The batteries were indeed charging, and we could use the boat's electricity at last. The freezer, which had seemed broken as its temperature rose before we lost power, apparently had too little sustenance to turn on the compressor, but was now cooling fast. (A lesson I hope we never need to use.)

Rich had other work and was headed for a vacation in San Diego with family but took notes about what needed doing, said he'd return after December 15. With that, we cleaned *Lea Scotia* pretty well. Jim, a dock guy, pumped the holding tank. Jenny worked hard; I left out the various alternators for Rich to have checked. Made our way to Vero and dinner, then on to a hotel near the airport in Tampa.

2 December Wednesday

An 8:30 flight to Baltimore; arrived Boston 3:30. Took a Lyft to Ipswich where we gathered Jenny's car and, after three weeks, drove home.

Lessons for an Old Man

We leave behind in Florida an eventful month, our metaphorical voyage transformed into a harrowing trial. Doubts about the boat, the idea of living aboard in Florida, my competence all are afoot. Meanwhile the Bean is for sale in a red-hot market. Odd that, during a time when so much is shut down, our lives are changing quickly and profoundly.

Back in May when the voyage was nothing but an incipient metaphor, I wrote, of a home bartender

> *A vital part of your work will be to keep your ship, your world, off the rocks (although we'll often take our cocktails on the rocks). You'll want to watch for the lee shore of anxiety, looking ahead and calculating the prospects of storms and other perils you will face. Caring for the crew begins with caring for yourself, which in the context of a bar means knowing and, usually, observing limits.*

My failures to understand limits are laid naked in this Diary. Limits come in many forms: exhaustion, time, capabilities, a tired boat, preying strangers, electricity meters, a poorly tied knot, malchance, and alcohol in the wrong place at the wrong time. The last is the worst because the most controllable.

If driving after drinking is stupid, for the captain of a vessel, drinking while sailing is unforgiveable. After what had gone before, the night we lost power and I drunkenly stumbled around the deck has left me dismayed, broken in ways that may not heal. It's true enough that alcohol temporarily relieves us of our cares. For a captain at sea, however, the ironclad rule of responsibility for crew and boat is that any refuge that dulls judgment must be shunned.

With that admission, declaration, promise, now ashore, I need a drink.

How about Sawyers?

Part IV: Strange New World

3 December Thursday

At last life is returning to normal. Sort of. Did things I like: worked out; took the motorcycle to the liquor store for gin, as Alex and company had drunk most of it; tended fires in the wood stoves; began a gumbo from leftover turkey; read the paper; met Meg's new dog Fred; learned of our neighbor Patrick's infidelity in Korea and his plan to marry his paramour; and in Tux2 found a new cocktail.

Could any cocktail have a more poetic name than Pale End of the Day, whose evocative power frames the mood for when and how we drink? I loved this one before ever preparing it, and although I shook a drink that calls for stirring, was not disappointed. Its clear, pale-yellow hue, sweetness with a hint of tart, gentle strength (for its main ingredient is vermouth) make the Pale End of the Day (such a pleasure to type the words) just the drink for a night you ease into after a day that doesn't need to be forgotten.

Pale End of the Day

2 ozs blanc vermouth (Dolin Blanc. There are others, but they are not easily found and Dolin is excellent anyway)

3/4 oz London dry gin (I started with Sipsmith and preferred it to Plymouth. Really any London dry should be fine if not too juniper forward. Beefeater will be my next one. Sapphire should be excellent)

3/4 oz pear or peach liqueur (thought we had Mathilde Poire but that is in Florida where we are not. We had peach, and it was terrific)

Prep: Stir with lots of ice until the stirring glass is frosty. Strain and serve in a chilled coupe. Pear or peach slice for garnish if you have it. No garnish if not.

Simplicity itself. Note that you can easily make a larger dose by increasing the ingredients proportionally without damaging yourself. E.g. 3 ozs vermouth to 1.25 ozs gin and liqueur. That way you won't have to make as many.

4 December Friday

Steve Poore wants my thinking on the New Orleans classic, the Sazerac, a drink I've mostly avoided in these pages. But the Sazerac is an imperative, and for a New Orleans native, a sacrament. Here goes.

I've spent a lot of time at the fabulous Sazerac Bar in the Roosevelt Hotel, once sharing a table with the singer Lou Rawls, who was appearing there in the Blue Room. But I've never been perfectly happy with the Sazeracs the very able bartenders turned out, mostly because they aren't cold enough to suit me. Also, the bar uses Sazerac rye, fitting, but not great. Years ago, I stole two glasses from the bar, which are single, as opposed to double, rocks glasses, and they are among the Bean's most prized and useful glassware. Today I had the remnants of a bottle of Sazerac rye.

Sazerac

The key to this drink is its preparation. The ingredients are carved in stone (well, you can take your pick of rye or, by the way, cognac), absinthe (or an approximation such as Herbsaint or Pernod), Peychaud's bitters, sugar, and lemon peel garnish, but how you assemble them is all.

Step 1. Fill the glass you will drink from with ice and set it aside. Better yet, keep the glasses in your freezer, though at the Bean this is inefficient because the bar and freezer are far apart. A single-rocks glass is best, but a double is fine. The Sazerac Bar does not chill the glasses, I guess because they serve so many, and that omission is, in my view, fatal.

Step 2. To a mixing glass, add 2 ozs rye (after the Sazerac was gone, used Old Overholt, which is much better and, of course, cheap. Many New Orleans bars do the same.)

Step 3. 3 dashes Peychaud's Bitters (real 1/8 tsp dashes, so 3/8 tsp). Some New Orleans bartenders like to use Peychaud's and Angostura bitters, and if you do, the ratio should be at least 3:1, that is 3 dashes of Peychaud's to 1 dash of Angostura.)

Step 4. 1 barspoon superfine sugar or a cube (the standard) or simple syrup

Step 5. Without yet adding ice, stir, or muddle if using a cube, to dissolve the sugar. Then add ice and stir for at least 20 seconds but 30 or even more will be better.

Step 6. Pour the ice out of the single-rocks glass or take the glass out of the freezer. Dry it a bit if needed. If you have a mister, use it to coat the glass with absinthe. If not, pour in a teaspoonful and swirl it around the glass. Drink the extra (or toss it, but why would a sane person do that?).

Step 7. Strain the mix of rye, bitters, and sugar into your glass. Spritz with a twist of lemon and rub the peel around the rim, then drop the lemon peel into the glass.

Oh, New Orleans.

The city forever claims any distinction for which it can make even an implausible case. The origin of the word cocktail, local lore has it, comes from Monsieur Antoine Amedie Peychaud, who served his bitters in a *coquetier*, a French egg cup, which evolved into the word we use today. Since he invented the word for cocktail, let's go ahead and cite the Sazerac, which originated in New Orleans no earlier than the 1860s and probably later, as the original cocktail. At the time, by the way, the Sazerac was cognac based, fitting given its French Quarter birth. But a plague killed most cognac vines in France, leading to rye as the substitute, though you certainly can use either and rightly call the result a Sazerac.

Finally, you'll have observed that the Sazerac is much like an Old Fashioned, though served up rather than on the rocks, and is a drinker's drink. One could go so far as to say the absinthe in a Sazerac plays the role of a cherry or a bit of orange in an Old Fashioned. Absinthe went missing by fiat for nearly all of the 20th Century and was replaced by Pernod or, in New Orleans, the locally made Herbsaint. Absinthe is better.

For many, in a world without other choices, one or the other—Sazerac or Old Fashioned— would suffice. What higher praise can there be?

5 December Saturday

Starting to feel like we're home. A pleasant, snowy day. How about a Ward 8, a Boston cocktail?

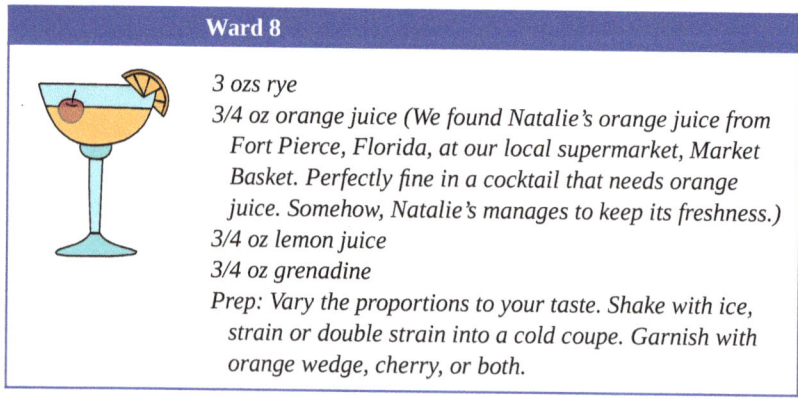

Ward 8

3 ozs rye
3/4 oz orange juice (We found Natalie's orange juice from Fort Pierce, Florida, at our local supermarket, Market Basket. Perfectly fine in a cocktail that needs orange juice. Somehow, Natalie's manages to keep its freshness.)
3/4 oz lemon juice
3/4 oz grenadine
Prep: Vary the proportions to your taste. Shake with ice, strain or double strain into a cold coupe. Garnish with orange wedge, cherry, or both.

A delicious cocktail from a city that should have many more to call its own. If not a classic, only because bartenders or cocktail advisors get the proportions wrong, typically shorting either the orange juice, which really works here, or the grenadine. Try this recipe, which should come close to filling most coupes. You could go with 2 ozs rye and 1/2 oz of the other ingredients, but why would you?

Welcome to New England.

6 December Sunday

Worked around the house, did some sewing, bought badly needed rye. Made the best gumbo—turkey and andouille—I've ever cooked. Ate early, but began as follows:

The Monte Carlo is a classic cocktail that, I thought, we'd had before, but it appears nowhere else in the diary. And the Monte Carlo deserves to be a classic.

Monte Carlo

2 ozs rye (Old Overholt)
1/2 oz DOM Benedictine
2 dashes Angostura Bitters (real 1/8 tsp dashes, or about
*   six shakes each from my shaker bottles)*
Prep: Stir, pour ice and everything into a single-rocks
*   glass. Garnish with lemon twist.*

Built like a Sazerac or an Old Fashioned, but with Benedictine as the sweetener, this one has a life of its own.

We both loved this one, but Jenny probably even more than me, which is quite a bit. Here's a cocktail that could be a regular for us.

Anyway, once the gumbo, rice, and French bread were ready, we needed a new cocktail, and decided on Jamie Boudreau's Nirvana, which we loved in July. The trick with this one is that no one has Amer Picon. Last time I used Amaro Nardini and Punt e Mes, and the entry says they were great. But not as great as tonight's:

Nirvana

2 ozs rye (Old Overholt 90 proof. Boudreau insists you
*   need 100 proof or it is too sweet. I'm here to say that*
*   ain't so.)*
1 oz Averna Amaro (this one, to me, is dark and bitter
*   enough to counter the sweet perfectly. I'm staying with it.)*
1/4 Luxardo Maraschino Liqueur
1/4 oz DOM Benedictine
1 real dash Boker's Bitters.
Prep: Stir, pour ice and all into a double-rocks glass.
*   Garnish with an orange twist.*

Even better than its cousin, sister, Monte Carlo. The amaro is key and makes this a first-rate candidate for the decanter. I'll return to Nirvana often.

7 December Monday—Pearl Harbor Day (only more people died today of Coronavirus than died at Pearl Harbor)

And the Boxcar War

It occurs to me on a day when a great war began for the country, now that we're in New Hampshire, to consider the result of our little Boxcar War. After the city fathers and mothers agreed to allow an extra thirty days for Tim and Beth to remain in the boxcar, with the likelihood, if not promise, of longer if needed, the weather began to cool enough that Tim was ready to go south. He hates to be cold. We had already made clear that we would sell the Bean, tried to find a place in Maine to re-settle all of us with the boxcar, failed, and moved to buy *Lea Scotia* in Tampa. We decided to look for a place to rent in the vicinity of Warner or perhaps Portsmouth, while Tim and Beth investigated campgrounds that permitted long-term stays, especially along the coast. Ultimately, however, Sandy Beach in Contoocook, a short distance from where we have lived for almost 25 years, looked reasonably priced, available, and had the advantage of being close to Chi, the carpenter who had built the boxcar and who would help set it up. Beth rented a spot for the coming summer, and Chi came for the boxcar, housing it on his property over winter. Beth and Tim moved in with us until leaving for Florida about October 12, well short of the deadline they had been granted.

The removal of the boxcar proved, first, that it was no tiny house. That is, Chi built it to conform to rules for an RV, which means it is licensed to be on the road. Our neighbors had insisted it was a tiny house, which is to say, stationary. Who can say whether the fact was a source of happiness or disappointment to our angry neighbors?

The For Sale sign at the Bean demonstrated that we planned to leave and the boxcar, as a result, would not return. Meanwhile, on Facebook and personally, many people in Warner and nearby expressed outrage at the mistreatment of J's parents and at the notion that the boxcar was anything but an adornment. One of our neighbors, Meg Stewart, gathered signatures to send to the selectmen in support of both the Goodriches specifically and of allowing tiny houses on one's property for relatives in general. A community activist, David Bates, studied the legal barriers and took up the cause directly with the selectmen in support of amending the town's bylaws to allow what we had done. Other neighbors, George and Joan Packard, had studied tiny houses in California, made films about them, were delighted and heartened to see the boxcar, and joined Meg's cause.

That said, although not liking to harbor grudges, I remain angry at the mean-spirits of people who formerly were friends, even close friends. Especially traitorous seemed our neighbor Beverly, a widow who had posed as a potential buyer of one of Chi's "tiny houses," had dined with us many times, been an original fan of the Luggnuts, accepted as a gift from us our Mason & Hamlin piano, and called on Jennifer more than once in distress. Before the boxcar arrived, we'd planted trees so that from her porch, she would hardly see it.

It is astonishing that with nothing to lose, with no reasonable cause except an imagined offense to their eyes, people who take freedom to do as they please as a fundamental right will try their best to disrupt, if not persecute, an elderly couple who share their politics and party and who could be, well, who could be them. Perplexing. Let's have a drink.

Stayed with the Monte Carlo, indeed three of them. Altered the recipe slightly to 2.25 ozs Old Overholt and used two (real) dashes each of Angostura and Peychaud's bitters. (Again, a real dash from my bitters containers requires six shakes.) Same 1/2 oz Benedictine.

A classic improved. And indeed, I'm thinking this could be my go-to drink at good bars.

8 December Tuesday

Every night I have hard dreams about the boat, the journey to Stuart. New cocktails feel like a way of getting back to the life we'd been living. From Canon, here is tonight's loveliness:

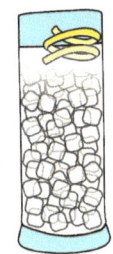

Bohemian French 75

1.5 ozs gin (Beefeater)
1/2 oz St Germain (this elderflower liqueur is underused.
  I've long deployed it in gin and tonics to good effect, but
  don't think I've ever made an official cocktail with it.
  Well, that's probably not true. But not many of them.)
1/2 oz lemon juice (or half a lemon)
1/4 oz simple syrup
2 ozs (or so) prosecco or champagne
1/4 oz absinthe
Prep: Pour the gin, St Germain, lemon juice and simple
  syrup into a shaker with ice. Shake hard. Pour ice and
  everything into a pilsener or a Collins glass. Fill to
  about 1/2 to 1/4 inch from the top with the prosecco or
  champagne, and then float the absinthe, garnish with a
  lemon twist.

A Jamie Boudreau drink, or at least from his book *Canon Cocktails*. The first sip brings you to a close encounter with the absinthe and is breathtaking. After that, the combination is balanced, nuanced, yet strong tasting, a fine cocktail that deserves many iterations. And we had two, but then, I wanted a tequila drink, perhaps because the two 16-oz Margaritas at Sailor's Return in Stuart seemed to share about 1 oz of tequila. Remember the Alamo, page 118, *The Canon Cocktail Book*:

Remember the Alamo

1/4 oz absinthe
1.5 ozs reposado tequila (Jose Cuervo)
1 oz Punt e Mes
1/4 oz Luxardo Maraschino Liqueur (the recipe calls for
  Cherry Heering)
2 dashes Angostura bitters (i.e. 12 shakes)
Mist a cocktail glass with absinthe. Add the other
  ingredients to a mixing glass with ice, stir, strain into the
  cocktail glass. Garnish with the cherry.

Another fine cocktail that deserves remembering.

9 December Wednesday

Intended not to drink, but Jean, Jenny's mother, is here, and Jenny needed something. Jean takes her scotch with ice and a bit of water. So, why don't we try a scotch cocktail, and what better place to begin than a classic, the Rob Roy.

As a teenager, scotch, especially The Famous Grouse, was my go-to spirit. I'd gotten sick on cheap bourbon and on awful vodka and been wasted on tequila. But I was never sick on scotch. As a young man, I'd been tutored in Inverness by an old Scotsman on how to drink whisky, in his estimation, best done neat with beer, an express ticket to that delightful lifting of the spirits and, if one liked, beyond. As to beyond, one night of whisky and beer at the Newton Hotel led to two memorable evenings with a widow, Jane Oliver. Thus, long before single malts made themselves felt on American shores, I learned to savor the mighty Glens, -morangie first, and later Glens -livet and -fiddich, before moving on to even finer whiskys such as Lagavulin, Macallan, and the lady scotch, Dalwhinnie.

But first beer and then cocktails, and along the way the great cost of single malts sidelined my interest. Dr. Cocktail has a scotch cocktail or two that I've tried, and the Ol' Bean Bar always has Drambuie on hand in case someone asks for a Rusty Nail, though no one ever has.

It was without high expectations that I opened the patient Famous Grouse to pour a Rob Roy and discovered a great classic.

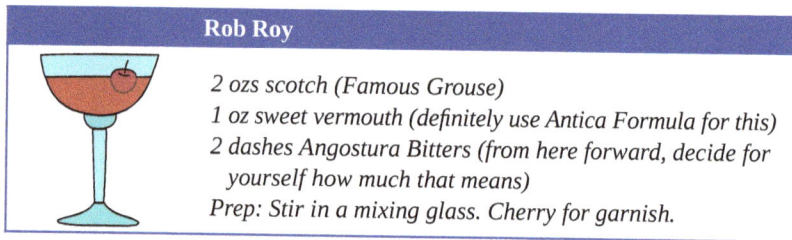

Rob Roy

2 ozs scotch (Famous Grouse)
1 oz sweet vermouth (definitely use Antica Formula for this)
2 dashes Angostura Bitters (from here forward, decide for
* yourself how much that means)*
Prep: Stir in a mixing glass. Cherry for garnish.

Who knew? Who knew that scotch could result in a great, simple, three-ingredient cocktail, a Manhattan made with scotch rather than rye? Who knew a Rob Roy was this excellent and did not require Drambuie? And if not, who knows what to do with the patient Drambuie that's been awaiting a Rob Roy? Oh, right, make a Rusty Nail.

It's mainly the bitters and Antica Formula, I think. But the scotch, in a subdued way, works. I'd order this in a bar, but they need Antica Formula, and they need to understand what a dash is.

Beyond that the Rob Roy deserves a single-malt test, perhaps several, although, come to think of it, that would be a costly experiment.

10 December Thursday

Often when I've had a revelatory cocktail one night, we'll go back to it the next to see whether it was something about the night or the cocktail itself that was excellent. So again, Rob Roys, my first with Chickory Pecan Bitters. Bad idea. For the second went back to Angostura.

11 December Friday

Drank a couple beers with an Indian dinner but that's all.

12 December Saturday

At a kind of birthday for me, dined at the Bean with Marge and Doug, and Susan and her new man Keith. I had elaborate plans for cocktails, especially Espresso Martinis, which Marge loves, but they didn't quite work out. For me the gathering was largely to tell Marge and Doug the story of our recent voyage, by way of declaring our experience sailing "Downeast" last year wasn't so bad. Thought it could make Doug feel better. Turned out, on the way over, Doug, who has Alzheimer's, asked Marge, "Who is David and who is Jennifer, and how do we know them?"

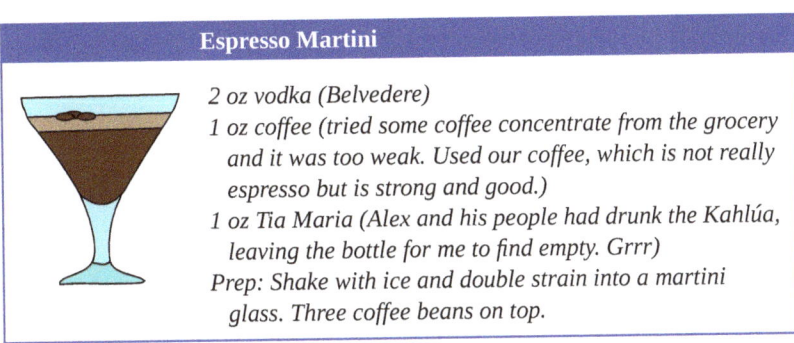

Espresso Martini

2 oz vodka (Belvedere)
1 oz coffee (tried some coffee concentrate from the grocery
  and it was too weak. Used our coffee, which is not really
  espresso but is strong and good.)
1 oz Tia Maria (Alex and his people had drunk the Kahlúa,
  leaving the bottle for me to find empty. Grrr)
Prep: Shake with ice and double strain into a martini
  glass. Three coffee beans on top.

Marge claimed to like it then switched to wine. I didn't try it. Jenny had a Monte Carlo, and I had a Pale End of the Day, or, rather, two of them, a good party drink because its vermouth base means it is not strong, and its taste is divine.

13 December Sunday—My birthday. 71 years. YIKES!

I used to think that living until 72 was a fair deal, long enough that one who did should not feel cheated of time. Now, I'd prefer to go longer. What do you expect?

Might try that Espresso Martini tonight, just to see…

Oh, the Espresso Martini! It's a game changer. The key was a tip on our coffee from Greg of "How to Drink." He explains that the Italian pot we use does not yield espresso, not enough pressure. But a couple years back my brother Danny sent us beans from his friend Margot Brignac, who roasts coffee and has a little company called Flamjeaux. The coffee was great, and we've been getting it from Margot ever since.

Greg, however, persuaded me that the coffee in our pot's basket might be tamped down to yield something stronger. I ground the beans, tamped them and filled the basket and tamped some more. Poured the coffee into a cream pitcher and put it in the freezer to take the heat off. And then

Espresso Martini (Redux)

2 ozs vodka (the Polish Belvedere. We do not keep vodka at the Bean. I consider it the spirit for people who dislike spirits. But last year in London we had a Polish vodka that was great. So here we are)

1 oz coffee liqueur (Tia Maria is what we have. Will get more Kahlúa)

1 oz coffee (Flamjeaux brewed in our Italian pot on the stove. The pot is a Bialetti. What you need is the Bialetti one cup, $23 from Amazon. No need for a bigger one as you'll just waste coffee. Of course, you could buy a $500 or more espresso maker. But trust me, you won't need it.)

Prep: Pour the ingredients into a shaker, add ice, shake hard, double strain (says Greg) into a Martini glass. The frothy top (delicious) will support the three coffee beans you must use for garnish.

As you sip the cocktail, now and again a bean will float into your mouth. Chew it and drink at the same time. Delicious. The sweet drink makes the bitter bean better (my first cocktail tongue twister!) in the way chocolate-covered coffee beans taste great.

Here's the thing. You get the immediate effects of alcohol, but you also get the enlivening effects of caffeine. In the cocktail world, I've found nothing else like this.

Happy birthday.

14 December Monday

The Ol' Bean Tavern is Sold

Today a good offer came, and we sold the Ol' Bean Tavern. Heartbreaking, in that we love the old tavern and its memories. But the time comes. We've found a place to rent that looks just right as it is nearby and has plenty of space. I guess the neighbors will think they've run us out of town and good riddance. Welcome to 71?

Jenny loves a Manhattan, but in the spirit of the moment, how about something a bit different, say, the Red Hook, or a modified Red Hook. Modified? The Tux2 recipe calls for sweet vermouth, and without looking further, I chose the red vermouth that is the one we go to automatically, Carpano Antica Formula. Wrong.

The recipe actually calls for the deeper, more bitter Punt e Mes. Ah well. I'll add that on a second try. For this one, we added just a half-dash (three shakes) of Angostura. Jenny right away proclaimed it improved, and I think a whole dash or two would have improved it more.

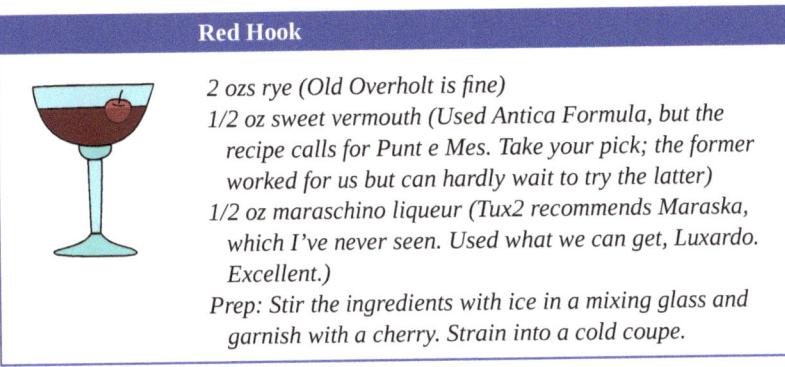

Red Hook

2 ozs rye (Old Overholt is fine)
1/2 oz sweet vermouth (Used Antica Formula, but the
recipe calls for Punt e Mes. Take your pick; the former
worked for us but can hardly wait to try the latter)
1/2 oz maraschino liqueur (Tux2 recommends Maraska,
which I've never seen. Used what we can get, Luxardo.
Excellent.)
Prep: Stir the ingredients with ice in a mixing glass and
garnish with a cherry. Strain into a cold coupe.

One of those cocktails that you can work with to finely adjust its taste to yours. According to *Death & Company's Cocktail Codex*, Manhattans are in the Martini family, especially in their ability to present more sweet or more bitter, more flavored or stripped down, but all quite simply are indeed Martini-like. We've tested the standard Manhattan, the Black Manhattan, and now the Red Hook, and other cocktails in the family, finding all of them a pleasure. Best to keep plenty of rye on hand.

15 December Tuesday

The Rob Roy was so good a few days ago that, when I stumbled on the Scotch Dram in *Death & Company* and saw that it specifies Drambuie, which has been slowly evaporating from its bottle after years of neglect, we had no choice but to take the night off from a night off from drinking:

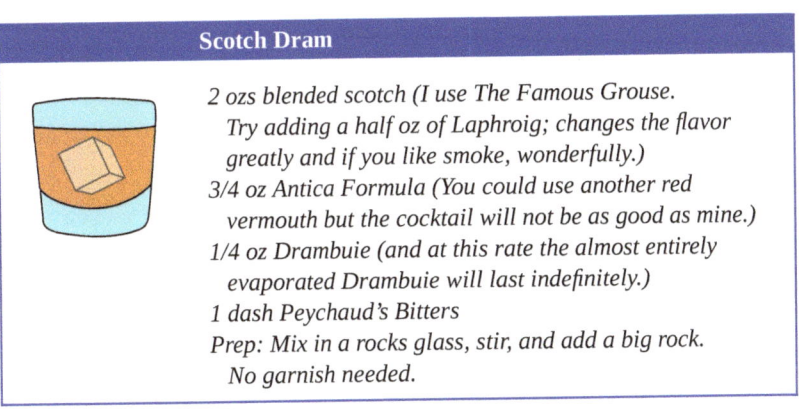

Scotch Dram

2 ozs blended scotch (I use The Famous Grouse.
Try adding a half oz of Laphroig; changes the flavor
greatly and if you like smoke, wonderfully.)
3/4 oz Antica Formula (You could use another red
vermouth but the cocktail will not be as good as mine.)
1/4 oz Drambuie (and at this rate the almost entirely
evaporated Drambuie will last indefinitely.)
1 dash Peychaud's Bitters
Prep: Mix in a rocks glass, stir, and add a big rock.
No garnish needed.

Love it. And at last we have a use for Drambuie! Don't you like the play on words?

16 December Wednesday

The last time we asked the bartender to make us Millionaires was March 30, as the pandemic was just getting started. Tonight, while we won't be millionaires, the sale of the Ol' Bean should put some money in our pockets, so the cocktail seems made for the occasion, as we process the idea of moving on.

Millionaire (Today's beginning recipe)

2 ozs Pirat dark rum
1 oz Plymouth Sloe Gin
1 oz apricot brandy (bottom-shelf "apricot-flavored" is fine)
1 oz lime juice
1/4 oz raspberry syrup
Prep: Shake and strain into a cold coupe; garnish with a
*   lime wedge or wheel.*

By now, we've drunk many dozens of cocktails together, and nearly always they are classifiable. I'd say the Millionaire, however, is *sui generis*, making it all the more interesting. You could call it a sour, but it would stand alone in relying on sloe gin, probably the key ingredient, certainly not a replaceable one, and then you've got the apricot brandy, which is not brandy but a liqueur. Call it a sour if you must; it does have lime; but I'm sticking with *sui generis*.

And with that, the complications begin. The recipe above adapts Dr. Cocktail's by adding the raspberry syrup because, despite his insistence, the drink is too sour without it, or at least not sweet enough. He also specifies Myers's rum, or Jamaican rum (Appleton would be another) as does Harry Craddock in *The Savoy Cocktail Book* of 1930, the first appearance of this drink. I tried a Haitian rum, Bermuda rum, Nicaraguan rum—all dark and all fine. Way back in March I declared Pusser's Rum from BVI my favorite. And on the last of the three incarnations last night, I used an ounce of Flor de Caña and an ounce of Goslings 151, which turned an already powerful drink into, well, a knockout (I mean that literally).

17 December Thursday

… continued

Harry Craddock presents his version of the Millionaire we have been discussing and calls it "No. 1." Then he gives us "No. 2," but it looked so unlikely that we went with the most common version, found on the Internet, this one at Liquor.com.

Millionaire (No. Who Knows?), **Bourbon Millionaire**

1/2 oz raspberry syrup (the recipe calls for grenadine.
*   Need to make some)*
1/4 oz absinthe (the recipe calls for Ricard Anisette.
*   See note below.)*
3/4 oz Grand Marnier
2 ozs bourbon (Elijah Craig)
1/2 lemon
1 oz egg white
Prep: Dry shake to emulsify the egg white, then shake
*   with ice. Strain into a cold coupe and garnish with*
*   ground nutmeg. This is by far the most common version*
*   I've found. Very Christmassy.*

And it is not good. Potent, tasty, but a taste that appeals to neither Jenny nor to me. No more of the Bourbon Millionaire. On the other hand, replacing anisette with absinthe was deviation enough that in reality this wasn't really a Bourbon Millionaire. Ah well.

What about the Gin Millionaire Harry Craddock calls No. 2? We'll see, but perhaps no time soon. Sorry, Harry.

Anisette/Absinthe: What's the Difference?

What's the difference between anisette and absinthe? Anisette is a liqueur and is sweet; it contains sugar. Absinthe is dry. Both rely on anise for their licorice flavor. Absinthe is quite strong, anisette not so much.

18 December Friday

With Christmas a week away I'm under pressure to discover just the right Christmas cocktail. Ideas come to mind. A Last Word because its monkish Chartreuse and the finality of its name imply Christmas. Or how about, And to All a Goodnight, whose strength, from bourbon and tequila, should help us sleep despite the anticipation of Santa's arrival. By contrast, tonight we'll try a coffee cocktail, the Revolver, because it is dark, deep, and should help us to stay awake on a Friday.

Revolver
 *2 ozs bourbon (the original calls for Bulleit, which I don't have. How about Woodford Reserve for a start?)* *1/2 oz coffee liqueur (at last, Kahlúa is in the house)* *2 dashes orange bitters* *Prep: Combine over ice and stir for at least 15 seconds. Garnish with a flamed orange peel.*

According to Tux2, the drink has attained "borderline modern-classic status." But it wasn't interesting, too thin, certainly no Christmas libation.

As a result, I made And to All a Goodnight, but this one didn't work either.

19 December Saturday

At Rick and Ruth's, outdoors and in the 20s; happily, Rick had a wood-burning jet engine of a fire-pit that, mostly, kept us warm, at least half of us (the front half or the back half) at a time. But the cold did curtail our drinking.

20 December Sunday

Tomorrow is the year's shortest day. We x-country skied with Brick and Laura, tried to get ready for the inspection of our house tomorrow on behalf of the buyers. But mostly, I fretted about a Christmas cocktail, and found one.

I'd given the Boulevardier some thought, so when Al sent the cocktail menu from the Sazerac in New

Orleans, and the drink was among their offerings, it had to be tried. Except, turns out, I tried it July 22 with effusive praise, which was not nearly enough.

Skipping to its Christmas credentials, the beautiful red conferred by all three spirits is heavenly; I guess red can be heavenly, but who can say? And then you can garnish this beauty with lemon, cherry, orange, or even lime. I love the taste imparted by a lemon twist with the peel rubbed around the rim.

Or you can hang a lime twist over the rim and there you have Christmas in a glass. You never see lime peel as a garnish. It has no gustatory value; the rind has little in the way of oils to express. But the green against the red. That's the Christmas Boulevardier.

21 December Monday

Denis for dinner; the 12-Mile Limit our cocktail. Late in this awful year, it is good to suggest some of the best cocktails we discovered as a small means of declaring not everything about 2020 was evil. Of course, as we do, Donald Trump is busily trying to overthrow the election, promoting evidence-less conspiracy theories made up whole cloth by one Sidney Powell and suggestions of martial law by Michael Flynn, a man he recently pardoned after having been convicted of lying to the FBI. Perhaps less consequential, but for two boats we have been unable to obtain papers from the US Coast Guard that prove them documented. When we sail, I assume it is illegally, at least within 12 miles of the US coast.

In the spirit of legal defiance, we offer the 12-Mile Limit as a 2020 favorite. A Prohibition cocktail, it is of a genre created to mock a stupid law. It is dangerous (3 spirits) and doubly, or triply, so because delicious. If Trump were to impose martial law, we'd drink a couple of these, load our guns, sail either down from Maine or up from Florida to Washington, DC, and invade, staying outside the 12-mile limit en route, until turning toward land.

Here's the recipe for two drinks to be served in champagne flutes:

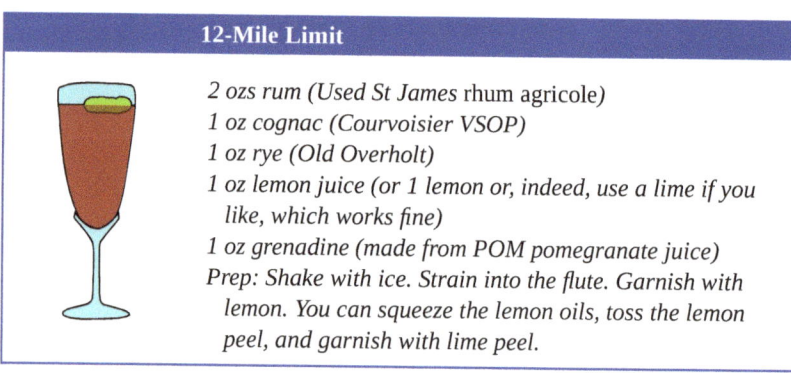

12-Mile Limit
2 ozs rum (Used St James rhum agricole)
1 oz cognac (Courvoisier VSOP)
1 oz rye (Old Overholt)
1 oz lemon juice (or 1 lemon or, indeed, use a lime if you like, which works fine)
1 oz grenadine (made from POM pomegranate juice)
Prep: Shake with ice. Strain into the flute. Garnish with lemon. You can squeeze the lemon oils, toss the lemon peel, and garnish with lime peel.

The drink is red and with the lime peel, the very spirit of a Christmas invasion.

22 December Tuesday

No drinks, but a ski along the river paths on our deep snow. The house inspection turned up a need to strengthen a structural timber, a project that could be expensive, ruining sleep.

23 December Wednesday

Going to Ipswich, and back, for dinner with Jean. She'll be alone on Christmas, fearing Covid infection. Made up an Old Fashioned of Eagle Rare, Angostura Bitters, and maple syrup that was pretty good.

I've done some research that shows the Boulevardier, our Christmas cocktail this year, is among a group of drinks that deserve attention, beginning with the Old Pal, perhaps culminating in the Negroni, and comprising the 1794, 1795, and the Rum Negroni.

24 December Thursday—Christmas Eve

Our last in the Ol' Bean, where for more than a decade we've spent the evening with our neighbors the Greasons. Back then Al and their three children believed in Santa Claus. Tonight, three of them 19, one 17, hover around the bar, starting with the 12-Mile Limit I was making before moving to the Corpse Reviver No. 2s Al loves. And on they went.

The gathering was proscribed as Covid rates have soared. We debated long with ourselves about whether to have it. The four teens became five, hard drinking, when Max showed up. Who knows what'll happen? All that said, Al was calm and strong. He's okay as a drinker, from what I've seen, enjoys it, loves a good cocktail, but typically doesn't go too far. That is a load off for us.

Day after tomorrow, Jenny and I return to Florida, see what boat living is like.

25 December Friday—Christmas 2020

Rain on the snow and warming into the 50s are making the outdoors foggy and humid. In front of the Christmas tree Al and Skylar brought in and, with Jenny, decorated, I'm listening to *Hipsters Holiday No.2*, made by our friend Stephen Pugh. With the other two *Hipsters Holidays*, they comprise the greatest collection of Christmas music of all time. Just proposed to Rick that the Luggnuts make a 2021 Christmas album of 15-20 of the songs from the three Hipsters.

But back to the Boulevardier Groupo (shall we call it that?).

The Boulevardier Groupo

William "Sparrow" Robertson, sportswriter, claimed to have invented the Old Pal in 1887. In his obituary, *Time* wrote, "the most remarkable columnist of them all—the Paris Herald's cocky, antique, legend-crusted, peewee William Harrison Robertson, universally known as the 'Sparrow', relied on neither grammar nor syntax." His claim is probably untrue, but he was a distinguished tippler, so maybe it wasn't.

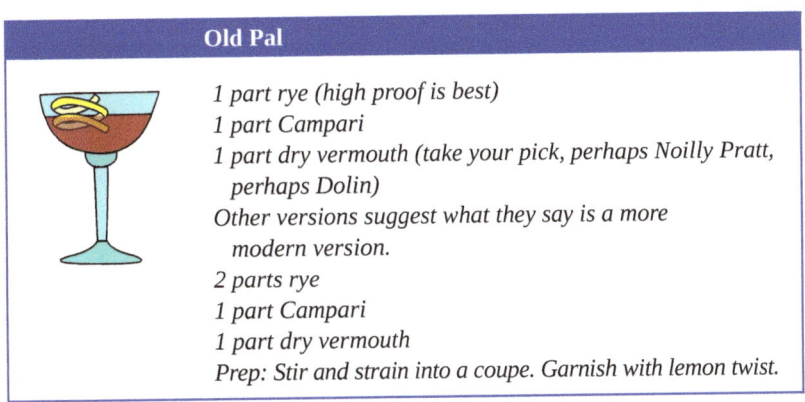

Old Pal

1 part rye (high proof is best)
1 part Campari
1 part dry vermouth (take your pick, perhaps Noilly Pratt, perhaps Dolin)
Other versions suggest what they say is a more modern version.
2 parts rye
1 part Campari
1 part dry vermouth
Prep: Stir and strain into a coupe. Garnish with lemon twist.

Harry MacElhone of Harry's New York Bar in Paris first published the recipes for both the Old Pal and Boulevardier in 1930. The Boulevardier comes from another American patron of MacElhone's bar, Erskine Gwynne, who published the *Boulevardier* literary magazine (1927-1932), which patrons of *la rive gauche*, including Hemingway, Fitzgerald, Stein, and others of the expatriate American cognoscenti of the 1930s, for whom alcoholism was pretty much a requirement, would have regarded with interest.

But we are far from finished. A more modern, more Manhattan-like take on these cocktails is the 1794.

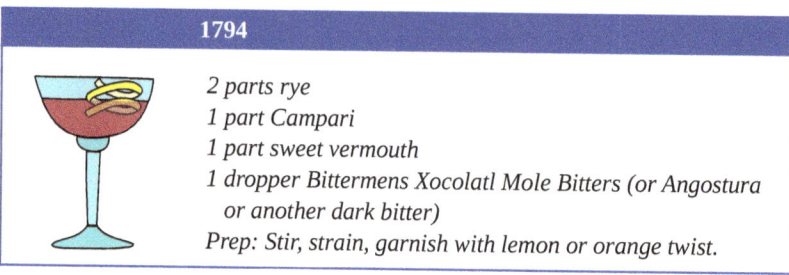

1794

2 parts rye
1 part Campari
1 part sweet vermouth
1 dropper Bittermens Xocolatl Mole Bitters (or Angostura
   or another dark bitter)
Prep: Stir, strain, garnish with lemon or orange twist.

A fine play on the Perfect Manhattan.

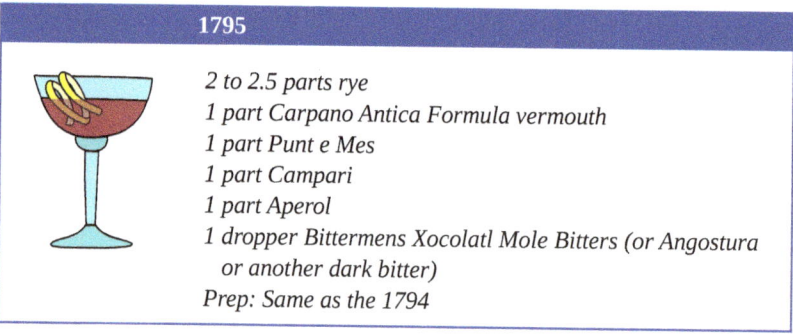

1795

2 to 2.5 parts rye
1 part Carpano Antica Formula vermouth
1 part Punt e Mes
1 part Campari
1 part Aperol
1 dropper Bittermens Xocolatl Mole Bitters (or Angostura
   or another dark bitter)
Prep: Same as the 1794

Sounds complicated though not exotic. The idea is to balance the two vermouths, one bitter (Punt e Mes), one sweet (Carpano Antica) against the two amari, one strong (Campari) one mild (Aperol).

And we cannot, must not omit, leave out, or forget the…

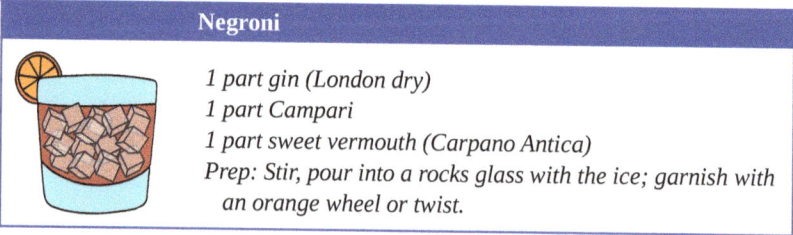

Negroni

1 part gin (London dry)
1 part Campari
1 part sweet vermouth (Carpano Antica)
Prep: Stir, pour into a rocks glass with the ice; garnish with
   an orange wheel or twist.

Some say the Negroni comes later than the Old Pal or Boulevardier, some say it comes before. No one, however, argues that the grandfather to the entire group, the fittingly named Americano, originating in Milan in the 1860s, came first.

Americano
 2 parts Campari 2 parts sweet vermouth Prep: Serve over ice. Top with club soda. Garnish with an orange wheel or twist.

As a final measure, for last call, let's add the Aperol Spritz. Aperol is the little sister of Campari, similar but much milder. The spritz, like the Americano, is a fresh, summery cocktail without a lot of alcohol

Aperol Spritz
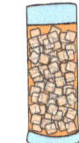 2 parts Aperol 2 parts prosecco 0.5 to 1 part club soda Prep: Mix in a Collins glass filled with ice and lightly stir.

And who knows, there could be others. Note that the common and key ingredient is Campari, with Aperol substituting in a couple. These amari are wonderfully versatile and, though assertive, manage to work together with any number of spirits and combinations. Keep them, handy.

That said, we drank none of these Christmas Day… and shame on us. However, Alex got three books on cocktail making for Christmas, one of them by Boston food writer J.M. Hirsch, who inscribed our copy of *Shake, Strain, Done*, with, "A good cocktail really does make us sexier and smarter!" Hirsch takes as his premise that at home you will lack ingredients and sometimes the know-how to make cocktails like the ones at, say, *Death & Company*. The ingredients part is a reality I've complained about in these pages. His solution is to invent a lot of new cocktails that don't require obscure ingredients and to remake classics, but with simpler, or easier to find, ingredients. The result is fun.

Al served as bartender. My first drink was a Corpse Reviver, but rather than washing the glass with absinthe, Hirsch recommends a fennel concoction. We used absinthe. He suggests dry white wine rather than Lillet Blanc. We used the latter. And he uses no lemon. We added lemon after tasting it without (ugh to that). Not a great start. Since when are lemons hard to find?

With dinner we switched to champagne, so that's all the experience I have to date. And oh, Al made me another called, perhaps, Always Spring, gin and Liqueur 43. Probably something else, but quite good. Will get details… or thought I would, but it cannot be found.

26 December Saturday

Flew at 5:25 AM from Manchester to Baltimore. Layover until 10:40, and then flew to Rochester (yes, backwards) where we were grounded for above an hour because so many flights were going to Tampa. As a result of the southward migration, Southwest filled the plane up, every seat, no open middles. We're weathering the delay by staying aboard, which is perhaps safer than being in the terminal. Who knows when we'll arrive?

We made our way to my car and drove across Florida, starving, finally succumbed at 8:00 pm or so and pulled into a Mexican restaurant, clearly a dive, but only two customers, until we ordered, and then every wretched, angry kid of color in Florida descended on the place. Ate as fast as possible and bailed out, pretty sure we must have Covid.

27 December Sunday

Aboard *Lea Scotia* after a harrowing—really, harrowing—trip down. Jenny has felt bad all day. But we worked on the boat, in my case unsuccessfully, shopped for necessities, and came back for a chili Jenny made. I reached back into the Covid Cocktail file and found her favorite, the Swanky Panky (see May 13, 2020). And my, my, my who could know that 1/4 tsp (2 dashes) of anything, here Fernet Branca, could change worlds. Such a great, bitter, yet sweet drink.

Here, now, I am declaring it the "Cocktail Diary Drink of the Year." And more than that, it fits perfectly into the Boulevardier-Negroni family. I mean rye and gin; red vermouth; amaro.

Ain't serendipity lovely?

28 December Monday

A deeply frustrating and satisfying day. The aft head has been baffling for a while, though at least not stinking, and we're not supposed to use it in port anyway because it does not empty into a holding tank, a practice on older boats. Freshwater, which we last filled on leaving Key West, began to run short, so I filled the tanks, coming to understand that the inlet to them is unaffected by what I do with the outlets (duuuhhh). But then the main freshwater pump below the sink kept running. And, sure enough, the filter leaked.

I removed it. The pump, and filter, are Italian. Jenny began a fruitless search for a replacement. I texted Bucky to ask if we might have a spare aboard, and he quickly sent me to likely places forward.

But no luck, except we did have a used Jabsco filter that at least had the same-size female fittings on both sides. But before trying it, we had to get our Covid tests at CVS and from there went up the road to West Marine, which had no Italian filters whatsoever.

To make the used Jabsco fit, I had to move the pump just a couple of inches, which was easily done. And wonder of wonders, installing the filter proved straightforward, easy really. And holy of holies, the new one did not leak; the water has been working fine (I'm writing on the morning of December 30) ever since.

Monday evening, we sat on deck, drank a Westmalle Dubbel, a Trappist ale, and played guitar. Lovely. Below we dined on fresh black-eyed peas and rice and drank an Anchor Steam Christmas Beer. Maybe things are improving?

29 December Tuesday

In some respects, our day centered on being prepared for a 6:30 PM video call with Steve and Rochelle. In the morning we traveled to our storage locker and set our bikes free. After a couple of false starts we went for what turned out to be a long ride, lost part of the time. And after lunch and a nap, I went to the gym here at the marina. We dined on bbq steak and chicken with baked potatoes and were ready to talk in the nick of time. The drink of the evening, our Christmas drink, was a Boulevardier, with which all four of us seemed mostly happy.

At last, we met David, my namesake (he really is) a sturdy youth of 23 who seems serious, and based on his description of how he is waiting out the plague, careful. Pretty different from Al.

Jenny, however, hasn't felt well since we arrived, raising fears, given the entry to Florida, of Covid infection. She thinks it is a sinus infection. We hope so and await our test results.

30 December Wednesday

Our 25th, silver, wedding anniversary. It's a deeply worn cliche that the years fly past, at least happy ones as ours have been, and even difficult ones, as 2020 is for most everyone in the wide world. Here we are on a beautiful sailboat, skies clear, air cool, lucky just to be. We've reserved a table at the Black Marlin in Stuart for dinner, a place that looks like the kind we love. And they are said to have experienced bartenders who make fine cocktails.

Looking to move all systems ahead, Jenny cleaned, I checked oil and anti-freeze in the engine and genset. We ran the two new ACs, which worked perfectly. I added anti-freeze and oil to the genset and thought it best to run it for a while. Flipped to on. Let the glow plug heat up briefly, raised the start switch, heard one click, and lost all DC power on the boat. No lights, water, refrigeration, bilge pump, gas—nothing. Deeply discouraging.

Yesterday we played, touched nothing, what we used worked, especially the water. Today what should have been a routine matter, one that needs to be reliable, led to what feels like disaster. We are, essentially, back where we were when we landed at this marina. Waiting for Rich Forbes, the marine electrician who has been so helpful and responsive. Meanwhile I sit here powerless, the second sailboat gambit looking ever more questionable.

Rich came, and in a short time traced the problem to the switch that directs power from the house batteries or starter battery. It was set to "0." It needs to be set to "2." And once Rich made that one small change, magically, everything worked again. Really, I should have been able to figure this out.

For dinner it was the Black Marlin, and the cocktails were superlative. First had a barrel-aged Manhattan. Excellent. Next an Applewood-smoked Old Fashioned, which was beyond excellent, served with a piece of bacon on a wide toothpick and a jigger of nuts and candy. Completely lovely. We'll go back, in part so that I can watch this drink get made. And note the companionship of food and drink, each made better by the other, a topic I too often neglect.

The end of the evening was as wonderful as the beginning, over which I will draw the veil of discretion.

31 December Thursday—New Year's Eve; Last Day of 2020

A pretty good bike ride at the end of which I fell but somehow avoided real injury. Continued to organize spare parts and tools aboard and have made great progress. Found a spare filter for the water at a very good chandlery. And now awaiting Tim and Beth, for whom I plan to make Swanky Pankys.

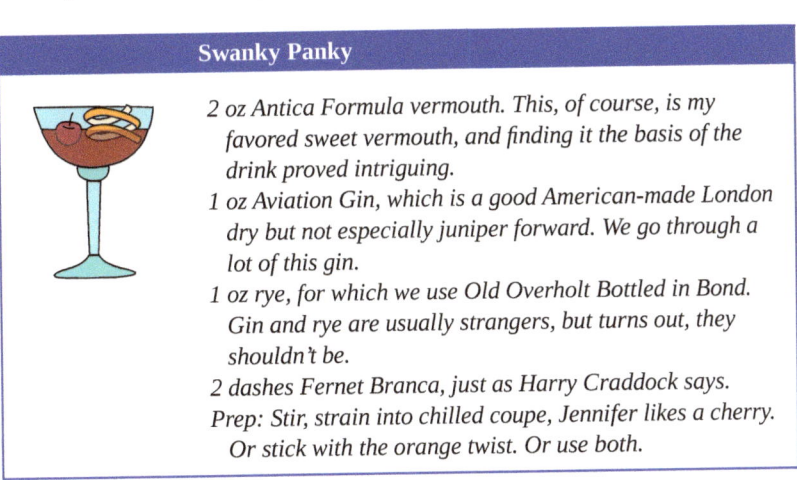

Swanky Panky

2 oz Antica Formula vermouth. This, of course, is my favored sweet vermouth, and finding it the basis of the drink proved intriguing.
1 oz Aviation Gin, which is a good American-made London dry but not especially juniper forward. We go through a lot of this gin.
1 oz rye, for which we use Old Overholt Bottled in Bond. Gin and rye are usually strangers, but turns out, they shouldn't be.
2 dashes Fernet Branca, just as Harry Craddock says.
Prep: Stir, strain into chilled coupe, Jennifer likes a cherry. Or stick with the orange twist. Or use both.

A fitting end to 2020, a year no one will miss.

1 January Friday 2021

Jenny and I had a bike ride; one of the highlights of being here is riding through winter in short pants and sleeves. Have a good path outside our marina, and easily ride to Savannah State Park, a lovely place north of here with trails. In all a good, hard ride.

Tim and Beth didn't show; they had the day confused, though it is New Year's Day. We expected them for dinner. When, prompted, they finally came, and we drank Swanky Pankys, which quickly got everyone laughing. For good luck I made Cajun Hoppin Jean, a version of black-eyed peas; tasty, whether or not it proves lucky.

Beth's son Aaron, an ardent Trump man, has a bad case of Covid. He says he is recovering, but no energy and no sense of smell or taste. Says it's the worst thing he's ever had. Meanwhile Beth's right hand is badly swollen, her arm virtually immobile. The tentative diagnosis is carpal tunnel. She's feeling old.

2 January Saturday

Intended to run errands but derailed because Beth's arm left her unable to do simple tasks, so over we went to help with washing and folding, shopping for groceries, throwing out recyclables. Dined on Thai takeout and drank a couple Sam Adams's.

3 January Sunday

Last day of Jenny's time off; we intended to sail. But the tide was so low that the oysters were above water, which they hate, our boat in only 4.5 feet, and we need 6.5 feet! Another sailor with a similar boat advised against going out, so we rode bikes instead, beginning in a state park south of here. Lovely terrain and vegetation, and Jenny scared herself running over the tail of a big snake, probably a corn snake. She feels bad.

Went to a taco place to pick up lunch and were furious about two families, including the children, who descended without masks. Had to be a political statement; lots of Trumpkins hereabouts. I'm surprised we aren't hearing of more fistfights over this. Afterward went to Totally Liquored and tonight hope to have a new cocktail.

Which we did, and quite good.

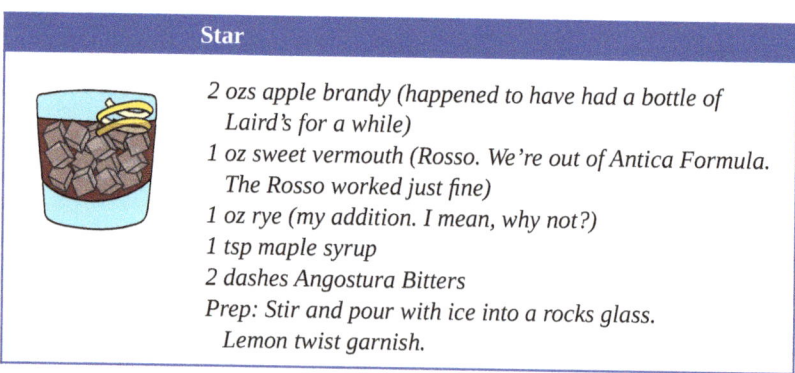

Star	
	2 ozs apple brandy (happened to have had a bottle of Laird's for a while)
	1 oz sweet vermouth (Rosso. We're out of Antica Formula. The Rosso worked just fine)
	1 oz rye (my addition. I mean, why not?)
	1 tsp maple syrup
	2 dashes Angostura Bitters
	Prep: Stir and pour with ice into a rocks glass. Lemon twist garnish.

Except for the apple brandy and the maple syrup, this is a Manhattan. The apple brandy was delightful, giving the Star a delicate fruity smell. Jenny drank this one.

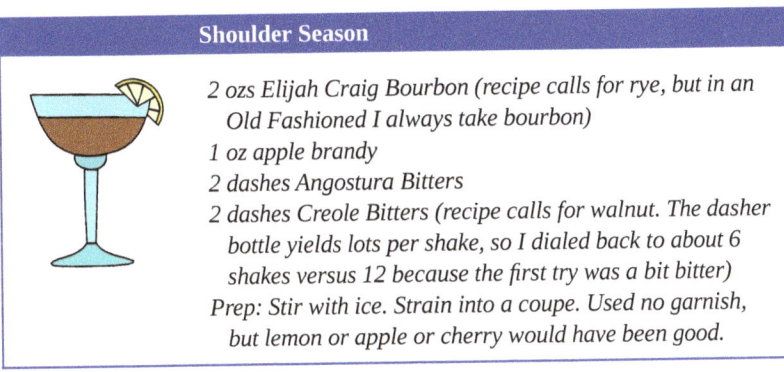

Shoulder Season

2 ozs Elijah Craig Bourbon *(recipe calls for rye, but in an*
  Old Fashioned I always take bourbon)
1 oz apple brandy
2 dashes Angostura Bitters
2 dashes Creole Bitters *(recipe calls for walnut. The dasher*
  bottle yields lots per shake, so I dialed back to about 6
  shakes versus 12 because the first try was a bit bitter)
Prep: Stir with ice. Strain into a coupe. Used no garnish,
  but lemon or apple or cherry would have been good.

Here is a fine riff on an Old Fashioned. As with the Star, the apple brandy is a poignant addition to an old favorite. Powerful.

4 January Monday

The day began when Rich the electrician came by. Jenny and I started the engine yesterday, and at first it looked fine, leapt into action. I'm sure I looked at the tach, and it showed 1000 or so rpms. I did something and looked again, but the tach wasn't working. When I went to shut down the engine, the stop button did not work, a problem Al and I faced in Key West, and so I knew how to stop the engine from below. None of the engine instrumentation (tach, oil pressure, water temperature) worked.

Today, Rich tried to start the engine, and nothing happened when he turned the key. He got it going quickly, but why seemed as much a mystery to him as to me. And all of the instrumentation, except the ever elusive idiot light for the alternator, worked.

Now, as I write, a loud hum courses through the boat. No clue what it is. Sounds electrical, comes and goes, you can feel it in the rigging, and it is loudest in the aft cabin. Could be, I suppose, something going on in the marina. But it could be something going on in this apparently spirit-riddled vessel of ours. I look through the boat for the source; steel bottles in the stern, what look like compressors in the engine room are mysteries to me. The batteries don't seem right, only half charged, but they read fully charged. And I don't know where to start to figure this out. The hum is new, never heard it till this afternoon.

Planned not to drink, but the day has been disheartening, and we need to use up some lemons and limes. Necessity being the mother of invention, and scarcity forcing us to shift for ourselves with the limited bar aboard, here's a new cocktail Jenny and I are drinking right now:

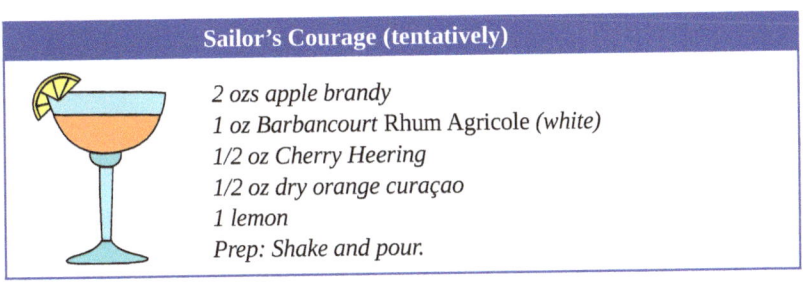

Sailor's Courage (tentatively)

2 ozs apple brandy
1 oz *Barbancourt* Rhum Agricole *(white)*
1/2 oz *Cherry Heering*
1/2 oz *dry orange curaçao*
1 lemon
Prep: Shake and pour.

Pretty good we think.

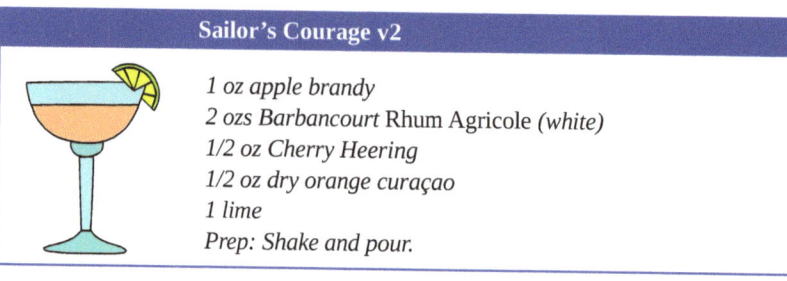

Better. Really good. And I'm feeling better. The mystery noise went away about 5:00 pm. Could be ghosts bed down early.

Sailors need courage, perhaps more of the time than most. Courage to run the ship when others depend on them. Courage to stay awake on a long, rough night. Courage to keep looking, thinking, when baffled by the myriad mysteries.

Strong drink helps, at times anyway. Tonight is one of them. Sailor's Courage. I'll need more of it.

5 January Tuesday

Spent a long time on the phone with Bucky today hoping to understand better the electrical system and monitoring of it. Helped some. Bucky, however, believes that the alternator for this boat needs to have an external, configurable voltage regulator. Without one, he thinks, the nature of lithium-ion batteries will cause the alternator to work at full capacity all of the time, which, he thinks, will burn it up. If so, it is another expensive, discouraging setback. What to do?

Have a good dinner. Pan fried steak. Heavy salt and pepper, smoking oil, turn it after 30 seconds. Better than bbq of a steak. But no cocktails.

6 January Wednesday

A unique day in the history of the republic. Yesterday, Georgians voted Reverend Raphael Warnock to the Senate and at present, Jon Ossoff appears more likely than not—with no guarantee—to win the other Georgia Senate seat, flipping the body to Democrats, turning Mitch McConnell into a back bencher, and denying two odious, pandering Republicans places they thought were theirs for the asking. Shine on Georgia!

This afternoon Congress convenes to count electoral votes and officially declare (again, really) Joe Biden the next president. But, of course, Donald Trump has lined up a group of Trumpkins to thwart the clear will of the people in that Biden won by more than 7,000,000 votes and has an electoral College advantage of 306-234. Neither is inconsequential.

Of urgent importance here is that the Trumpkins have floated completely refuted lies about the "stolen" election, and millions of people believe them. They believe it despite no evidence to support their conviction, even as one lie after another has been demonstrated to have no basis. As a result, the power and importance of the first amendment, of free speech itself, are now in question. If the president can use his power, as he did during a forever famous hour-long phone call to the head of Georgia elections on the weekend, to insist that the lies he believes are true, and if millions follow his lead, what becomes of the republic?

And sure enough, after a Trump speech near the White House decrying the "rigged election" as he has for two months, abetted at every step by almost the entire Republican political establishment, the Trumpkins marched to the capitol. As we watched the speeches in the Senate, fatuous opposition by people like Ted Cruz using an analogy to the 1877-78 (I think) intervention in the vote that resulted in the end of Reconstruction and beginning of Jim Crow as his example for why an election commission should be appointed, suddenly odd movement on the Senate floor and soon the disappearance of Mike Pence, escorted away by large Secret Service types, signaled something.

Thanks to YouTube, one could easily switch to reports from the Capitol grounds where we watched a mob storm the Capitol steps, break windows and doors, and soon, roam the halls of Congress. Their depredations will be in the history books; the people I saw looked clueless about what to do next, rough and ignorant, true deplorables. But the thing is, for two months Trump has lied to them about the election, claiming he won in a landslide, and so many, even most, believed they were saving democracy. The woman shot to death by Capitol Police realistically was murdered by Donald Trump.

We headed to Tim and Beth's for the night where I expected, quietly, to celebrate the coup's failure with some drinking featuring the new Sailor's Courage and the much loved Pisco Sour. Here's to Biden, Warnock, and Ossoff! Shine perishing republic! We stuck with the Pisco Sours. And I wonder, why not the same recipe with rum? (Which, it turns out, I had made here and named the Vero Rum Sour, declaring it better than the pisco version. So much for memory.)

By the time we went to bed, Congress had reconvened after the entire building was swept to ensure no lurking insurrectionists or their bombs had been left behind. I was as mesmerized as during the Watergate hearings and watched deep into the night. The presentation was surreal, out of a bad science fiction movie about End Times (sounds like a new cocktail) in that everyone except most of the people during their speeches, wore masks. They wore masks! Even the Republicans wore masks.

7 January Thursday

In their self-serving declarations about the power of democracy, the Republicans who spoke in favor of disqualifying electors, decried the mob. But how cynical, given that even then they were empowering the Trumpkins by leaving them with nothing to believe except that the doomed attempt to overturn the election legislatively needed insurrection to carry out its aims. The Republicans in the House, a much less polished, much more sketchy lot, are too many to name. But I'll record the Senators who acceded to this tactic: Josh Hawley of Missouri, Ted Cruz of Texas, John Kennedy of Louisiana, Roger Marshall of Kansas, Cindy Hyde-Smith of Mississippi, Tommy Tuberville of Alabama. A seventh, whose name I can't find at the moment, voted with them in favor of decertifying Pennsylvania's electors.

Many speeches were good on the side that stood for upholding the election and smartly wiped away the supposed objections to things such as Pennsylvania allowing mail-in ballots. First, a Republican legislature voted to do it. Second, if it was illegal, why did no one take it to court before the election? Third, only because Trump lost the state is it being examined now. Had he won, do you think the Republicans would have objected to its electors? How cynical.

The most powerful speech of the night came from Mitt Romney, who, as we know, was the only Republican Senator with the courage to vote to remove Trump from office after the impeachment. Romney, perhaps thinking of his father George Romney's record as a man of conviction, humorously invoking the sorrow of his own loss in running for president, declared that Donald Trump alone was responsible for the insurrection. He began by describing himself as heartbroken that people in countries striving for freedom, looking to us as an example, saw the events of the day. He continued,

> *Now we gather due to a selfish man's injured pride and the outrage of supporters who*
> *he has deliberately misinformed for the past two months and stirred to action this*
> *very morning. What happened here today was an insurrection incited by the President*
> *of the United States... For any who remain insistent on an audit in order to satisfy*
> *the many people who believe that the election was stolen, I'd offer this perspective.*

No congressional audit is ever going to convince these voters, particularly when the president will continue to say that the election was stolen. The best way we can show respect for the voters who are upset is by telling them the truth.

Meanwhile, of course, the right-wing media on Fox and elsewhere promoted the unsupported, and almost surely unsupportable, notion that Antifa actors posing as Trump supporters were responsible for the attack on the Capitol. And you know, again, this pandering of lies rather than a real attempt to see the truth, makes us wonder. The first amendment now appears paradoxical, on one hand, proliferating lies that would undo democracy, and on the other, enabling us to speak out against overreaching government. Could be this means a republic is no longer viable under the thinking of the Enlightenment, that, as in other ways, our technologies have so outstripped our primitive brains we will inevitably destroy ourselves.

I think you probably should have a drink. How about an End Times, if one exists?

End Times
?
?
?
?
?
?

8 January Friday

Because lots of cameras were in the Capitol, we can see that the marauders included many white supremacist/QAnon types, not Antifa followers, and many were not simply misled citizens. The motives and ends were mixed, but it sounds as if those hoping for a civil war were over-represented.

More important, and a partial result, is that this appears, we are hopeful, to be the death knell of Trump's sway. Since he descended the golden stairs at Trump Tower and identified immigration of Mexican rapists as probably the greatest problem we face, we liberals have seen Trump as unfit. For many of us, he was so obviously unfit that only if Republicans nominated him rather than one of the other candidates, would Hillary Clinton, the worst nominee possible, stand a chance of winning. Well, we were at least right about his unfitness. All the while we have puzzled over how intelligent Republicans, and I'll call my brother Denis one of them, could support him. Lots of Republicans in the chattering class moved away from his destructiveness and lies. But not Denis.

Now I think the reason for staying with the man was that his followers feared immigrants, at least Denis did, despite relying for years on the unsurpassed help of Thai and Cambodian housekeepers. Probably more important, they believed that he would strip away regulations, that they would be able to act freely. Business would love it, and citizens would not be burdened by the chains of government. Their hatred of masks and other pandemic restrictions are evidence to them that government edicts are like a bad father telling you how to live your life. Denis detests politicians, especially Democratic ones, thinks they're universally dishonest and outrageously out to tell him what to do. I have some hope now that Trump's crimes may at last be so egregious that he'll understand the lies outweigh the freedom. But who can say? Denis certainly has not.

Enough politics. Tonight we're for cocktails, especially another iteration of Sailor's Courage and a faceoff between a Pisco Sour and a Rum Sour. Oh boy! The republic still stands.

We worked on the Sailor's Courage, using Flor de Caña in Jennifer's rather than Barbancourt. Jennifer preferred the former, me the latter. Hard to say if this cocktail has real possibilities. I keep thinking a bit of grenadine might be a good idea.

9 January Saturday

Last night our friend Faith Minton sent notice that the woman who defeated her for a seat in the State House was one of 33 Republicans to vote against a resolution condemning the pillaging of the Capitol in Washington. A little drunk and pretty repulsed, I wrote this to Representative Natalie Wells:

David Swords <daswords1@gmail.com>
Fri, Jan 8, 10:15 PM (13 hours ago)
to nataliewells4nh, bcc: minton.faith

Dear Representative Wells:

One of the best things about politics in New Hampshire is that either party can comprehend when the other has gone too far. While it has taken years, tragic incompetence, absurd self-pity, and vast sustained lies from President Trump, hardly anyone except the most willfully blind remains who cannot see his criminal behavior. Hardly anyone, that is, except you and 32 colleagues in the New Hampshire House. How depressing.

Do you believe that this election was stolen? Surely, you're smarter than that. Do you believe calling people to invade the capitol in hopes of derailing Congress from its Constitutional duty is right? I suppose you might, but if so, you are by definition a totalitarian.

And perhaps you are. Could be the caring, skeptical, Yankee Republican party of New Hampshire has been body-snatched by Trumpkins.

If so, if you are one of these mindless, maybe racist, surely blind automatons who follow this bedeviled, selfish man wherever he goes, a plague on your house.

Sincerely,
David Swords

She said in an email reply that she placed the vote by mistake and couldn't recall it. I suppose incompetence is an excuse?

Had lunch with Tim and Beth at Conky Joe's in Jensen Beach, not far from us. Excellent place. Drank a Hemingway Daiquiri that was strong and passable but nothing great. Could not really taste the grapefruit juice.

One thing I've realized about living aboard is that we seldom need to search for things. We've put them in places where they tend to stay, don't have a lot of things compared with shore life, and so can lay hands on stuff easily. It's a great feeling, one I'll explore as we move along.

10 January Sunday

Our first sail since we arrived here. All went well, the trip to the ocean (about 1.5 hours), a pleasant sail, the trip back upriver (about 3 hours from the time we began to head in), until we reached our slip in the latter stages of the falling tide. We ran aground. Backed up. Tried again. Again aground. Tried a new direction into the main area of our part of the harbor. Aground.

We finally gave up, went around to a slip where the occupant was gone and lay there for the night after alerting the marina. Apparently, we can expect this during low tides, and in future will stay at the fuel dock until the water comes up. For this we pay $1,000 a month.

The good news was that we were forced to maneuver a lot in close quarters without mishap. The docking between two big yachts went well, and getting to our slip at high tide next morning was easy, though we again touched bottom on the way in.

At any rate, we celebrated, or I did anyway, with Pisco and Rum Sours, the latter made with Flor de Caña. Rather than simple syrup, used agave, which seems a better fit. Both were excellent, and I really don't prefer one to the other.

11 January Monday

A new radio, solar controller, hooking up solar panels, and $2k plus later, we're tired. Went to Anthony's Coal Fired Pizza, a chain we'd never heard of, and dined on one of the best pizzas we've ever eaten, in a dark, lovely restaurant with few people and ample room. Glasses of good red wine with the pizza led me to wonder if a cocktail would have been better, and I cannot say.

But back at the boat, I finished off the pisco with a sour that tasted like dessert. And after watching a series about female relationships, *Dead to Me*, that Jenny likes, watched about half of Arnold Schwarzenegger's *Total Recall*.

It is a serious film and especially pertinent. In it, Arnold is a man whose memory of past misdeeds on behalf of a corrupt government has been erased, and his is a struggle to find the truth and to learn who he is. One would think any honest Republican would be on the same mission today, though, alas, most are not. Hope to finish the movie tonight.

Watching this was brought on by Arnold's excellent video calling Republicans to account based on their support of Trump, whom he despises. The two have much in common. They are about the same age, have long been in the public eye, made names for themselves through stardom in television and film, and have been regarded as successful, turning to politics relatively late. The differences, however, may be more instructive.

Trump grew up in a wealthy family in NYC in easy circumstances and learned his ways from a dishonest father who gave him his start with what most of us would call a fortune. Trump stayed out of the military thanks to "bone spurs." Arnold's father, by contrast, was a broken and angry WWII veteran of the German army who was a drunk and beat his children. Arnold grew up in post-war Austria, made his name first as the most successful bodybuilder of all time, which required grueling, painful dedication. Then, he surprisingly became a successful actor, first in *Stay Hungry*, but most famously in *The Terminator*. If Trump pretended to be "himself," a successful tycoon with business genius, which he was not, Arnold used who he was to portray authentically characters that either are dangerous villains or great heroes. In the Trump video, where he recounted Kristallnacht and the ravages of WWII on Germany, Arnold was a true hero.

12 January Tuesday

Let's find an appropriate drink with which to toast Arnold tonight. Already I've eaten Linzer tart from Jennifer's bakery in Stuart today. Very Austrian.

Finished sewing parts of the dodger so that it should keep the instruments dry and hold together. The stitching is old, rotten. But for now, we'll make do.

The drink of the night was a Fernet Manhattan. Not Austrian. Not even the Black Manhattan I thought it was. That is, the Black calls for Amaro Averna, which I'd forgotten and which we lack aboard. I blithely used 1 oz of the Fernet Branca, 2 of rye, a lot of Creole Bitters in Jenny's and, oh my, it was bitter. Had to add agave, which worked just fine and made her happy. Did the same with mine and went lighter on the bitters. It's worth noting that some brands of bitters come in bottles that supply a far larger dose per dash than Angostura. Watch for this and, probably, cut back based on your instinct.

13 January Wednesday

Donald Trump is being impeached again. I'm just hoping that this is prelude to the Biden administration's being able to work with Republicans, if not in the House, at least in the Senate. He and McConnell have had a conversation that sounds as if it went well and in which McConnell averred that he believed Trump's actions last week, and his repudiation of any responsibility now, are impeachable.

We're off to Tim and Beth's this evening. In all, I feel better about boat living, less needing to get off, than last week. Things are taking shape in general. So goes our little life here.

Months ago, I proposed a Vieux Carré substitute that made use of ingredients you have rather than ones you may lack. But rather than look back, let's look forward. How about fashioning a Vieux Carré-like cocktail. Perhaps bourbon or rye, apple brandy or calvados, sweet vermouth, Cherry Heering, and a couple of bitters? Intriguing? Down the road, will let you know how this turns out.

Meanwhile, Beth had a new cookbook which had this recipe:

Smokey the Bear

2 ozs smoky bourbon, which we did not have. In fact, we had no bourbon and used Old Overholt 100 proof Bottled in Bond rye.
1 oz lemon juice, or the juice of one lemon
1 oz agave, but we had only simple syrup
1 Amarena cherry, and I do not know what these are, but we had some excellent Italian cherries. Amarena at least sounds Italian.
Prep: Shake, pour ice and everything into a double rocks glass, rather than straining and pouring over new ice. New ice seems like such a waste. And for good measure I added Peychaud's Bitters on top, which were delicious and colorful.

The drink is a rarity. That is, you don't often find bourbon or rye with citrus, and it was great! Not pretty, that is, until the Peychaud's. But oh, how tasty. I'd drink these anytime, and notably, the rye was not smoky. I guess a smoky bourbon could be good, but why bother. The drink is good enough as is, or how about a smoky scotch, say Laphroig?

And Trump was again impeached with the help of 10 honest Republicans.

14 January Thursday

Looks as if we'll store *Lea Scotia* in Florida through the summer. Bringing her up this year feels too complicated. Tim and I had a mission to find a place, in Fort Pierce, to hurricane-proof the boat. We did and then dined at the Harbor View (I think that is the name).

The staff did not wear masks, which as the new more contagious variant makes the rounds seems ignorant, angry. I'm wondering as well whether as people are vaccinated, they will give up mask wearing, which will lead those without vaccinations to do the same. So many unpredictable scenarios yet to be played out.

At any rate, got back to the boat and took a night off from cocktails.

15 January Friday

Made plans to return to New Hampshire two weeks from today, which feels good. We'll be packing, spending our last nights in the Bean, which does not feel good. I've been disassembling and greasing winches, which need it badly. We're hoping to sail through a long weekend.

And I need a drink. It is high time for a Whiskey Sour.

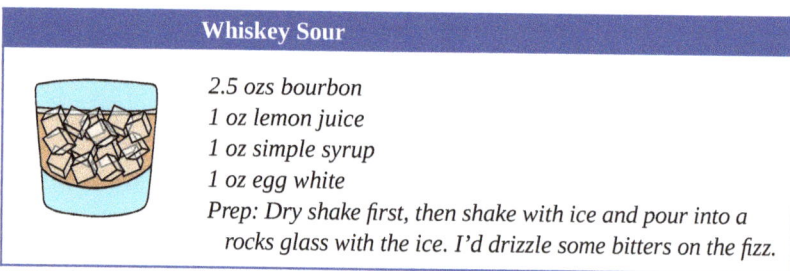

Whiskey Sour

2.5 ozs bourbon
1 oz lemon juice
1 oz simple syrup
1 oz egg white
Prep: Dry shake first, then shake with ice and pour into a
rocks glass with the ice. I'd drizzle some bitters on the fizz.

Delicious. And it works fine, in my view, without the egg white, but works fine with it. No wonder this is a classic. Simple. And surprise, the so-called "Smokey Bear" I made at Beth's, without the smoky whiskey, was, ta da, a Whiskey Sour, including the drizzled bitters. This lemon (and lime is fine too) formula is ancient, classic, standard. High time for a Whiskey Sour?

I'd already had one, just didn't know it.

16 January Saturday

Jenny wanted one of our standbys, so it was back to Manhattan. But it seemed a moment to fine tune.

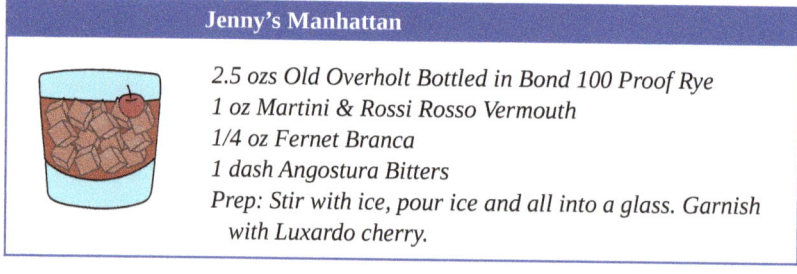

Jenny's Manhattan

2.5 ozs Old Overholt Bottled in Bond 100 Proof Rye
1 oz Martini & Rossi Rosso Vermouth
1/4 oz Fernet Branca
1 dash Angostura Bitters
Prep: Stir with ice, pour ice and all into a glass. Garnish
with Luxardo cherry.

She loved it. A very robust Manhattan, dark, the Fernet Branca giving the drink a bitterness she prefers.

My Manhattan

1.5 ozs Old Overholt
1.5 ozs Calvados Morin (I love this Calvados. It's better
than Laird's Applejack.)
1 oz Martini & Rossi Rosso Vermouth
1/4 oz Fernet Branca
1 dash Angostura Bitters
Prep: Stir with ice, pour ice and all into a glass. Garnish
with Luxardo Cherry.

Less powerful tasting than Jenny's thanks to the Calvados. And fruity, with a fine scent. This may in fact be, for me, the perfect Manhattan. And it does harken to the idea I've had of rearranging the Vieux Carré. Maybe try some Peychaud's Bitters, when I get some, to make the More Perfect Manhattan.

17 January Sunday

Drank some wine and a beer. Boring.

18 January Monday—MLK Day

Tried to sail with Tim and Beth but were stuck in our slip, the water too low. Our deck must be 6 inches or so above the dock or our keel is in the mud. Ah well, we had lunch aboard, went for a walk during which Tim was slow and amusing, threatening to tilt with trees that jumped into his blind path. He really is blind now. When he talks to you, his eyes look out in a general direction rather than at you. He's a brave man for letting himself be guided.

After they left, J and I went to Best Buy looking for help with our Internet connection aboard. They had nothing to say. We remembered that with an extension cord, perhaps our router could be on deck, and if so, it might bring in connections to the marina wi-fi. Reluctantly, off we went to Lowe's, a bit of a hike.

We returned to *Lea Scotia* tired, but I moved the router on deck anyway and used the extension cord through a porthole to power it. After some effort in the Pepwave Soho router's interface, we connected to the wi-fi, and it's been working like a charm since. We even watched a TV show on the iPad. Jenny is about to start her week's work, so we'll know soon enough whether this set-up is effective.

But let's get to what's important. We were having one of our favorite simple meals, tamales from Trader Joe's, and I'd begun to think Margaritas would suit us. We have nice limes, and it's been a while. But then I recalled the grapefruit from Fresh Market, a beautiful specimen of the fruit. And we have a 1.75-liter bottle of Flor de Caña white rum. With those in mind, the drink of the evening became proper Hemingway Daiquiris.

The thing that has mostly kept me from this drink is cutting up the grapefruit in a way that it can be squeezed. You can't desiccate half a grapefruit in a lemon squeezer. So, I halved, quartered, eighth-ed (?) the grapefruit and used our smaller squeezer, the one for limes, because the pieces fit compactly into it, enabling a hard, effective delivery of grapefruit juice. The best approach is to squeeze the whole grapefruit while you're at it, which gave us enough juice for the evening with some left over for Jenny to drink down as we finished up. You would not want to try to keep the fresh juice. The most common cherry liqueur for this cocktail is Luxardo, which we lack aboard, but Cherry Heering is fine.

The combination of a delicious rum, a fine cherry liqueur, wonderful specimens of lime and grapefruit yield a fabulous cocktail. As I have with so many, I'm calling this one of my favorites. The deep red color, the slightly sour but not bitter touch on the tongue, the background sweetness of the Cherry Heering, make this complex yet smooth. Papa Hemingway is said to have preferred his daiquiri with as little sugar as possible because the sugar got in the way of the alcohol. True or not, the alcohol does its work just fine even though the drink has no huge measure of it. Jenny doesn't care for a sweet drink, likes her fruit, so this one suited her well.

In all, then, despite the bad beginning aground in our slip, the day and evening proved a triumph.

19 January Tuesday

Took a break, anticipating the celebration of Joe Biden and Kamala Harris's inauguration. Couple of Anchor Christmas beers.

20 January 2021 Wednesday—Inauguration Day

Amy Klobuchar set the tone. Happy, witty, spirited, all underpinned by real depth. Lady Gaga sang a memorable Star-spangled Banner and Jennifer Lopez introduced Spanish into her "This Land is Our Land." Joe Biden's speech was honest, about our predicament and about how we got here. He's a man you can trust if you allow yourself.

Amanda Gorman, ablaze in a yellow overcoat that gave a shimmer to her bronze skin, hair held high by a red bun and gold markers above her forehead, smile bright, hands that were punctuation, the Junior Poet Laureate, performed her poem, "The Hill We Climb," more memorably, beautifully, poignantly, than any poem I've ever seen or heard at an inauguration. The day was one of poetry in so far as meaningful symbols danced everywhere, and everyone seemed deeply aware of their presence and personal contribution to the themes of the day, especially unity. But thanks to Amanda Gorman, the most meaningful symbol was words—their importance, after being devalued for so long by a man and an administration that were almost deliberately deaf, that used them only as weapons, that rang hollow in nearly every moment owing to their disregard for truth. Amanda Gorman's poem looked forward to what we strive to be rather than the phony lurch backward that has been peddled these four years. If it is words as much as anything that distinguish humans, we can thank Amanda Gorman for their renaissance.

I suggested champagne, but Steve Poore rightly preferred Presidentes. At Tim and Beth's, we returned to Hemingway Daiquiris.

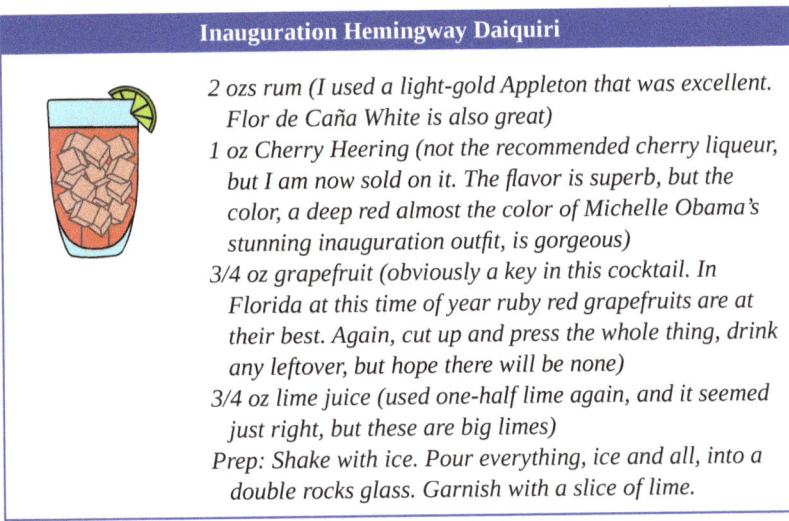

Inauguration Hemingway Daiquiri

2 ozs rum (I used a light-gold Appleton that was excellent. Flor de Caña White is also great)

1 oz Cherry Heering (not the recommended cherry liqueur, but I am now sold on it. The flavor is superb, but the color, a deep red almost the color of Michelle Obama's stunning inauguration outfit, is gorgeous)

3/4 oz grapefruit (obviously a key in this cocktail. In Florida at this time of year ruby red grapefruits are at their best. Again, cut up and press the whole thing, drink any leftover, but hope there will be none)

3/4 oz lime juice (used one-half lime again, and it seemed just right, but these are big limes)

Prep: Shake with ice. Pour everything, ice and all, into a double rocks glass. Garnish with a slice of lime.

A perfect drink to end a day of perfect promise. As Hillary Clinton proposed: Amanda Gorman, 2036.

21 January Thursday—A New Day

Turned in the paperwork for *Lea Scotia* to be on the hard over summer and mailed the lease for our rental house in Bradford. Back on the boat, needed a drink, and as usual, Jenny led us to Manhattan-like cocktails.

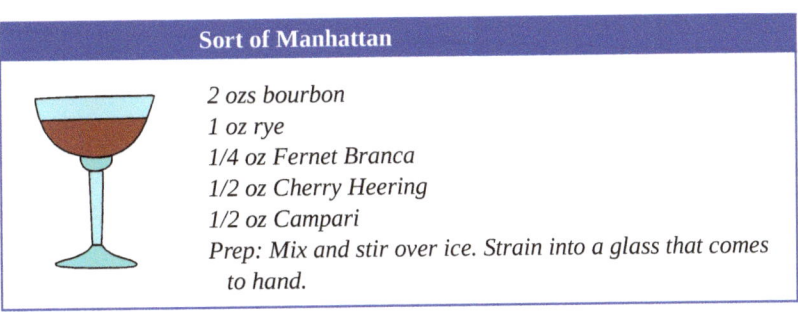

Sort of Manhattan

2 ozs bourbon
1 oz rye
1/4 oz Fernet Branca
1/2 oz Cherry Heering
1/2 oz Campari
Prep: Mix and stir over ice. Strain into a glass that comes to hand.

A vermouth-less Manhattan that was pretty good, lots of potent whiskey. Cherry Heering, which I'm ever more partial to, stands in for the sweet vermouth. Everything else is bitter. Not sure the combination of whiskies is useful.

22 January Friday

Outfitted our dinghy with its outboard and jetted across the broad St Lucie River to downtown Stuart, where they conveniently have a visitor's dock. Walked ashore and dined in the window of an excellent restaurant, where we had salad and pasta and loved every bite. J drank Zinfandel and I drank Palm, a beer I thought was from Charleston, or at least from South Carolina. But it's a beer from 1747, Belgium, a lighter version of an abbey beer that was perfect.

We walked the lovely Stuart Healthy Trail, avoiding Covid as best we could and rode the dinghy back across in the dark to *Lea Scotia*.

23 January Saturday

We're stuck in our slip again, owing to unusually shallow water. Or, to say truth, it could be I prefer staying in the slip to sailing. Hard to say. But let's assume the best, which is that I'm no sailing coward, and the water really is shallow.

At any rate, we did a Jeff Sixpack Shuffle in the gym and then raced up the Greenway for our bicycle ride. Came back, showered, dressed, went off to Bed, Bath and Beyond for a hair catcher. Saved the best part of shopping for post-lunch sandwiches from Honey Baked Ham, then we walked down the strip mall to Totally Liquored. Jenny keeps me from spending her 401K on spirits, though we bought Green Chartreuse, which is pretty much all anyone can afford.

> ### Mr. Black
>
> *As we were heading out, a stand in the Totally Liquored store was promoting "Mr. Black." This is an Australian coffee liqueur, a replacement for sweeter coffee liqueurs such as Kahlúa. Well, being a man ahead of his time, I'd already bought a bottle that, or so I thought, lived somewhere aboard* Lea Scotia. *It was delicious. The woman promoting Mr. Black said you can drink it straight or over ice or add it to any cream liqueur. I said we had a boat and heard it was better in an espresso martini than other coffee liqueur because not as sweet. She enthusiastically agreed. And, she said, "On a Sunday morning, you can have it over vanilla ice cream."*
>
> *As we walked away to allow space for an enthusiastic couple who overheard some of our conversation, she said, alluding to her all-black outfit, "And obviously, I am Mrs. Black."*

And so she is. Happily, we have a bottle aboard; starting tonight about 4:30, we're exploring Mr. Black Negronis (too sweet) and Mr. Black Old Fashioneds (fine with me).

24 January Sunday

Stuck again in our slip by unusually low tides, we invited Tim and Beth for a walk and lunch. Walked the Healthy Trail in Stuart, slowly because Tim can't talk and walk together, adding up to about half of said trail. Back to *Lea Scotia*, where J made salad and yellow rice while I bbq'ed salmon, which Tim loves, on deck. Beth drank a Mr. Black Old Fashioned.

We've had the cocktail that follows, but perhaps not well made, and tonight's were excellent...

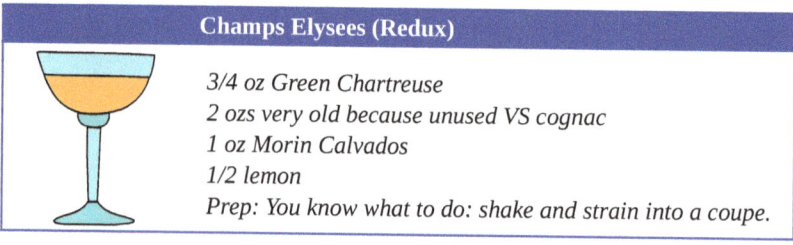

Champs Elysees (Redux)

3/4 oz Green Chartreuse
2 ozs very old because unused VS cognac
1 oz Morin Calvados
1/2 lemon
Prep: You know what to do: shake and strain into a coupe.

J had hers without the calvados, with more (2.5 ozs) cognac, and as always liked her version better. But I love this Morin Calvados, had two, which are strong, and am writing tonight mostly on a blurry keyboard.

25 January Monday

Dined at Anthony's Coal Fired Pizza and drank a bit of wine. That's it. Spent the day on boat projects, such as improving the table in the cockpit, making it steadier, stronger, level.

Screwed up my vaccination. After I signed up with NH.gov, they sent an email explaining that "when it arrived" the form from the US CDC for getting an appointment needed to be filled out carefully. The form would arrive by email in the next few days. Problem was the form had already arrived. I found it today, several days later, and when I went to sign up for the vaccine, the earliest date was 12 March. Drat the luck! Toys with our plans to return to Florida shortly after 1 March to the point that we're not sure what to do.

Surprisingly to us, we like the Florida winter. We're here at The Harborage Marina among true yachts, mostly motor-driven, 70 to 100 feet, I'd guess, lots of them designed to rise out of the water and plane at 20 knots or more. Think of the power needed to do that; think of the fuel!

Our sailboat, grand to us, is Gulliver among the Brobdingnags. The residents of these yachts are mostly retired people. They tie their boats stern toward the dock, enabling them to see and talk with one another from their aft decks. Each afternoon into evening, they take cocktails on their deck dining tables beginning at about 4:00 PM, swapping conversation across transoms. With no data except stereotypes, I'm guessing the cocktails of these pretty rich, by capitalist standards very successful, cruisers are mostly vodka and almost universally uninteresting. If any ever chance to light on this page, here's a suggestion, that tonight gives J and me an excuse to try out our improved cockpit table and perhaps raise our social status:

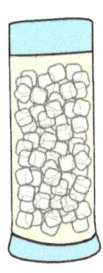

Royal Bermuda Yacht Club

3 ozs rum (a dark gold or darker rum from some island is best, say Appleton of Jamaica or Goslings of Bermuda)
1 oz dry orange curaçao (Pierre Ferrand)
1 oz falernum (Taylor's. Is there another?)
1 oz lime juice
Prep: Shake and pour ice and all into a pilsener, double rocks, or beer glass. If your yacht measures more than 70 feet, (1) have someone do the pouring for you and (2) prefer monogrammed crystal.

This is the yachtsmen's version of Planter's Punch but taken on deck rather than veranda. The Bermuda Yacht Club is the third outside English shores to be titled "Royal."

Falernum and the Seagoing Bar

Falernum, not universally known but available at Totally Liquored, reasonably priced, especially by boat standards, has many tiki applications and should be in every seagoing bar. (I'm considering illegal sales of Taylor's Falernum off the stern of Lea Scotia once this deserving cocktail becomes the toast of yachting tipplers.)

26 January Tuesday

Beginning to think about leaving, which we'll do tomorrow after Jenny finishes work, staying at Tim and Beth's Wednesday and Thursday, flying home Friday, non-stop, to Manchester-Boston Regional Airport.

The job now is to get the boat ready to be stored, and besides making sure she's closed-up, I am concerned about the electrical system. For reasons I don't fathom, the charger does not turn on automatically when the SOC (state of charge) drops below a certain point. Probably need to speak to the manufacturer of the controller. My life…

	7:00AM	10:00AM
DC Volts	13.1	13.1 ("Full Charge")
DC Amps	-7.8	-3.6
Amp Hrs	25.65/213.88/307.52	Same
SOC	57%	100%

Anyway, I got a Seattle computer nerd at Magnum Energy who must have been lonely. Did not want to get off the phone. But he changed a lot of settings. And now we'll see.

My life. How about a San Martin?

Way back on May 2, I discoursed about how varied recipes for this fine cocktail are and promised to experiment with different possibilities. Many variations use Chartreuse, and now we have a bottle. Except, oh, a San Martin is also known as a Martinez. So yeah, it can be anything, a drink that changes its name and contents according to today's bartender.

Hold on, change of menu, one of the finest prerogatives of the home bartender. At the end of the day, the time has arrived to reprise the Sawyer. We lack orange bitters, which I never taste anyway and so made enough without orange bittering to fill a thermos. We gathered two plastic glasses with stems and in our dinghy set out across the St Lucie River for Stuart on a lovely calm evening. Tied up at the public dock and took the short walk ashore to a bench overlooking the river toward our marina. The drinks were delicious, and we couldn't resist taking phone photos till the Sawyers were gone, mostly to my head, and the sky nearly dark with a bright, almost full moon.

Walked back to our dinghy, climbed aboard, the engine started, then killed, and that was it. No motor. What had been a perfect evening turned into a tough paddle across the broad St Lucie, taking I'd guess a half hour, perhaps 45 minutes.

The engine is a 9 hp Mercury. We spent about $400 getting it tuned up before leaving Ruskin. This is a model that other people we know, including a couple who stopped by on the Stuart dock to recall their cruising life, have found unreliable. We have the old, loud, oil burning, British Seagull in our storage locker. If I cannot get the Mercury going on my own, we're getting rid of it and, sensibly, either going with the Seagull or going Japanese.

Jenny, by the way, did not complain about rowing across. She is a seagoing woman.

27 January Wednesday

Tried to get the starter rope on the dinghy to pull through, the problem that thwarted us last night. No luck, so I proceeded with the pretty complicated job of using our manual crane to take the outboard off, thinking we'd keep it on deck till returning, then consider next steps. As soon as I lifted the engine off the transom, the problem that stopped us last night was obvious: bowline lodged in the propellor. Our bowline. Entirely my fault for being sloppy. A rookie mistake. A drunk's mistake, we might add. And sure enough, the starter rope easily pulls through; the engine is fine.

Lesson? Mariners cannot afford to be sloppy, or they will be hoist on their own petard, unable to pull their own rope. It's a lesson I should have learned that night in November. As my daddy used to say, "David, some people never learn."

Spent much of the day preparing to leave *Lea Scotia* for a month or more and then drove to Tim and Beth's where we drank Corpse Reviver No 3s. That's right, our corpses needed reviving; we lacked some No.2 ingredients, and so we made do.

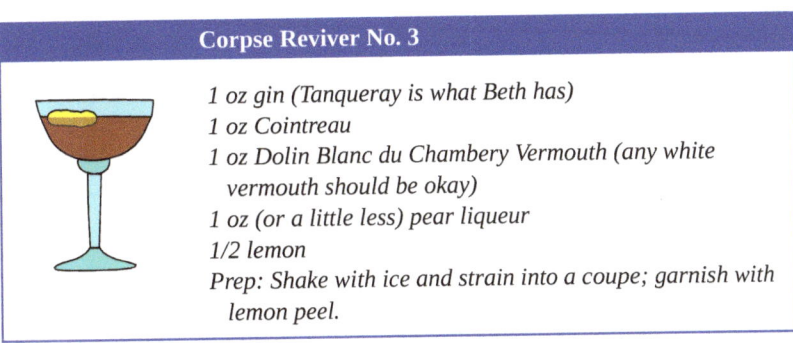

Corpse Reviver No. 3

1 oz gin (Tanqueray is what Beth has)
1 oz Cointreau
1 oz Dolin Blanc du Chambery Vermouth (any white
*   vermouth should be okay)*
1 oz (or a little less) pear liqueur
1/2 lemon
Prep: Shake with ice and strain into a coupe; garnish with
*   lemon peel.*

No Lillet Blanc or Cocchi Americano. No absinthe. The pear gives a subtle, sweet scent instead of the sterner absinthe licorice, and the Dolin vermouth is a fine substitute for Lillet Blanc. The lemon played a smaller role and perhaps the drink could have used more. That said, all of us were very pleased with the result and may well have more Thursday.

28 January Thursday

Yes, bought Lillet Blanc and a fine 124 proof French absinthe (Lucid) and made the Corpse Reviver No. 2 for Beth, Jenny, and Tim, Corpse Reviver No. 3 for me. Beth and I agreed that we prefer No. 3. It is sweeter, thanks to the Cointreau, Dolin Blanc, and pear liqueur. The No. 2 has an edge of sour. Yet both are remarkably good, as Tim, who drank two, said many times. Made for a very pleasant evening.

A few sips into the Corpse Revivers, and many, many other drinks, I begin to feel them. By the end of the first, the delightful effects of alcohol have asserted themselves, a feeling of lightness in which conversation is easier, perhaps more fun and imaginative. On to the second, a night only improves. By then dinner comes out, as it must, and for me anyway, a few bites of food greatly diminish the felt effects of the alcohol. Once that happens, I seldom move along to a third, from which we can draw lessons such as don't drink and eat or do drink and eat or just do what you will while not forgetting the bowline.

The first time I felt the effects of alcohol was when I was about 10 years old. My mother and her father were always estranged, but he had invited my parents, and for some reason me with them, to a large party at his grand inherited house in the Garden District of New Orleans. As I came into the chandelier-lit living-room, he motioned to one of the Black waiters to come over, hand me a glass of pink champagne with a lump of sugar releasing bubbles extravagantly in the bottom. I drank it off quickly because it was sweet, effervescent, delicious and felt its heightening effects as I did. By the time my glass was empty, Grandfather Watson had moved on to other guests, but the waiter kindly stopped to ask if I'd care for another.

"Could I have a pink one with sugar in the bottom?" I asked. To which he replied, "Why, yes sir, I'll see to it myself."

And he did, initiating me into a state of grace in which I was comfortable among adult strangers; included and treated like a man; all the while feeling lighter, gayer, better than I'd ever felt. Some fine things never change.

January 29 Friday

Back in New Hampshire, our last times at the Ol' Bean.
The Pegu Club, invented in Burma during the British Empire, the club and drink were the provenance of the high-born British. In this century, the Pegu Club was reborn as an influential cocktail bar in New York City but closed early in the pandemic. Here's to the memory of a place I never visited.

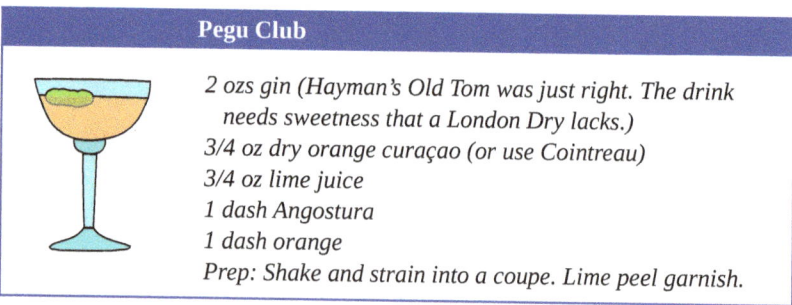

Pegu Club
2 ozs gin (Hayman's Old Tom was just right. The drink needs sweetness that a London Dry lacks.) 3/4 oz dry orange curaçao (or use Cointreau) 3/4 oz lime juice 1 dash Angostura 1 dash orange Prep: Shake and strain into a coupe. Lime peel garnish.

Drank two and found the Old Tom, which is nearly all the gin left after Al and his people depleted our supplies, was perfect. Al liked them as well, observed they are not unlike Corpse Revivers.

Now, however, I feel like a stranger in our house. It looks spare. Went into my closet to see the hanging clothes. They are familiar but not friends. Al seems good. And Skylar was pleasant. They're boat people as are we. And they showed us examples of the absurd prices people are paying for boats. Al thinks he could get $15K for the ski boat we bought, I'd guess 10 years ago, for $9K, but he doesn't want to sell her because he can't afford an upgrade.

The spareness of the house is for the best. The Ol' Bean is sold, and we'll move in three weeks, packing beforehand. Yet, the boxes of records Sharon Marshal sent back after I'd donated them to the University of

Alberta 20 years ago were old friends, many remembered, a few strangers. Mainly, the classical musicians in what is mostly a classical collection are nearly all dead, or near it, a seamless progression of dedication and talent to the great music of our culture down the centuries, captured on vinyl for the first time in the 50s and 60s as close to the original as we yet know how to record. They'll be Al's now if he wants them. Past, present, future feel inseparable. And discrete.

I recall as a boy, on the toilet, reading a book about dinosaurs (always read on the toilet) at our house in Houston. The book, a gift from our great aunt Ola, was old, perhaps written in the 1930s. Our dad, a geologist, had a sense of geological time. And I wrote in that book something to the effect that, "Here is a book I hope my grandchildren will learn from and enjoy as I have." The book is long gone, pulped or something. The grandchildren, Dom, Jon, and Travis are now real. That sense of time as inexorable grows stronger. Moving from the grand Bean to a rented, smaller place. Living on a boat in Florida. Watching Tim decline. The virus and the Republicans.

On the covers of the vinyl albums, artists Ellis Marsalis, Jesse Winchester, Emil Gilels, and so many others stand alive, looking as if they will remain forever. And, hmmm, perhaps they will.

Jenny is asleep. Our bed feels like home.

30 January Saturday—My Dad's 90th Birthday

Last night we got home to a decimated bar at the Ol' Bean, the result of 5 weeks absence with the liquor in teenage hands. But Al had bought very fine limes, and the youths had left the Old Tom gin alone. So, the Pegu Clubs were possible.

The New Natural Bartender

In making the drinks I was aware, perhaps for the first time, of the facility that these months of consistent bartending have built in what we could now call my "style." I know where to reach and what to reach for, both in the sense of where things are in my bar (and Al has kept them in order while depleting the booze) but also with a sense of how the where and what combine in preparing a cocktail. All coming naturally, which jigger to use; how to measure into and then combine the shaker, one side with ingredients, the other with ice; how to break it and strain without spillage. In the eyes of family, and eventually guests, I look like a bartender, which is not bragging but means to suggest, so do you.

In honor of Bobby/Papa/my father, who died in 2007, we drank an Old Fashioned as follows:

Old Fashioned 90

In a double rocks glass add one dash each of Angostura, Peychaud's, and orange bitters—that is, four to six good shakes each.

Add one or two barspoons (I prefer one) of warmed maple syrup.

Add a barspoon or two of the liquor from a jar of Luxardo Maraschino cherries.

Stir for a while with a little bourbon until blended well.

Add one large clear cube to the glass. Fill to near the top with bourbon and stir again. Garnish with a cherry.

This is a great Old Fashioned. Here's to Bobby. We wish he were with us for his 90th.

31 January Sunday, 1 February Monday

Today begins our last month at the Ol' Bean, and we start packing. It's very sad, and I'll need a strong drink. I'm thinking that it's a night, snowstorm expected, to go back to the Cobbler's Dream for the first time since June.

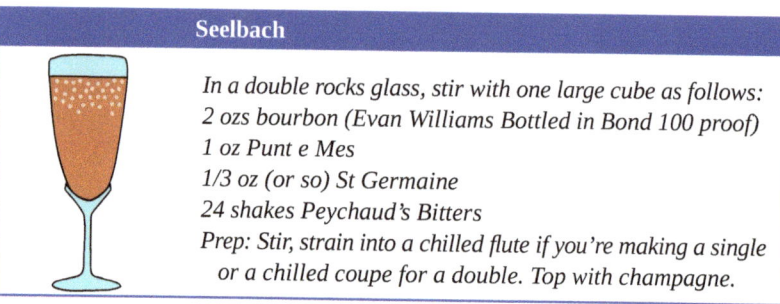

Cobbler's Dream (Redux)
1.5 ozs rye *1 oz sweet vermouth, in particular Punt e Mes* *.25 oz elderflower liqueur* *1 or 2 dashes of Peychaud's Bitters* *Prep: Served up in a coupe that has been coated with*   *absinthe. Garnish with a cherry.*

Seelbach
In a double rocks glass, stir with one large cube as follows: *2 ozs bourbon (Evan Williams Bottled in Bond 100 proof)* *1 oz Punt e Mes* *1/3 oz (or so) St Germaine* *24 shakes Peychaud's Bitters* *Prep: Stir, strain into a chilled flute if you're making a single*   *or a chilled coupe for a double. Top with champagne.*

I think it needed Angostura. But let's move to the real matter.

When I go to the trouble of making a cocktail, and when among all the prospects this one is elected for a night, I want it to be good. As a result, it is easy to presume it is good, to wish it good, to depress any discordance in favor of what we like.

But, you know, the Seelbach and Cobbler's Dream are oddities. My daddy used to say, "It's easier for most people to climb a tree and believe a lie than it is to stand on the ground and see the truth." This is not the easiest equivalence to grasp. Try this.

It's easier to think tonight's Seelbach is good as we sip it rather than throw out the booze and make something else, so why not persuade ourselves that this strange combination merits getting through, enjoying how the alcohol makes us feel, write something that does no worse than damn with faint praise, and move on.

In essence, then, I'll try harder to know the truth of what is good, to detect ones that screech, to be a better guide. And, you might say, damn, he says this now?

2 February Tuesday

We'll get back to things new directly, but tonight we're returning to the Millionaire for two reasons. One spirit the teens ignored while Jenny and I were away from the Bean for five weeks was Plymouth Sloe Gin, which is apparently unobtainable in Florida, perhaps because blackthorns don't grow there, piquing Floridian pride. And, we have beautiful New Hampshire (well, we bought them in New Hampshire) limes. Tonight's is the 16 December version:

Millionaire (Redux)
2 ozs dark rum (in December used Pirat's. Tonight it is the Haitian rhum, St James.) *1 oz Plymouth Sloe Gin* *1 oz apricot brandy (bottom shelf is fine)* *1 lime* *1/4 oz raspberry syrup* *Prep: Shake with ice and strain into a coupe.*

Sloe Gin and the Millionaire

How many cocktails combine gin, or sloe gin, and rum? A thorough, even exhaustive search of the Internet turns up only one, the Millionaire. In England, at least, sloe gin is not neglected. Our English friends might at this moment be drinking Sloe Gin Hot Chocolate or a Sloe Gin Negroni, the former in keeping with their taste for, well, possibilities whose virtues elude the rest of us, the latter at least interesting. At Christmas, mercifully closely behind us for now and only distantly ahead, Mulled Sloe Gin is possibly the tradition of many an English family. On this side of the Atlantic, where sloe gin is not readily obtainable (or, as noted, possibly banned in certain states), we would not want to use this unique, vital ingredient promiscuously.

The Christmas use makes some sense because sloes ripen on blackthorn hedge rows in autumn, must be harvested and imbued with gin, and surely by Christmas everyone is bursting to try the year's batch, however its purveyor presents it, perhaps with pigeon pie or the like. On our side of the Atlantic, I'm for making it illegal to use our scant supply for anything but Millionaires.

3 February Wednesday

At sea.

4 February Thursday

Lacked one ingredient or another for at least four cocktails I had in mind to try tonight, new ones, although it turns out, one of them, La Chaparra, we've had. If we recalled everything we've had, less would remain for us to re-invent, possibly only 17,864,392,600 or so. (See the Introduction and H.L.Mencken.)

I'd bought a nice ruby red grapefruit today, New Hampshire citrus improving in every way, no doubt soon we'll be able to buy sloes, and you may recall the delightful Hemingway Daiquiri. Here is a Mexican riff on it:

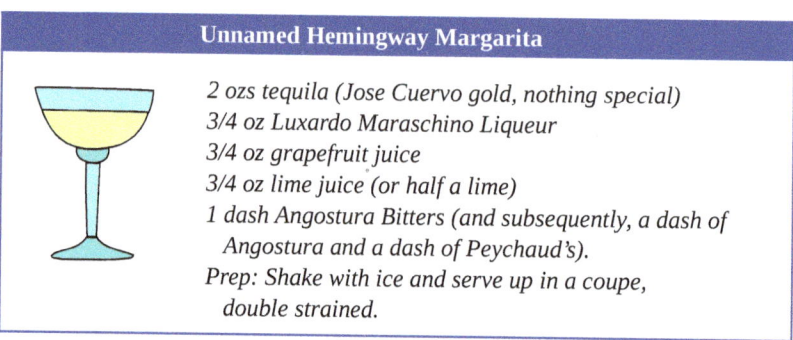

Unnamed Hemingway Margarita

2 ozs tequila (Jose Cuervo gold, nothing special)
3/4 oz Luxardo Maraschino Liqueur
3/4 oz grapefruit juice
3/4 oz lime juice (or half a lime)
1 dash Angostura Bitters (and subsequently, a dash of
*   Angostura and a dash of Peychaud's).*
Prep: Shake with ice and serve up in a coupe,
*   double strained.*

Curious, isn't it? The first sip was disappointing, not much flavor. But with the second, the tequila came through strongly, much more strongly I'd say than spirits do in most cocktails. The ingredients here, then, do not hide, may even bring forward, the base flavor. Don't like the taste of tequila? Steer clear of this. The cocktail is not too sweet, but sweet enough. The grapefruit is much more present than the lime, a good thing. The bitters? You know, I think they help. Might be smart to try one sans bitters. But is it possible that the bitters smooth the cocktail somehow? Maybe more likely is that they deepen it.

Hemingway could have turned his boat *Pilar* west, and instead of traveling to Cuba, which from Key West was a fair bit closer, might have gotten to Mexico. If he had, we'd probably be drinking a Hemingway Margarita. We'll need to see how he would have liked it on the rocks.

And tonight's dinner, by the way, is tacos, which I'm going to start before moving to a second trial of this promising, newly invented, sour.

5 February Friday

A snowy trek to the NH Liquor Store and Market Basket ensured we had ingredients for any of last night's missed prospects. Jenny was more than ready to drink, and I laid out the recipes for a Rio Bravo and a Paddington to her. Without pause, she chose the first.

A Rio Bravo is one of two cocktails I know about that deploy cachaça, the Brazilian national spirit, as their base, the other being the Caipirinha, far better known and the national cocktail of Brazil, where all but a negligible number are drunk each year. The number imbibed in Brazil, however, more than makes up for the neglect among other countries.

We have had a tall unopened bottle of cachaça atop the highest shelf of the Bean bar, in an overlooking position, for a couple of years. As some songwriter wrote, "Tonight's the night."

Rio Bravo

2 ozs cachaça (Our until now unopened bottle is "51,"
the only cachaça I could find at the NH Liquor store.
Not cheap only because rare, this bottle of clear spirit is
unaged, virtually raw)
3/4 oz orgeat (I love orgeat and too few recipes use it.
Here is a chance to go deeply into our large bottle.)
1 lime
2 or so slices of pickled ginger (recipes call for thinly
sliced fresh ginger. Go for it. But the pickled seems fine.
You might even drop in a piece as garnish.)
Orange zest and orange peel for garnish.
Prep: Put the cachaça, orgeat, and ginger into a shaker
and muddle with force to release the flavor of the ginger.
Add the lime and shake like hell, to a samba beat if you're
able. Strain into a coupe. Top with the orange zest and
orange peel for garnish (plus, perhaps, pickled ginger).

Oh, brave new world that has such cocktails in it! Jenny and I both were smitten. This is one of those "too good" drinks (wink, wink) that could lead to trouble on the lawn or elsewhere. However, we have no clue as to how cachaça tastes, unless it tastes like orgeat, lime, and orange zest. But cachaça is rum.

Yep. As Jenny said, rum is smoother, but the Rio Bravo is just as dangerous. I'd say, however, as much an advocate as I am for Barbancourt White Rum and Flor de Caña, the cheap cachaça, in part because it is rough, suits the cocktail. Orgeat is so smooth, so soothing, that it needs a little roughness.

6 February Saturday

Again, looking for the new. Here we have one from *Death & Company*, perhaps the first time ever that the rickety, rustic Ol' Bean has every indicated ingredient to hand.

Green Chartreuse
1.5 ozs Beefeater Gin
1/2 oz Aperol
1/2 oz lime juice
1/2 oz grapefruit juice
1/2 oz simple syrup
Prep: Swirl the Chartreuse in a cold coupe and toss it, they say, then shake the other ingredients and strain them into the coated vessel without garnish.
Here's what the Bean does:
2.5 ozs Beefeater
1 oz each Aperol, lime juice, grapefruit juice, and simple syrup.
Prep: Shake with ice. In the cold coupe, swirl the Green Chartreuse, leaving what is left in the bottom. Strain the rest into the glass and love what you have made.

But to love it even more, replace the Aperol with Campari. And try different sweeteners. We liked raspberry liqueur. The cocktail was much more dominating with Campari, yet the raspberry, which did not make it sweet, came through. Both versions were fine, but the power of the Campari was not so overwhelming that you had something close to a Negroni. This gypsy's eyes transfixed in their own way.

7 February Super Bowl Sunday

Last night we watched *Apollo 11*, a documentary film about the first voyage to the moon in July 1969, more than 50 years ago. It was obviously the culmination of President Kennedy's enjoinment at Rice Stadium in September 1962:

> But if I were to say, my fellow citizens, that we shall send to the moon, 240,000 miles away from the control station in Houston, a giant rocket more than 300 feet tall, the length of this football field, made of new metal alloys, some of which have not yet been invented, capable of standing heat and stresses several times more than have ever been experienced, fitted together with a precision better than the finest watch, carrying all the equipment needed for propulsion, guidance, control, communications, food and survival, on an untried mission, to an unknown celestial body, and then return it safely to earth, re-entering the atmosphere at speeds of over 25,000 miles per hour, causing heat about half that of the temperature of the sun—almost as hot as it is here today—and do all this, and do it right, and do it first before this decade is out—then we must be bold.

The power of the documentary is that it shows the fulfillment of Kennedy's prophecy. In the film, hundreds of engineers and scientists watch their rudimentary computers as if each were an infant in their special care, as the giant rocket and all of the interconnecting problems that had to be solved unerringly unfold in their immense complexity and the United States succeeds, not only as the United States, but as the representative of all humanity. This was a government project, a story the world watched over the decade of setbacks and successes, and I think the world was breathless that July evening, or morning depending on where you stood, as Neal Armstrong said, "One small step for man, one giant leap for mankind."

So many lessons. The power of a story and of being a player in the story. The United States in its daring and in its clear role as the representative of what democracy could accomplish was then a model and beacon for the world. The job of government was to be the engine that brought together the resources and solved the disparate problems Kennedy laid out. And the boldness, as he said, of even trying and of trying within a narrow time in a peaceful, enlarging adventure by an entire people may have been unique. The film made it easy to understand why the United States was for decades after admired, envied, feared, loved, and seen as the hope of the world.

Tonight, many of us will watch the Pandemic Super Bowl only because Tom Brady, through age, endurance, intelligence, concentration, gifts, and boldness stands alone on this night representing what America, and an American despite much tarnish, can be if he guides a team of committed people with care and with daring. I hope he, they, we, win. It'll be a far better story.

(Next day: Brady led the Buccaneers of Tampa Bay to win this most trying of Super Bowls. May this help bring us all back to what we can be.)

A Super Bowl without drinking may seem odd but concentrated attention. The game went the way I'd hoped from the time I found a way to tune in, middle of the first quarter.

8 February Monday

Surely the Paddington deserves a try. And, for a date Wednesday with Rick and Ruth, I'll need to learn to prepare a good Hot Buttered Rum. Why? It's cold and we'll be outdoors. Rick's jet-engine burner will help, but as it warms us from the outside, the evening will go better if a cocktail warms us from the inside.

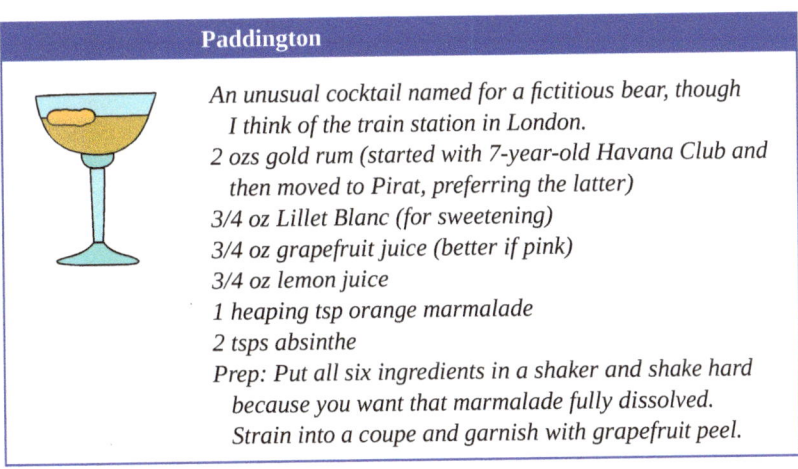

Paddington

An unusual cocktail named for a fictitious bear, though I think of the train station in London.
2 ozs gold rum (started with 7-year-old Havana Club and then moved to Pirat, preferring the latter)
3/4 oz Lillet Blanc (for sweetening)
3/4 oz grapefruit juice (better if pink)
3/4 oz lemon juice
1 heaping tsp orange marmalade
2 tsps absinthe
Prep: Put all six ingredients in a shaker and shake hard because you want that marmalade fully dissolved. Strain into a coupe and garnish with grapefruit peel.

First taste was disappointing, the cocktail seeming thin. Not tasty. Al didn't like the absinthe, but that's just him. And then as the cocktail settled into the glass and my tastebuds awoke, excellent. Indeed, here's a hypothesis.

The Effect of Shaking on Cocktails

Shaking introduces lots of air into a mix. But the air has no flavor of its own (we hope) and dilutes the flavor of the ingredients. Once the drink settles into its glass, the air bubbles burst and escape, leaving a richer tasting confection behind, in which the, here six, ingredients quickly sort out their relationship to one another and the blend that they now comprise.

Now that's science! Or probably not, though it is true that as I drank, the Paddington grew perceptibly better until near the end I was taking tiny sips to save what was left and once none, of course I had another.

After the first Paddington had taken its place in my stomach and I'd made a second, dinner needed preparing. I'd bought a large piece of fresh Icelandic cod and decided to pan fry it on the stove. Bad idea. Cod is flaky and as soon as it began to heat, fell apart despite my every effort to hold it together. I know nothing, except what I learned from this bad experience, about cod. Better save the pan frying for your trout.

Once we'd dined and I'd made a token effort to clean up, it seemed time for a Hot Buttered Rum.

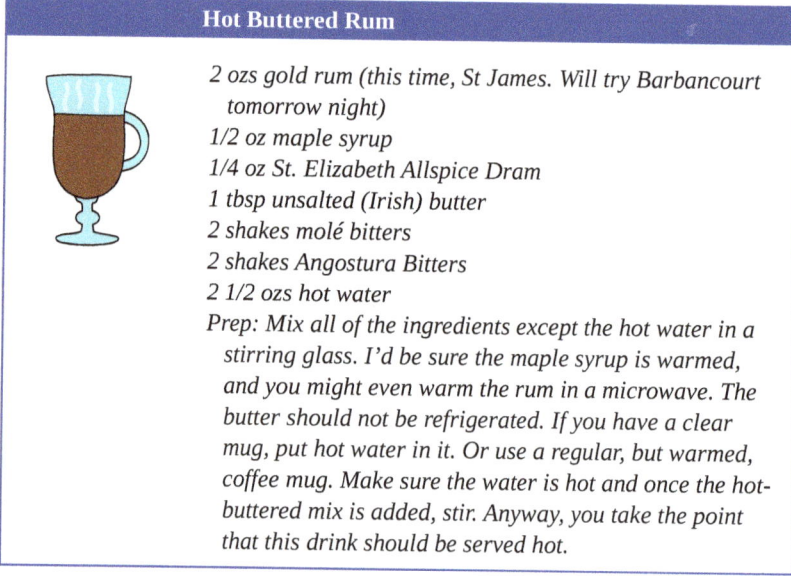

Hot Buttered Rum

2 ozs gold rum (this time, St James. Will try Barbancourt tomorrow night)
1/2 oz maple syrup
1/4 oz St. Elizabeth Allspice Dram
1 tbsp unsalted (Irish) butter
2 shakes molé bitters
2 shakes Angostura Bitters
2 1/2 ozs hot water
Prep: Mix all of the ingredients except the hot water in a stirring glass. I'd be sure the maple syrup is warmed, and you might even warm the rum in a microwave. The butter should not be refrigerated. If you have a clear mug, put hot water in it. Or use a regular, but warmed, coffee mug. Make sure the water is hot and once the hot-buttered mix is added, stir. Anyway, you take the point that this drink should be served hot.

And it will cool as you drink, but this is so good, even when you get to the dregs it will be so tasty, and you will have been so warmed, that the last cool sips will taste just fine.

9 February Tuesday—Second Impeachment Trial Begins

The number of Covid cases and deaths is going down. At 1:00 pm the impeachment trial of Donald Trump begins in the Senate. We wish him the worst possible verdict, which, sadly for the long-term health of our republic, is unlikely to play out. From the House impeachment managers, we expect a compelling case that makes the Republican Senators who vote to exculpate look absurd, and in histories down the ages, like the cowards and calculators we know them to be. What's to drink?

10 February Wednesday

For dinner at Rick and Ruth's, made Rio Bravos and Hot Buttered Rum. The latter was especially delicious. It was delicious because hot, because the butter was well integrated into the mix, and because the recipe is excellent (even though I forgot the cinnamon sticks).

The impeachment was powerful. The House Democrats are making their case in a compelling way without flourishes, very carefully, using a point-by-point approach to show how once Trump saw his deficit in the polls, he began to say that the only way he could lose is if the election were "rigged." He said it continually and refused to say he would leave office peacefully if he lost. A revelation was that the January 6 rally in DC was originally set for after the inauguration, but according to the House managers, it was Trump who asked it to be moved to the specific day and time that the electoral votes were being counted in the House and Senate.

This trial specifically improves the efficiency of my packing here at the Bean. Because I have it to listen to, I can pack lots more boxes than without!

We were inside at Rick and Ruth's, wearing masks some of the time and well separate mostly, proving that none of us really knows how to manage socializing during this long, long pandemic. But we tried.

11 February Thursday

The House Managers concluded their case today. The Trump defense starts tomorrow. It is hard to imagine they can mount anything close to a believable defense. And while this is a night when I should take a break from drinking, I feel strongly tempted. Just saying.

Poet's Dream

First had this the night of 2 November, where I wrote,

> *The fateful election is tomorrow. Both sides are nervous, even scared. Certainly, the day is a culmination and the end of a weight we've all borne through the primaries, pandemic, conventions, and the campaign itself. Both sides are rather sure that if the other wins, the American experiment in democracy ends.*

Little did we know that Trump's assault on the American Dream was far from ended, even though he was to lose!

2 ozs dry gin (Tanqueray)
3/4 oz Dolin Dry Vermouth
1/4 oz Benedictine
2 dashes orange bitters (on cocktail two, I used 1 dash
  each of orange and Peychaud's. Much better!)
Prep: Stir and strain into a Nick & Nora glass.
  Express and garnish with a lemon twist.

The drink is strong and I'm no real fan of it. But served in a double rocks glass with one big cube it is striking to see. And its potency helped.

12 February Friday

Toward More Decantered Cocktails

Long ago, in September, we briefly explored what we're calling "Decantered Cocktails." The Mother-in-Law was the first and is quite good. The idea is to mix the ingredients, store them in a lovely decanter or a plain bottle, and have them at the ready for pouring with no fuss, any time. The key is to use ingredients that will not spoil or mold. But we did not get very far, so it is time to revive the idea.

Summer cocktails typically rely on citrus, the most perishable of ingredients. You must use fresh citrus squeezed today. Additionally, vermouth, which should be refrigerated after opening, is a poor choice. Sugars such as simple syrup, grenadine, and maple syrup will mold in time unless you use commercial versions that are chemically disinfected, although a bit of vodka—and this is possibly the best use for most vodka—preserves them for a much longer time.

We're down, then, to amari, liqueurs, bitters and fortified wine to support the base spirits with which we begin. It is straightforward to make an excellent Manhattan with rye, amaro, and bitters that will last indefinitely. No reason to disallow keeping a decantered cocktail in the refrigerator, by the way, which means you could use vermouth. And no reason to disallow fresh garnish, such as orange, lemon, or what you have. But to begin, let's try not to do that. Other sweetener possibilities that won't mold include Cherry Heering (one of my favorites), Luxardo Maraschino Liqueur, Benedictine, orgeat. Liqueurs should include Chartreuse.

So how about, say, a Decantered Old Fashioned? How would we approach it?

First, Luxardo Cherries and their juice will not spoil, so that is one source of sweetener. A bit of dry curaçao could add orange flavor, which I like; we might use ample Angostura Bitters and a good bourbon, such as the dry, inexpensive Evan Williams 100 Proof Bottled in Bond. This is like the classic Fancy Free (bourbon, Luxardo Maraschino, Angostura and orange bitters). Or, how about a Monte Carlo (see 6 December).

2 ozs rye (Old Overholt)
1/2 oz DOM Benedictine
2 dashes Angostura Bitters (real 1/8 tsp dashes, or about six
  shakes each)
Prep: Mix and stir the ingredients then pour them over a
  large rock.

Simple, lasting, delicious.

Or an

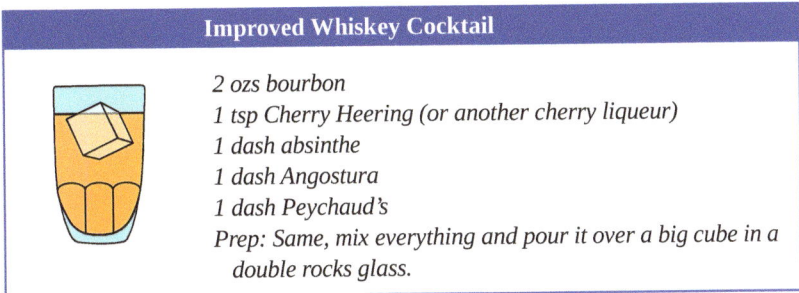

Improved Whiskey Cocktail

2 ozs bourbon
1 tsp Cherry Heering (or another cherry liqueur)
1 dash absinthe
1 dash Angostura
1 dash Peychaud's
Prep: Same, mix everything and pour it over a big cube in a
*   double rocks glass.*

Enough. If we keep going I'll never sober up. But this will get us started on the trail to a comprehensive set of decantered cocktails.

13 February Saturday

A last night of revelry with Al and Skylar plus Max here at the Bean, where time is oh so short. I'd set aside several nearly empty bottles that we don't want to carry to the new house and thought, let's use them. We'll call this the One-of-a-Kind cocktail.

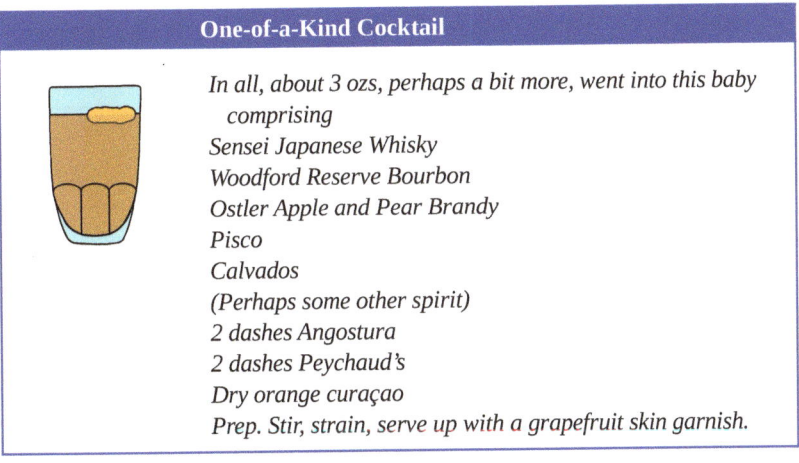

One-of-a-Kind Cocktail

In all, about 3 ozs, perhaps a bit more, went into this baby
*   comprising*
Sensei Japanese Whisky
Woodford Reserve Bourbon
Ostler Apple and Pear Brandy
Pisco
Calvados
(Perhaps some other spirit)
2 dashes Angostura
2 dashes Peychaud's
Dry orange curaçao
Prep. Stir, strain, serve up with a grapefruit skin garnish.

Surprisingly drinkable. Leads me to think that as in cooking, if you have a sense of what goes together and a sense of proportionality and know what you like—as in how sweet—you can make do with nearly anything. Not surprisingly, this cocktail packed a wallop, as people used to say, kind of needed after the Republicans acquitted Trump of the worst crimes a president can commit, hoping to seize the office for himself and, one can only assume, his heirs. This will sound like a foolish conspiracy theory, but I believe his plan was either (a) for Mike Pence, faced with an overrun Capitol, to stop the electoral vote count; declare the count impossible; and hand the counting to the House, where each state would get one vote. There are more red than blue states, so Trump would stay in office, or (b) to have Pence "the traitor" killed

("Hang Mike Pence," they shouted), declare martial law, and hang on to power that way.

At any rate, I drank the One of a Kind in my Sazerac glass and thought, why not follow with a Sazerac? And I did. To refresh your memory:

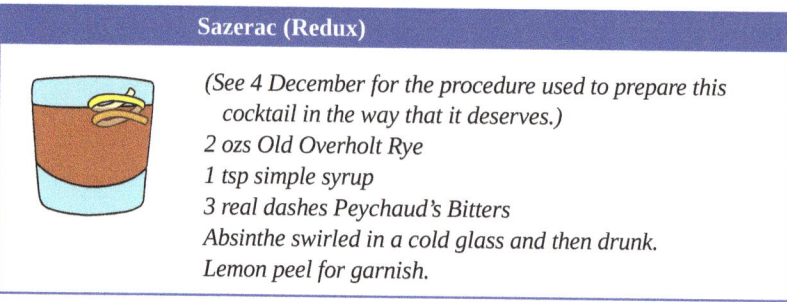

Sazerac (Redux)

(See 4 December for the procedure used to prepare this cocktail in the way that it deserves.)
2 ozs Old Overholt Rye
1 tsp simple syrup
3 real dashes Peychaud's Bitters
Absinthe swirled in a cold glass and then drunk.
Lemon peel for garnish.

Occurred to me I'd never had a Sazerac with "real" dashes of bitters. And sure enough, when a dash is 1/8 tsp you get a much better drink! Tried a second with Peychaud's and Creole Bitters, and it was fine too.

We finished the night with a cocktail that Al makes for Skylar so consistently that when we returned from Florida, the Bean was dead out of the ingredients.

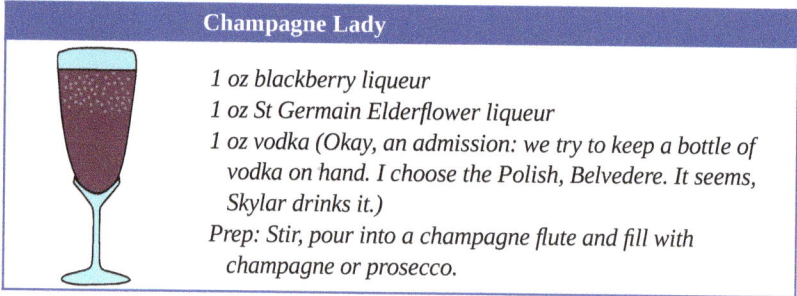

Champagne Lady

1 oz blackberry liqueur
1 oz St Germain Elderflower liqueur
1 oz vodka (Okay, an admission: we try to keep a bottle of vodka on hand. I choose the Polish, Belvedere. It seems, Skylar drinks it.)
Prep: Stir, pour into a champagne flute and fill with champagne or prosecco.

Easy to like. As with most vodka cocktails, a drink that you feel but that is not in the least boozy.

14 February Sunday—Valentine's Day

We observed no real rituals but given our packing tasks, the day was fine nonetheless. As for cocktails, a new one:

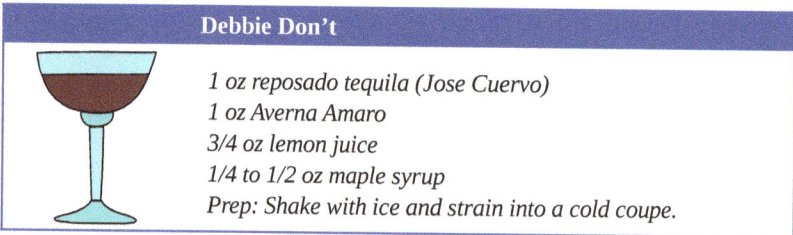

Debbie Don't

1 oz reposado tequila (Jose Cuervo)
1 oz Averna Amaro
3/4 oz lemon juice
1/4 to 1/2 oz maple syrup
Prep: Shake with ice and strain into a cold coupe.

As Tux2 says, a crowd pleaser, and not one I would have dreamed up. The far-flung ingredients—

tequila from Mexico, Amaro from Italy, lemon from Florida, maple syrup from New Hampshire—are no natural combination. But put them together, shake them up, strain into a coupe, and they are magic.

15 February Monday

As she does when asked what to drink, Jenny favored a dark cocktail. These amount to anything in the Manhattan to Old Fashioned family, and we quickly settled on the Nirvana, a Jamie Boudreau creation that you may recall:

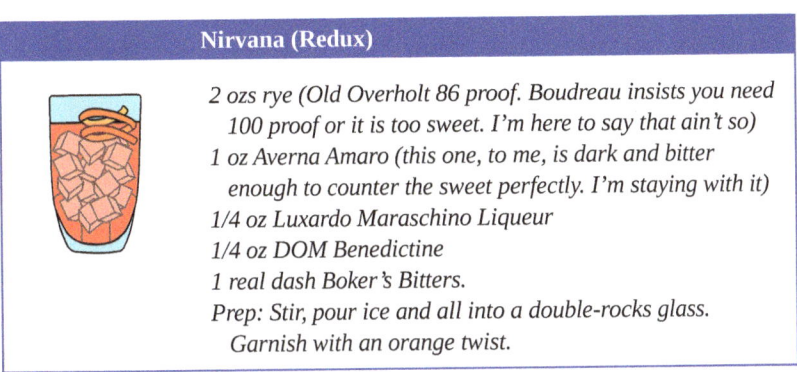

Nirvana (Redux)
2 ozs rye (Old Overholt 86 proof. Boudreau insists you need 100 proof or it is too sweet. I'm here to say that ain't so)
1 oz Averna Amaro (this one, to me, is dark and bitter enough to counter the sweet perfectly. I'm staying with it)
1/4 oz Luxardo Maraschino Liqueur
1/4 oz DOM Benedictine
1 real dash Boker's Bitters.
Prep: Stir, pour ice and all into a double-rocks glass. Garnish with an orange twist.

Next, we followed the recipe for the first one, except used Creole bitters in place of Boker's, and a grapefruit twist with a cherry instead of orange. And, while I made Jenny's with rye, mine used Elijah Craig bourbon. She preferred hers; I, mine.

In two other iterations I replaced the Luxardo with Grand Marnier Cherry Liqueur, going light on the two sweeteners, keeping each short of 1/4 oz. I replaced the Creole bitters with Peychaud's and liked that version a lot. In the final Nirvana replaced the Averna Amaro with Amaro Nardini and liked it best of all. Used lemon as the garnish, which proved better than grapefruit.

Put differently, this cocktail invites a lot of tinkering. But once dialed in to your satisfaction, you have an excellent candidate for a Decantered Cocktail, which I will make shortly. Imagine on any evening you like, putting a big cube in a double rocks glass, pouring a healthy dose of medicine, and sending yourself off to nirvana with virtually no mess or fuss.

16 February Tuesday—Mardi Gras

And yes, we tinkered and decantered, the latter using the Elijah Craig-Peychaud-Nardini-lemon twist (once in the glass) approach. I put one large clear cube in a double rocks glass and filled her up, ummm, more than once. It is easy, so easy, bordering on too easy—but we won't go that far—to pour and simply add a twist. I did not drink the whole decanter, and it really was a small one as I seemed to have packed every other vessel.

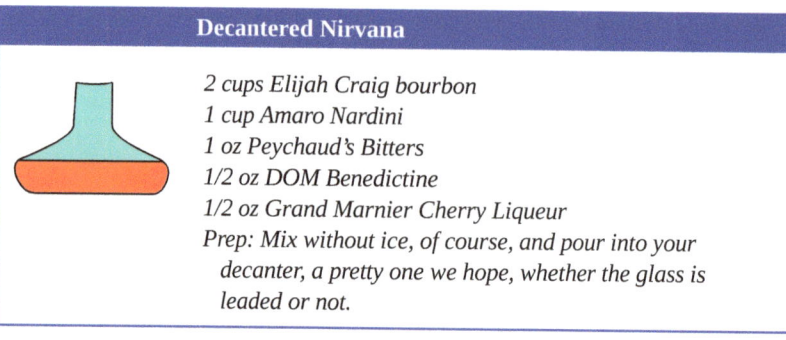

Decantered Nirvana

2 cups Elijah Craig bourbon
1 cup Amaro Nardini
1 oz Peychaud's Bitters
1/2 oz DOM Benedictine
1/2 oz Grand Marnier Cherry Liqueur
Prep: Mix without ice, of course, and pour into your
decanter, a pretty one we hope, whether the glass is
leaded or not.

Perhaps too sweet, but nonetheless a treat.

As for Mardi Gras, down in my hometown where the temperatures are icy, the celebration has been called off because of Covid. And if the present keeps to the past, if the city really froze, exposed pipes under thousands of houses will have burst. Instead of foreheads smudged by ash on Ash Wednesday, you'll have mud as residents try to become plumbers to fix the broken pipes up under their houses. Much cooler here, of course, and we got no broken pipes.

17 February Wednesday

As I write, it is Sunday 21 February. A hiatus, an interstice (apparently correctly spelled). On the 17th, I drank something, but not much, or so I believe, knowing that Rick and Ruth were coming to bid the Bean farewell. And by day I made shrimp creole for our dinner.

18 February Thursday

We sat in the pub. Ruth drank the Last Word, Rick what we'll call a Nardini Nirvana. Jenny and I drank Old Fashioned 90s. We talked, reminisced, dined on shrimp creole and Ruth's bread, were joined by Al. Rick preferred the rye version, with less Benedictine and Luxardo Maraschino than the decantered bourbon attempt. I'm sure he's right. I drank too much to know.

19 February Friday

And on Friday I was hungover. Perhaps not massively, but memorably enough that it is Sunday night, and I haven't drunk a cocktail since Thursday. Friday Al and I rented the trucks we'd need to move, and I packed up the Bean Bar, cleared the shelves of booze. Brick brought us the most delicious scallops, pasta, and salad for dinner, and I opened a bottle of Klinker Brick, a Zinfandel we've always liked.

Our last night in the Bean, now one more rent in the fabric of our lives.

20 February Saturday

Today we moved, after 16 years in the Ol' Bean Tavern, helping Al grow up and me grow old. Al brought in Sam, Skylar, Kyle, Noah, and Brodie to help us move, and the movers had Bob, Dan, Jess, and a fellow whose name I never got. Took all of us and Jenny the day, working without break, and still much remains at the Bean to be done. Meanwhile, the three-car garage at our Lake Massasecum house is amassed with stuff, a chaotic galaxy, perhaps of ten or fifty times more stuff than we removed from *Lea Scotia* just a few months back.

Our first night in the rented house on Davis Road in Bradford near the lake, a house we like considerably and are lucky that Jenny found. Neighbors left a welcoming bottle of wine, but we had no cocktail.

21 February Sunday

We dined at Denis's tonight—gumbo, fabulous bread, cheesecake and French silk pie—him, exhausted by a full-house weekend and us with two houses in such disorder that in neither could I find the strength to mine the ingredients to make a soothing cocktail. Indeed, I found that Jenny had unloaded a box of what I'd call "essential spirits" in a closet in the downstairs bathroom, about as near to our proposed bar as a Darwinian is to an evangelical. Broke my spirit.

22 February Monday

The fast is broken. Revolver is one for which we had the pretty simple ingredients in places where they could be found. Back on 18 December, I complained that this was "too thin." Turns out, when you haven't had a cocktail in days, "too thin" transforms to "just about perfect." It was sweet, but who cared? Had no orange for garnish, but a cherry was just fine. Probably this one would be better with Mr. Black, and when we return to Florida, where our boat stores Mr. Black, we'll find out.

Revolver (Redux)

2 ozs bourbon
1/2 oz coffee liqueur (Kahlúa is in the house)
2 dashes orange bitters
Prep: Combine over ice and stir for at least 15 seconds.
Garnish with a flamed orange peel if you can.

Flaming Citrus and Smoking an Old Fashioned

Not a lot, but a few cocktails call for flaming citrus or, say, rosemary, and lots of high-end cocktail bars are serving a Smoked Old Fashioned. The implement to use for flaming and smoking is a propane torch. I use ours at the Bean to start fires in woodstoves. But if you hold a citrus wheel with a pair of metal tongs and fire up the torch, it does a splendid job of scorching. For a Smoked Old Fashioned, get a piece of oak, cedar, cherry, hickory, or apple about the size of a small cutting board. Aim your torch and start a fire on the wood. Put the glass you'll use for the Smoked Old Fashioned upside down over the burning, smoking wood, which will extinguish the fire. Meanwhile, make the Old Fashioned you like in your stirring glass and pour it quickly into the smoky glass. Have fun.

23 February Tuesday

The bar in our new digs wasn't working. Too dark, too low, too far from a sink. I moved the tools to our kitchen and now choose a cocktail for the night, delivering the spirits to the tools, gin and Green Chartreuse for a Last Word… the lime and ice were already in the kitchen. Worked fine.

But in trying to figure out the bar, realized we had a beautiful cherry wine rack at the Ol' Bean, and here we have a wall where a woodstove has been ejected because we renters can't be trusted by insurance companies to burn a fire (Please don't mention smoking Old Fashioned to them.). The wine rack fits snugly, and I realized that the guy who made the wine rack, our friend Heston, could make a bar to go next to it, which, as it happens, is adjacent to the kitchen. Altogether this is more logistical than you care to know. But the bar, a top priority in this all-consuming move, while it will never be up to the Bean's high standard, is a project that requires ingenuity where our experience will in due course yield a setting we can love.

And the Last Words were perfect for the night. I like to use one lime and about 1 3/4 ozs of both gin and Green Chartreuse. The limes are small right now, or I'd go for 2 ozs of each. I drank two, felt them pleasantly, then did some moving work with Al, and had a third later, which easily revived the pleasant ecstasy. Was an unusual way to drink for me, but not a bad one.

24 February Wednesday

The gigantic move continued with a fleet of Al's friends helping shift stuff around and load truck and trailers. Yes, many hands make light work. But tonight, no drinking. Rick and Ruth are bringing dinner tomorrow to the new house, so I need to (1) stay sober tonight and (2) find appropriate cocktails for tomorrow. Perhaps

Corpse Revivers
La Chaparra
Hemingway Daiquiri
Gypsy Eyes
Millionaire
?

25 February Thursday

We apparently celebrated my mother's birthday, July 18, with La Chaparra, and my enthusiastic review suggests this summer cocktail deserves refreshing, perhaps as a way of encouraging summer along. And who knows, we may experiment with the formulas, using, for example, different citrus while muddling the peel.

La Chaparra (Redux)

1 lime peel. Skin a lime peel in the latitudinal direction getting a fair bit of it.

1 tsp simple syrup or a little less

2 ozs rum (I used Cruzan aged from St Croix, which was great. If you can get Havana Club 3-year-old, that is where to start. Lots of experimentation possible)

1 oz red vermouth (Dolin Red. But I'd love to try this with Antica Formula, Punt e Mes, or an Amaro. Again, possibilities)

Prep: Put the lime peel in your stir glass with the simple syrup and muddle, not hard, but assertively. You want to break the lime oils and essence free. Add ice, vermouth, and rum. Stir until frosty cold and then strain into a cold coupe. Once the drink is in the glass, discard the ice and use the muddled lime peel as garnish.

In the new configuration, new bar, we must, as Rick Lugg, our evening's guest along with Ruth, said, "move things [i.e., cocktail parts] from place to place." I was, however, after experiments earlier in the week, prepared for the inefficiencies. Here, and this is far more important than one recipe, is the process:

1. Choose a cocktail. Tonight's offering is La Chaparra.
2. Thus, tonight rum is the operative spirit, gold or dark, probably not white. But with rum those colors signal different new-world outposts from Venezuela to BVI.
3. Sweet vermouth is the flavor director in this cocktail. Dolin Rouge is a first-rate place to begin. Antica Formula has bottom, but it is also sweet, so be moderate. Punt e Mes, the deepest vermouth, desires attention.
4. Flay half a lime latitudinally. Not every reader will decipher this instruction but follow your best guess.

See what I mean? Gather the rums and vermouth you aim to try, skin a lime, have cold coupes and ice handy, along with a measuring spoon, lime flayer (ie., a knife), muddler, sugar or simple syrup, and ice. In this scenario, don't give the guests much choice, as was our approach for the evening.

How did it go? Naturally a man of my experience tested the cocktail beforehand, and it came up to our very high standards. We chose the rums and vermouth artfully. Havana Club, Cruzan, St James; Dolin, Antica Formula; fast-dissolving sugar in place of simple syrup, nothing too daring, but lightly experimental.

Yet, Rick and Ruth did not appear to be in the mood for much drinking, had one apiece, and then all of us switched to prosecco they'd brought along. They brought us dinner from Siam Orchid, and I ate like a starving man, as my daddy used to say. But were the Las Chaparras satisfying? Cannot say.

26 February Friday

Dined with Marge and Doug at the Lakeside Tavern in Hopkinton. No Mai Tai this time, a much safer, marginally acceptable Manhattan. Well, two Manhattans. Nothing to say about them except it's a shame restaurants do not try to do better.

27 February Saturday

With Al and Skylar we worked again till broke like rotten sticks—a hard, hard day getting out of the Bean. And except for a few last things, we were done, the house beautifully clean. All of us returned exhausted to the new place, got a second wind, went to dinner, and came home, where Al and I wanted a cocktail. We leave Wednesday for Florida and have citrus that should not be wasted, in particular, a grapefruit. We went for something new, the 212, named for Manhattan's most common area code.

212

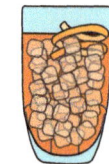

2 ozs reposado tequila (Jose Cuervo)
1 oz Aperol
2 ozs grapefruit juice (ruby red)
Prep: Combine, shake, double strain into a cold double-
rocks glass filled with ice. You can add soda water
(I would not) and should garnish with a grapefruit twist.

Both of us loved the drink. It's a summer cocktail, but so what? It's a crowd pleaser in the vein of a Debbie Don't, lovely in the glass, a bright orange, almost red. It's simple and thanks to the Aperol more bitter than sweet. May have another Sunday. And what about substituting Campari for Aperol? Or how about Cynar? Not sure why I think this last a good idea but may have a go.

28 February Sunday—Last Day at the Bean

We'd cleared everything Saturday, a hard day when snow became rain, and we worked to exhaustion. Sunday was easier, and Jenny and I had a last top-to-bottom look at the Bean, memories traveling with us. In truth, I've been gone since about last Monday. Our things are in the new place, and, it seems, they are us more than the walls in which they dwelt. Jenny and Al have found this harder.

Our former neighbors Jim and Stephanie brought us dinner. We made them drinks, the 212, and for Jim a couple of Nirvanas. Jim is a Trumpkin, and arrived with, as he'd say, some Jack in him. He was readier than normal to be angry about the election, I thought, and we'd never argued, only joked, about our differences. Happily, again we moved on.

As Jenny and I were going upstairs last night we asked the kids (Al, Skylar, Max) if they wanted to join us watching Tom Hanks' new film, *News of the World*. Al's reply was a question, asking if we were, "Going to watch a movie with that pedophile in it?"

Shocked, I asked what he meant. He said their friend Kyle had shown photos or online evidence that Hanks was a pedophile, that QAnon said so. I exploded. I demanded their evidence. He said they'd seen the evidence online. I demanded they produce it. He then said they were making a joke. I demanded Skylar produce it. Al, threateningly, commanded I not talk to his girlfriend that way. In short, the night fell apart.

Now we've all apologized. Al and Skylar have found who and what QAnon is. I apologized for my fierce anger, horrible behavior. They apologized for alleging anything QAnon said could be true.

And Jenny and I watched *News of the World*, together. I loved it.

The blow up came about, I think, because Al and Skylar are politically like us, and I was shocked, repelled, horrified that they could accept something so unlikely about a good person based on evidence presented by a kid who I believe to have right-wing roots. It was as if they had been body snatched. Perhaps my anger was appropriate, and could be that they'll be more careful in forming opinions driven by politics? One can yet hope in these imperiled times.

No drinking.

1 March 2021 Monday

Hung pictures in our rented home and toured the new owners through the Ol' Bean. But let's go right to cocktails, or almost to them. Have you noticed that serious drunks are often thin? Here's a theory about why and a healthy derivation:

As I've warned from time to time in the diary, if you have a drink, feel the alcohol, then dine, the effects of the alcohol rapidly dissipate. We want to taste a cocktail, certainly, but more importantly we want to feel it. Undoing the narcotic effect as soon as achieved seems wasteful, counter, needless. Yet we don't want to waste away our bodies by fasting, as happens to the serious drunk.

My latest approach is to dine in the late afternoon up until about 5:00, then start cocktail hour at 6:00 p.m. The food tides you over but does not interfere with the joy of the alcohol. Later, having had as much fun as you can stand, eat a bedtime snack or just wait till next morning. I'm testing this approach further. [Note to the reader: Dining in the late afternoon soon proved unworkable. Better to drink first, then decide whether you want food, I'm guessing.]

Tonight's cocktails began with a Triple Viesper (sp?), sent by Mel.

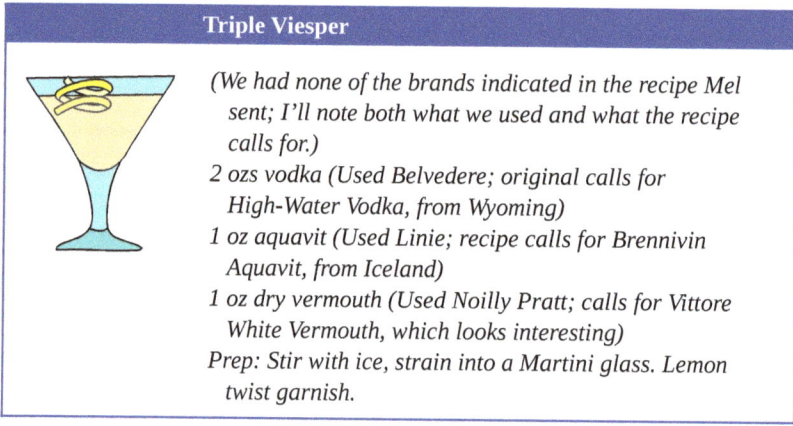

Triple Viesper

(We had none of the brands indicated in the recipe Mel sent; I'll note both what we used and what the recipe calls for.)
2 ozs vodka (Used Belvedere; original calls for High-Water Vodka, from Wyoming)
1 oz aquavit (Used Linie; recipe calls for Brennivin Aquavit, from Iceland)
1 oz dry vermouth (Used Noilly Pratt; calls for Vittore White Vermouth, which looks interesting)
Prep: Stir with ice, strain into a Martini glass. Lemon twist garnish.

Mel loved this cocktail, and perhaps it is all in the specific brands, perhaps in the setting where she experienced it, a New Orleans restaurant. That said, based on their origins and price, the brands I used look comparable. Yet, I didn't love the substitutes. Obviously, this is a Bond Vesper knockoff (except, why the "i" in Viesper?). Perhaps gin could replace vodka? A dash or two of orange bitters would help.

With that, needing to use up the citrus before we leave for Florida, I looked in Tux2 and discovered the Mariner's Ghost, a complicated tiki cocktail he/she invented. While we lacked key ingredients, such as mango, and I did not want to bother with dark and light rum, or grapefruit juice, or a lime (used lemon), the Ghost of a Ghost is remarkably good:

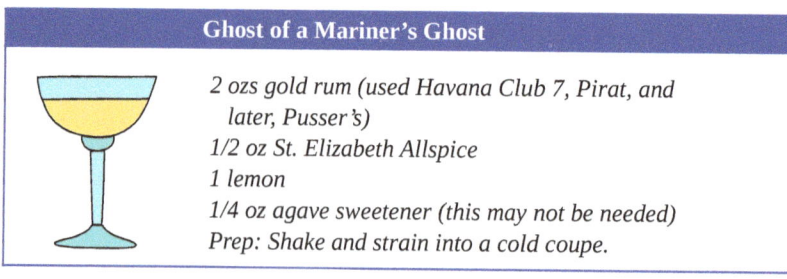

Ghost of a Mariner's Ghost

2 ozs gold rum (used Havana Club 7, Pirat, and later, Pusser's)
1/2 oz St. Elizabeth Allspice
1 lemon
1/4 oz agave sweetener (this may not be needed)
Prep: Shake and strain into a cold coupe.

Simple. And very, very delicious. The allspice is magic. You could, as Tux2 recommends for the mother ghost, strain into a double rocks glass and add ice. But in winter (the wind chill is -15°F today) who needs ice? And the cocktail has a warm, welcome gold hue, thanks to the rum and allspice.

Allspice Dram

This liqueur is much underrated, and I berate myself each time the allspice berries bought last summer show up in the spice cabinet unused. The neglect is especially deserving of criticism because St. Elizabeth is hard to find. Even the Totally Liquored franchise stores are inconsistent in carrying it; the one near Stuart does not, sadly. A homemade alternative could sell quite a lot, and at least one would never need to run short. Or an outfit like Difford's, which makes a big bottle of orgeat, could do the same with allspice dram.

Anyway, I'm eager to research allspice dram, which is to say to make some once in Florida; to perfect the promise of the Ghost of a Mariner's Ghost; and to further investigate healthy early-evening dining as a means of prolonging the effects of cocktails, if not life itself.

2 March 2021 Tuesday—Deadly Cold

Ran into a tree today in Skylar's car. Was driving on Hwy 114 near Blaisdell Lake when a dead maple, knocked down by the very strong winds of the past couple days, loomed immediately. Swerved hard left, but the tree whacked the right front, broke a blinker and dented the car. New car too. But happily, not ours.

Why was I driving Skylar's car? Al and Skylar had our car, so I borrowed hers. Curiously, Al had backed into and damaged her car, so I added to the total repair bill. How lucky can you get?

Our friends Dan and Laurie Morrissey came by in the evening, and in fact I was looking for their summer house on Blaisdell Lake and thinking about Laurie's poem, recently published in *Appalachia Magazine*, when the tree appeared. The poem is a fine one, called, "Polar Vortex." One reason for the night's visit was to test Dan's new Perfect Manhattan, which we've named the Perfect Dubliner because made with Irish Whiskey:

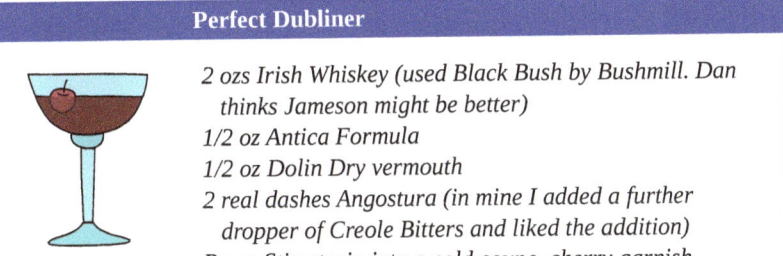

Perfect Dubliner
2 ozs Irish Whiskey (used Black Bush by Bushmill. Dan thinks Jameson might be better)
1/2 oz Antica Formula
1/2 oz Dolin Dry vermouth
2 real dashes Angostura (in mine I added a further dropper of Creole Bitters and liked the addition)
Prep: Stir, strain into a cold coupe, cherry garnish.

As you'd expect, given the characteristics of Irish Whiskey, this is a mellow Manhattan. The whiskey comes through subtly. Maybe a summer or winter afternoon Manhattan, not that it lacks strength. Made me also think a similar approach with a blended scotch such as The Famous Grouse would be interesting, surely worth a try. (Note: That would be a Perfect Rob Roy, of course.)

3 March 2021 Wednesday—Travis's Birthday

Here we are at 30,000 feet, bumpy, on our way to Orlando and life aboard ship. Warmth ahead. The move from the Ol' Bean took about all the energy we could muster for a solid month and in some ways for months before. We spent the summer paying to have a new chimney built, repairing sills and clapboards, tossing irretrievably useless stuff; in fall, buying a new boat and sailing her around Florida with problems we've noted, organizing that boat and acclimating to life aboard (that part being surprisingly easy); and then the final push to move from the Bean and relocate near Lake Massasecum. Truly, the Bean was too big, and this smaller, tighter house suits us and looks like a gallery with our artwork, much of it acquired to fill the massive wall space at the Ol' Bean.

Back in Florida after an easy trip, we drove to Tim and Beth's. Beth needed a cocktail because without me, she'd had none. I wanted a Swearengen Sling, but perusal of the ingredients showed we'd have to make do. Here's the list: Jack Daniel's, Amaro Nardini (so far so good), pear liqueur, grapefruit juice, a bit of juice from Italian cherries.

I cut up and squeezed the ruby red grapefruit. The cocktail, called by Beth a Vero Sunset, is as follows:

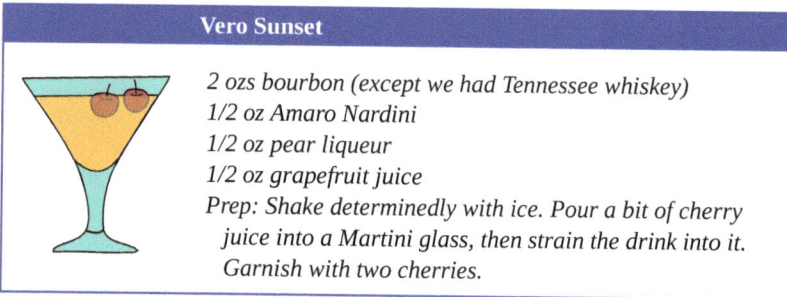

Vero Sunset

2 ozs bourbon (except we had Tennessee whiskey)
1/2 oz Amaro Nardini
1/2 oz pear liqueur
1/2 oz grapefruit juice
Prep: Shake determinedly with ice. Pour a bit of cherry juice into a Martini glass, then strain the drink into it. Garnish with two cherries.

The Sorcery of Cocktails

This did not seem likely to be great, but sorcery has its way. Rather than dull brown, as the bubbles subsided, the cocktail turned a golden hue accented by the cherry juice at bottom as if the sun were sinking below the verge. And to be truthful, it was a pleasure. Beth had a second; I had a third. The taste of the pear came through but so did the whiskey. The drink was just sweet enough and, while the grapefruit was not obvious, I think it key and a better choice than lemon or lime, though this will require experiment.

Most of all, the Vero Sunset is a good example of how rewarding it is in the world of cocktails to make do. Afterward, Jenny drove us to our boat, which was in excellent shape, clean, orderly, and after Jenny suffered excruciating pain in what has become a worrisome arm or shoulder impingement, we slept on the water comfortably, thanks to the promiscuously warm Florida winter weather.

4 March 2021 Thursday

Jenny and I have fought rarely during our marriage of 25 years. But the move seems to have unhinged us, and we are finding ways to disagree, today about money, my worst subject. I like to spend it; she is careful. After our incident this evening, a description of which we'll discreetly omit from these pages, we dined in the cockpit. Our friend Jim came by to say the boss (i.e., the dockmaster) has offered us slip A36, deeper, closer in, next to other sailboats. We're taking it in hope that the deeper water means we can sail more often.

The drink of the night was a real Swearengen Sling (below and on 8 August):

Swearengen Sling

2 ozs bourbon (used Wild Turkey 101 for both)
1/2 oz amaro (the recipe calls for Amaro Nonino, which I
*   don't have. In mine, used Amaro Nardini; in Jenny's, used*
*   Liquor Strega. Both excellent. I'd hoped the Strega would*
*   lend its yellow color to the cocktail, but it did not. I'm not*
*   quite sure whether I like its look, its color.)*
1/2 oz Cherry Heering
1/2 oz lemon juice (used 1/2 lemon for each drink)
1/2 oz simple syrup
2 cherries (the recipe calls for brandied, but we had only
*   Luxardo Maraschino, which were fine. You can easily*
*   make brandied cherries, and it could be worth doing as*
*   well as inexpensive.)*
Prep: Muddle the two cherries in a shaker. Add ice and the
*   other ingredients. Shake. Strain into a rocks glass with*
*   ice. Add a cherry for garnish and serve with a straw.*

I modified it: served up or with a little ice from the shaker; did not muddle cherries but used syrup from the now empty jar; used no simple syrup, as this is sweet enough. And it was good. But in truth, I think it was no better than the Vero Sunset and not as pretty.

But here is the kicker (an expression I don't recall ever using before). Rather than cut another lemon and use only half, I replaced citrus with bitters, specifically Creole Bitters by Bittermens. Jenny tried it and declared she preferred it to the original, identifying herself as a "Manhattan girl." What we've got here is a Bitter Swearengen. I think Al would approve.

Citrus and Bitters
Think about it. Most cocktails that use citrus lack bitters. The two seem to serve a similar function as spice and to ameliorate the sweetness of other ingredients. So why can't we from time to time replace the one with the other, perhaps in either direction? (In Florida, my friend Steve says, we'll need to keep quiet about replacing citrus or risk a bad end.)

A Manhattan with lemon in place of bitters? Hmmm.

5 March 2021 Friday

It's time to say, and I've avoided it, that we're coming to the close of this diary. We've got enough cocktails, for a year anyway. It may be worth adding, if a bit boastful, that three nights running we've built new or partly new cocktails, all of them good. In other words, we should all have a sense of what mixes well together.

March 23 marks a year's worth of entries that began about two weeks into the pandemic lock down. Vaccines are ever more available, and lots of people we know have had theirs; I'm due March 27 and might be able to get one sooner. With an end in mind, what have we learned, not just about cocktails, but about surviving a pandemic sane? Here's the first thing.

How to Survive a Pandemic

It is invaluable to have something to look forward to every day. The worst period of this pandemic was the week I went on the wagon. The cocktails, which are innately uplifting, focused the hour each day. What will I make? Do we have the ingredients? What's appropriate for the day?

And then there is the first taste, often disappointing, especially if we haven't waited for a shaken cocktail to settle. But then, somewhere into that first drink, the alcohol rises; we feel lighter, happier, freer. Maybe those dissident right-wing boys should get off the Bud Light and have a real drink.

That's a start. Let's see what tomorrow brings. For dinner, by the way, Jenny and I shared a large bottle of the dark, malty, St Bernardus Abt 12, Belgian, one of the great beers of the world.

6 March 2021 Saturday

A relaxed rainy day, the first rain we've seen in Florida this year, since the last hurricane rolled through in November. Dined with J's family, including Beth's daughter, Christine, at Conchy Joe's, where I love their version of the Hemingway Daiquiri, which has lime and grapefruit, light and dark rum, and simple syrup. It's powerful.

In the evening, J and I tried a new cocktail, the Paper Plane.

Paper Plane
1 oz bourbon (Evan Williams 100 proof) 1 oz Amaro Nonino 1 oz Campari (the recipe calls for Aperol, which we do not have aboard) 1 oz lemon juice (Out of lemon, on a second used lime) Prep: Shake. Poured into our new rocks glasses with the ice from the shaker. No garnish.

Delicious. Why would you use Aperol? The lime was at least as good as the lemon. A good riff on the Boulevardier.

7 March 2021 Sunday

During a FaceTime call with Steve and Rochelle, Jenny and I drank plain old Manhattans while they drank Nirvanas. Both good choices, I'd say. We have not moved our boat to the new deeper slip today because the wind is blistering strong and looks as if it will continue strong tomorrow, so we hope to move Tuesday morning.

What We Have Learned

Back to what we've learned this year: When to shake, when to stir. A dash is much more than a shake. Grenadine should be made from POM pomegranate juice. Simple syrup; agave; grenadine; raspberry, honey, orgeat, cane, and maple syrups; DOM Benedictine;

Luxardo; and others are sweeteners that have their place. Often, when a drink calls for ice, just pour what you've used to shake or stir into the glass. When using an absinthe rinse, drink the over-pour rather than toss it. Citrus does not need refrigerating until squeezed. Often half a lemon is enough but a whole lime. Lemon and lime are mostly interchangeable or can be miscegenated (spell check seems to believe that's a word). When using grapefruit, cut up and juice the whole thing all at one time. Drinks with an entire ounce of bitters are divine and possibly healthful.

I went into the year expecting to find a few cocktails that would be my drinks, the way I often prefer either a New England IPA or a monkish Belgian. Instead, discovered dozens of drinks I love and that many are better suited for summer or winter than others.

Learning, in other words, has helped make the pandemic endurable and could make its effects durable.

8 March 2021 Monday

No drinks except a Fat Tire beer with tamales from Trader Joe's. Bad Internet. Remember the mystery noise aboard *Lea Scotia* from a while back? Perhaps roar is a better description. The night was tough owing to a strong wind from our stern which sets up harmonic vibrations in the mast. This happens in tall buildings and in some boats with aluminum masts, I suspect when the masts are especially tall, as ours is, and it seems related to the in-mast furling of our mainsail. The phenomenon is called a Karman vortex street, for which I think we'll name a bad-tasting, and if possible noisy, cocktail.

In boats the cause is mast pumping, which may be controllable with our never used running backstays. Here's a description from Wikipedia, which I cite for its highly descriptive unintelligibility:

> In fluid dynamics, a Karman vortex street is a repeating pattern of swirling vortices, caused by a process known as vortex shedding, which is responsible for the unsteady separation of flow of a fluid around blunt bodies.

Somehow, we have to prevent the eddies from interacting on the downwind side. If not, since the sound is loud and will disturb other mariners, we will be intensely hated in port.

9 March 2021 Tuesday

For now, however, I'm sitting in the marina laundromat waiting for clothes to wash, after moving to a new, and we think better, slip today. I'm editing the cocktail diary and have arrived at September 15, the morning I awoke after a bad fight with Jenny and spontaneously offered that, "Maybe we need a second sailboat." And here we are.

Things have not worked out as we thought in many respects. Beth's daughter, Christine, came down from Nashville, and she lives with Beth and Tim. As a result, Beth doesn't need us to look after Tim when she heads off for physical therapy. Late in the year, Beth injured her right arm probably playing the one round of golf she's tried in years. The injury left her right hand nearly useless and her whole arm weak. In February she finally got enough attention from her doctor that he operated. So far, however, the arm hasn't noticeably improved.

At any rate, Christine stays with Tim, buoys Beth's spirits, and makes our presence superfluous most of the time. Luckily, we like living on the boat and are surprised at how agreeable we find Stuart.

Tonight, we'll have no Karman Vortex Cocktail. Instead, it'll be something good, very good, I'm thinking with grapefruit. Or how about a Réveillon? Or a Spruce Goose?

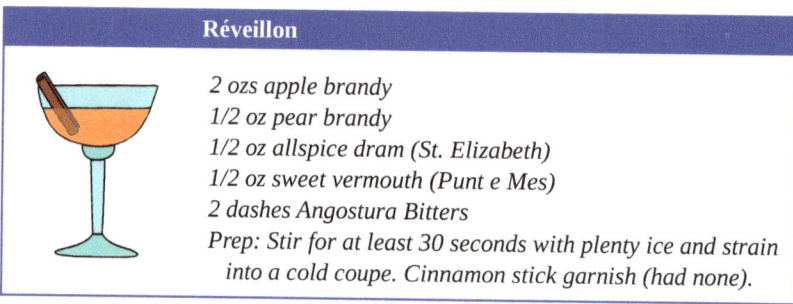

Réveillon
2 ozs apple brandy
1/2 oz pear brandy
1/2 oz allspice dram (St. Elizabeth)
1/2 oz sweet vermouth (Punt e Mes)
2 dashes Angostura Bitters
Prep: Stir for at least 30 seconds with plenty ice and strain into a cold coupe. Cinnamon stick garnish (had none).

The Réveillons seemed right for celebrating where we are, and they were good. I'd run out to Totally Liquored for pear brandy, but what I found wasn't as tasty as I'd hoped. For me, pear liqueur may be the better choice. What's the difference?

Brandy or Liqueur?
A brandy is liquor distilled from grapes, apples, what have you, or pears. A liqueur is a spirit (perhaps based on pear for pear liqueur, though not necessarily), plus sugar and pear flavoring. It is thicker, sweeter than brandy and to my taste, has more the flavor of the original fruit. But still, a Réveillon is a fine cocktail however you pear it or however it a-pears.

During the first we walked the docks and took pleasure in our new slip because it suits the boat. We are tied as if in a spiderweb so that no side touches and squeals against a dock, and we're protected from the waves. Other boats are less fortunate. We also appreciated *Lea Scotia's* design. The Taswell 43 really is a high-end boat, in design and build, for its time, and I'd say generally ahead of most boats of the era. She has the comfort of modern boats but, to our eyes, is much better looking. But enough bragging.

I drank the other two Réveillons aboard during a lovely, but brief evening. Was fast asleep by 9:30, which makes for a long sleep. And waking in the night, the relative quiet of this slip was notable and put a smile on my sleepy face.

10 March 2021 Wednesday

Thanks to our long sleep we were up and on our bikes by 6:30. On returning, I volunteered to get pastries from Jennifer's bakery while Jenny showered and made coffee.

Downtown Stuart confuses me. It's a river city, and like other river cities, say Boston or my hometown New Orleans, the streets meander. I recall in the 90s in Calgary a big laugh on a blistering cold night because all the streets running north-south are numbers and the ones that run east-west are letters. None of them is anything but a straight line. That's a prairie for you

Anyway, in Stuart I've been unable to figure out a direct route onto Ocean Blvd. where the bakery lives, and when I reach downtown, turn left, am always unsure whether Ocean is to my right or to my left. Today I drove to the end of Martin Luther King Blvd. where instinct told me Ocean was to the right and experience told me Ocean was to the left.

It is unusual for me to choose experience over instinct, but I did, and experience was right. Perhaps tonight's cocktail will reflect the same right-thinking choice. Where does Sailor's Courage fit?

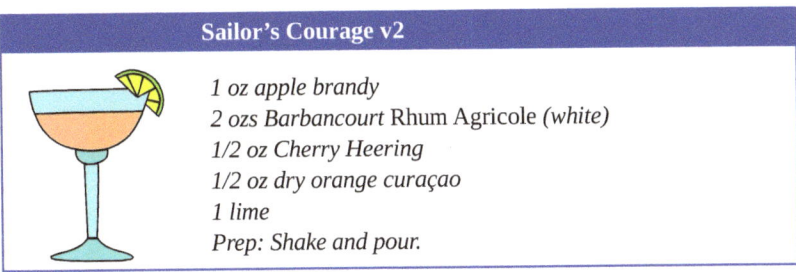

Sailor's Courage v2

1 oz apple brandy
2 ozs Barbancourt Rhum Agricole (white)
1/2 oz Cherry Heering
1/2 oz dry orange curaçao
1 lime
Prep: Shake and pour.

Instinct? Experience? Delicious.

Late by our standards. Jenny is asleep below. We've had what is for us a normal evening, and easy, tonight pre-made dinner of twin stuffed potatoes. I'm in the cockpit. Watched episodes, of a British series, *Mum*. The Theme Song, "When I'm Gone," is what I hope someone will play to remember me. I'd best learn it just in case. The wind has shifted enough that our mast isn't howling. That's a relief.

But I want to say that too much of this diary has been superficial. Cocktails make us feel better. And tonight's Sailor's Courage deserved sipping because so good and so good at making us feel better. Guess I'd say, however, that chemically lifting everything to make the broken world feel livable is no real help, is chimerical. We could do more, try to say more.

I hope the wind keeps blowing from the east, not the southeast. If I can… if it does, will sleep till morning.

11 March 2021 Thursday

It didn't fit yesterday's menu, but today went right to the Hemingway Daiquiri prepared as I believe it is by Conchy Joe's. A few words about that.

First, unlike almost any other bar in these parts, they use fresh citrus. Makes all the difference. Their version is dry, I think because like us they use Cherry Heering as the sweetener. As do they, I used dark rum (Flor de Caña gold) and white rum, beginning with Flor de Caña white but moved to Barbancourt as in the past. And the Barbancourt was much better; I believe may be a secret to Conchy Joe's. When Covid allows, we'll go sit at that bar and watch how this cocktail is made by them. It is beginning to look like a favorite.

12 March 2021 Friday

We slept last night, mostly vortex free, but first thing this morning it started and was so loud that Jenny's colleagues were bothered by it during their Zoom meeting.

Meanwhile, I was out acting on a cure. Step one was to get the right rope to fill the slot in the mast. I thought 1 inch and went to Chapman's Marine Supply where a nice fellow cut a one-foot piece of 1-inch nylon anchor line and gave it to me to try. They had nothing that would serve as slides to keep the rope tight against the slot along its 60-foot length. He sent me along to the store that sells inflatables and other supplies for sailors. But that place had nothing and sent me to a sail loft, where a rigger recommended an online outfit. I needed results today.

Lowe's was nearby, and I decided to comb the store slowly with an open mind to find or fabricate slides that would serve. To this end, I began in the garden center and worked my way aisle by aisle to plumbing.

Along the way several possibilities presented themselves, and I became at least a Lowe's novitiate. In plumbing, nylon pipe holders that would surround the rope and that have tabs meant to be screwed into wood that could serve as slides looked like they would do the trick.

Back at *Lea Scotia*, the 1-inch rope appeared too thick, a bit of a mystery since a piece of 3/4 inch dock line was slightly too narrow the night before. The slides could be made to fit, but I had to cut the tabs shorter and cut spacers so that they could squeeze into the slot.

Back at Lowe's I bought 3/4-inch slides, a diamond cutting wheel and some bits for a Dremel tool. At Chapman's got 65 feet of 3/4 inch nylon line.

Back at the boat I went to work. The 3/4-inch line and slides were perfect. I sewed a sling on the end of the line to which a halyard could be hooked to haul the rig up the mast. I cut and shaped one of the slides to be sure it would fit the rope snugly, could be torqued into the slot, and then would not break being hauled up the mast. Decided to use a slide every six feet. On the dock, Dremel in hand, cut and drilled each of the ten slides. Then, with them in my pocket, climbed high enough on the mast to put each slide around the rope, hauling it up with a halyard just enough to be sure it all worked.

Once all seemed ready, attached a slide to the rope with a 1/2-inch stainless screw, pulled the assembly 6 feet higher, and attached another, until the assembly was tight against the slot in the mast all the way to its top.

And lordy, lordy… it worked! The dreaded, sleep-depriving, nerve-breaking vortex street, a deadly ghost, has disappeared. All is quiet below.

Making Do

But you may ask how this trip deep into the weeds of sailor making-do relates to cocktails? At sea, or even in port, being able to figure things out is a fact of every sailor's life. And I believe it is a critical ability for a home bartender. We often do not have and cannot always get the ingredients cocktails call for. So we make do, solve the problem of what to drink rather than be swallowed by the vortex on the street of Want.

13 March 2021 Saturday

Spruce Goose. Had been awhile. But Tim and Beth always have a cabinet of alcohol that no one, except me in a small way, has planned. I wanted something Beth hadn't had. And somehow, because they did have the ingredients, except honey-syrup which I quickly made, we went to the Spruce Goose.

It's a cocktail I love, as noted 18 September, for its large dose of Angostura (1/4 oz) its 1/2 lime (needs no more than that), the 1/2 oz of honey syrup, and 2 ozs of gin (Tanqueray is what they have). The Goose solved my problem of what to make, of making something we had not had, and of an outstanding cocktail.

So yes, going back to yesterday, and before, going back to Philip Henslowe, the theater manager in *Shakespeare in Love*, somehow things tend to work out. Unless you're dealing with electricity on a boat.

14 March 2021 Sunday

To lunch with Tim and Beth; Beth's daughter, Christine; and Jenny's uncle and aunt, Hoyt and Sally. The restaurant, Crabby's in Fort Pierce, a new member of a Florida chain, was large and airy. But the food was bad. I drank two beers that were tolerable and had a taste of Crabby's signature rum punch. It was awful. And that was it for drinking and dining. My stomach was off, hernia a bit bothersome.

    What have we learned this year? It's not inflexible, but a rule is never order a citrus drink, perhaps any drink, at a chain restaurant unless you know for a fact that they insist on fresh citrus. And even one-off restaurants are likely to cheat. An exception, in Concord, New Hampshire, is Hermanos. There, pretty much the only drink people order is a Margarita. They squeeze lime and make a good one. If their life were more complicated, as most are, I hate to think of the ruinous shortcuts they might take. And life would be the worse for those shortcuts. We home bartenders oh so naturally forswear shortcuts!

15 March 2021 Monday— "Beware the Ides of March."

    We were going to Starbucks for coffee and a pastry, had not much to eat aboard, and I was hungry after missing dinner, only to find the car battery dead. A Lyft took me to an auto parts store, and soon I'll install the new battery.

    What We Have Learned (continued)

    But here's another lesson: Use the events of the day to think about a cocktail for the night, perhaps invented, perhaps traditional. What would an Ides of March cocktail be? Think with me.

    Last week I bought an Italian Brandy called Tuaca thinking a recipe I'd seen called for it. No such recipe has appeared. I have no clue about the taste of this Tuaca, but how about adding an amaro and even a sweet vermouth? If it works, or not, we'll hoist a glass and exclaim "Et tu Brute?!"

    Here goes. We're drinking what we call Tuaca Manhattans.

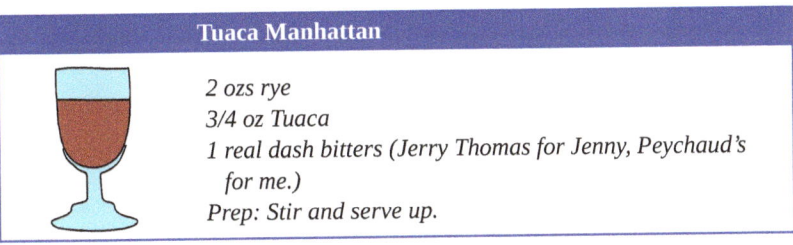

Tuaca Manhattan

2 ozs rye
3/4 oz Tuaca
1 real dash bitters (Jerry Thomas for Jenny, Peychaud's
    for me.)
Prep: Stir and serve up.

    We agreed my version was better than Jenny's. But considering Tuaca is as old as Lorenzo the Magnificent, both were okay, if not pretty good. She prefers a darker Manhattan; I probably do as well. We were at least happy.

    Et tu, Brute?

16 March 2021 Tuesday—Laundry Day

    Yes, Tuesday seems to be laundry day. Why not? And as I sit watching over the machines, editing this diary, the entry for 2 October comes up in which I describe my hopes for our boat *Lea Scotia* the day before I came to this marina looking for a slip. And good gracious, here we are, everything, really, which we learned today includes our ability not to be taxed on the money we used to buy her, which came from a 401K and an IRA, I mean, here we are! And *Lea Scotia* has lived up to all I'd hoped. Okay not all. Perhaps not most. Some of what I'd hoped!

Making Do with Aquafaba

Tonight, something with citrus. Based on the Pisco Sour, this cocktail calls for egg white. But we have none, and while I could go for some, let's try it without that ingredient. I just found in a FedEx store, Sother Teague's, *I'm Just Here for the Drinks*. One reason I believe this book to be a good one is that Teague says you can substitute the water from a can of chickpeas for egg white and won't know the difference. He calls this aquafaba.

We have a can of chickpeas. You throw the peas away (I don't much like chickpeas) or perhaps grind them up, but keep the juice, the aquafaba.

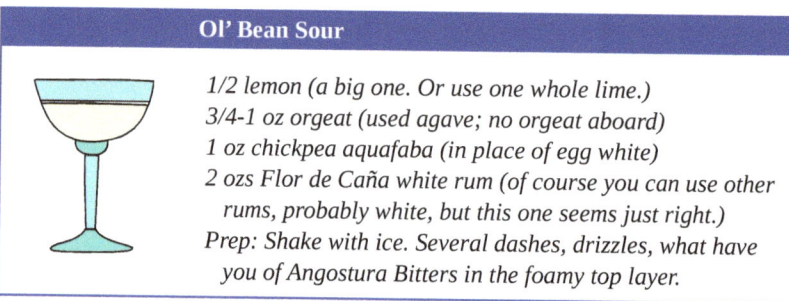

Ol' Bean Sour

1/2 lemon (a big one. Or use one whole lime.)
3/4-1 oz orgeat (used agave; no orgeat aboard)
1 oz chickpea aquafaba (in place of egg white)
2 ozs Flor de Caña white rum (of course you can use other rums, probably white, but this one seems just right.)
Prep: Shake with ice. Several dashes, drizzles, what have you of Angostura Bitters in the foamy top layer.

Aquafaba continued

Tasted good. The aquafaba had no flavor of its own, a good thing. And it added foam, which you need for drizzling the bitters. Let's call it a success, with a caveat. Egg white kind of thickens, adds body. Aquafaba does not. But if someone is vegan or, say, allergic to egg white, as is our friend Susan, aquafaba is a replacement. Susan loves a whiskey sour, and we all know the cocktail is better with egg-white, which she cannot have.

Well, we'll have to try the Aquafaba in a Whiskey Sour. Meanwhile, thank goodness for chickpeas. Never thought I'd say that.

17 March 2021 Wednesday—St Patrick's Day

Descended at least in part from the Irish, shared a Chimay with J on the Irish day of days, and that without enthusiasm, perhaps a first in this long pandemic. Quite the surprise.

18 March 2021 Thursday

The "rage for order" is a title used for books and albums probably because it is a paradox, rage being the opposite of an orderly way, an orderly mind. Which is where Jenny and I find ourselves aboard *Lea Scotia*.

Jenny's rage for order is always about what is visible. She hates cluttered counters, or on a boat, a cockpit cluttered with tools, wants things out of sight. She hates too many cars in a neighborhood, wants them garaged. As I was off to pick up Al and Skylar at the Orlando Airport, Jenny saw the organized but vivid pieces of my current projects in the cockpit, including tools and polishes and oil, and put them away. The cockpit is now a marvel of the shipshape.

But where did these things go? Behind closed doors, hatches, covers, I cannot really say where, except not in the places I've tried to devise for them either categorically (where would they be in Lowe's?) or where they fit, or any other—to me—discernible criterion of organization except their already mentioned invisibility.

My gripe here, and it is a gripe based on experience and on an unpardonable irritation, is that on a boat, where space is strictly limited, and where laying hands on what you need when it is needed can be important, the rage for order in appearance creates massive disorder under the covers.

So much for gripes. Tonight, we had the Sailor's Courage, in which I used a quarter ounce more Cherry Heering than in the past and grapefruit as well as lime. It's unquestionably a good cocktail.

19 March 2021 Friday—Last Day of Winter

Time for tequila, but how about tequila with egg white? Should work. Could resemble a Pisco Sour or an Ol' Bean Sour. Citrus of course. And bitters. For good measure, add pear brandy. Why? Because we have some. Let's call it a…

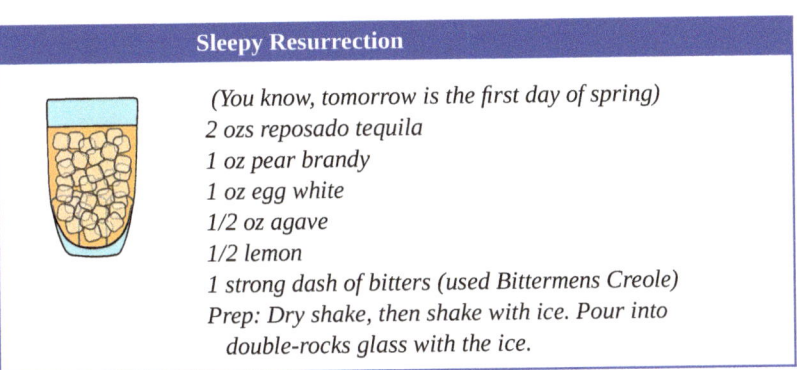

Sleepy Resurrection

(You know, tomorrow is the first day of spring)
2 ozs reposado tequila
1 oz pear brandy
1 oz egg white
1/2 oz agave
1/2 lemon
1 strong dash of bitters (used Bittermens Creole)
Prep: Dry shake, then shake with ice. Pour into
*   double-rocks glass with the ice.*

You'll be surprised that, beneath the froth, the cocktail is a lovely pink. And it is tasty, I think in an early spring way. Not sure we or anyone will ever make this one again, but it goes to show you can cobble together an acceptable cocktail without much trial and error (the first was too sweet and grapefruit did not suit it; the second was fine).

20 March 2021 Saturday—Spring Equinox

Lunch at Conchy Joe's, my favorite. Tonight, Al and I drank Hemingway Daiquiris in which I favored the darker rum, Appleton Estate 2:1 over Flor de Caña. Excellent, we both thought.

But the drink of the night, though only Jenny had one, was the Ms. Jenny Manhattan. It is based on an idea earlier in the week, substituting Amaro Nonino, which is expensive, for red vermouth or another amaro. And it is now her favorite and her namesake:

<table>
<tr><td colspan="2">Ms. Jenny Manhattan</td></tr>
<tr><td></td><td>2 ozs rye
1 oz Amaro Nonino
1 heavy dash of bitters (Angostura)
Prep: Add a bit of cherry juice and a cherry or two or
    three as garnish. Stir and pour into a single-rocks glass.</td></tr>
</table>

This is a great Manhattan. Amaro Nonino is quite versatile, and we're glad to have it.

21 March 2021 Sunday

Eventful. Skylar's dad tested positive for Covid, so we're anxiously awaiting her results to know whether we must all quarantine. Such a drag. But, with Al's excellent help, found the leak in our dinghy, repaired it, and the two youths are off in it. They've already seen a half dozen dolphins. Jenny is doing errands, and I'm aboard about to look for a next project. Lovely day and perfect temperature. This Florida weather is Edenic.

The reason for keeping a diary, noted by almost every writer who matters, is that writing preserves what the mind forgets. Tonight we've read aloud entries that track our voyage from Key West to this harbor, most of which would be lost without the diary. I'm alone in the cockpit of *Lea Scotia*, just finished drinking a second Stepmother-in-Law, having read to Jenny, Skylar, and Al the entries for our voyage from Key West. Turns out that on the fateful night when we lost all electrical power, I thought I was asleep down below, but was drunkenly asleep in the cockpit. By reading the diary to the people who were aboard, we learned the truth.

Two Stepmothers-in-Law for me, one for Jenny, one for Al. It's a fine cocktail, and appropriate as it ended our voyage.

<table>
<tr><td colspan="2">Stepmother-in-Law</td></tr>
<tr><td></td><td>1 oz Amaro Nonino
1 oz Mathilde Poire Liqueur
1 scant tsp Cherry Heering liqueur
3 ozs Woodford Reserve bourbon
2 dashes Peychaud's Bitters
2 dashes Angostura Bitters</td></tr>
</table>

Strong, you say. It is a Stepmother-in-Law, man!

What We Have Learned (continued)

Note the order of ingredients listed above. Over the year this has become the order I use just about always. The amaro, liqueur, and sweetener are thick or sweet; the bourbon, I believe, cleans the jigger. And the bitters are a kind of garnish. Most important, having an order that you stick to helps avoid forgetting an ingredient, something I used to do often and almost never do now.

22 March 2021 Monday

Today marks 365 days since the first entry in this diary. I missed some days, but not many. Could have been more contemplative most days, but here's what we have. Later today, I'm flying to New Hampshire where I'm scheduled for the Covid vaccine, first of what will probably be two shots.

A year ago, I didn't know about the existence of Stuart, Florida; The Harborage Yacht Club and Marina, where I'm sitting in the laundromat; or *Lea Scotia*, aboard which we live. The pandemic was two weeks old, and every trip to the grocery seemed perilous. But the New Hampshire Liquor Store was open for business and got plenty of ours. Despite the pandemic, and in some ways because of it, this has been an adventurous year for us.

We did a poor job of quarantining, a word I even have trouble remembering, seeming to come up with "sequestered" instead when called to describe our situation. We've been responsible in our way, mostly (though not entirely) avoiding restaurants and getting tests at CVS after flights. We've worn masks diligently when in public.

But we have flown several times, have had friends and family into our house and boat maskless, have been around unfettered and mostly unmasked young people. We've had some brushes with Covid that we know about, the most recent in which Skylar's father tested positive while she, having left home after he began to feel symptoms, is staying aboard with us. Today we learned she tested negative.

The thing that has suffered most for me is songwriting. Could be I'm just done, but I hope not. With luck, it'll turn out that the year has had enough adventure to need processing, to need time. I have continued to play and sing and, who knows, might have improved a bit.

I've learned a few things about drinking. Lately, for example, I've been less keen to feel the effects of drink, the high of a night's first cocktail, than in the past. On the other hand, not drinking on a night is rare for me, and I find excuses to make a cocktail.

I've learned a lot about cocktails, their history, making them, what I like. An unspoken goal last year was to learn to make a few I liked best, but that changed quickly to a wide-ranging interest in trying possibilities. One result has been the discovery of lots of ingredients, for example falernum in the summer, allspice dram, many amari, new vermouths, Suze, orgeat, and Cherry Heering recently. It has become clear that when a cocktail calls for a new ingredient, a substitute in the same vein will usually work just about as well. At first, thinking I preferred stirred cocktails, I shied away from shaken ones. Could be the influence of Florida, but citrus is more likely to be present than not most nights, at least down here. For quite a while I stayed away altogether from grapefruit, but now love it, especially in a Hemingway Daiquiri, and have learned how to cut it.

It is the rare restaurant that goes to the trouble of making good cocktails. Bartenders usually seem to know less about liquor than you'd expect. Their knowledge is mostly driven by local taste, which seems to mean lots of vodka and a few standards, some of them remarkably awful when made without art. Even Mexican restaurants, where Margaritas are the preponderance of what is ordered, seldom seem to go to the trouble of preparing good ones. Too bad.

The voyage metaphor, especially a voyage of discovery with the end unknown, has held up in surprising ways. Goodness, we had a real and surprisingly fraught voyage after buying *Lea Scotia*; some of those problems remain unsolved. Cocktails have been essential to calming and forgetting after hard days. If the sea can be bleak, tedious, an unending sight in every direction, the anticipation of a cocktail at night breaks the spell of tedium. The ration of rum or of grog in the British Navy, a tradition hundreds of years old, surely had much the same role as a cocktail during our pandemic. Ultimately, we've discovered Florida in winter where the weather is Edenic and to our surprise, that's enough to bring us back, and, "Like Stout Cortez, silent on a peak in Darien," we are spellbound. With that, here's a new one to me, but a classic, that you will love…

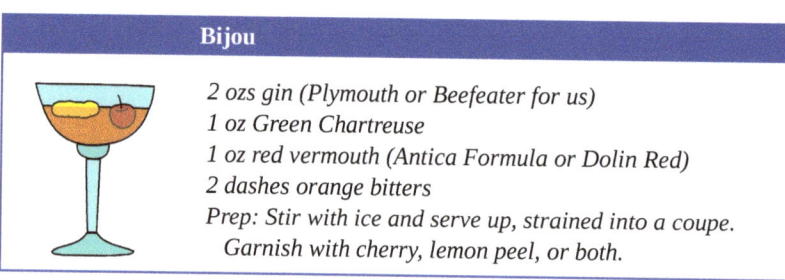

Bijou	
	2 ozs gin (Plymouth or Beefeater for us)
	1 oz Green Chartreuse
	1 oz red vermouth (Antica Formula or Dolin Red)
	2 dashes orange bitters
	Prep: Stir with ice and serve up, strained into a coupe.
	Garnish with cherry, lemon peel, or both.

A jewel.

23 March 2021 Tuesday—A New Year

We thought we were done, but damn, there is more to say. For example, back on land in our new home in New Hampshire, I've rediscovered how you make a drink is important. All the stuff about just pouring the ice into your glass… forget it. I've not chilled glasses for a while. Mistake.

<table>
<tr><td colspan="2">Dark Horse</td></tr>
<tr>
<td></td>
<td>

2.5 ozs dark rum (Barbancourt 15-year-old is perfect)
1 oz calvados
1 oz Amaro Nardini (first drink I've found that calls
*   specifically for this fine amaro)*
1 oz Grand Marnier (an esteemed ingredient seldom used
*   in cocktails)*
Prep: Stir over ice and strain into a chilled coupe.
*   No garnish.*

</td>
</tr>
</table>

A fine cocktail, even a go-to cocktail. We'll see.

24 March 2021 Wednesday

No drinking. Had a ramble in the New Hampshire woods with Brick, birding. The highlight was Hooded Mergansers on the Warner River. They are beauties, male and female, and were courting, so in their best plumage.

Brick and I caught up. Told me about taking Zoom pedal-steel guitar lessons from a young man who knows and plays with members of the Grateful Dead, Brick's all-time favorite. I told him about the LPs, listening to Felix Slatkin conduct Borodin and Ippolitov-Ivanov at the Hollywood Bowl, a recording of my dad's from the 50s. Brick taught Daniel Slatkin, Felix's grandson, Leonard's son, and played music with him. Ain't the world tiny sometimes?

Got most of the second-floor storage area at least something like organized, but there is lots more to do.

Guess I'll keep writing. One important lesson is how much fun and how illuminating it is to read entries months later. Writers who advise us to keep diaries aren't entirely wrong.

25 March 2021 Thursday

Dinner with Denis, and fun. Explained my gun licensing idea as described in a letter to the *Concord Monitor:*

> *To the Editor:*
>
> *We liberals need to stop talking about "gun control," which goes nowhere, and try proposing something that seems tolerable to gun fanciers. For example, could the two camps agree to treat gun owning like driving?*
>
> *To drive a car or boat or fly an airplane you take a course, pass a test, get a license. No one complains. Suppose to use the guns people hunt with—shotguns and hunting rifles—you take a course, pass a test, get a license?*
>
> *Let's say you want to carry a pistol for self-protection. You'd need a separate course that requires additional commitment because now you're going to carry a weapon in public places. This seems comparable to obtaining a motorcycle endorsement.*
>
> *For those who want assault weapons, just as for those who drive big trucks, captain*

ships, or fly using only instruments, you'd need still more training, again an expense, a commitment, and a means of keeping all of us safer. Anyone who feels the need can still own assault rifles. Yet, if you are around others who handle such weapons wouldn't it be reassuring to know that they are trained and licensed?

Such an approach would mean that a 21-year-old cannot spontaneously buy an assault weapon and start shooting. I'm guessing that most shooters lack the discipline to get a license.

This isn't a cure all, but some form of it might be acceptable to most gun owners. They all have driver's licenses, and I'm guessing they are happy that others have them as well.

David Swords
Bradford

To this I'd add that you would need no license to own and shoot a musket that loads with a ramrod and powder horn, whether rifle or pistol. These were the weapons our forefathers had in mind when they wrote the Second Amendment, so let the Second Amendment continue to protect them with no requirements of the gun owner.

Anyway, dropped by Denis's and came home to listen to music, the Emperor Concerto in particular played by Rudolph Serkin, and made an Older Old Fashioned.

Older Old Fashioned (Redux)

At least 3 ozs bourbon (Evan Williams 100 proof Bottled in Bond)
2 dashes Angostura Bitters
Lightly smashed a bit of lemon and a cherry; used cherry juice to sweeten
One large clear ice cube
Prep: Fill glass with bourbon and stir. Lemon twist also rubbed around the rim of a double rocks glass.

This was a heavenly Older Old Fashioned, perhaps my best. The lemon seemed to add a lot of flavor and complexity.

26 March 2021 Friday

No drinking. Covid shot no.1 tomorrow morning. Hooray! It has been good to be here, especially in the new house, which I think is beautiful. Continued to organize but have a way to go. Discovered a space below the garage that is great for things like lawn equipment, making the garage less crowded. It's kind of a crowning, or more accurately, foundational, touch on a place that has absorbed our mass of stuff brilliantly.

27 March 2021 Saturday—Pfizer Vaccine No. 1

A big moment that reminded me of standing in line in the dark as a boy of, maybe, 10 to get the magic sugar cube with the polio vaccine. In the South, for us Houston, and knowing polio survivors, this was a release from fear. We still had the Soviet Union and nuclear weapons, bomb drills diving beneath our desks, but even though my dad had recently flown jets in the Air Force to protect us from the evil commies, polio was more immediate and insidious.

Near a fire outdoors, dined at Brick and Laura's watching snipe do their sky dance. A delicious spatchcocked chicken. I made Whiskey Sours hoping to improve on the boozy drinks from our canoe excursion last summer. But batch-made, kept in a thermos, the egg white was, ugh, slimy. Gained no converts.

28 March 2021 Sunday

Great breakfast at Denis's—eggs Victoria and his unsurpassable beignets—then flew to Florida with Charles Getchell. Realized on the flight that I'd left my computer behind. Seemed likely that loss would end the diary. But here we are, thanks to the magic of the internet and the tiny digital keys of a cellphone.

Drank some pretty good Cigar City beers with dinner and a Fuller's afterward.

29 March 2021 Monday—Spring Training

The language of the American pastime is Spanish. In my lifetime baseball has gone from a white man's sport to a brown man's sport. Why? Could be that, like boxing, baseball is a way out and up. The path to major leagues is usually long and uncertain. As Bob Dylan wrote, "When you got nuthin, you got nuthin to lose."

The Astros and Washington Nationals share a training park in Palm Beach, where Charles and I took ourselves for their final game of spring training. We arrived early and collected home run balls during batting practice.

I read that the Chinese see us as decadent, a society in decline. Surrounded by yachts in this harbor, it's hard to call them wrong. But I'd add that the will, drive of immigrants, many of whom polish these boats, could stretch our run by a few years.

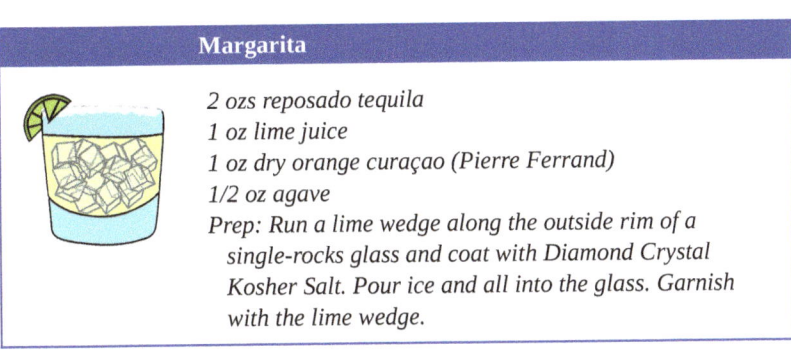

Margarita
2 ozs reposado tequila 1 oz lime juice 1 oz dry orange curaçao (Pierre Ferrand) 1/2 oz agave Prep: Run a lime wedge along the outside rim of a single-rocks glass and coat with Diamond Crystal Kosher Salt. Pour ice and all into the glass. Garnish with the lime wedge.

An undeniably good Margarita.

30 March 2021 Tuesday

In the cockpit drinking a

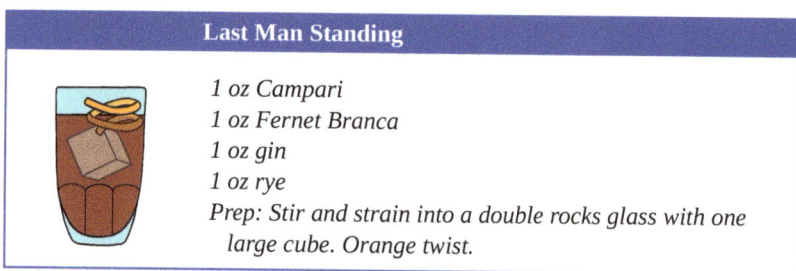

Last Man Standing	
	1 oz Campari
	1 oz Fernet Branca
	1 oz gin
	1 oz rye
	Prep: Stir and strain into a double rocks glass with one large cube. Orange twist.

Mighty fine, an expression my father used. And that's all I have to say.

31 March 2021 Wednesday

Back to the Margaritas, and they were excellent. Discovered the British Hornblower series and I'm hooked, especially while drinking a scurvy-preventing Margarita.

Spent much of the day replacing an exhaust fan in the galley. Thought it through creatively, installed the fan and ductwork. Tied into an existing switch in the galley, and "Tah dah," the fan was in upside down, sucking air in, not out. Disassembled the day's work. So goes "triumph."

1 April 2021 Thursday—Opening Day, which is to say, April Fool's Day

That hopeful moment, especially after last year when everything went wrong. Today, only the weather went wrong; Red Sox rained out.

Drank a pretty bad Vero Sunset and an excellent

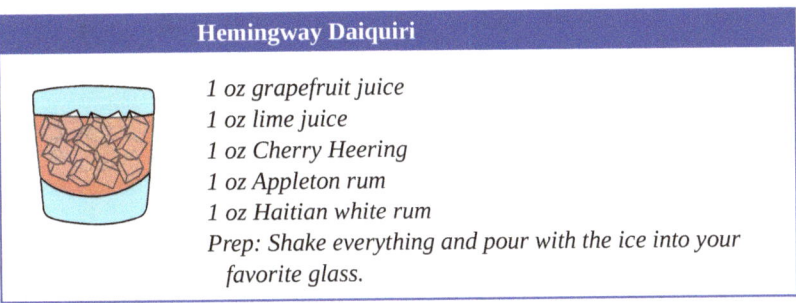

Hemingway Daiquiri

1 oz grapefruit juice
1 oz lime juice
1 oz Cherry Heering
1 oz Appleton rum
1 oz Haitian white rum
Prep: Shake everything and pour with the ice into your favorite glass.

Easy. One of my favorites.

2 April 2021 Friday

Today the Red Sox lost to the Orioles. The Sox look to be bad.

I figured out a good way to set up a solar vent for summer on a dorade. Huh? We're starting to prepare to leave *Lea Scotia* for the summer. She'll be "on the hard," as we mariners say, at a yard in Fort Pierce. Ashore is safer than tied up during hurricane season. But reliable electricity to the boat in a yard is unlikely, which means she'll be closed and windless in the humid, fetid Florida summer, a petri dish for mold. The vent is a small solar-powered fan that either brings outside air in or the reverse and keeps the air moving a bit, which helps against mold. We'll take other steps as well, so the preparations will be drawn out.

We drank Jennifer's favorite, the immortal Swanky Panky.

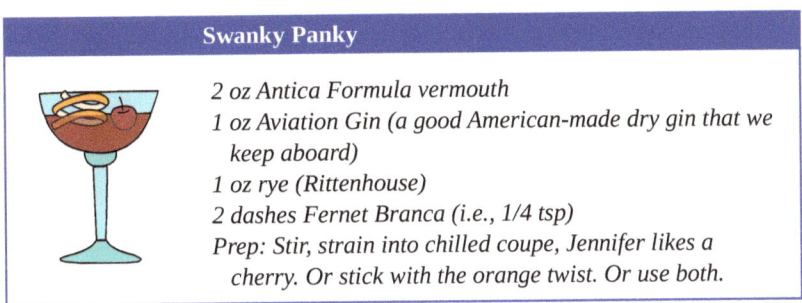

Swanky Panky

2 oz Antica Formula vermouth
1 oz Aviation Gin (a good American-made dry gin that we keep aboard)
1 oz rye (Rittenhouse)
2 dashes Fernet Branca (i.e., 1/4 tsp)
Prep: Stir, strain into chilled coupe, Jennifer likes a cherry. Or stick with the orange twist. Or use both.

3 April 2021 Saturday

While the ill-fated Red Sox were losing to the O's, we entertained Beth, Tim, and Beth's daughter, Christine, aboard. The drink, Three Dots and a Dash, is a great one that we'd ignored for far too long. Won't happen again.

4 April 2021 Sunday

J and I shared a Westmalle Dubbel, one of my favorite Belgian Trappist beers. Back in the 80s in Brussels, on a Saturday morning in the Grand Place, a beautiful Walloon I was courting introduced me to Trappist beers, starting with Orval. After drinking two, I weaved my way to the train for Paris, forever in her debt and in thrall to these beers.

The Trouble with IPAs

The recent brewpub renaissance in New England, and the U.S. more generally, has emphasized hops, where we live, New England double IPAs, whose intense hops seem to be the equivalent of catnip for many humans. The Trappist beers, as strong as these IPAs, emphasize malt instead. One result of this new hops preference is that the great Belgians are relatively, sadly neglected. Let me mention, then, three abbeys in the motherland, which are Orval (gold valley, and the story of the gold ring is worth knowing); Westmalle; and Chimay, the best known. An abbey near Worcester in Massachusetts, brews Spencer, a fine beer in the traditional Trappist style and worth seeking out. The Belgians are the world's greatest chefs in my view, and these ales (they are all ales, not lagers) are as good a complement to any great meal as a well-chosen cocktail.

And that's all we drank. Meanwhile, the Red Sox lost their third in a row. Can they go 0-162?

5 April 2021 Monday

One of only two cocktail books aboard is *Canon*, which I don't love but which includes makeable gems by Jamie Boudreau. The Union Club is one.

In New Hampshire I have avoided, mostly, drinks that include orange juice. Navel oranges have not been reliably good; Valencia oranges are good but hard to find; and bottled orange juice, even expensive brands that are "not from concentrate," does not work.

But here in Florida, Natalie's is fresh, sweet, and in the Union Club marries with the Campari beautifully (hence the name?). Together with the bourbon and Cherry Heering, you get one of those cocktails that has lots of flavors waiting for the alert senses to uncover. This one is easy to make, and as long as I can restrain myself from drinking all of the Natalie's at breakfast, I'll serve it often… at least in Florida.

[Note: Natalie's is now available in New Hampshire making it likely to be distributed nationally. Worth looking for.]

6 April 2021 Tuesday—Noises, Boats, and Darwin

Lots of stuff today. We have a haul-out date of April 30, a Friday, at 12:30, high tide. Being in the right place at high tide is one worry, but the summer is a bigger one owing to the prospect of sun damage along with mold and mildew. And hurricanes.

Living aboard has been lovely, above all, perhaps, thanks to the weather. Yet, life aboard has its worries. Noise is one of them. Not the neighbors but noises the boat itself makes. Remember the Karman vortex street?

Years ago, during the period when Jenny and I first met, just before reading Daniel Dennet's *Darwin's Dangerous Idea*, I asked myself what I believed to be ultimate causes and the best explanations for life. You need to believe in something, and gods were no help, but natural selection was. In that period, and ever since, lots of thinkers have turned to Darwin's idea as the "universal solvent" that answers many puzzles. What's this got to do with boats?

Even in a quiet, commodious harbor such as ours, life aboard a boat feels much more like life in the wilderness, with its dangers, than life ashore in a house. The boat moves; the wind often makes it groan and creak. At night clacking noises below the hull—we've been told they are small shrimp or barnacles—at first kept Jenny awake (not me).

I recall realizing years ago that living in a forest, where myriad sounds could befuddle us if we tried to make sense of all of them, having the ability to filter and to parse from the rest what seemed imminently dangerous would be an advantage. So it is on a boat. We barely hear the shrimp, or barnacles, now; the battery charger going on and off at night; or the bilge pump. We understand when the freshwater pump is signaling it's time to change tanks, the sump pump filter is clogged, or the holding tank for the head needs pumping out. In all, I think our senses are naturally more alert here because life seems at least a bit more precarious. Come to think of it, this is why I wanted a sailboat in the first place.

For dinner we took the dinghy across the St. Lucie River and dined at the Riverside Cafe and Oyster Bar, me on Maine oysters, a fine salad, and softshell crabs cooked in wine and butter, the last one of my favorite foods in the world. Washed everything down with the fine Belgian Palm Beer. We motored back across, and for dessert I made the drink, finally discovered in *Canon*, that calls for Tuaca.

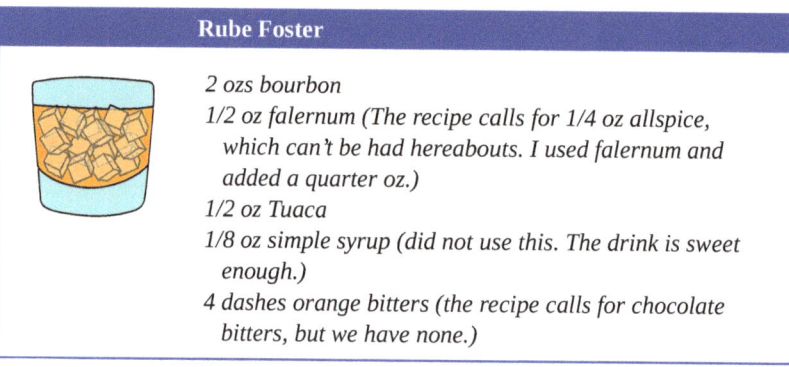

Rube Foster

2 ozs bourbon

1/2 oz falernum (The recipe calls for 1/4 oz allspice, which can't be had hereabouts. I used falernum and added a quarter oz.)

1/2 oz Tuaca

1/8 oz simple syrup (did not use this. The drink is sweet enough.)

4 dashes orange bitters (the recipe calls for chocolate bitters, but we have none.)

Hmmm. Not really a Rube Foster is it? Let's call it either a Rube Goldberg Foster or a Rube Falernum. Still, quite good.

7 April 2021 Wednesday—Shopping for Booze

It's frustrating, and I love it. Most any cocktail recipe book will have way too many drinks requiring ingredients you won't have and cannot get. Some of those ingredients will need to be made by you if you want them, say a bourbon infused with something. I have not been tempted to do this. (Once I was. A neighbor gave us a pile of jalapeno peppers. I cut them in half and stuffed three into a half-empty quart bottle of tequila. Left for no more than an hour and owwwww it was hot! Still, 1 oz tequila with 1 oz jalapeno-infused tequila in a Margarita turns a hot-weather cocktail into a tongue warmer.)

But the bigger problem is liquor stores. Except in the most cosmopolitan places, they sell to people whose experience of cocktails is far, far… far smaller than yours. The stores can't afford bottles of amari that sit on the shelves, and as they must, stock for what their people want, such as Tito's "handmade" vodka. Now, I've conspicuously avoided vodka, with a couple of exceptions, for a year. We mostly keep a bottle of Polish Belvedere on hand to handmake grenadine or simple syrup because a teaspoon of it helps keep sugary things from growing mold. And Al uses the Belvedere up for, well, I don't know what for.

Meanwhile, let's go to a classic in the whiskey sour family whose ingredients can be found most anywhere, simply the:

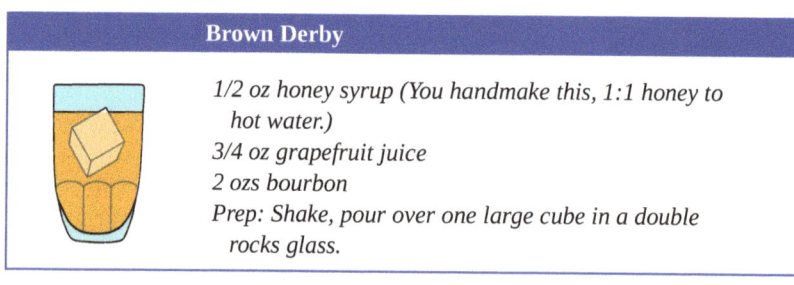

Brown Derby

1/2 oz honey syrup (You handmake this, 1:1 honey to hot water.)

3/4 oz grapefruit juice

2 ozs bourbon

Prep: Shake, pour over one large cube in a double rocks glass.

What do you think?

8 April 2021 Thursday

Humans, civilization are an experiment, Darwin would say. The environment in which a system of government begins inevitably changes, and in the case of *Homo sapiens*, is changed, by us. As a result, insisting on an "originalist" interpretation of a more than 200-year-old document, which for all its still valid ideas cannot address today's vastly different environment, seems sure to bring disaster and failure. The cliche that something or someone is a "dinosaur" means that their old ways do not suit their environment. In this sense conservative originalists on the Supreme Court and in Congress are "genuine dinosaurs," as the song "Alley Oop" describes that famous caveman's chauffeur. The truths of governing are not immutable. Natural selection—in which adaptation to the present enables the possibility of a future—is as firm a truth as you get in the world of living things on planet earth.

My point? We would not want a square-rigged 18th-Century boat to live on. Think of the noises! Why do we accept an 18th-Century system of government? All of which is no more than an introduction to today's cocktail. George Washington is said to have gotten his recipe for apple brandy, which he sold at Mt Vernon, from Laird's, America's oldest distillery.

Washington (Stubborn as a) Mule

 *2 ozs Laird's Apple Brandy (used a high-end one with a label filled in by hand. Really good)*
1/2 oz lime juice
3 dashes Angostura bitters (here, 6 shakes were about right)
Prep: Shake and pour. Add ice and ginger beer to fill the glass. Lime wedge garnish.

From *Canon*, this simple cocktail is excellent. As to bitters, I have been giving bad advice and over bittering. Here one could tell based on the photo in *Canon*, where the drink is much lighter than my first 12-shake version. Even at 6 shakes mine were deeper red. But they were also delicious.

9 April 2021 Friday

Jenny wanted a Manhattan, but I wanted a Petruchio, which we've had before but not for a while, and I'm the bartender. She got what she wanted, and so did I. We're a both-and family, it seems.

About Campari

The *Canon recipe for the Petruchio calls for Aperol, and having none, I used its stronger sister, Campari. Let's talk about Campari. We know that it works with gin, as in the Negroni, but it works just as well with bourbon, rye, apple brandy, even mezcal. The Boulevardier and the recent Union Club are good examples, but many others appear in these pages.*
We ultimately decided Campari was the best amaro for our decantered Mother-in-Law.
Its bitterness is especially valuable, since many amari, ironically—the word means bitter— are sweet. When you're looking for an ingredient that might work in an experiment, Campari should be high on the list.

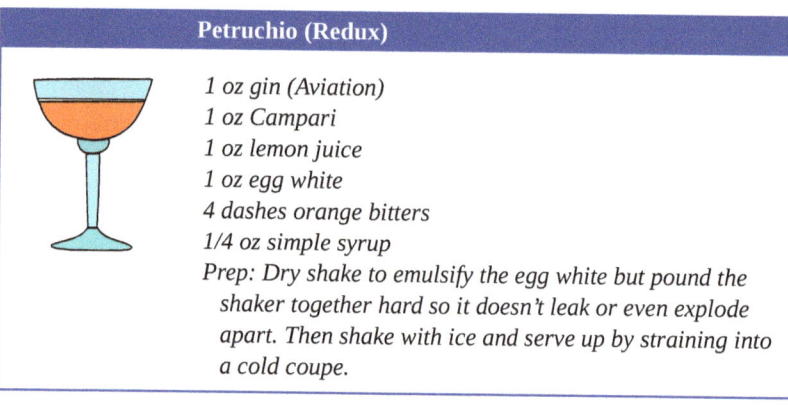

Petruchio (Redux)

1 oz gin (Aviation)
1 oz Campari
1 oz lemon juice
1 oz egg white
4 dashes orange bitters
1/4 oz simple syrup
Prep: Dry shake to emulsify the egg white but pound the
shaker together hard so it doesn't leak or even explode
apart. Then shake with ice and serve up by straining into
a cold coupe.

Lovely to look at as the bubbles fade. Delicious. Summer in a glass.

10 April 2021 Saturday

Dined at Tim and Beth's, choosing the Petruchio for Beth as the cocktail of the week, which she loved. And at long, long last, began our first steps toward allspice dram with a full cup of berries.

Allspice Dram

1. *Break up the allspice berries with a mortar and pestle or in, say, a coffee grinder (our approach), but don't grind to powder.*
2. *Put the pieces in a Mason jar, and add a fifth of rum, for us Appleton 8-year-old.*
3. *Let the mixture soak for 10 days, giving it a daily shake.*

And then we'll see. The recipe is Chuck Taggart's of Hurricane and Mother-in-Law fame.

You cannot buy Allspice Dram in Florida, so who knows, perhaps thousands of cocktailiers will come to Tim and Beth's door for ours?

11 April 2021 Sunday

Lunch at Conchy Joe's where Beth and I drank our usual Hemingway Daiquiri. Her other son in law, Mark, had flown in from Nashville, as unpretentious a fellow as I've ever met.

12 April 2021 Monday—Blue Monday

Mondays are hard, blue days. I'm thinking the voyage around Key West really did result, for me, in a mini-PTSD. Nervous, especially about sailing, and depressed more often than usual.

The recipe, however, as far as I know is not stolen, but original. If it is any good, which I won't speak to, we can have a naming contest.

14 April 2021 Wednesday

Another new one; cannot say why.

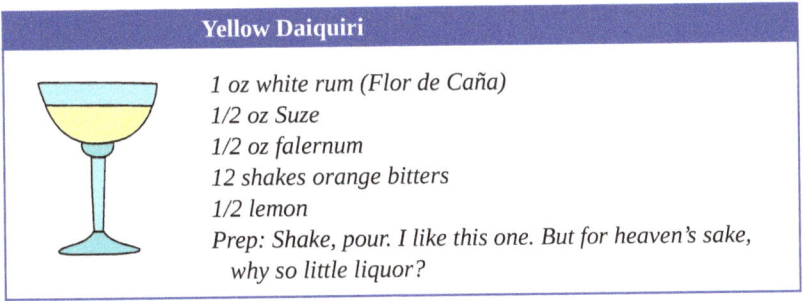

Yellow Daiquiri
1 oz white rum (Flor de Caña) 1/2 oz Suze 1/2 oz falernum 12 shakes orange bitters 1/2 lemon Prep: Shake, pour. I like this one. But for heaven's sake,   why so little liquor?

Well, it was an experiment. If you like it, double everything except perhaps the bitters.

15 April 2021 Thursday—Walmart

I've been preparing for hauling out, trying to protect *Lea Scotia* from the southern sun and summer. We know about hurricanes. But UV ravages boats from the outside and the heat and damp mildews them inside, which I've said before, but it is on my worried mind a lot.

Bucky left behind a world of products that could help with the sun. For the summer, I've been trying to get to an approach that uses a new solar panel connected to a cheap battery, to a solar controller, to cheap 12-volt fans, the "cheap" stuff in this description from Walmart, rather than West Marine or another chandlery.

The fans, which oscillate, were less than $13 each, the battery less than $70. The cheap fans will be supplemented by solar vent fans that suck air out of here and one 12-volt vent fan that runs on our house batteries.

Anyway, thanks to Spaceship Walmart, *Lea Scotia* may survive the environment of a Florida summer, which is more hostile than space.

16 April 2021 Friday—Sailing

At last, we sailed. But not before sticky buns at Jennifer's and a bagel at a cafe where we found Natalie's grapefruit juice.

The sail was a mess. We had the main and small jib flying in a light breeze. The main was problematic because I had the running backstays in the wrong place, which had them pinching the main. Got that sorted, unfurled the genoa and before we knew, it was falling.

In devising the flute stopper (the rope that prevents the Karman vortex street), I had looked at various lines that run up the mast. Could not really tell what most were for and apparently failed to re-cleat the genoa halyard, so down came the sail.

Was able to bundle it on deck. We got the other sails furled and headed in, back up the St Lucie River. Spent time in the Intracoastal Waterway looking for an anchorage, but the water on either side was way too shallow. Backtracked and went up the St Lucie to a spot where we'd seen a couple sailboats at anchor. That's where we stayed the night. The multi-million-dollar homes of the Treasure Coast loomed above us; we were their front yard, and anchoring is free.

We had a make-do dinner but most important, tried out Natalie's grapefruit juice in Hemingway Daiquiris. We were nearer to the channel than we liked, but after a frenzy of boats passing us at dusk, spent a quiet, pleasantly cool night… with one exception: a noise. I recorded because it was everywhere, loud, and I had no clue about its cause. But we didn't sink.

17 April 2021 Saturday—The Dolphins Appear

Up early, we addressed and hoisted the Genoa, raised anchor, headed down river. In a light breeze we got about halfway to the Gulfstream before turning back to reach our slip at high tide, which we easily did.

On the way out, a school of small pantropical dolphins swam under the bow and around the boat for a while. Soon after, two and then four of the much larger bottlenose dolphins joined us. Jenny talked to them while I took a video. In it the clear blue water is gorgeous, the dolphins sleek and lithe. When they break the surface, it is as if they briefly enter our dimension and look startlingly real.

The sail was grand, the trip upriver smooth, and we docked without mishap. Perhaps in celebration we drank Jennifer's favorite, Manhattans, and I'm staking the reputation I do not have by saying that a Manhattan cannot be better than:

Lea Scotia Manhattan
 2 ozs Old Overholt 1 oz Antica Formula vermouth 10-12 shakes Peychaud's Bitters Prep: Stir and pour with the ice or serve up. Garnish with a Luxardo cherry.

18 April 2021 Sunday—Vaccine 2

Jenny is a week or so behind, but today I am fully vaccinated thanks to CVS in Stuart. A year ago, I'd never heard of Stuart. Today, owing to the pandemic and Tim's health challenges, we live here on a sailboat. A year ago, we had no notion that a vaccine would be invented, approved, rushed to citizens—at least in the U.S.—with life-giving consequences, though it may fall short of its promise thanks to the poisoned political atmosphere in the country.

Is there a vaccine cocktail?

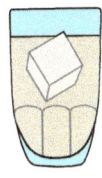

Penicillin

2 ozs blended scotch (Famous Grouse or what you will)
3/4 oz lemon juice
3/4 oz honey syrup (1:1 honey to water)
3 slices fresh ginger
1/4 oz smoky scotch (such as Laphroig)
Prep: Muddle the ginger hard in a shaker to break loose
*   its flavor and aroma. Add the Famous Grouse, lemon,*
*   and honey syrup (I love honey syrup in almost any*
*   cocktail, don't you know). Shake and strain into a*
*   double-rocks glass with one large cube. Float the smoky*
*   scotch on top.*

Last I had one of these was at the Harvey Nichols posh department store in London just before the pandemic struck. Aboard, we lacked several ingredients, but the occasion called for a special effort, Totally Liquored is nearby, and post-vaccine I felt celebratory.

The aroma of the smoke followed, but the pungent flavor is heaven on earth. After the second you will be fully vaccinated, safe from your teeming brain. Drink a third and you'll be safe from most anything. However, as Harry Craddock said of another cocktail (the Penicillin was awaiting invention), "Four of these taken in swift succession will unrevive the [potential] corpse again" (*The Savoy Cocktail Book*, page 52).

19 April 2021 Monday

Aviation. I'm thinking we missed this one till now because we're sailors. The Aviation, or sometimes L'Aviation, suggesting its French origin, is a classic that disappeared and that many believe should not be missed. Others, by contrast, have no interest in this, by their lights, prehistoric cocktail. It is old. And Creme de Violette disappeared for a long time, came back as a cheap, seldom used, mixing ingredient.

No more. It may not be creme, but Tempus Fugit's Liqueur de Violettes, which includes a recipe for the Aviation on the label, is excellent. Drink up and enjoy the wild blue yonder:

Aviation

3/4 oz Liqueur de Violettes (Tempus Fugit)
3/4 oz Maraschino liqueur (Luxardo. Our ship's stores are
*   ever increasing. Not a bad thing; alcohol is lighter than*
*   water. You can use Cheery Heering in a pinch, but the*
*   cocktail is much darker.)*
2 ozs London dry gin (or, obviously, the American dry
*   Aviation gin)*
3/4 oz lemon juice
Prep: Shake and serve up in a cold coupe. No garnish.

Looks like a pink sky or if not, still lovely. A bit sour, which Jenny and I both approve. Most cocktails are sweet, and the difference here is welcome. Sometimes the old ways are the best.

20 April 2021 Tuesday

At sea.

21 April 2021 Wednesday

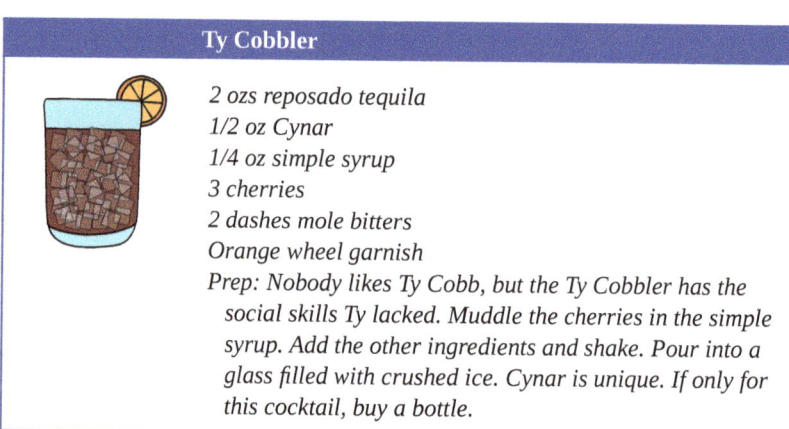

Ty Cobbler

2 ozs reposado tequila
1/2 oz Cynar
1/4 oz simple syrup
3 cherries
2 dashes mole bitters
Orange wheel garnish
Prep: Nobody likes Ty Cobb, but the Ty Cobbler has the social skills Ty lacked. Muddle the cherries in the simple syrup. Add the other ingredients and shake. Pour into a glass filled with crushed ice. Cynar is unique. If only for this cocktail, buy a bottle.

22 April 2021 Wednesday

Yesterday a jury found Derrick Chauvin guilty of murdering George Floyd. African Americans suffer daily at the hands of police, always have. But I seem to want to mention that while the danger posed by police is often a matter of racism, it is also a matter of power in the hands of people ill-suited and poorly trained to have life and death authority over anyone. Here's my example.

At seventeen, I hitchhiked from New Orleans to Montreal to see the 1967 World's Fair. Coming back, I was broke and nearly home, late in the night, exhausted, no cars coming, and fell asleep by the side of the road outside St Francisville, Louisiana.

I was awakened by headlights and a figure looming over me, in a broad-brimmed hat, rifle in hand. My hair was long at a time when this symbolized liberal-yellow-pacifist to state troopers in the South. The trooper ordered me to my feet and to spread my legs, put my hands as far as they would reach on the trunk of his car, which is when I said something like, "Why are you being such a dick?" Mistake. As a lesson he had the town jail lock me up, booked but without charges, for ten days.

The days were not wasted. Each morning breakfast arrived in a bucket with a pack of Target tobacco and rolling paper. One of my two cellmates, a trustee who'd spent most of his life in prison, taught me to roll cigarettes, a valued skill in college. The cells were segregated. At night, the jailers let Black prisoners out to visit us, and we swapped things like comic books and stories through the bars of our cell. Came to know each other a bit. When the Black prisoners heard why I was there, talking back to a cop, everyone hushed, looked at me, shook their heads as if to say, "This is the dumbest white boy ever. Maybe it comes with the hair."

When the jail released me, another cop drove me back out to Highway 61 (and it really was Hwy 61). As I left the car he said, "Boy, you best not come back here. Understand?"

Let me know when it's safe to return.

23 April 2021 Friday

We leave the water a week from today, sailing up to Fort Pierce the day before. We'll lay at anchor just off the boatyard with a short ride to the dock where they will pull us out at 12:30 pm, high tide. The week for me requires taking things off the boat that we won't miss the next few days and storing them in an air-conditioned locker we've rented to protect against mildew. In all, the week promises to be not unlike leaving the Bean, which is to say, rather miserable but with concerns about making mistakes that will jeopardize *Lea Scotia* and our things.

Let's think about something else, say, a good cocktail.

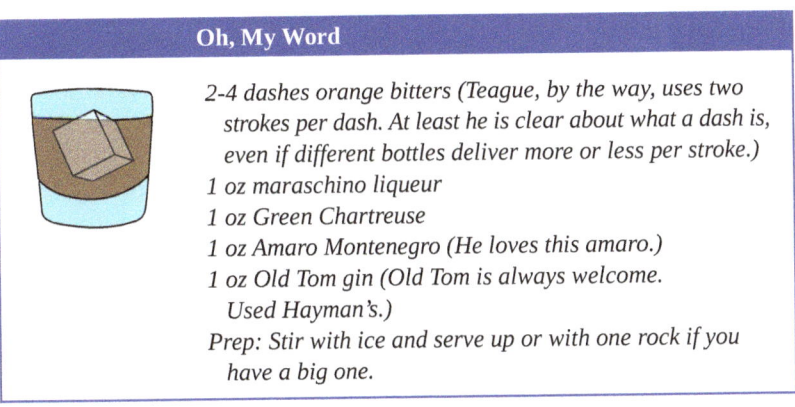

Oh, My Word

2-4 dashes orange bitters (Teague, by the way, uses two strokes per dash. At least he is clear about what a dash is, even if different bottles deliver more or less per stroke.)
1 oz maraschino liqueur
1 oz Green Chartreuse
1 oz Amaro Montenegro (He loves this amaro.)
1 oz Old Tom gin (Old Tom is always welcome. Used Hayman's.)
Prep: Stir with ice and serve up or with one rock if you have a big one.

A variation on the Last Word. Remember Sother Teague and aquafaba? Teague's recipes typically are simpler than you'll find in most cocktail books, yet artful. He presents the bartender's point of view, in this recipe, for example, prescribing .75 oz of each of the main ingredients, to which we home bartenders take exception.

Perhaps not as good as the classic Last Word, which is less sweet and lets the Chartreuse come through more fully. But just fine.

24 April 2021 Saturday

Let's begin with a cocktail. Or with beignets. Before leaving New Hampshire, I went to my brother's inn for beignets, a New Orleans specialty that Denis recreated through long experimentation, which, come to think of it, may run in the family. Without bias, I say Denis's are better than any beignet you can find in our native city.

Pineapple Corer

With the beignets, I ate some of the pineapple he had out for his guests. He uses a tool called a pineapple corer to pull the meat out of a fresh pineapple. On his advice I ordered an inexpensive stainless-steel version and bought a green-looking pineapple at Publix. It ripened, turned yellow, and today I broke out the corer, which works like a charm. I mean it's really fun to use.

The pineapple was perfect, sweet, delicious. Hence today's choice of cocktail, which originated in Cuba.

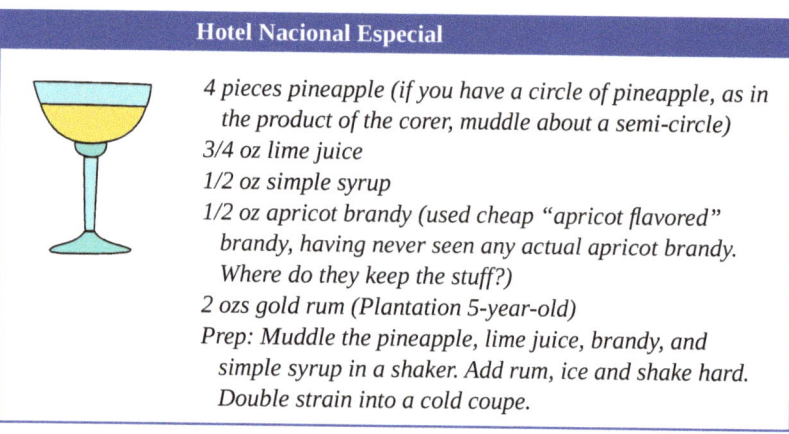

Hotel Nacional Especial

4 pieces pineapple (if you have a circle of pineapple, as in the product of the corer, muddle about a semi-circle)
3/4 oz lime juice
1/2 oz simple syrup
1/2 oz apricot brandy (used cheap "apricot flavored" brandy, having never seen any actual apricot brandy. Where do they keep the stuff?)
2 ozs gold rum (Plantation 5-year-old)
Prep: Muddle the pineapple, lime juice, brandy, and simple syrup in a shaker. Add rum, ice and shake hard. Double strain into a cold coupe.

Delicious. Tried variations such as using peach liqueur, honey syrup and lemon, two dashes of orange bitters, a kind of all-yellow theme. Equally delicious. Even with an inferior New England rum, delicious.

Have I said, "delicious"?

25 April 2021 Sunday

One of the best parts of living aboard a boat in Florida over winter is exercise. J and I find it easy to wake early, either go to the gym or ride our bikes, and return to the boat in time for her first of many Zoom calls. On a Sunday, typically, we just ride, usually longer than during the week, and often we'll cross bridges over the ICW (Intracoastal Waterway), which rise 65 feet, a height that in Florida feels mountainous. Today our ride included a stop for pastries at Jennifer's, my favorite bakery. Cyclists require calories, and Jennifer's obliges.

Back at the boat, our neighbors from Buffalo delivered the week's ration of fresh conch. And we showered, dressed, went off for our last meal with Beth and Tim at Conchy Joe's where, predictably, some of us drank Hemingway Daiquiris. All in all, a pleasant beginning to the end of this chapter.

26 April 2021 Monday

More of the same, that is, preparing to leave, with visits to the storage unit; to West Marine and Lowe's for desiccant that we'll put around the boat to reduce humidity when she is closed up; and to Totally Liquored for Aperol, key to the *Death & Company* cocktail I've wanted for some time:

> ### Gypsy Eyes (Redux)
>
> *As is often true, we'll raise the amounts of ingredients for the home bartender but keep the proportions.*
> *2.5 ozs gin (Aviation)*
> *1 oz Aperol (but you can use Campari)*
> *1 oz lime juice*
> *1 oz grapefruit juice*
> *3/4 oz simple syrup*
> *Green Chartreuse*
> *Prep: Pour Chartreuse into a cold coupe and swish it around then drink it off (or toss it, but the stuff is $70 a bottle and made by monks). Shake the other ingredients with ice and strain into the Chartreused coupe.*

Crowd Pleasers

Once, a guest at the Bean turned up her nose when I said Gypsy Eyes, cocktail of the evening, included gin. She preferred vodka. I used vodka. The Belvedere. Next day she asked for the recipe. Her husband sent a photo of two Gypsy Eyes on their patio table next to a vase of flowers. Made with vodka, I guess.

Because people who don't like spirits often will drink vodka (and so believe they like spirits) a couple of cocktails in which you could substitute vodka for gin, but also for white rum, can be valuable. You'll have satisfied customers and, who knows, perhaps some will give the spirit native to the cocktail a try. Helping people to widen their vision seems mostly a very good thing.

27 April 2021 Tuesday

J and I paid a farewell visit to a bar we like in Stuart whose name I've never known because we typically enter through a backdoor to avoid a make-up store that gathers you in if you try the front. This is, after all, the Treasure Coast. The time we made the front-door mistake, a pretty, peppy saleswoman grabbed Jenny and applied some age-defying make-up to the skin around her right eye, then asked me to judge which eye looked better. On cue, I said "the right" of course.

In we went for the full treatment, both of us, and after we'd "talked her down" from $600 for a syringe of the magic formula to the special price of $150, we both looked years younger, with a follow-up treatment included in this Treasure Coast package. A week or so later we returned, looking younger still— me especially— from the every-other-night applications of our bargain make-up syringe. Only this time another pretty, peppy salesperson applied laser light—red, green, blue, and maybe gold—offering to sell us this miracle light machine for $10,000, though before buying we "talked her down" to $3,000. Just kidding. We did not buy. Why would we? I already looked about 14.

Today, having avoided further age-reducing miracles by the backdoor, we found our way to a bar in the oddly organized, unnamed restaurant. They keep this bar behind curtains because, and this is a trend you may have seen in your town, it is dressed to be a Prohibition speakeasy. The irony is that, unlike during

Prohibition, the cocktails in such places are both interesting and well made, or at least they are in the two I have visited. The cocktail that leaped out at us, because we love allspice dram, which cannot be bought in Florida, was a Lion's Tail:

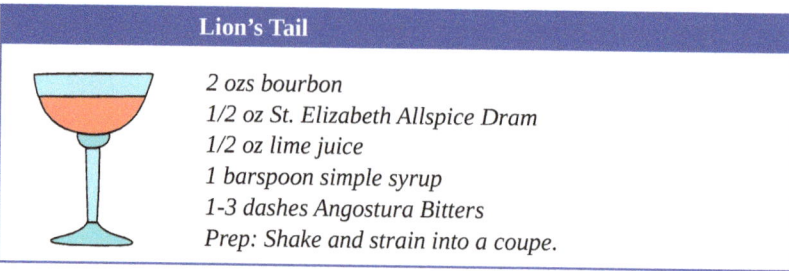

Lion's Tail

2 ozs bourbon
1/2 oz St. Elizabeth Allspice Dram
1/2 oz lime juice
1 barspoon simple syrup
1-3 dashes Angostura Bitters
Prep: Shake and strain into a coupe.

Very nice. We felt like a couple of youthful scofflaws.

28 April 2021 Wednesday

The teak has been oiled, the deck waxed, both with as many of the dozens of bottles of boat anti-aging formulas Bucky kept aboard as I had arm strength to apply. Hope they work. We waxed ourselves this last night in our slip, to which we expect to return in the fall, with Ward 8s, a rye-based (or bourbon, scotch, Canadian, Irish) Boston cocktail to celebrate our imminent return to New England:

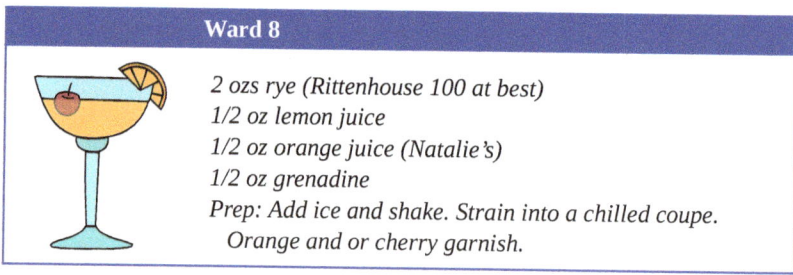

Ward 8

2 ozs rye (Rittenhouse 100 at best)
1/2 oz lemon juice
1/2 oz orange juice (Natalie's)
1/2 oz grenadine
Prep: Add ice and shake. Strain into a chilled coupe.
   Orange and or cherry garnish.

A version of whiskey sour, perhaps the best version for getting waxed.

Part V: Going Home

29 April 2021 Thursday—Leaving Stuart

At high tide, warmed the engine, then with the help of willing neighbors, untied, gathered our dock lines aboard, and backed out of the slip. Went as far as I could astern toward the line of boats behind us. Put her in forward, and to reverse the motion of the boat, gave her some throttle. We shot forward, and I threw her in reverse, throttling back to stop the sudden momentum. But we continued shooting forward... crashed into the dock, neighbors doing their best to hold us off. And the boat kept pushing forward until, frenzied, I finally shut down the engine.

Under the circumstances, quite common in marinas, your first emotion is embarrassment for being clumsy, incompetent. Beyond whatever mistakes I made, our neighbor Greg Rogers, who with his wife Marie have lived aboard sailboats for more than 30 years, quickly confirmed that simpler, perhaps more likely failures—such as that the shift cable had detached from the transmission—were not culpable. The transmission itself was trashed.

What to do? The tide was high and waits for no indecision. Before the pandemic our friend Charlie Belden, who worked for TowBoatUS until committing suicide last May, advised us to buy their unlimited towing package because it was bargain priced and could prove useful, even for a sailboat, under myriad circumstances. Thank you, Charlie.

While I dithered about other courses, Jennifer insisted we call TowBoatUS, and I did. Unlike in Key West, they promptly answered, and soon a boat was on its way. The captain was grumpy, especially when he learned we needed to be towed 25 miles, the maximum range their insurance allowed, to Fort Pierce. But he knew his job and in a feat of maneuvering in tight quarters, pulled us out of the slip, lashed us to his boat, made way to the St Lucie River as she stuck on bottom a couple times, and we were on our way to the Intracoastal Waterway. If you own a boat that goes out on the ocean, follow Captain Charlie's advice. Get towing insurance.

Being towed is a sailor's most inglorious fate. Other sailors assume you must be an idiot because sailboats sail, don't need engines. The tow took two, three hours, maybe 30 years. Along the way, nearing the destination, our Stuart-based captain handed us, helpless, off to a younger captain from Fort Pierce. He towed us to the anchorage and even helped make sure our anchor held before leaving for the night, promising to return in the morning.

Maybe we drank that evening. Perhaps we ate. I cannot say.

30 April 2021 Friday

True to his word, the young captain sent another TowBoatUS our way next morning, allowing ample time to arrive at the dock where we were to be hoisted at 12:30. Water was barely deep enough to get the slings set, but the experienced hoist operators knew their work and plucked us out.

Standing in the rain, watching your sailboat hang in the air is an odd moment. It is unnatural. On the other hand, it's also a relief, especially, I'd say, with a busted transmission that you've got no ideas about how to repair or replace. Once the crew had power-washed the bottom, we left the yard for Tim and Beth's. I'd had enough.

Enough, however, is never enough, I guess, and soon was texting Greg to ask his ideas about what to do with the transmission. He was clear that only one place, Transmission Marine in Fort Lauderdale, would or even could do what we needed. Job 1 was to remove the transmission and deliver it to them.

Cocktails? Sorely needed. Pisco Sours.

1, 2, 3 May 2021 Saturday, Sunday, Monday

Best laid plans, as they say, "gang aft aglay," even on Mayday. I'd hoped to finish preparing *Lea Scotia* for our departure for New Hampshire, but the transmission changed those plans. With Greg's help by way of texts, I began three miserable days in spaces so tight a jockey could hardly fit; drenched in sweat, hands beat and bloodied; ready to give up many times when the rusted, frozen, immovable bolts would not budge; taking out bits of the engine I'd have no clue about how to put back, creating uncertainty within uncertainty; finally getting the transmission off the engine only to discover it could not squeeze through the narrow space to come out of the bilge; diving back down to take it apart; and at long, long last pulling the blasted, broken thing out; knowing even then that putting a new or repaired transmission back, whenever that might be, would be beyond my abilities. Uncertainty, ambiguity, worry. We move on.

Bill at Transmission Marine explained the complexity of replacing a transmission no longer made, but thank goodness, said to bring it to Fort Lauderdale, Tuesday's mission.

4 May 2021 Tuesday

A long drive somewhere and back, when you know exactly how far, have no doubt about the way, is therapeutic. The handoff of the transmission was outdoors and resulted in no claim check of any sort. They have the old one and will let me know down the line costs and timing if repairs are possible.

On the return trip I had lunch at a Thai restaurant where I'd dined once before on the outskirts of Palm Beach Gardens. Something about a good meal not rushed when you're hungry and have put a cap, if only for the moment, on an exhausting effort, is restorative. Drank ginger tea, which I love.

5 May 2021 Wednesday—Cinco de Mayo

Closed up the boat. Connected the Walmart battery to its solar panel in the cockpit and to the cheap fans in the cabin. Will check tomorrow to see if the panel is adequately recharging the battery. Seems like a night for tequila.

Here's a cocktail Beth had in mind and had gone out of her way to have what we needed on hand.

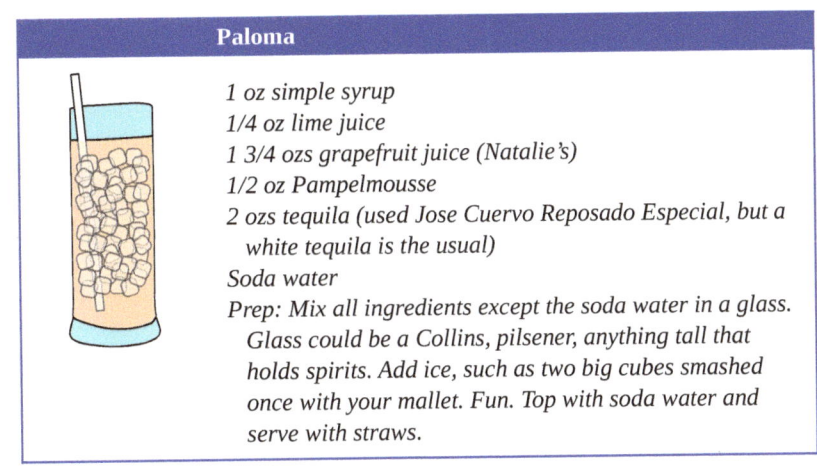

Paloma
1 oz simple syrup
1/4 oz lime juice
1 3/4 ozs grapefruit juice (Natalie's)
1/2 oz Pampelmousse
2 ozs tequila (used Jose Cuervo Reposado Especial, but a white tequila is the usual)
Soda water
Prep: Mix all ingredients except the soda water in a glass. Glass could be a Collins, pilsener, anything tall that holds spirits. Add ice, such as two big cubes smashed once with your mallet. Fun. Top with soda water and serve with straws.

Perfect when it is warm in Florida and proves Cinco de Mayo is not a holiday invented only for drinking Margaritas.

6 May 2021 Thursday

The battery is charging fine by way of the solar panel, the air in the cabin moving. Set out the desiccant, neatened the boat, opened every closet and drawer. Loaded cushions in my car for the trip to New Hampshire, where I plan to recover them over summer. (Sewing is vastly more satisfying than removing transmissions.)

Head north tomorrow. Tonight, we try our homemade allspice in a Lion's Tail.

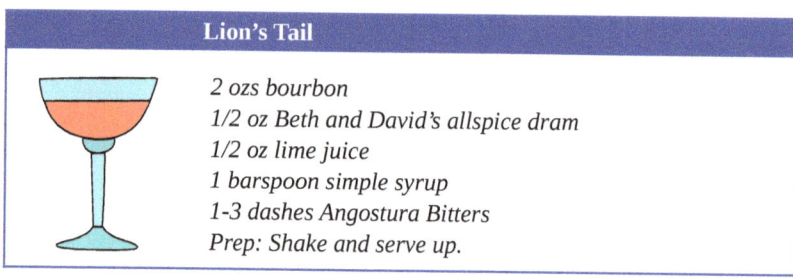

Lion's Tail
2 ozs bourbon   1/2 oz Beth and David's allspice dram   1/2 oz lime juice   1 barspoon simple syrup   1-3 dashes Angostura Bitters   Prep: Shake and serve up.

How good can good be? Our allspice is stronger, darker, lots darker, than St. Elizabeth. You could use half as much, I believe.

Get a good night's sleep.

7 May 2021 Friday

I left Stuart, and Florida, much as I arrived. The trip down came as a hurricane threatened our new boat, the voyage from Tampa to Stuart, beset with breakage and doubt, began, perhaps you recall, with a day aground. Its bookend, leaving our Stuart marina under tow was humiliating, and now the transmission and, really, the engine itself are questions. Will *Lea Scotia* come through the summer well enough to be habitable in the fall? Who knows? Some questions are best left behind to be faced another time, forgotten in the moment or they pester and plague while you're helpless to address them. A liberal arts education, of little help in making life financially viable, offers other lines of thought. Songs. Poems. Politics…

On the road I travel hard, stop only for fuel and for dinner at a Cracker Barrel, spend the night in a cheap motel outside Richmond. Only, not so cheap. The vaccine has begun to set people free. Traffic in places was heavy today. Everything seems to be opening. It is spring.

8 May 2021 Saturday

On the road early, I begin by refueling. Through Washington, traffic is thick, indeed, all the way through Baltimore. Somehow, even roads annoyingly full of cars seem transparent, make me feel lighthearted. People moving about feels like a curse has lifted.

And I manage to make good time. Stymied by traffic at the George Washington Bridge, I don't cross, head north along the Palisades to the Tappan Zee Bridge, which has light traffic. Crossing the Hudson, soon traveling east toward Hartford on Hwy 84, cars are thick, every few miles we slow to a crawl, but the speed picks up, slows, picks up, until I turn north on I-91.

Massachusetts comes quickly, traffic thins, I'm in Vermont and flying, almost alone on the road. On the north end of Brattleboro, I leave the interstate for highway 9 to Keene, New Hampshire, and then on highway 202 soon reach Henniker, "the only one on earth," turn north on 114, and in a few minutes I'm home, the new home, the barely familiar home. It is late afternoon. I've bought a frozen pizza.

The journey ends, our journey—yours and mine—tonight, here, alone. Or, well, alone together. Jenny will fly north in a couple of days with her father while Beth drives with her son. I'll pick J and Tim up at the Manchester airport.

Tonight, it is just you and me. Can I offer you a drink?

Let's have an Old Fashioned. Or would you prefer a Martini? No doubt Al has made good use of our booze, but these we surely can mix in any version you like. An Older Old Fashioned? Use a slice of lemon and a cherry, pressed lightly in the double-rocks glass, not muddled? Good idea. Slightly warmed maple syrup, two, three barspoons. Heavy Angostura, say, six, okay eight, hard shakes. A couple shakes of Peychaud's? Ahh, Wild Turkey 101. Stir. Look, we've got a few large clear cubes. Stir again. Sip. Oh my. Good thinking, dear reader.

Let's sit together listening to an old LP of Emil Gilels playing the "Moonlight Sonata." The years float on the notes, but let's recall this year, the one we've shared, for a few measures. "The light begins to flicker from the rocks;/The long day wanes; the slow moon climbs;/The deep rolls round with many voices" (Tennyson, "*Ulysses*").

Do you feel it, the Old Fashioned? Me too. I'm going to sit back here in the moonlight, enjoy the bourbon, and your lovely company. We'll have another presently.

Until then... Thank you for being here.

# # #

Afterword, May 2024

Recently, I finished reading the manuscript of this book for the first time since summer 2022. Steve Poore and I had edited and delivered it to a company for layout and design to be available on Amazon, in print or Kindle editions. The result was an expensive embarrassment quickly pulled. The thing looked terrible. I moved on, spending time recording an album of original songs with my friend Brick Moltz and about two dozen musicians. The gent who laid out the liner notes, Kristian Gustafson, did such good work that we asked him to help us with the book. And here it is. (Oh, the album is *The Window* and you can find it on all of the streaming services. Hmm. Buy a copy of the print version of this book and get a CD of the album free!)

the window
perfectly good old men
david swords & brick moltz

It's been almost exactly three years since we ended the cocktail diary together after a long drive from Florida to New Hampshire, with Old Fashioneds and the "Moonlight Sonata," in the living-room of our newly rented house. A series of events, including voyages and crashes along the east coast, find me writing from our new home in Williamsburg, Virginia, where we have moved lot, stock, and sailboat this past week.

The new house has a bar (see photo). It's not grand and ancient like the Ol' Bean, but it is no afterthought. My love of cocktails and the pleasures of thinking and writing about them are undiminished. I have become a licensed bartender, and we both know a lot more about setting up and tending a home bar than when we began this journey.

Meanwhile, you will have noticed that since the pandemic most every restaurant and bar has its own list of increasingly expensive, usually weak, often terrible cocktails. The mark-up on booze, they've rediscovered, makes cocktails the most profitable offering of many a food-service business.

I too tried to turn cocktails into capitalism with excellent help but poor results. With the financial backing of friends, we tried a podcast; named our home bar *Chimes at Midnight*, from a line by Sir John Falstaff in Henry 1V, Part 2; and wrote articles for Substack. We promoted the Falstaffian motto to, "Forswear thin potations." I sewed Lewis bags from used sails, especially a mainsail I'd cut to pieces at Cape Fear, that include a Chimes decal. These are, by the way, probably the finest Lewis bags made, indestructible, and because Dacron is slick, ice slides easily from them into a shaker… oh, there I go, lapsing back into capitalism.

Since the beginning of the cocktail diary, the vast superiority of home bartending to buying cocktails has been clear. As a final word on the subject, and as a way codify what we do, here are the…

Ten Commandments of Home Bartending

1. Forswear thin potations. That is, mostly keep original proportions, but upsize! Never fail to turn a recipe that calls for 3/4 oz of any or every ingredient into 1 oz, and when you like, turn 2 ozs into 3 ozs. The results will be happier parishioners, who sing your praises, less work for you, the pleasures of living by our motto.

2. Decide on a drink of the night, whether home alone or for guests. As evening comes, decide on a cocktail, gather the ingredients, and if they include citrus, squeeze what you need into a bottle. Base your choice on any of many factors, such as: the season, the temperature, curiosity about something new or yearning for what is proven, your beloved's preference, tastes of any guests, and the ingredients you have on hand. One advantage is that memory plays almost no part. But a bigger advantage, useful to any home bartender, is that, rather than Jack and Coke or vodka and soda-water, guests discover, and invariably love, cocktails they would never know without you.

3. Experiment. Make do with what you've got and what you know. Which is to say, cocktails are not Platonic ideals; a recipe is not an inviolable dictate. For example, any cocktail that calls for sweet vermouth can be made with Antica Formula, Dolin Red, Punt e Mes, or any other. Or you can combine two sweet vermouths. Or you can substitute an amaro or amari. When you simply lack an ingredient or ingredients, try a substitute or substitutes. You'll seldom be disappointed.

4. Keep to a regular order for mixing so that you never, or rarely, forget to include an ingredient. Anything that will play against the main spirit, including vermouth, amari, and liqueurs goes in first. Next, I add the sweetener, such as simple syrup, grenadine, honey syrup, Benedictine, or orgeat. The main spirit or spirits are next, followed by citrus, and finally bitters and garnish. The order, in my mind, washes the jigger of the tastiest ingredients, which may or may not really matter. I do not add ice until all ingredients are in the stirring glass or shaker. Adding ice last decreases dilution. More important, if I am distracted the order helps guard against inadvertently omitting anything. And a dash is 1/8 teaspoon.

5. Use good ice, never refrigerator cubes. To this end, make big rocks (I recommend ClearlyFrozen, but other systems may be as good or better) and save the ice that comes from the hot water to crush in a [Chimes at Midnight] Lewis bag for the shaker. At the least, buy clear cocktail cubes at a grocery. A corollary to good ice is, keep ice and glasses cold. A small bar freezer is inexpensive. In preparing stirred cocktails I seldom use a stirring glass. Instead, mix the ingredients in a cold double-rocks glass and add a big rock last, swirling the combination about three rotations with your cocktail spoon.

6. Traveling cocktails will make you famous. When invited to dinner volunteer to bring one or two cocktails for the evening and make them in advance. Considering what you know about the likely preferences of your guests, typically make one cocktail with and one without citrus. Use portions by the cup rather than the jigger. You will soon discover that dinner invitations include requests for your famous traveling cocktails, not salad or dessert. Among the crowd pleasers that are largely unknown are the Royal Bermuda Yacht Club, Gypsy Eyes, Three Dots and a Dash, Crop Top, Spruce Goose, Dark Horse… Given that these days an Old Fashioned is the most ordered cocktail, your own take on it will surely impress many.

7. Do not be mesmerized by cocktail menus in bars and restaurants. You're better than they are. Almost every restaurant these days has a cocktail menu. Usually the drinks are expensive, weak, and use one, or sometimes all, inferior ingredients. You can learn by thinking about the combinations they invent or steal and now and again can take away ideas for a promising cocktail that you make in your own way and size at a fraction of the cost. The proportions to observe typically are 2 parts main spirit; 1 part liqueur, amaro, vermouth, etc.; 1 part citrus; 1-3 real dashes of bitters. Sweetener to taste, best tested by adding a quarter ounce (whether simple syrup, orgeat, honey or maple syrup, Benedictine, etc.) once the cocktail is built, then adjusting to suit you.

8. Keep a decantered cocktail (or two, or more) on hand. These use ingredients that will not spoil (no citrus, vermouth only if you know the decanter won't last for months). While such cocktails are dangerous, having them made and ready to pour improves a hard day measurably by making it easier. I like a decanter of Mother-in-Law, Cocktail de la Louisiane, and Manhattan. If you need, say, an Old Fashioned by the decanter (as my mother did for our father), keep it in the freezer so that your sweetener will not grow mold.

9. Consider some plan of moderation. I try, often unsuccessfully, to drink on the schedule that Steve (the editor of this book) and his wife Rochelle, mostly keep, drinking on Wednesday, Friday, and Saturday. They keep the evenings to two cocktails. Jenny likes this idea because she believes it healthier than drinking every night or most nights. Ever so reluctantly I take her point, especially when it is possible to cheat by having, say, a beer with dinner. For me, not drinking every night means cocktails taste even better on nights when we have them. (Don't tell Jenny, but they taste so good that I sometimes need a third or even fourth and might upsize dangerously.) Another approach could be to allow yourself only one cocktail a night. Jenny seems to follow this effortlessly.

10. Pair cocktails with food. You'll drink less wine, less beer. Again, if you keep to known limits, you'll sleep better and almost never suffer a headache. Oh, the food will taste better too. Among my favorites are cocktails in the Manhattan family with beef, especially roast or steak. For some reason I love an Aviation with pasta. Summer meals are good with almost any sour. Fish and Martinis are even better than peas and carrots.

Are you surprised that there are ten commandments for home bartenders? Well, wasn't Jesus a home bartender when he turned water into wine?

The End

Bibliography

(See Library of Congress Classification TX951)

Amis, Kingsley. *Everyday Drinking: The Distilled Kingsley Amis*. New York: Bloomsbury Publishing, 2021 ed. (first published 2008). Print.

Arnold, Dave. Liquid Intelligence: *The Art and Science of the Perfect Cocktail*. New York: W.W. Norton & Company, 2014. Print.

Boudreau, Jamie and James O. Fraioli. *The Canon Cocktail Book*. New York: Houghton Mifflin Harcourt, 2016. Print.

Carson, Gerald. *The Social History of Bourbon: An Unhurried Account of Our Star-Spangled America Drink*. New York: Dodd, Mead & Company, 1963. Print.

Craddock, Harry. *The Savoy Cocktail Book*. London: Constable & Co Ltd. London: Chancellor Press, 1930. Facsim. Ed., 1983. Print.

Day, Alex, Nick Fauchald, David Kaplan with Devon Tarby. *Cocktail Codex: Fundamentals, Formulas, Evolutions*. New York: Ten Speed Press, 2018. Print.

Doeser, Linda. *Classic and Contemporary Cocktails: The Essential Collection*. Bath, England: Parragon Publishing, 2005. Print.

Edmunds, Lowell. *The Silver Bullet: The Martini in American Civilization*. Contributions in American Studies, Number 52. Westport, CT: Greenwood Press, 1981. Print.

Embury, David A. *The Fine Art of Mixing Drinks*. Garden City, NY: Doubleday & Company, 1948. New York: Dolphin Books, 1961 edition. Print.

English, Camper. *Doctors and Distillers: The Remarkable Medicinal History of Beer, Wine, Spirits and Cocktails*. New York: Penguin Books, 2022. Print.

Foley, Ray, consulting ed. *The Bar Guide*. San Francisco: Weldon Owen, 1999. Print. The Williams Sonoma Guides. Print.

Forsyth, Mark. *A Short History of Drunkenness: How, Why, Where and When Humankind Has Got Merry from the Stone Age to the Present.* London: Penguin Books, 2017. Print.

Haigh, Ted (aka Dr. Cocktail). *Vintage Spirits and Forgotten Cocktails*. Beverly, MA: Quarry Books, 2009. Print.

Hellmich, Mittie. *Ultimate Bar Book: The Comprehensive Guide to Over 1,000 Cocktails*. San Francisco: Chronicle Books, 2006. Print.

Homer. *The Odyssey*. Translated by Emily Wilson. New York: W.W. Norton & Company, 2018. Ebook.

Jackson, Michael. *Michael Jackson's Complete Guide to Single-Malt Scotch. 2nd ed.* Philadelphia: Running Press Book Publishers, 1991. Print.

Johnson, Harry. *New and Improved Bartender's Manual or How to Mix Drinks of the Present Style*. New York: Harry Johnson, 1882. Online facsimile ed . at https://euvs-vintage-cocktail-books.cld.bz/1888-Harry-Johnson-s-new-and-improved-bartender-s-manual-1888/4/

Kaplan, David, Nick Fauchald, and Alex Day. *Death & Co.: Modern Classic Cocktails*. Berkeley, CA: Ten Speed Press, 2014. Print.

McCaffety, Kerri. *Obituary Cocktail: The Great Saloons of New Orleans*. Gretna, LA: Pelican Publishing Company, 2015. Print.

McElhone, Harry. *Barflies and Cocktails*. 2008 facsimile ed. New York: Cocktail Kingdom, LLC, 1927. Print.

McLafferty, Clair. *The Classic Craft Cocktail Recipe Book*. Berkeley, CA: Rockridge Press, 2017. Print.

Mencken, H.L. *The American Language Supplement One*. New York: Alfred A. Knopf, 1977. Print.

Monti, Francois. *101 Cocktails to Try Before You Die*. London: Hachette, UK, 2016, 2018. Print.

Okrent, Daniel. *Last Call: The Rise and Fall of Prohibition*. New York: Scribner, 2010. Print.

Parsons, Brad Thomas. *Bitters: A Spirited History of a Classic Cure-All with Cocktails, Recipes & Formulas*. New York: Ten Speed Press, 2011. Print.

Parsons, Brad Thomas. *Last Call: bartenders on their one final drink and the late-night wisdom and rituals of closing time*. New York: Ten Speed Press, 2019. Print.

Pashley, Nicholas. *Notes on a Beer Mat*. Toronto: Polar Bear Press, 2001. Print.

Reiner, Julie with Kaitlyn Goalen. *The Craft Cocktail Party: Delicious Drinks for Every Occasion*. New York: Grand Central Life & Style, 2015. Print.

Roe, Charlie and Jim Schwenck. *The Home Bartender's Guide and Song Book*. 2015 facsimile. New York: Cocktail Kingdom, Inc., 1930. Print.

Saltz, Joanna and the Editors of Delish. *Delish Ultimate Cocktails: Why Limit Happy to an Hour*. New York: Hearst Home, 2020. Print.

Schofield, Joe and Daniel Schofield. *Schofield's Fine and Classic Cocktails*. London: Kyle Books, 2019. Print.

Simonson, Robert. *3-Ingredient Cocktails: An Opinionated Guide to the Most Enduring Drinks in the Cocktail Canon*. New York: Ten Speed Press, 2017. Print.

Slingerland, Edward. *Drunk: How We Sipped, Danced, and Stumbled Our Way to Civilization*. Boston: Little, Brown Spark, 2021. Print.

Teague, Sother. *I'm Just Here for the Drinks: A Guide to Spirits, Drinking and More then One Hundred Extraordinary Cocktails*. New York: Topix Media Lab, 2018. Print.

Thomas, Jerry. *How to Mix Drinks or the Bon Vivant's Companion*. New York: Dick & Fitzgerald, Publishers, 1862. Online facsimile ed . https://euvs-vintage-cocktail-books.cld.bz/1862-Bar-Tender-s-Guide-price-1-50-by-Jerry-Thomas/4/

Vermeire, Robert. *Cocktails: How to Mix Them*. London: Herbert Jenkins Ltd., 1924. Print.

Waller, James. *Drinkology: The Art and Science of the Cocktail*. New York: Stewart, Tabori & Chang, 2010. Print.

Williams, Elizabeth M and Charles McMillian. *Lift Your Spirits: A Celebratory History of Cocktail Culture in New Orleans*. Baton Rouge: Louisiana State University Press, 2016. Print.

Wondrich, David. Rev. ed. *Imbibe!* New York: Perigee Books, 2015. Print.

Wondrich, David with Noah Rothbaum, eds. *The Oxford Companion to Spirits and Cocktails*. New York: Oxford University Press, 2022. Print.

Index

Autobiography in which the Author Establishes His Credentials

New Orleans is, by some lights, world headquarters for cocktails. The city hosts Tales of the Cocktail, the grandest annual conference devoted to them; has a cocktail museum; and most important, on a per capita basis, thanks to Mardi Gras, music, and Catholicism, the inhabitants surely drink more than people of any other city one could name. My dad used to say, "Nearly all of my friends are alcoholics, many of them functional."

Born in New Orleans, at an early age I loved cocktails. When we were children, our parents encouraged us to order a Ramos Gin Fizz or Milk Punch on the rare occasions when we ate breakfast at Brennan's in the French Quarter. At sixteen I was a regular at a couple of French Quarter bars and another uptown. In graduate school at Tulane, along with a considerable group of likeminded literary scholars (including the editor of this book), most days ended in the bar nearest to the Howard Tilton Library.

The love of alcohol apparently has genetic origins. My great grandfather, sheriff of St Landry Parish in Louisiana, among other enlightened law-enforcement practices, flouted wrongheaded local ordinances by refusing to shutter "blind tigers," that is, proto-speakeasies, in his jurisdiction. In the early Twentieth Century, his son, my grandfather, lawyer and alcoholic, spent lunch hours at a French Quarter bar, where a gent could relieve himself, owing to the pissoir beneath the bar, without missing sip or sentence. His bar, along with him, was long gone by the time I ventured forth as a young Director of Communication for a large company headquartered in the city; for us, the bar and its convenient pissoir were replaced by Paul Prudhomme's Louisiana Kitchen, where lunchtime Mason Jar Martinis, garnished with an array of peppers, inspired our afternoon labor.

That job also began my international travel, first to Scotland, where in the 80's I devoted many evenings at the Nelson Hotel outside Nairn to the "mighty Glens," and learned from an old Scotsman to chase those single malts with a pint of ale. In Belgium I was lucky to discover the world's greatest beers, both for flavor and strength, making it practicable to shun virtually all American beers for decades.

Thanks to that acquired taste for fine beer and good whisky, I found the British Michael Jackson, whose books, over decades of world travel, guided me to the rare bars in far-flung cities where one could order acceptable spirits. In the early 90s, on the coldest winter night I'd ever imagined, walking into the face of a hurricane-force north wind, thanks to Jackson I lurched into Bottlescrew Billy's, joined their Around-the-World Beer Club, and on later visits smuggled them single malts unavailable in Calgary in return for evenings of free drinks and insights into curling. Once, I was lucky enough to cross paths with Jackson at the Gingerman in Houston where he taught me to order two beers at once so that the second had time to warm up, reveal its flavors. Very British.

For a time, while I was a management consultant to companies such as General Electric and Mobil, my brilliant boss used alcohol as social medicine to bring forth needed dialogue and hard truths. Later, selling books to academic libraries, whether deep in the small hours of morning in Dubai or listening to mariachis in Guadalajara, alcohol helped build trust, friendships, and business. As a sales manager for three companies, Yankee Book Peddler, which brought Jenny and me to New Hampshire and a group of friends and bandmates who love a cocktail; Blackwell, where I divided time between Oxford and Portland, Oregon (oh my, aged cocktails at Clyde Commons); and Ebook Library of Australia, a small group who loved one another's company and declared the Sidecar to be our cocktail, my career was replete with memorable colleagues and customers who loved to drink.

When you're lucky enough to have had a career that is much more adventure than drudgery, retirement can be frightening. But we lived in a fine bar, the 18th Century Ol' Bean Tavern, and a colleague had given me Ted Haigh's *Forgotten Cocktails*, which I quickly explored as if it were the Galapagos Islands. Even so, a salesman sometimes unwittingly becomes the road; sitting on beach or barstool, even with a Maiden's Blush in hand, will not serve every need. So, Jenny agreed to a sailboat, for us quite a big one that could travel the Atlantic, fostering dreams of traveling further.

It was not, however, until the Covid 19 Pandemic of 2020 and 2021, with time on my hands and liquor stores designated essential businesses, that cocktails and the cocktail diary magically proved to be primary, daily sources of joy, order, ideas, conversation, anticipation, and salvation. You hold in your hands the story of those cocktails and how to make them. Dr. Johnson, a serious tippler, wrote, "None but a fool ever wrote for anything but money." Less fortunate than me, he held in his hands, without ever discovering it, a subject that can make writing worth more than money.

Jenny and I live in Bradford, New Hampshire; sail out of Salem, Massachusetts; and during winters when we can go south, live aboard our boat, *Lea Scotia*, in Stuart, Florida. Juliet, Melanie (along with our son in law CJ), and Alexander are our children. All love a cocktail, and the last is a professional bartender. As yet uncertain about the grandboys, we are hopeful that those apples won't fall far from the tree.

w.ingramcontent.com/pod-product-compliance
tning Source LLC
bersburg PA
W041508120626
ICB00018B/2351